UNDER THE EDITORSHIP OF

William C. Holbrook

HAMPDEN–SYDNEY COLLEGE

READING FRENCH
in the Arts and Sciences
3rd Edition

EDWARD M. STACK
NORTH CAROLINA STATE UNIVERSITY

HOUGHTON MIFFLIN COMPANY • BOSTON
DALLAS • GENEVA, ILLINOIS • HOPEWELL, NEW JERSEY • PALO ALTO • LONDON

Acknowledgments

The selections reprinted in this book are used by permission of the proprietors of their respective copyrights. The author wishes to give special thanks to the following publishers and author for permission to reproduce the selections listed below in this new edition of the text.

Ariel Alexandre, "Prévision de la Gêne due au Bruit autour des Aéroports," from *Anthropologie Appliquée,* April, 1970. Used by permission of the publisher.
Raymond Bouillenne, pages 722–723, *Phytobiologie,* 1946. Reprinted by permission of Masson S.A., Paris.
J.E. Courtois and L. Manet, "Recherches sur la Phytase. Les Phytases du Colibacille," from *Bulletin de la Société de Chimie Biologique,* numbers 3–4, 1952. Reprinted by permission of the author.

Printed in the U. S. A.

ISBN: 0-395-27505-9

CONTENTS ⎿⎯⎯⎯⎯⎯⎯⎯

I

French Vocabulary · Cognates and False Friends · Articles · Plurals

II

Adjectives · Expressions of Quantity · Numbers · Contractions

v

III

Past Participles · Adverbs · Attributes · Present Tense

IV

Subject Pronouns · Reflexive Verbs · *dont* · Multiple Modifiers · Participle-Preposition Linkage · Infinitives · Impersonal Verbs

V

Negative Forms of Verbs · ne . . . que Construction · tenir*

VI

Personal Pronouns Used as Subjects · Present Tense · Recognition of Future and Conditional System

VII

Special Future and Conditional Stems of Irregular Verbs · Past Tenses · Translation of the Imperfect Tense · avoir*

VIII
Object Pronouns · être*

IX
Present Participles · Comparisons · celui · prendre* · faire*

X
Inverted Word Order · faire (faire) Construction · mettre* · savoir* · pouvoir* · voir*

XI

Supplemental Auxiliary Verbs · *lequel* · *en* · *vouloir** · *devoir** · *aller**

XII

Past Definite Tense · Expressions of Time · *depuis, il y a . . . que* Constructions · *venir** · *venir de*

XIII

Relative Pronouns · Importance of Gender for Meaning · *tout* · *ouvrir**

XIV

Adjectives with Variable Meanings · Possessive Adjectives · y · Conjunctions

XV

Disjunctive Pronouns · Imperatives · *aussi*

XVI

Present Subjunctive · *servir**

XVII

Compound Tenses · Interrogatives · *ne* Used Alone

Appendices

PREFACE

The purpose of this book is to provide an effective means of teaching students, in one college semester, to understand written French. No previous knowledge of the language is assumed, no conversation or composition exercises are provided.

Proficiency in understanding a foreign language, like any other skill, is attained by establishing a method and by applying that method persistently. One definite method is described in the Introduction; drills on structure follow each lesson in order to fix newly learned techniques; extensive connected passages of French call for the persistent application of what has been learned. The "Integrated Tests" which parallel each lesson may be used for evaluation of progress, and they contain transitional material from one lesson to the next.

Vocabulary is supplied in the footnotes on each page as well as in a complete end vocabulary. Cognates are omitted from the footnotes, as are words previously used and words whose meaning should be deduced from the context.

The connected reading passages are intentionally heterogeneous, for it is desirable to call the attention of students in technical and scientific fields to the values of non-technical literature, just as students in the humanities should become aware of the method and precision of scientific description. Though this is certainly not a text for the teaching of literature, physics, or philosophy, the variety of the readings provided may help students to understand the synthesis of intellectual endeavor among educated men. And in view of the tremendous contributions of France to the culture and scientific advancement of modern civilization, it is appropriate that students should be introduced to that synthesis through the French language.

In this edition I have substituted several new reading selections for others, added or improved a few grammatical presentations, honed the exercises, and added reading comprehension exercises for seven of the longer reading texts. The symbol ✕ has been placed beside the titles of the seven reading texts for which reading comprehension exercises have been provided.

Raleigh, North Carolina   EDWARD M. STACK

INTRODUCTION | To the Student

This textbook differs from most French texts in that it is designed solely to teach you to *read* and *translate*. A saving of time and energy is made for you by omitting much grammar and other instructional material which is usually included, but which is necessary only if the purpose of the book is to teach composition and conversation in addition to reading. This, then, is a book in which the grammatical information is very *selective;* only what you actually need to accomplish your goal has been retained.

Three main tasks lie ahead of you: (1) learning a vocabulary, (2) learning the structural organization of French, i.e. word-order, and (3) learning to discriminate between verb tenses. There is a method for accomplishing each of those tasks; that method is outlined here, and incorporated into the instructional material of the book.

ORGANIZATION OF THE BOOK. — This text has seventeen lessons, each calculated to be approximately a week's work in class (not counting outside preparation). The rate of progress depends upon your teacher's estimate of the situation, of course, and you may spend more or less time as he sees fit. Each lesson contains explanations, with examples; short fragmentary exercises to fix the principles explained; longer sentences; and connected readings. For each lesson there is one (or two, in the case of the first few lessons) *Integrated Test* at the back of the book. Your teacher may assign this as homework, or he may actually use it as a test. In any case it is important to try the exercises in the tests, because they contain material which is planted there to make your mental wheels grind into action, and to cause some creative thinking — not just memory work.

Like most books, this one is equipped with a storehouse of reference material: the Appendices. Get into the habit of referring to them for verb forms, numbers, and other information. Use the Index to refer back easily to material already covered which you need to re-check. A small dictionary (called an "end vocabulary") is also at the back of the book for finding the meaning of French words which you have forgotten, or for which you have tried but failed to "invent" a probable meaning.

VOCABULARY. — Learning new words is a feat partially of memory, and partially of an imaginative ability to deduce the probable meaning of a word from the *context* (the surroundings) in which it is found. The lessons begin with deceptively easy French words called "cognates," which cause no difficulty. Soon, however, there are words which you will be explicitly asked to memorize.

Memorization of frequently used words is part of the spadework of language learning, just as learning the multiplication table is a necessary prelude to being able to perform simple arithmetical functions. It is not very exciting, but it can lead to amazing results if properly done.

How should you memorize the words you are called upon to recognize time after time? A good method is to use vocabulary cards, which you can make yourself.

Vocabulary Cards. — Cut a number of slips of paper of equal size. On one side write the French word you wish to learn; on the other side, its English equivalent. (You should start this system at once, so that you will not have too great a number to make all at the same time.)

Now pile the "cards" in a single pile, French words up. Glance at the first word, tell yourself its English equivalent, and then turn the card over to check your accuracy. At this point you begin placing used cards in two piles: (1) Pile "A" is where you place cards which you have correctly identified, and (2) Pile "B" is where you place those cards which you got wrong, or hesitated over.

Go through the entire pile, sorting into piles "A" and "B" as you give the English meanings.

Next time through, concentrate on Pile "B," and see if you can't get some of them into an "A" pile this time. Continue as often as possible in this fashion. WARNING: Always shuffle the cards in a pile before you start through them; if you do not, you may learn the *sequence* of words, rather than the words themselves.

Review the "A" pile once every two or three days, or the words in that pile may sneakily revert to "B" status. Keep them in "A" condition by frequent review. Carry a few "B" slips around with you, and go through them while loafing between classes, waiting for the bus, or at other odd moments.

Vocabulary by Logical Deduction. — Read a whole sentence or paragraph entirely through before even attempting a translation. This first "rough" reading will orient you as to the general subject matter, even though you do not know all the details.

Next re-read the first sentence of the paragraph; now that you know the general orientation of the whole paragraph, the first sentence will now fit into a definite scheme of meaning which will aid you in deducing the meaning of any words you do not definitely know. It is at this point that you are *emphatically encouraged to make an educated guess* at the probable meaning, and say it boldly.

Take an example. Suppose that the rough reading of the paragraph you are to translate is evidently about the solar system. The first sentence you can translate readily, except for one word, as follows:

"The planets revolve around **une étoile . . .**"

WARNING! Don't stop just because you don't know the meaning of **une étoile**; don't bother to look in the vocabulary. *Read on!* You may get a clue! All right: you read

"The planets revolve around **une étoile** which is called the Sun."

Now reflect for a moment and deduce logically what that unknown French word *must be.* Did you say, "a cigar"? "a doghouse"? What, then? Of course, it is "a star." It takes only a small acquaintance with the subject to deduce meaning, and that is what you probably do all the time in reading English, to save trips to the dictionary.

Cognates. — The first lesson deals with those French words which you already know, like *nation, observation,* and *résumé.* You will not need to make vocabulary cards nor deduce meanings for these, as they are already part of your working vocabulary.

False Friends. — The "false friends" *look* as if we knew them, but they are often traitors, and mean something else. They are marked with a dagger (†) on their first few appearances, just to warn you. They should be placed on vocabulary cards and learned with their correct meanings.

An example is the word *vase:* see it in action in the sentence

"John slipped and fell in the **vase**."

Logical deduction tells us that it seems unlikely that this means a piece of ceramic pottery that John fell into. However, as John *could* have fallen into almost anything from a vat of sulphuric acid to Niagara Falls (unless we are given *more* context), there is no way but to know that **vase** means *mud.* False Friends must be memorized.

FOOTNOTE VOCABULARY. — New words are given in the form of footnotes, in the order they appear on the page. The key to them is the number in brackets at the beginning of the sentence or paragraph you are reading. If a new word is not listed, it means either (a) you should already know it, as it has appeared before, or (b) you are expected to make a clever logical deduction of the meaning. In either case, you may find the word in the end vocabulary — but only as a last resort!

STUDY METHODS. — It is important that you practice French *regularly* and *frequently.* Try to do some reading *every* day. It has been very definitely proved that a little every day is more effective than a lot on just one day. In other words, an hour every day is better than seven hours one day a week.

METHOD OF PRESENTATION OF MATERIAL. — The structure of the French language is presented in definite stages in this text. These stages of development are

1. NOUN-ADJECTIVE GROUP, or basic unit of thought, which starts with a core, or a noun and its article:

> (la **nation**)   *the nation*

These noun-adjective groups are built to larger units by the addition of adjectival modifiers, thus:

> (la nation **américaine**)   *the American nation*
> (la **grande** nation **américaine**)   *the great American nation*
> (cette nation **à géographie diverse**) *this nation with diversified geography*

The noun-adjective group is converted into a prepositional phrase by placing a preposition in front:

> (de la nation américaine)   *of the American nation*

2. SENTENCE (or CLAUSE) GROUPS are formed by inserting a VERB between two familiar NOUN-ADJECTIVE GROUPS:

> (La nation américaine) **possède** (un gouvernement démocratique).
> (*The American nation*) *possesses* (*a democratic government*).

3. ADVERBS are introduced to give more subtle distinctions:

(Cette **assez** grande nation)	*This **rather** large nation*
possède **déjà**	***already** possesses*
(un gouvernement **complètement** démocratique.)	*a **completely** democratic government.*

Other slight variations are introduced systematically, and finally the time-relationship is varied in the verb *tense*.

TRANSLATIONS. — An English translation of a French passage must have the following characteristics:

1. It must be in **excellent English**, devoid of traces of French word order. It should sound as if you composed it originally in English. There need not be an English word for every French word, because

2. It must **present the entire *idea*** of the French passage. You must read each French sentence, and then provide an English one which conveys the same idea in English. It must not add any ideas (or interpretations), nor omit any.

3. It **must not change the time** (verb tense) of the French (with a few exceptions explained later), as this would be a mutilation of an important part of the idea.

Your command of English will be taxed in the selection of the *mot juste* (the exactly appropriate word); and the writing of a translation is a creative act which is separate from and more difficult than merely reading and understanding *in French*. (You should soon develop the ability to read through a French passage and tell the general meaning without attempting a sentence-by-sentence translation.)

I mentioned that there need not be a word-for-word correspondence of French and English. To do this kind of so-called "literal" translation is to do a poor translation. For example, in reading a letter from a French business firm, you find at the end the following sentence:

Veuillez agréer, cher Monsieur, l'expression de nos sentiments distingués.

A literal (i.e. bad) translation of this is:

Kindly accept, dear Sir, the expression of our distinguished sentiments.

This way of ending a letter is positively hilarious in English, but the intent of the French writer was quite serious. He was merely using the customary final formula. The correct English phrase which serves the same purpose in a letter, and which is the proper translation of the long French formula, is "Yours truly."

In summary, then, attack the job ahead seriously and conscientiously. Use vocabulary cards for words which you find recurring frequently, and those in special lists which are marked for you to learn. Be bold in deducing meanings by context, shunning reliance on the vocabulary. Don't be afraid to make mistakes — they are fine in the learning process, and they make the classroom cheerful. Beware of the false friends†, and take comfort in the cognates. The method is ready-made, so just follow the book and take your teacher's comments as a means of improving what you are doing; after all, you are the one who is solely responsible for your progress.

READING SELECTIONS

Chapter

1

French Vocabulary
Cognates and False Friends
Article · Plurals

1. General

The main task in gaining a reading knowledge of French, at the outset, is to learn the words which will appear most often in the material we plan to read. This stock of words, or *vocabulary,* consists of two parts: (1) words common to all kinds of writing, regardless of the subject matter, and (2) words peculiar to a particular field of study, such as psychology or chemistry.

The first type is obviously important to everybody, and it is with the COMMON VOCABULARY AND STRUCTURE that this text deals. Specialized vocabularies can quickly be built in your own fields of interest after the groundwork has been laid. Readings used here will concentrate on common vocabulary and fundamentals of structure. The explanation of technical terms like *cyclotron* and *mytosis* would fall within the scope of a course in physics or botany, but here we will content ourselves with reading and translating, leaving the explanation of these terms to the specialists in a class.

Fortunately you all already possess a fairly large French vocabulary! There are many French words which are the same (or nearly the same) in spelling and meaning as English words; these are called *cognates,* and may safely be translated by their English equivalents.

On the other hand, there are among these similar-looking words a few traitors (called the "false friends") which mean something quite different from what they *appear* to mean. The only way to avoid being stabbed in the back by one of these *faux amis* is to be forewarned, and to know them thoroughly. As an example, the word *expérience* looks like a cognate, but it does not always mean "experience"! It means something important to all scientists, however: *experiment.*

The false friends will be marked with reminding dagger (†) in the text for the first few appearances. Thereafter you are on your own to defend yourself against them. (List in §3).

2. Cognates

These French words closely resemble English ones, and may usually be translated by the English words they look like. Many terms pertaining to science, architecture,

1

law, music, society, and military organization came into English from the French terms.

a. *Exact Cognates.* These are words which are spelled exactly like the English equivalent. They may ordinarily be translated by the English cognate, although some have *additional* meanings in French:

table	village	train
résumé	colonel	auto
fiancé	lieutenant	boulevard
amateur	général	dose
restaurant	sabotage	édifice
plan	capture	danger
rare	week-end	influence

b. *Cognates ending in -ion.* Almost all English words ending in **-ion** are exact cognates of French words (all feminine gender):

construction	pénétration	décoration
agitation	bifurcation	confusion
déviation	diffraction	direction
distribution	émission	introduction
investigation	possession	complication

c. *Cognates ending in -ie.* Many French nouns can be recognized in their English form by substituting *-y* for the **-ie** ending:

géographie	géométrie	géologie
énergie	psychologie	sociologie
théorie	océanographie	photographie

d. *Cognates ending in -é.* Some French words ending in **-é** may be recognized in their English form by substituting *-y:*

beauté	identité	obscurité

e. *Cognates ending in -ique.* Many French words ending in **-ique** correspond to English words ending in *-ic* or *-ical:*

HAVING ENGLISH EQUIVALENTS IN *-ic:*

électrique	Atlantique	magnétique
spécifique	géométrique	dynamique
métallique	cosmique	énigmatique

HAVING ENGLISH EQUIVALENTS IN *-ical:*

optique	mécanique	physique
symétrique	mathématique	identique

f. *Cognates containing the circumflex accent* [^]. The circumflex accent often indicates that the letter s was formerly written after the letter having this accent:

forêt (= forest)   hôpital (= hospital)   île (= isle)

This fact sometimes helps recognize the meaning of the French words bearing such accents.

3. False Friends (†)

Words which *look* like English words, but which **must not** be translated as cognates. Learn them thoroughly. Here are a few important ones to learn at once:

FRENCH	MEANING	FRENCH	MEANING
actuel, actuelle	present-day, current	éditeur	publisher
actuellement	currently, at present	expérience	experiment (or experience)
apparition	appearance	évidemment	obviously
as	ace (cards; flyer)	inconvénient	disadvantage
axe	axis	important,-e	large
but	purpose, goal	journée	day
cap	cape (*Geog.*)	large	wide
car	for; because	lecture	reading
chair	flesh	or	now; but
commodité	convenience	partie, la	part
conférence	lecture	phrase	sentence
court, -e	short	physicien	physicist
davantage	more	sensibilité	sensitivity
demander	to ask for	tour, le	turn, tour
		tour, la	tower

4. Definite Article ("the") *le, la, l', les*

These four words are all translated *the* in reading French. The first three are used with singular nouns; the word **les** is used for plural nouns, and is easy to remember because of the final **-s**.

The reason for the different forms is in their use:
    le is used before *masculine* nouns — **le cas**
    la is used before *feminine* nouns — **la table**
    l' is used before *any singular noun* beginning with a *vowel* sound — l'énergie
    les is used before *any plural noun,* regardless of gender —
        les cas   **les tables**   **les énergies**

le plan	the plan	**les** plans	the plans
la table	the table	**les** tables	the tables
l'expérience	the experiment	**les** expériences	the experiments

In *general* statements do not translate: *la liberté est précieuse* (*Liberty* is precious).

5. Gender

All French nouns are arbitrarily classified as *masculine* or *feminine* in grammatical gender. A few nouns have either gender. Nouns designating persons usually (but not always) correspond in gender to the sex of the person. The nouns designating *objects* have a gender which cannot usually be deduced, and must therefore be learned by all who wish to write or speak French. The gender is important for making adjectives *agree* (§12), but need not be studied in detail by those interested only in *reading* French. (Nouns ending in **-tion** are feminine.)

The gender of nouns is indicated in the vocabulary as
follows: nm. = *masculine* noun, e.g., **le plan**
         nf. = *feminine* noun, e.g., **la table**

EXERCISES
Series A (§§1–5)

Translate into English.   (Give the gender of each *noun* where possible.)

I.
1. le président
2. le général
3. le secrétaire
4. le consul
5. la capitale
6. le ministre
7. le lieutenant
8. le sergent
9. le capitaine
10. l'armée

11. la nation
12. l'architecte
13. le musicien
14. la cathédrale
15. l'édifice
16. le coton
17. l'animal
18. la théorie
19. le tissu
20. l'extrémité

21. la condition
22. le but†
23. l'expérience†
24. la science
25. l'élément
26. l'océan
27. la possibilité
28. l'hémisphère
29. la géologie
30. l'inconvénient†

II.
31. caractéristique
32. catastrophique
33. électronique
34. énigmatique
35. cylindrique
36. géométrique

37. physique
38. identique
39. automatique
40. métallique
41. historique
42. pathologique

43. biologique
44. astronomique
45. sociologique
46. comique
47. magnifique
48. brique

III.
49. les présidents
50. les ministres
51. les armées
52. les nations
53. les architectes
54. les économistes

55. les musiciens
56. les théories
57. les extrémités
58. les conditions
59. les buts†
60. les expériences†

61. les sciences
62. les océans
63. les possibilités
64. les inconvénients†
65. les lames†
66. les axes†

IV.
67. l'empereur
68. les empereurs
69. spécifique
70. l'agitation
71. élégant
72. l'élégance
73. la série
74. oblique
75. la décoration
76. les décorations
77. les expériences†
78. les difficultés
79. la dose
80. les buts†

81. théorique
82. la perception
83. les conférences†
84. la densité
85. les circuits
86. extrême
87. les corrections
88. la correction
89. tangible
90. extérieur
91. la transmission
92. or†
93. la nature
94. l'éditeur†

95. la commodité†
96. actuellement†
97. cosmique
98. Pacifique
99. large†
100. le cap†
101. les caps†
102. les déviations
103. l'attraction
104. la comète
105. les comètes
106. la solution
107. les proportions
108. la variation

Test I B, pages 181–182

6. Indefinite Article *un, une, des*

The words **un** and **une** mean *a* (*an*). **Un** appears before masculine singular nouns; **une** before feminine singular nouns. **Des** means *some,* is used before plural nouns of both genders, and usually need not be translated at all.

un moyen	a means	des moyens	(some) means
un plan	a plan	des plans	(some) plans
une raison	a reason	des raisons	(some) reasons

In questions, **des** = *any:* Avez-vous des livres? Have you any books?

7. Plurals of Nouns

Normally nouns are made plural by adding **-s** to the basic singular form found in dictionaries:

un fait	a fact	des faits	(some) facts
le jour	the day	les jours	the days

Special cases. Some nouns, in their singular form, already end in **-s, -x,** or **-z.** They *look* like plurals in the singular form; and the plural form remains the same. Upon seeing nouns, check the accompanying article to verify whether they are singular or plural.

les | cas | the cases (*pl.*)   le | cas | the case (*s.*)

Here are some common nouns whose singular form already carries a plural-like ending:

le cas	the case	les cas	the cases
le fils	the son	les fils	the sons
le poids	the weight	les poids	the weights
le gaz	the gas	les gaz	the gases
le nez	the nose	les nez	the noses
le choix	the choice	les choix	the choices

8. Irregular Plurals of Nouns

It will be observed that nouns ending in **-s, -x,** and **-z** are usually plural, although those listed in §7 are exceptional. When in doubt, check to see whether the accompanying article is plural (i.e., ends in **-s**).

a. Although most nouns simply add **-s** to form the plural, it is quite usual for nouns ending in **-au** and **-eu** to add the old form of the plural, **-x:**

le niveau	the level	les niveaux	the levels
un niveau	a level	des niveaux	(some) levels
le rameau	the branch	les rameaux	the branches

b. Nouns ending in **-al** usually change the **-l** to **-u** and add **-x:**

un animal	an animal	des animaux	(some) animals
un journal	a newspaper	des journaux	(some) newspapers
le minéral	the mineral	les minéraux	the minerals

c. Totally different plurals occur in a few cases:

un œil   an eye   des yeux   (some) eyes

9. Prepositions

The following prepositions indicating position should be memorized:

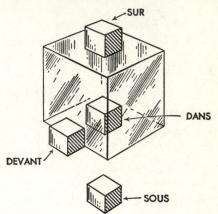

dans	in (contained within)
sur	on (on the surface of)
sous	under
devant	in front of, before
derrière	behind
à côté de	beside
entre	between
vers	towards

EXERCISES

Series B (§§6–9)

Translate the following:

I.
1. un président
2. un général
3. un secrétaire
4. une capitale
5. une armée
6. une théorie
7. des théories
8. un fait
9. des faits
10. un but†

11. des présidents
12. des généraux
13. des musiciens
14. une cathédrale
15. des cathédrales
16. des buts†
17. des journaux
18. des poids
19. un poids
20. un niveau

21. des conditions
22. une condition
23. des expériences†
24. une science
25. des sciences
26. des niveaux
27. une possibilité
28. des possibilités
29. un inconvénient†
30. des inconvénients†

II.
31. derrière le sergent
32. sur la table
33. sous une table
34. devant les tables
35. sur l'océan
36. sous l'océan
37. sous la condition
38. dans la solution
39. à côté de l'éditeur†
40. à côté des éditeurs†

41. derrière la cathédrale
42. devant le fait
43. dans le cas
44. dans les cas
45. dans les journaux
46. dans le journal
47. sous un poids
48. sous des poids
49. sous le poids
50. sur un rameau

III. 51. à côté des musiciens
    52. sur les extrémités
    53. sous des conditions
    54. derrière l'édifice
    55. devant un choix
    56. des fils
    57. un fils
    58. les fils
    59. dans la nature
    60. dans les expériences
    61. une perception
    62. des perceptions
    63. un but
    64. des buts
    65. un moyen
    66. des moyens
    67. le moyen
    68. les moyens
    69. une attraction
    70. des attractions
    71. l'attraction
    72. les attractions
    73. dans le gaz
    74. dans un gaz
    75. dans les gaz
    76. dans des gaz
    77. un résumé
    78. des résumés
    79. dans le résumé
    80. des villages

81. dans les villages
82. le weekend
83. les weekends
84. un weekend
85. le golf
86. le football
87. une complication
88. un coefficient
89. des concepts
90. le concept
91. le médecin
92. les médecins
93. des professeurs
94. un ingénieur
95. une opération
96. des opérations
97. un œil
98. des yeux
99. un téléphone
100. la télévision
101. des influences
102. sous des influences
103. le flux
104. un orchestre
105. des orchestres
106. derrière l'orchestre
107. sur le podium
108. dans les autos
109. des théâtres
110. dans les théâtres

Test I B, pages 183–184

Chapter

Adjectives: Position
and Agreement

10. Adjectives

An *adjective* is a word whose chief function is to *limit* and *define more precisely* the meaning of a noun. This function may be demonstrated by noticing the progressive limitation in the following series. (Refer to the squares in the adjoining figure.)

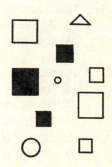

a. Look at the SQUARES.
(You look at all of them as an entity when the noun is used alone.)

b. Look at the WHITE squares.
(When one adjective is used, our attention is already greatly concentrated.)

c. Look at the SMALL WHITE squares.
(Two adjectives further define which squares we should observe.)

d. Look at the TOP SMALL WHITE square.
(Just *one* of the seven squares is eligible to receive our attention.)

11. Position of Adjectives

Adjectives normally *follow* the noun they limit. In translating, we restore English order by skipping over the noun to the adjective, then returning to read the noun:

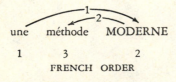

une	méthode	MODERNE		a	MODERN	method
1	3	2		1	2	3
	FRENCH ORDER				ENGLISH ORDER	

le plateau CONTINENTAL   the CONTINENTAL plateau

12. Agreement of Adjectives

Adjectives agree in gender and number with the noun they qualify. The basic form listed in vocabularies is *masculine singular*. This form is made feminine by adding -e; either masculine or feminine form may be made plural by adding -s. Hence most adjectives have four possible forms:

	SINGULAR	PLURAL
Masculine	grand	grands
Feminine	grande	grandes

The reader need not be able to form these agreements, as the work has already been done by the French writers. Note, however, that the correspondence of gender and number helps show to what noun an adjective applies:

un fait intéressant (*m.s.*)   des faits intéressants (*m.pl.*)
une table intéressante (*f.s.*)   des tables intéressantes (*f.pl.*)

a. Adjectives ending in -e in the basic form. Some adjectives like **magnifique**, **autre** (*other*), and **jeune** (*young*) end in an unaccented -e; these do *not* add another -e for the feminine: both *m.* and *f.* singular are the same, and *m.* and *f.* plural are the same.

un plan   **magnifique**   des plans   **magnifiques**
une table   **magnifique**   des tables   **magnifiques**

b. Adjectives ending in -s or -x in the basic form. These adjectives already have a plural-like ending in the masculine singular, and do not change in the masculine plural:

un homme   **heureux**   des hommes   **heureux**
une femme   heureuse   des femmes   heureuses

Note that adjectives ending in -x change the -x to -s before adding the characteristic feminine ending -e: **heureux** (*m.*), **heureuse** (*f.*) *happy*.

13. Prepositions

Learn the following prepositions:

avec	with	**à**	to; at, in (a city)
sans	without	**de**	of; from
par	by; through		(**d'** before a vowel or mute *h*.)

EXERCISES
Series A (§§10–13)

Translate into English. Find the words you do not know in the vocabulary at the back of the book.

I.
1. une possibilité historique
2. des possibilités historiques
3. un but† utile
4. des buts inutiles
5. des cas pathologiques
6. un plan géométrique
7. une cathédrale historique
8. une machine automatique
9. des machines automatiques
10. un économiste énigmatique
11. une expérience† biologique
12. un cas identique
13. un tube cylindrique
14. des minéraux métalliques
15. des théories contradictoires
16. une difficulté énorme
17. des difficultés énormes
18. un diamètre critique
19. un cas extrême
20. des constatations certaines
21. un fait intéressant
22. un moyen efficace
23. une structure magnifique
24. la théorie comique
25. des théories ridicules
26. la musique dynamique
27. l'Institut national
28. la construction intérieure
29. les théories actuelles†
30. un plan circulaire

II.
31. par la science physique
32. de l'hypothèse newtonienne
33. de l'architecture byzantine
34. sans occupations sérieuses
35. à la collection complète
36. avec une pression verticale
37. avec la machine automatique
38. d'une exagération mortelle
39. de l'état naturel
40. dans le mouvement scientifique
41. une monotonie insupportable
42. des cellules photoélectriques
43. à l'océan Pacifique
44. de la forme ancestrale
45. des résultats [results] variables
46. sans résultat
47. des cas importants
48. avec la révolution annuelle
    de la planète
49. de composition identique
50. des systèmes différents
51. des parties actives
52. le poids atomique
53. à l'élément simple
54. de l'hémisphère nord [northern]
55. des cas favorables
56. le but principal
57. le résultat principal
58. par l'expérience originale
59. dans l'océan Atlantique
60. par un moyen empirique
61. sans l'orchestre symphonique
62. à côté d'une structure magnifique
63. la partie méridionale [southern]

Test II A, pages 185–186

14. Preceding Expressions

Although most adjectives *follow* the noun in noun-adjective groups (§11), there are some which habitually precede the noun (§15). Certain other expressions ordinarily are also found before the noun and can be translated in the order in which they appear: **expressions of quantity** such as *many, several, some* (§16), **possessive adjectives** such as *my, your, our* (§17), and **numbers** (§18).

Sometimes an adjective not normally preceding will be placed before the noun for stylistic or emphatic purposes; but this should cause no difficulty in translation, as all adjectives in a group must be translated before the noun anyway.

EXAMPLES: une **nouvelle** machine   (nouvelle is listed in §15)

beaucoup de café   EXPRESSION OF QUANTITY
much coffee

ma machine à écrire   POSSESSIVE ADJECTIVE
my typewriter

trois machines à écrire   NUMBER
three typewriters

15. Normally Preceding Adjectives

The following adjectives usually precede the noun in a noun-adjective group. As they are very frequently encountered, they should be learned thoroughly as a part of everyday vocabulary in all fields.

bon, -ne[1]	good	vieux, vieil**, vieille	old
mauvais, -e	bad	beau, bel**, belle	fine, beautiful
grand, -e	big	nouveau, nouvel**, nouvelle	new
petit, -e	small	ce, cet**, cette	this
jeune	young	autre	other
		même	same

LESS IMPORTANT

joli, -e	pretty		bas, -se	low
haut, -e	high		long, -ue	long

** These four forms are alternate masculine singular forms, used when a masculine noun begins with a vowel or mute *h*:

un **bel** arbre	a beautiful tree	**cet h**omme	this man
un **vieil** homme	an old man	un **nouvel** élève	a new student

Three forms are listed for these adjectives. The first two are masculine; the last (always ending in **-e** like every other feminine adjective) is feminine singular.

16. Expressions of Quantity

Learn the following expressions of quantity:

plusieurs	several	assez de	enough
quelques	a few	trop de	too much, too many
la plupart des	most (of the)	peu de	very few, very little
bien des	many, much, lots of	plus de	more
beaucoup de	many; much	moins de	less; fewer

1. **bon, -ne.** This system of notation indicates that the basic masculine form is **bon.** The feminine is formed by adding the letters following the dash: **bonne.** The plurals are formed by adding **-s** to either *m.* or *f.* as desired.

Note that the feminine form always ends in an unaccented **-e,** however irregular the spelling may be.

17. Possessive Adjectives

Learn the following third-person possessive adjectives:

son (with masculine singular nouns) his, her, its
       (and before *fs.* nouns beginning with a vowel: **son université, son école**)
 sa (with feminine singular nouns) his, her, its
ses (with plural nouns, *f.* or *m.*) his, her, its
leur (with singular nouns, *f.* or *m.*) their
leurs (with plural nouns, *f.* or *m.*) their

EXAMPLES

son poids (*m.*)	his weight; her weight; its weight
sa table (*f.*)	his table; her table; its table
ses tables (*f.*)	his tables; her tables; its tables
leur plan (*m.*)	their plan
leurs théories (*f.*)	their theories

18. Numbers 1–10; 100, 1000

The following numbers should be learned:

un, une	one	**premier, première**	first
deux	two	**second, deuxième**	second
trois	three	**troisième**	third
quatre	four	**quatrième**	fourth
cinq	five	**cinquième**	fifth
six	six	**sixième**	sixth
sept	seven	**septième**	seventh
huit	eight	**huitième**	eighth
neuf	nine	**neuvième**	ninth
dix	ten	**dixième**	tenth
cent	one hundred	**centième**	100th
mille	one thousand	**millième**	1000th

The numbers in the first column are called CARDINAL NUMBERS; those in the second, since they indicate order, are ORDINAL NUMBERS. Most ordinal numbers are distinguished by the ending **-ième**. (See Appendix D for a more complete list.)

19. Contractions

The prepositions **à** (*to, at*) and **de** (*of, from*) combine with the articles **le** and **les** as follows:

au = (à + le)	*to the, at the*	**du** = (de + le)	*of the, from the*
aux = (à + les)	*to the, at the*	**des** = (de + les)	*of the, from the*

NOTE: **des** means (a) *of the,* (b) *from the,* or (c) *some* [§6]. The context of the sentence in which it appears will indicate which to use.

EXERCISES
Series B (§§14–19)

I. Translate into English:

1. la grande pyramide
2. le nouveau style
3. du nouveau style (*2 ways*)
4. des talents (*3 ways*)
5. de grands talents [2]
6. de nouveaux développements
7. cette grande pyramide
8. ce nouveau plan
9. ce vieil homme
10. cet arbre
11. des arbres (*3 ways*)
12. beaucoup d'arbres [3]
13. trop d'arbres [3]
14. trois arbres
15. trois grands arbres
16. un long boulevard
17. plusieurs résultats intéressants
18. quelques grands dangers
19. trop d'énergie [3]
20. moins de diffraction
21. moins d'arbres
22. une belle rue [*street*]
23. une rue large†
24. un autre cas
25. une autre rue
26. trois autres expériences†
27. une longue rue
28. de longues rues intéressantes [2]
29. une vieille théorie
30. un mauvais ministre
31. un petit animal
32. un grand animal
33. six musiciens
34. six petites corrections
35. un bel arbre
36. un bel homme
37. ce grand danger
38. cette longue rue
39. du grand danger
40. des obstacles naturels
41. ces longues rues
42. ces beaux édifices
43. cet édifice imposant
44. cet autre édifice ridicule
45. l'état [*state*] naturel
46. les étoiles [*stars*] fixes
47. cette presse hydraulique
48. ces presses hydrauliques
49. ces autres presses hydrauliques
50. l'univers physique
51. un autre état
52. les nouvelles positions
53. de nouvelles expériences [2]
54. aux nouveaux états
55. au nouvel état
56. de la grande attraction
57. de longues expériences [2]
58. la partie active
59. des crises industrielles
60. par une courte méthode

II. Exercise on Contractions (§19). Translate the **boldface** words into good English. Some partitives have been included (*some*).

61. (We have seen) **des pyramides.**
62. (There are) **des pyramides** (in Egypt).

---

2. When **de** alone appears in front of an adjective, disregard it, or use "some."
3. **de** becomes **d'** before a vowel or a mute *h*.

63. (The sides) **des pyramides** (are rough).
64. (Moving away) **des pyramides,** (we found water).
65. (What is your opinion) **du nouveau style?**
66. (The trend is away) **du nouveau style.**
67. (There is a man who has) **des talents.**
68. (Let's examine the indicator) **de l'instrument.**
69. (The indicators) **des instruments** (are broken).
70. (We have) **des instruments** (in the laboratory).
71. (We are returning) **du théâtre.**
72. (The stage) **du théâtre** (is large).
73. (He is going) **au théâtre.**
74. (This is oxygen) **à l'état liquide.**
75. (This play has been seen) **aux théâtres** (of Paris).
76. **Des lignes sinueuses** (represent rivers on this map).
77. (He is referring) **aux phénomènes isolés** (of just one experiment).

III. Expressions of Quantity and Numbers. Translate into English:

78. plusieurs symphonies excellentes
79. quelques bâtiments gothiques
80. beaucoup de possibilités intéressantes
81. assez de machines automatiques
82. moins de danger
83. bien des cas pathologiques
84. beaucoup de cas pathologiques
85. peu de pression horizontale
86. la plupart des expériences biologiques

87. dix théories sérieuses
88. la neuvième théorie considérée ici
89. huit grands arbres magnifiques
90. la huitième symphonie de Beethoven
91. sept mois [*months*] agréables
92. le septième mois de l'année
93. trois plumes [*feathers*] rouges
94. quatre roses
95. trois sortes de roses

IV. Possessive adjectives (§17). Translate:

96. ses théories intéressantes
97. son état solide
98. sa pression verticale
99. leur architecture moderne
100. leurs buts
101. leur nouveau plan
102. leurs résultats intéressants
103. son état liquide

104. leurs études
105. leurs échantillons [*samples*]
106. sa méthode perfectionnée
107. leur maison neuve [*brand-new*]
108. sa petite maison
109. ses symphonies romantiques
110. leur action inattendue [*unexpected*]

Test II B, pages 189–190

Chapter

III

20. Verb Listings

Verbs, which indicate some kind of action, are listed in dictionaries in the infinitive form (e.g., **examiner** *to examine;* **développer** *to develop*). The characteristic feature of the English infinitive is that it is preceded by the word *to.*

a. *Infinitive Types.* There are three main types of regular French infinitives. They are classified by the ending of the infinitive as (1) **-er** type, (2) **-ir** type, and (3) **-re** type. The first type is by far the most common kind.

> (1) **arriv/*er***   to arrive; to happen
> (2) **fin/*ir***   to finish
> (3) **vend/*re***   to sell

b. *Verb Parts.* A verb form consists of a *stem* and an *ending.* Remove the infinitive ending; the stem remains:

> arriv / er
> STEM   ENDING (infinitive)

The *stem* of a regular verb is found in *all forms of the verb,* and provides a sure means of identifying it. [IRREGULAR verbs do not have unchanging stems, and must be learned more thoroughly.]

21. Past Participles

Past participles of verbs are used in all compound tenses (to be examined later), and may be used as adjectives. To determine the English meaning of a past participle, say to yourself "I have . . . " and the form of the verb in question which naturally fits this phrase. For example, to determine the past participle of *to sell* (an infinitive), say "I have . . . sold." *Sold* is the past participle of *to sell.* (We shall use the abbreviation *pp.*)

a. *Formation of the Past Participle.* Drop the infinitive ending of the verb, and add the ending for the past participle:

	VERB TYPE	ADD *pp.* ENDING
(1)	-er	-é
(2)	-ir	-i
(3)	-re	-u

15

EXAMPLES:

(1)	observ/er	to observe	pp.	observé	observed
(2)	bât/ir	to build	pp.	bâti	built
(3)	rend/re	to render	pp.	rendu	rendered

b. *Use of the Past Participle as Adjective.* Observe the use of these past participles:

un fait **observé**	an observed fact
la méthode **perfectionnée**	the perfected method
les faits **observés**	the observed facts
les methodes **perfectionnées**	the perfected methods

The above examples indicate that past participles used as **adjectives** follow the rule for agreement (§12), by adding -e for the feminine, -s for the plurals.

c. *Past Participle as Predicate Adjective.* Note the following examples of agreement of past participles after the verb **est** *is* and after **sont** *are:*

Le fait est **observé**	The fact is observed.
Les faits sont **observés**.	The facts are observed.
La méthode est **perfectionnée**.	The method is perfected.
Les méthodes sont **perfectionnées**.	The methods are perfected.

This arrangement may occur with any verb (such as **paraît** *appears*) which takes a predicate adjective.

Cette méthode paraît **perfectionnée**.

EXERCISES

Series A (§§20–21)

Translate into English. Look up words you do not know in the vocabulary.

I.
1. arrivé (*2 ways*)
2. finie
3. vendu
4. vendues
5. examinés
6. développée
7. bâties
8. rendu
9. rendue
10. perfectionnées
11. accéléré
12. pénétrées
13. accompagné
14. diminuées
15. enrichie

II.
16. l'architecte est fatigué
17. l'accident est observé
18. la construction est finie
19. la maison est vendue
20. les maisons sont vendues
21. les résultats examinés
22. un circuit développé
23. une désintégration accélérée
24. un mélange enrichi
25. un échantillon composé
26. des phénomènes isolés
27. la vapeur condensée
28. le béton [*concrete*] armé
29. un effort concentré
30. une particule désintégrée
31. une quantité déterminée
32. une résistance éliminée
33. l'hypothèse compliquée

14. **diminu/er** *v.* to diminish 25. **échantillon** *nm.* sample; **compos/er** *v.* to compound
27. **vapeur** *nf.* steam; vapor 28. **arm/er** *v.* to arm; to reinforce

34. beaucoup d'hypothèses compliquées
35. plusieurs difficultés éliminées
36. sur une autre surface unie

37. sous la forme différenciée
38. cet état évolué du poisson
39. La désintégration est accélérée.

40. La désintégration est très [*very*] accélérée.
41. Le circuit est examiné.
42. Les circuits sont examinés.
43. Le mélange est enrichi.
44. C'est [*It is*] un mélange enrichi de gaz.
45. Plusieurs phénomènes sont isolés.
46. Quelques-uns des édifices baroques sont très beaux.
47. Bien des cathédrales sont gothiques.
48. La littérature de la France est d'un intérêt extraordinaire.
49. La physique nucléaire est très compliquée.
50. Le grand Sphinx de Gisèh (Égypte) est énigmatique.
51. Les comètes ont [*have*] des orbites allongés.
52. La particule a [*has*] un mouvement accéléré dans le cyclotron.
53. Le nez de Cléopâtre a un intérêt historique.
54. Un triangle isocèle a deux côtés égaux.
55. C'est une hypothèse actuellement éliminée.
56. La Terre a un axe incliné.

III. Before translating the following sentences, divide each into sense-making noun-groups by placing parentheses around (a) nouns with their articles and adjectives and (b) prepositional phrases. For example:

57. La difficulté énorme **de** la distribution générale **de** ce produit est un inconvénient considérable.

The words in **boldface** type are prepositions, and indicate the beginning of a prepositional phrase. Enclosing groups in parentheses, we have

57. (La difficulté énorme) (**de** la distribution générale) (**de** ce produit) est (un inconvénient considérable.)

Only the verb **est** is left out of the groups. Now it is easy to translate each group as was done in the earlier exercises; but this time we will build a whole sentence.

58. Le but de ces expériences est la résolution de quelques problèmes compliqués.
59. La lecture† générale est un devoir nécessaire aux personnes cultivées.
60. Ce bâtiment magnifique est bâti en béton armé.
61. Le terrain choisi est extrêmement défavorable à la construction désirée.

36. **uni, -e** *adj.* smooth   38. **état** *nm.* state; **évolu/er** *v.* to evolve; **poisson** *nm.* fish 43. **mélange** *nm.* mixture 44. **de** with 49. **physique** *nf.* Physics 51. **allong/er** *v.* to elongate 53. **intérêt** *nm.* interest 54. **côté** *nm.* side; **égal, -e** *adj.* equal 57. **produit** *nm.* product 58. **résolution** *nf.* solution 59. **devoir** *nm.* duty   60. **bâtiment** *nm.* building; **bât/ir** *v.* to build; **béton** *nm.* concrete   61. **terrain** *nm.* building-site; **chois/ir** *v.* to choose, to select; **défavorable** *adj.* unfavorable

62. La première symphonie de Saint-Saëns est très bien connue.
63. Dans les symphonies, les mouvements rapides sont gâtés dans une salle de théâtre trop grande. (**gâter = to spoil**)
64. Une bonne bibliothèque est essentielle à la lecture.†
65. La cybernétique est une nouvelle science qui traite des machines automatiques.
66. La sociologie est une science moderne qui traite des phénomènes sociaux.
67. Une partie compliquée de la science physique est la physique nucléaire.

Test III A, pages 191–192

22. Adverbs

Adverbs have already been used in the exercises to qualify verbs and adjectives:

un mouvement **très** accéléré	a **very** (much) accelerated movement
un terrain **extrêmement** défavorable	an **extremely** unfavorable site

Adverbs are placed (a) before an adjective or (b) after a verb. Many adverbs which end in **-ment** (like the English *-ly*) are placed almost anywhere.

Learn the following important adverbs:

très	very	**plus**	more
bien	well; very	**moins**	less
trop	too much; too	**tant**	so; so much
assez	rather	**à peu près**	approximately
beaucoup	very much		

Note the effect of adverbs on the meaning of adjectives:

un **grand** animal	a big animal
un *très* **grand** animal	a **very** big animal
un **cas intéressant**	an interesting case
un cas *assez* intéressant	a **rather** interesting case
un **nombre réduit**	a reduced number
un nombre *considérablement* réduit	a **considerably** reduced number
l'eau **profonde**	deep water
l'eau *moins* profonde	shallower water ("less deep")

NOTE: The adverb **peu** is sometimes a signal to translate the following adjective by its *antonym;* the translation *not so* (*adj.*) may also apply:

l'eau **profonde**	deep water
l'eau *peu* profonde	**shallow** water
un événement **important**	an important event
un événement *peu* important	an unimportant event
un animal *peu* féroce	**not so** ferocious an animal

63. **salle de théâtre** *nf.* auditorium   64. **bibliothèque** *nf.* library   65. **qui** which, who; **cybernétique** *nf.*   Cybernetics (*a branch of engineering dealing with automatic machines*)   66. **social, -e** *adj.* social

23. Attributes: *à-* and *de-* phrases

Prepositional phrases beginning with à or **de,** or with a contraction of one of these (§19), often serve as a single adjective with a noun:

des moteurs (à pétrole)	gasoline motors
une lampe (à huile)	an oil lamp
une machine (à écrire)	a typewriter ("a machine for writing")
un animal (à quatre pattes)	a four-footed animal
un bateau (à vapeur)	a steamboat
une galerie (de peinture)	an art gallery
une salle (de réunion)	a meeting-room
le hall (de réception)	the reception hall

24. Materials: *en* or *de*

To indicate the material of which an object is made, a prepositional phrase beginning with **en** or **de** is often used after the name of the object:

une maison (en brique)	a brick house
une montre (en or)	a gold watch
un bâtiment (en béton armé)	a reinforced-concrete structure
des planchers (de béton)	concrete floors

25. Regular Verbs, Present Tense (3rd person)

The present tense of regular verbs is formed from the *stem* (§20) plus the following endings:

In French a verb *must* have a noun or pronoun subject; otherwise it is an imperative (p. 126).

VERB TYPE		-er	-ir	-re
ENDINGS	he, she, it (*s.*)	-e	-it	(stem only)
	they (*pl.*)	-ent	-issent	-ent

EXAMPLES:

(1) arriv/er:	Les musiciens arrivent.	The musicians **are arriving.**
	Le général arrive.	The general **is arriving.**
(2) fin/ir:	Le physicien finit l'expérience.	The physicist **is finishing** the experiment.
	Les physiciens finissent l'expérience.	The physicists **are finishing** the experiment.
(3) vend/re:	Le professeur **vend** sa maison.	The professor **is selling** his house.
	Les professeurs vend**ent** leurs maisons.	The professors **are selling** their houses.

The present tense may be translated into English so as to indicate that the action is *taking place* at the moment, or that it *usually takes place*:

$$\text{il finit} = \begin{cases} \text{he is finishing} & \text{(right now)} \\ \text{he finishes} & \text{(habitually)} \\ \text{he does finish} & \text{(for questions: Does he finish . . . ?)} \end{cases}$$

EXERCISES

Series B (§§22–25)

I. Translate (see §22)

1. un gaz raréfié; un gaz très raréfié; plusieurs gaz raréfiés
2. une cathédrale énorme; une très grande cathédrale
3. dans un milieu différent; un milieu légèrement différent; au milieu du lac
4. pour la partie essentielle; pour la partie la plus essentielle
5. par des vibrations; par les vibrations rapides; par des vibrations extrêmement rapides
6. un corps répandu dans la nature; un corps plus répandu dans la nature
7. la plupart des minéraux; bien des minéraux; plusieurs minéraux
8. une partie active; une partie plus active; la partie la plus active
9. un polygone irrégulier; quelques polygones considérablement irréguliers
10. cette évaluation exacte; cette évaluation assez exacte; ces évaluations plus exactes
11. quatre arrangements possibles; cinq arrangements également possibles
12. un globe sphérique; un globe à peu près sphérique
13. la célèbre comète de Halley; la comète la plus célèbre; une comète moins célèbre
14. une variation importante; des variations moins importantes
15. plusieurs systèmes différents; plusieurs systèmes entièrement différents; quelques systèmes légèrement différents
16. tant de matières homogènes; tant de matières exclusivement homogènes
17. bien des sections étroites; bien des sections assez étroites
18. un pays démocratique; tous les pays démocratiques; tous les pays actuellement démocratiques
19. une vague haute; une vague très haute; les vagues les plus hautes
20. de l'eau profonde; de l'eau moins profonde; de l'eau peu profonde
21. une hypothèse raisonnable; une hypothèse plus raisonnable; l'hypothèse la plus raisonnable

II. Translate (see §§23; 24):

22. des bateaux à vapeur
23. plusieurs machines à écrire

1. **raréfi/er** *v.* to rarefy; to thin out   3. **milieu** *nm.* environment; **légèrement** *adv.* slightly; **au milieu de** in the middle of; **lac** *nm.* lake   6. **corps** *nm.* substance; **répand/re** *v.* to spread; **répandu** *pp.* widespread   8. See Adjective comparisons, page 52.   9. **polygone** *nm.* polygon (*Geom.*)   11. **également** *adv.* equally   13. **célèbre** *adj.* famous   16. **homogène** *adj.* homogeneous   17. **étroit,-e** *adj.* narrow **pays** *nm.* country   19. **vague** *nf.* wave   21. **raisonnable** *adj.* reasonable; **la plus** the most   22 **bateau** *nm.* boat; ship; **vapeur** *nf.* *vapor, steam*   23. **écrire*** *v.* to write
*Irregular verb

24. un plancher de béton

25. une salle de réunion

26. une salle à manger

27. des relais d'une extrême sensibilité

28. un monsieur peu intelligent

29. des basiliques à charpente

30. des horloges à pendule

31. une salle à voûte plate

32. des coupoles en brique

33. une machine à structure simple

34. une rétine à structure assez simple

35. une étoile à dimensions colossales

36. des noyaux à polarité chromatiques

37. d'une nation à géographie diverse

38. deux petites îles cultivées

39. trois moteurs à pétrole

40. une symphonie à quatre mouvements; une symphonie a quatre mouvements

41. un homme à cheveux noirs; cet [*this*] homme a les cheveux noirs

III. **Translate** (see §25). Give two translations for each verb in the present tense, unless the sense of the statement makes it clear that only one of the two possibilities is correct. Omit "the" in generalities like No. 46, *L'oxygène*.

42. Un miroir donne l'image des objets placés devant lui.

43. Les miroirs donnent les images des objets placés devant eux.

44. Plusieurs physiciens considèrent ce cas compliqué.

45. La construction des instruments de musique repose sur les propriétés vibratoires de l'air.

46. L'oxygène existe dans l'air et dans la constitution des végétaux et des animaux.

47. Le cultivateur fournit de l'azote au sol sous forme d'engrais.

48. L'oxygène forme la partie active de l'air atmosphérique.

49. Les mathématiciens classent l'algèbre parmi les mathématiques pures.

50. La géométrie mesure l'étendue. Les géomètres mesurent l'étendue.

51. Les musiciens fournissent de la musique au public.

52. Les architectes préparent les plans des nouveaux bâtiments.

53. Les psychologues étudient les phénomènes de l'âme.

24. **plancher** *nm.* floor; **béton** *nm.* concrete   25. **réunion** *nf.* meeting; **salle** *nf.* room   26. **mang/er** *v.* to eat   27. **relai** *nm.* relay (*Mech.*)   29. **charpente** *nf.* frame, carpentry work   30. **horloge** *nf.* clock; **pendule** *nm.* pendulum   31. **voûte** *nf.* vault, arch; **plat, -e** *adj.* flat   32. **coupole** *nf.* dome, cupola   34. **rétine** *nf.* retina (*of eye*)   35. **étoile** *nf.* star   36. **noyau** *nm.* nucleus   41. **cheveux** *nm.* hair; **noir, -e** *adj.* black   42. **devant lui** before it; **donn/er** *v.* to give   43. **devant eux** before them   44. **physicien** *nm.* physicist   46. **constitution†** *nf.* composition, make-up; **végétal** *nm.* vegetation   47. **fourn/ir** *v.* to supply, to furnish; **azote** *nm.* nitrogen; **engrais** *nm.* fertilizer; **sol** *nm.* soil   49. **parmi** *prep.* among   50. **étendue** *nf.* extent, size, area   53. **psychologue** *nm.* psychologist; **âme** *nf.* mind, soul

54. Les ingénieurs bâtissent des édifices, des ponts et des machines.
55. Un agent de police protège les individus du danger.
56. Les agents de police protègent le public général.
57. Les détectives recherchent les personnes dangereuses ou suspectes.
58. Les historiens sont des personnes qui examinent en détail les faits de l'histoire politique ou militaire.
59. Les généraux donnent beaucoup d'ordres nécessaires; les soldats exécutent les ordres de leurs officiers.
60. Les professeurs donnent des cours aux universités.
61. Les chimistes sont des personnes qui pratiquent la chimie; la chimie est une science exacte qui étudie la nature des corps.
62. Un sous-marin est un navire qui navigue sous la surface de la mer.
63. Un lycée est une école française qui ressemble peu aux high-schools des États-Unis.
64. Les trains transportent des marchandises au marché.
65. La locomotive est une machine qui remorque les voitures d'un train.

---

54. **ingénieur** *nm.* engineer; **pont** *nm.* bridge   55. **agent de police** *nm.* policeman
57. **recherch/er** *v.* to seek, look for   60. **cours** *nm.* course   61. **chimiste** *nm.* chemist; **pratiqu/er** *v.* to engage in; **chimie** *nf.* chemistry; **étudi/er** *v.* to study; **corps simple** *nm.* element (*Chem.*)
62. **sous-marin** *nm.* submarine; **navire** *nm.* ship; **navigu/er** *v.* to navigate; **mer** *nf.* sea
63. **lycée** *nm.* lycée (*French secondary school*); **école** *nf.* school; **français, -e** *adj.* French; **ressembl/er à** *v.* to resemble; **États-Unis** United States   64. **marché** *nm.* market
65. **remorqu/er** *v.* to tow   **voiture** *nf.* car

Test III B, pages 193–194

Chapter IV

Subject Pronouns · Reflexive Verbs

dont · Multiple Modifiers

Participle-Preposition Linkage

Infinitives · Impersonal Verbs

26. Subject Pronouns, 3rd Person

The pronouns which are used as subjects of third-person verbs (§25) are as follows:

SINGULAR

il	he *or* it (used in place of a masculine singular noun)
elle	she *or* it (used in place of a feminine singular noun)
on	one *or general, unspecific* "they" (sometimes written l'on)

PLURAL

ils }	they	(used in place of a masculine plural noun)
elles }		(used in place of a feminine plural noun)

EXAMPLES:

Le musicien arrive.   Il arrive. (*m.s.*)

Les musiciens arrivent.   Ils arrivent. (*m.pl.*)

La nation est grande.   Elle est grande. (*f.s.*)

Les nations sont grandes.   Elles sont grandes. (*f.pl.*)

EXAMPLES of the use of **on**. Change to passive: the OBJECT becomes SUBJECT:

On étudie ce cas.   ROUGH: One is studying this case.
BETTER: This case is being studied.

On finit l'expérience.   ROUGH: They are finishing the experiment.
BETTER: The experiment is being finished.

RULE: When the subject is **on**, a better translation is usually obtained by using the *direct object* as a subject, and making the action passive. (e.g., "is being" done)

27. Reflexive Verbs

a. *General.* Certain verbs are classified as *reflexive*, meaning that the action indicated is *reflected* back upon the doer. These verbs are listed with the reflexive

23

pronoun se in vocabularies. As an example, let us examine the verb lav/er *to wash*. Used in the regular way (*not* reflexively), we have:

Ce monsieur *lave* sa voiture.   This gentleman is washing his car.

The action here is performed upon the car, not upon the gentleman. However, with the reflexive verb *se* laver, we have:

Ce monsieur *se lave*.   This gentleman is washing himself.
                and
Ce monsieur *se lave* la figure.   This gentleman is washing his face.

In the last two examples, the reflexive pronoun indicates that the gentleman is performing the action upon *himself.*

b. *Translation of Reflexive Verbs.* With many reflexive verbs, a simple solution is to read se as a form of *to be* (*is* or *are*), and the verb itself as if it were the *past participle* (§21):

La lumière *se propage* ...   The light is propagated ...
Les maisons *se trouvent* ...   The houses are found ...
                                        (Literally: "*find themselves*")

28. *Dont* ("of which," "of whom") "whose"

This important word introduces a clause of a parenthetical nature within a sentence. Such a clause always begins with **dont** and ends just before a verb. In translating at first, it may be of assistance to isolate the **dont**-clause as has been done below:

Le monsieur / **dont** ils parlent / est malade.
The gentleman /   / is sick.   MAIN CLAUSE
                of whom they are speaking

The most useful translation of **dont** is *whose*. In English the word "whose" must be followed immediately by a NOUN. Therefore after translating **dont** as *whose,* go immediately to the next noun; translate the noun; return to the words skipped (if any) between **dont** and the noun.

EXAMPLES   (1) L'événement / **dont** LA PROBABILITÉ est cherchée / ...
                              1   2

                The event / **whose** PROBABILITY is being sought ...
                              1   2

              (2) Les données / **dont** il a examiné LA VALEUR / sont exactes.
                              1   2

                The data / **whose** VALUE he has examined / are accurate.
                          1   2

REMEMBER
After translating **dont,** go to the next NOUN.

EXERCISES

Series A (§§26–28)

I. Translate (§26):

1. La construction: elle est finie.
2. La littérature française: elle est extraordinaire.
3. Un triangle équilatéral: il a trois côtés égaux.
4. La Terre: elle a un axe incliné.
5. Les symphonies: elles ont quatre mouvements.
6. Les physiciens: ils finissent l'expérience.
7. Les musiciens: ils arrivent.
8. Les professeurs: ils parlent français.
9. Ces maisons: elles sont construites en brique.
10. L'expérience: elle est terminée.
11. On prépare les plans.
12. Dans une université on étudie les arts et les sciences.
13. Dans l'armée, on donne beaucoup d'ordres aux soldats.
14. On trouve de l'oxygène dans la constitution des végétaux.

II. Translate into polished English:

15. L'air atmosphérique se compose de plusieurs gaz.
16. La lumière se propage en ligne droite à une grande vitesse.
17. Cette règle se déduit de nos observations.
18. Ces cas se divisent en deux groupes.
19. Un rayon lumineux se réfléchit dans une seule direction.
20. Parmi les éléments qui se trouvent dans l'air sont le néon, le krypton et l'hélium.
21. La plupart des substances minérales se présentent sous des formes cristallines.
22. La surface du globe se compose de grandes masses de terres qu'on appelle des *continents*.
23. Le lac isolé *dont parle Rousseau* se trouve en Suisse.
24. Les problèmes *dont les difficultés sont grandes* sont résolus.
25. Les données *dont il a examiné la valeur* se trouvent sur la table.
26. Les agents de police, *dont l'honnêteté est certaine*, protègent le grand public.
27. Ce train, *dont la locomotive est électrique*, porte beaucoup de voyageurs.
28. Cette cathédrale, *dont la nef est très belle*, se trouve à Paris.
29. La composition *dont le troisième mouvement est très lent* est une symphonie de César Franck.
30. Le problème est plus simple si l'on divise les cas en deux catégories.

16. **en ligne droite** in a straight line; **vitesse** *nf.* speed, velocity   17. **règle** *nf.* rule; **déduit** *pp.* of **déduire*** to deduce; **nos** our   18. **divis/er** *v.* to divide.   19. **rayon** *nm.* ray; **lumineux** *adj.* light, luminous; **seul, -e** *adj.* single   20. **se trouv/er** *v.* to be found 22. **appel/er*** *v.* to call   23. **parl/er** *v.* to speak; **la Suisse** Switzerland   26. **honnêteté** *nf.* honesty   28. **nef** *nf.* nave; **se trouv/er** *v.* to be located   29. **lent** *adj.* slow

Test IV A, pages 195–197

READINGS

A. [30] La Lumière

[31] La lumière se propage en ligne droite avec une vitesse de 300.000 kilomètres par seconde. [32] Un rayon lumineux qui tombe sur un miroir se réfléchit dans une direction unique. [33] Grâce à cette réflexion, le miroir donne l'image des objets placés devant lui.

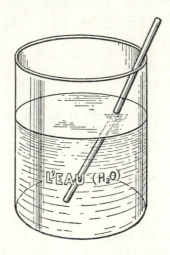

Effet de la réfraction: Un bâton plongé dans l'eau paraît brisé

[34] Un rayon lumineux change de direction lorsqu'il passe d'un milieu dans un milieu différent; on dit qu'il *se réfracte*. [35] C'est à cause de la réfraction qu'un bâton plongé dans l'eau paraît brisé.

B. [36] Le Son

[37] Le son est produit par des vibrations qui résultent de la compression de l'air. [38] Il parcourt l'air avec une vitesse de 340 mètres par seconde;

30. **lumière** *nf*. light   31. **300.000** *In French numbers, a comma is used as a decimal point; this period is the equivalent of our comma, used only to divide thousands.*   32. **tomb/er** *v*. to fall; **miroir** *nm*. mirror   33. **Grâce à** Because of, thanks to; **lui** it (*here*)   34. **lorsque** when; **milieu** *nm*. medium; environment; **dit** *v*. (*fr.* **dire***) says: **on dit** it is said   35. **à cause de** because of; **bâton** *nm*. stick; **bris/er** *v*. to break   36. **son** *nm*. sound   38. **parcour/ir*** *v*. to travel through

dans les liquides et surtout dans les solides, sa vitesse est plus grande. [39] Lorsque le son rencontre un obstacle, il est réfléchi et produit l'écho.

[40] La construction des instruments de musique repose sur les propriétés vibratoires des cordes tendues et de l'air.

C. Napoléon en Égypte

[41] Napoléon marche aux Pyramides; il crie à ses soldats: «Du haut de ces monuments quarante siècles ont les yeux fixés sur vous.» [42] Il entre au Caire. [43] Sa flotte saute en l'air à Aboukir, détruite à l'ancre par l'amiral anglais Horatio Nelson. [44] L'armée de l'Orient est séparée de l'Europe. [45] Julien de la Drôme, fils de Julien le Conventionnel, témoin du désastre, nous en donne la description minute par minute:

[46] «Il est sept heures; la nuit se fait; le feu redouble encore. [47] A neuf heures et quelques minutes le vaisseau a sauté. [48] Il est dix heures, le feu se ralentit, et la lune se lève à droite du lieu où vient de s'élever l'explosion du vaisseau.»

[49] Quelle scène mémorable! Bonaparte assis dans l'intérieur de la Pyramide de Chéops sur le sarcophage d'un Pharaon dont la momie avait disparu, et causant avec les muphtis et les imans!

[50] Voici la description du *Moniteur,* le 27 novembre 1798: «Aujourd'hui, 25 thermidor de l'an VI de la République française une et indivisible, le général en chef, accompagné de plusieurs officiers de l'état-major et de plusieurs membres de l'Institut national, s'est transporté à la grande pyramide, dite de Chéops, dans l'intérieur de laquelle il était attendu par plusieurs muphtis et imans, chargés de lui en montrer la construction intérieure.

[51] La dernière salle où arrive le général en chef est à voûte plate, et longue de 32 pieds sur 16 de large et 19 de haut. [52] On y trouve une grande caisse de granit d'environ 8 pieds de long sur 4 d'épaisseur, qui renfermait la

---

surtout *adv.* especially   39. **rencontr/er** *v.* to encounter; **produit** *pp.* of **produire*** to produce   40. **repos/er** *v.* to rest, to depend; **tendu** *pp.* of **tendre** to stretch   41. **cri/er** *v.* to shout; **haut** *nm.* height(s); **quarante** 40; **siècle** *nm.* century; **yeux** (§8c); **vous** *pron.* you   43. **flotte** *nf.* fleet; **saut/er** *v.* to explode; **détruire*** *v.* to destroy; **à l'ancre** at anchor; **anglais, -e** *adj.* English   45. **témoin** *nm.* witness; **nous** to us; **en** of it   46. **heures** *nf. pl.* o'clock; **la nuit se fait** night is falling; **feu** *nm.* firing; **encore** again   47. **vaisseau** *nm.* ship, vessel   48. **ralent/ir** *v.* to slow down; **lune** *nf.* moon; **se lev/er*** *v.* to rise; **à droite** to the right; **lieu** *nm.* place; **vient de** [+ *infinitive*] has just; **s'élev/er** *v.* to rise, (*here*) to occur   49. **quelle** what a; **assis** seated; **Pharaon** *nm.* Pharaoh; **momie** *nf.* mummy; **disparu** *pp.* of **disparaître*** to disappear; **avait** had; **causant** chatting (The ending -ant of verbs corresponds to the English *-ing*); **muphtis et imans** (*Moslem officials*)   50. **aujourd'hui** today; **thermidor, an VI** (*new month and year established by the revolutionaries*); **chef** chief; **de** by; **état-major** *nm.* General Staff; **dite** called, named; **laquelle** which; **était attendu** was being waited for; **en** of it; **montrer** *v.* to show   51. **où** where; **pied** *nm.* foot; **sur** (*in dimensions*) by; **de large** in width; **de haut** in height   52. **y** there; **caisse** *nf.* box, case; **environ** about; **sur** by (*in dimensions*); **épaisseur** *nf.* thickness; **renfermait** used to contain

momie d'un Pharaon. [53] Il s'assied sur le bloc de granit et commence une conversation avec les autres qui sont là.»

— CHATEAUBRIAND. *Mémoires d'Outre-Tombe*

D. [54] *Les Psychologues au travail*

[55] Les étudiants demandent souvent si la psychologie est une science. [56] Comparé avec les sciences comme l'astronomie, la géologie, la physique, la chimie ou la biologie, l'objet de la psychologie paraît bien différent et bien préoccupé de lui-même. [57] En outre, les problèmes psychologiques ont été pendant si longtemps étudiés du point de vue philosophique et non scientifique qu'on a des doutes bien naturels au sujet du caractère scientifique de la psychologie. [58] Même dans les universités la psychologie est parfois classée parmi les humanités et parfois parmi les sciences sociales. [59] Le caractère scientifique de la psychologie, comme de toute autre science, naturelle ou sociale, repose sur ses méthodes et non pas sur son objet. [60] Ses méthodes sont essentiellement les mêmes que celles des autres sciences naturelles, mais ·la nature de ses matières appelle des problèmes méthodologiques qui ne se posent pas pour les autres sciences. [61] Les psychologues utilisent des variantes des méthodes suivantes: 1° *observation directe;* 2° *méthode clinique;* 3° *expérimentation.* Une autre méthode qui peut être employée pour analyser et interpréter les résultats obtenus par une de ces trois méthodes, c'est 4° *la méthode statistique.*

— NORMAN L. MUNN. *Traité de Psychologie* (Payot, Paris)

29. Two or More Adjectives Qualifying a Single Noun

Several adjectives may qualify a single noun, making a rather large *noun-adjective group.* In French, many of these adjectives follow the noun, and must be restored to a position *before the noun* for good English style. It will be well to practice seeing a noun-adjective group as a whole, allowing the eye to take in this entire unit at once. Then, as you translate, say (or write) all the adjectives in the group before mentioning the noun itself.

EXAMPLES:

(1) une machine **compliquée**   a **complicated** machine
            ADJ.

---

53. **s'assied** sits down; **là** there   54. **psychologue** *nm.* = une personne qui s'occupe de la psychologie, *i.e.,* un psychologiste; **travail** *nm.* work   55. **étudiant** *nm.* = une personne qui étudie, un élève; **souvent** *adv.* often   56. **bien** *adv.* = très; **lui-même** itself   57. **en outre** moreover; **pendant si longtemps** for such a long time; **vue** view   58. **même** even; **parfois** *adv.* sometimes   59. **toute** every (cf. §72a, page 111); **non pas** not   60. **celles** *pn.* those (cf. §51, page 71); **appelle** *v.* "calls [up]," raises   61. **1°, 2°, 3°** *correspond to* 1st, 2nd, 3rd

(2) **une autre** machine **compliquée**   **another complicated** machine
     ADJ.   ADJ.

(3) **une autre** machine **automatique compliquée**   **another complicated**
     ADJ.   ADJ. (2)   ADJ. (1)   **automatic** machine

NOTE: With two adjectives following, translate in reverse order.

(4) **une autre nouvelle** machine (**compliquée** et **lourde**)
     ADJ.   ADJ.   ADJ.

      another new, (**complicated and heavy,**) machine   (not best English order)
      another complicated and **heavy new** machine   (slightly rearranged)

(5) **beaucoup de nouvelles** machines (**compliquées mais utiles**)
              ADJ.   ADJ.

      many (**complicated** but **useful**) new machines

Note in Examples 4 and 5 that two adjectives following a noun are often joined by et (*and*) or mais (*but*).

30. Participle-[Adjective]-Prepositional Phrase Linkage

We have seen participles used as adjectives (§21b). If a participle or an adjective is immediately followed by a preposition, read straight through in French word order. Compare:

(1) les données **observées**   the **observed** data
(2) les données/**observées** (**dans ce cas**)   the data/**observed** in this case
(1) des routes **commodes**   **convenient** highways
(2) des routes **commodes pour** les voitures   highways **convenient for** vehicles

31. Infinitives

Infinitives normally appear after a preposition, and are translated as follows:

a. *After* **pour** "in order to: to—"
     pour étudier   in order to study; to study
     pour expliquer   in order to explain; to explain
     pour pouvoir*   in order to be able; to be able

b. *After* **à** *and* **de:** "to—"
     à étudier   to study
     d'expliquer   to explain
     de remarquer   to notice

c. *After other prepositions:* "—ing"
     sans étudier   without studyING
     sans voir*   without seeING
     avant de remarquer   before noticING
     après avoir* étudié   after havING studied
     après être* arrivé   after havING (lit: "being") arrived;
                      after havING happened

d. After **il faut** *it is necessary*

$$\text{il faut étudier} \begin{cases} \text{it is necessary to study} \\ \text{studying is necessary} \\ [\textit{person involved}] \text{ must study} \end{cases}$$

32. Impersonal Verbs

Learn the following impersonal verbs:

il y a	there is *or* there are
il s'agit de	it concerns; it is a matter of
il paraît que	it appears that
il (en) reste	there remain(s)
il est possible que ⎱	
il se peut que ⎰	it is possible that
il importe que	it is important that

EXERCISES

Series B (§§29–32)

I. Translate (§29):

1. un seul fait; un seul fait certain; un seul fait bien certain.
2. une méthode; une vraie méthode; les vraies méthodes expérimentales.
3. un concert; des concerts quotidiens; de petits concerts quotidiens.
4. une hypothèse; une célèbre hypothèse; la célèbre hypothèse newtonienne.
5. un mètre; un mètre carré; mille mètres carrés.
6. le sentiment religieux; un sentiment religieux secret.
7. les symphonies; les magnifiques symphonies classiques; les magnifiques et célèbres symphonies de Haydn; les magnifiques et célèbres symphonies classiques de Haydn.
8. la musique moderne; la musique instrumentale; la musique instrumentale moderne.
9. des complications mécaniques; de nouvelles complications mécaniques.
10. unis de façon intime et indestructible.
11. des occupations simples; les occupations les plus simples
12. les motifs subtils et déshonnêtes.
13. le goût exquis et pur.
14. le bâtiment; le premier bâtiment; le premier bâtiment climatisé; le premier bâtiment d'habitation climatisé.
15. un système; un nouveau système; de nouveaux systèmes de climatisation.
16. la nouvelle découverte; une découverte entièrement nouvelle.

1. **fait** *nm.* fact; **seul, -e** *adj.* single   2. **vrai, -e** *adj.* true, real   3. **quotidien, -ne** *adj.* daily
5. **carré** *adj.* square   10. **uni, -e** *adj.* united, bound together   12. *prefix* **dés-** = *English*
dis-   13. **goût** *nm.* taste; **exquis, -e** *adj.* exquisite   14. **bâtiment d'habitation** *nm.* dwelling
(*not an office building*); **hermétique** *adj.* air-tight (*for air-conditioning*)   15. **climatisation** *nf.*
air-conditioning   16. **découverte** *nf.* discovery

17. la loi; les lois; les lois physiques et chimiques; les mêmes lois physiques et chimiques.
18. des obstacles naturels presque insurmontables.
19. des crises industrielles très inattendues.
20. une autre question; une autre question relative; cette autre nouvelle question relative à nos recherches.

II. Translate (§§30, 31, 32):

21. les données observées; les données observées *dans ce cas.*
22. une substance observée; une substance observée *dans ce mélange.*
23. il y a des forces accélérées; il y a des forces accélérées *vers les centres.*
24. il s'agit de plusieurs substances résistantes; il s'agit de plusieurs substances résistantes *aux hautes températures.*
25. C'est une question relative; c'est une question relative *aux problèmes actuels;* c'est une question totalement relative.
26. Il s'agit d'une nation importante et puissante.
27. Il s'agit de plusieurs méthodes difficiles mais utiles.
28. Il reste un autre cas intéressant et important.
29. Il s'agit de soixante échantillons étudiés en détail.
30. Il paraît que l'estomac du poisson est très dilatable.
31. Dans l'algèbre il s'agit de la résolution des questions relatives aux quantités en général.
32. Il reste quelques expériences à ompléter.
33. Il importe d'examiner ces moteurs à pétrole. (§23)
34. Il se peut que les moteurs à réaction soient très efficaces. (§23)
35. Le fait important est que la matière vivante est soumise partout aux mêmes lois physiques et chimiques.
36. Les personnes faibles manquent de sincérité.
37. Être ou ne pas être, voilà la question.
38. Il importe de chercher toujours la vérité.
39. Les physiciens examinent les données pour comprendre la théorie dont il s'agit.
40. Ce gaz a pour effet de modérer l'action de l'oxygène.
41. L'homme est visiblement fait pour penser; c'est toute sa dignité et tout son mérite, et tout son devoir est de penser comme il faut. Or† l'ordre de la pensée est de commencer par soi, et par son auteur et sa fin.—PASCAL. *Pensées*, 146.
42. La mémoire est nécessaire pour toutes les opérations de la raison.

17. **loi** *nf.* law; **même** *adj.* same (§15)   18. **palais** *nm.* palace; **royaux** *adj. pl.* royal   29. **échantillon** *nm.* sample   30. **estomac** *nm.* stomach; **poisson** *nm.* fish   34. **moteur à réaction** *nm.* jet engine; **soient** may be   35. **vivant, -e** *adj.* living; **soumis** *pp. of* **soumett/re*** to submit, to subject; **partout** *adv.* everywhere   36. **faible** *adj.* weak; **manqu/er de** to lack   37. **ne pas** not   38. **cherch/er** *v.* to seek; **vérité** *nf.* truth   39. **comprend/re*** *v.* to understand   40. **avoir* pour effet** to have as an effect; **l'oxygène** Do not translate the l'.   41. **fait** (*pp. of* **faire*** to make); **pens/er** *v.* to think; **tout, -e** *adj.* all; **devoir** *nm.* duty; **comme il faut** as it is necessary = properly; **soi** oneself; **auteur** *nm.* author (i.e., creator); **fin** *nf.* end

READINGS

A. L'Oxygène

[43] L'oxygène est, de tous les corps, le plus répandu dans la nature. [44] Il existe non seulement dans l'air, dont il forme à peu près le cinquième en volume, mais il constitue les huit neuvièmes de la masse de l'eau, et il entre dans la constitution des végétaux et des animaux; enfin la plupart des minéraux en contiennent.

B. L'Azote

[45] L'azote, gaz incolore, inodore et sans saveur, n'entretient ni la combustion ni la respiration. [46] Une bougie allumée placée dans un flacon ne contenant que de l'azote s'éteint. [47] Dans l'air ce gaz a pour effet de ralentir les combustions.

[48] L'azote entre dans la composition des végétaux et de la chair des animaux. [49] Il est indispensable à la vie des plantes. [50] La terre inculte en renferme toujours, mais en quantité insuffisante; le cultivateur doit lui en fournir sous forme d'engrais.

C. Dividing the Inheritance

[51] Un vieil Arabe est sur le point de mourir. Il appelle ses trois fils dans sa chambre pour leur dire comment il désire partager ses possessions. [52] Il dit à l'aîné que sa part sera la moitié, et au second fils que sa part sera un tiers. [53] Quant au cadet [= le fils le plus jeune], sa part sera un neuvième de tous les biens de son père.

[54] Après un certain temps, le père meurt. [55] Les trois frères se réunissent pour partager les biens de leur père. [56] D'abord il paraît qu'il n'y a pas de

---

43. **corps** *nm.* element; **répandu** *pp.* widespread   44. **non seulement** not only; **huit neuvièmes** eight-ninths; **l'eau** *nf.* water; **contiennent** contain   45. **saveur** taste; **entretient** supports; **ne** [VERB] **ni...ni** neither...nor   46. **bougie** *nf.* candle; **allum/er** *v.* to light; **flacon** *nm.* flask, bottle; **ne contenant que** containing only; **s'éteint*** goes out   47. **ralent/ir** *v.* to slow down   49. **vie** *nf.* life   50. **inculte** *adj.* uncultivated; **renferm/er** *v.* to contain; **en** some; **engrais** fertilizer   51. **mour/ir*** to die; **appel/er*** *v.* to call; **fils** *nm.* son; **dire*** *v.* to tell; **partag/er** *v.* to divide, to share   52. **aîné** *nm.* eldest; **sera** (*Future of* être*) will be; **moitié** *nf.* half; **tiers** *nm.* one-third   53. **quant à** as for; **cadet** *nm.* youngest; **bien** *nm.* property; **père** *nm.* father   54. **meurt** dies   55. **se réun/ir** *v.* to gather, to meet

problème, mais bientôt, quand il s'agit de partager les chameaux laissés par leur père, les fils sont très perplexes. [57] Il y a dix-sept (17) chameaux: impossible de diviser dix-sept par deux, trois, ou neuf, sans couper en morceaux quelques-uns des animaux.

[58] Les fils ne désirent pas tuer de chameaux, et ils ne désirent pas désobéir aux instructions de leur père. [59] Ils consultent donc un vieux derviche. [60] Il paraît que ce derviche est estimé de tout le monde à cause de sa sagesse.

[61] Le derviche est très agréable et intelligent. [62] Il désire aider les trois fils à trouver une solution à leur problème assez complexe. [63] Le lendemain il arrive chez eux, et il demande à examiner les chameaux. [64] Il range les chameaux devant lui, et il attache son propre chameau à côté des autres.

[65] — Écoutez-moi, dit-il. Il y a maintenant dix-huit chameaux. [66] Que chacun prenne sa part!

[67] L'aîné en prend neuf (la moitié de 18), le second fils six (un tiers de 18), et le cadet deux (un neuvième de 18). [68] Les fils sont très contents. [69] Alors le derviche remonte sur son chameau et part, laissant les trois fils très intrigués.

[70] — d'après F. B. CRAMPTON. *The All-In French Course* (Nelson)

56. **chameau** *nm.* camel; **laiss/er** *v.* to leave 57. **coup/er** *v.* to cut; **morceau** *nm.* piece 58. **tu/er** *v.* to kill; **obéir** *v.* to obey 60. **de** by; **tout le monde** everybody; **sagesse** *nf.* wisdom 63. **lendemain** *nm.* next day; **chez eux** at their house 64. **rang/er** *v.* to line up; **propre** (*before a noun*) own 65. **Écoutez-moi** Listen to me 66. **Que chacun prenne** Let each one take . . . 69. **part/ir*** to depart 70. **d'après** adapted from (*where some change or simplification has been made, as in this story*), or according to, from (simply indicating the source)

Chapter

V

Negative Forms of Verbs

ne ... que Construction

Irregular Verb *tenir* *

---

33. Negative Forms of Verbs: *ne* [VERB] *pas*

When a verb is preceded by the negative fragment **ne** and followed by the completion **pas,** the verb is understood to be negative in sense:

ne [VERB] **pas**

Il **ne** désire **pas**...	He does **not** desire...
Il **ne** paraît **pas** que...	It does **not** appear that...
Il **ne** s'agit **pas** de...	It is **not** a matter of...
Ils **ne** sont **pas** arrivés.	They have **not** arrivED.

The fragment **ne** is written **n'** before vowels and *h*'s:

Ils **n'**examinent **pas**...	They are **not** examining...
Il **n'**a **pas** examiné ce cas.	He has **not** examinED this case.
Ils **n'**ont **pas** fait cela.	They have **not** done that.
Il **n'**est **pas** possible que...	It is **not** possible that...
Ils **n'**habitent **pas** Paris.	They do **not** live in Paris.

---

34. Alternate Negative Terms

Although **ne** invariably appears before a verb which has a negative sense, the second element of the negation (the part which normally *follows* the verb) may be some other one than simply **pas.** The word **pas** may be replaced by one of several alternate terms to modify the meaning, as follows:

Il **ne** désire **rien.**	He wants **nothing.**	OR He doesn't want **anything.**
Il **ne** voit **personne.**	He sees **nobody.**	He doesn't see **anybody.**

* Verbs which are **irregular** are marked throughout this text with an asterisk (*). Most irregular forms are listed alphabetically in the end vocabulary.

		rien	nothing
		plus	no longer
		personne	not . . . anybody, nobody
NE	[VERB]	jamais	never
		guère	scarcely
		ni . . . ni	neither . . . nor
		aucun -e	
		nul -le	[+ NOUN] no [ITEM MENTIONED]

Il **ne** paraît **plus** que...	It **no longer** appears that . . .
Ils **n**'examinent **jamais**...	They **never** examine . . . .
Il **ne** s'agit **guère** de...	It is **scarcely** a matter of . . .
Ils **n**'aiment **ni** l'un **ni** l'autre.	They like **neither** one **nor** the other.
Il **n**'a **aucun** LIVRE.	He has **no** BOOK.
Il **n**'a **nulle** MÉTHODE.	He has **no** METHOD.

Some of these alternate terms are sometimes used as subjects of a sentence; they then appear first, and **ne** still appears *before the verb:*

Rien n'est arrivé.	**Nothing** has happenED.
Aucun CHEVALIER ne descend.	**No** knight comes down.
Personne ne me comprend.	**Nobody** understands me.

35. Negative Term Before Infinitives

Both elements of a negative term are found before infinitives:

Être ou **ne pas** être...	To be or **not** to be . . .
Il promet de **ne jamais** demander . . .	He promises **never** to ask...

36. Ne . . . que Construction: "only"

When **ne** precedes the verb, and the second element is **que** rather than one of the regular ones previously indicated, translate as follows: leave the verb *positive,* and translate **que** as *only.* **Que** *may* follow the verb at some distance.

ne [VERB] que "only"

Il a une méthode.	He has a method.
Il **n**'a **qu**'une méthode.	He has **only** one method.
Il **ne** s'agit **que** d'une expérience.	It concerns **only** an experiment.
Ils **n**'examinent **qu**'un seul échantillon.	They are examining **only** one sample.
Cet homme **ne** fait **que** parler.**	That man **only** talks.

When multiple negatives are used, translate **que** by *except:*
Il **ne** s'agit **guère que** de cette urne. Hardly anything **except** this urn is concerned.

When an action is to follow **que in the form of an infinitive, the main verb is usually a form of **faire*** *to do.*   This means, literally, *That man does nothing except talk;* hence **ne . . . que** could be translated *not* [do something] *except. . . .*

37. Irregular Verb *tenir** to hold

Irregular verbs cannot be recognized at all times by their stems (§20b), as there is often a high degree of dissimilarity between stems and infinitives. It is therefore expedient to learn the deviant forms as part of an irregular verb. Learn the following as part of **tenir***:

REGULAR   **ten-**   IRREGULAR   **tien-, tin-**

Study the following examples:

Il **tient** un livre.	He is holding a book. (PRESENT)
Ils **tiennent** des livres.	They are holding some books. (PRESENT)
Nous **tenons** un livre.	We are holding a book. (PRESENT)
Tenons un livre.	Let's hold a book. (IMPERATIVE)
Il **tint** un livre.	He held a book. (PAST DEFINITE)
Ils **tinrent** un livre.	They held a book. (PAST DEFINITE)

In the FUTURE TIME, note the letter **-R-** (as in the French word futu**R**) before the ending:

Il **tiendRa** un livre.	He will hold a book.
Nous **tiendRons** un livre.	We will hold a book.

Thus **tiendr-** can be called the *future stem* of **tenir***, and regardless of the ending it will be translated *will hold*. (This is also the Conditional stem, page 44.)

37a. Compounds of *tenir*. Having learned the two identifying stems for **tenir***, it will now be easy for us to recognize the following compounds of this verb:

REtenir*	to retain	*e.g.,* nous **retenons**	we retain, remember
OBtenir*	to obtain	il **obtient**	he obtains
CONtenir*	to contain	elle **contient**	it contains
MAINtenir*	to maintain	il **maintiendra**	it will maintain, he will maintain
ENTREtenir*	to support	**entretenons**	let's support
		il **entretient**	it supports

37b. Idiomatic Structure *tenir*à "to be anxious to [DO SOMETHING]" or "to place a high value [ON SOMETHING]"

Il **tient à** examiner cet échantillon.	He **is anxious to** examine this sample.
Nous **tenons à** notre avis.	We value our opinion; We **cling to** our opinion.

EXERCISES

Translate the following into good English:

I. 1. ils mesurent; ils ne mesurent pas; ils ne mesurent jamais.

    2. ils sont; ils ne sont pas; ils ne sont guère; ils ne sont jamais.

    3. elle étudie; elle n'étudie pas; elle n'étudie plus; elle **ne** fait qu'étudier.°

° Is used to remind you of special constructions studied.

4. il a; il n'a pas; il n'a rien; il **n'a que**° trois échantillons.

5. ils ont; ils n'ont pas; ils n'ont rien; ils n'ont aucun plan.

6. Cela ressemble à un lycée; cela ne ressemble pas à un lycée; cela ne ressemble guère à un lycée.

7. il navigue; il ne navigue jamais; il n'a pas navigué; il n'a jamais navigué.

8. La locomotive remorque le train; la locomotive ne remorque pas le train.

9. Nous préparons; nous ne préparons pas; nous ne préparons guère; nous ne préparons nulle expérience†; nous **ne** préparons **qu'une**° expérience; nous **ne** préparons d'habitude **qu'une**° expérience.

10. ils transportent; ils ne transportent rien; ils n'ont rien transporté.

11. il arrive; il n'arrive pas; il n'arrive jamais; il n'arrive plus; il n'est pas arrivé; elle n'est pas arrivée. [Translate this twice through: once using the sense *to arrive,* and once *to happen* if appropriate.]

12. ils finissent; ils ne finissent rien; ils ne finissent qu'une° partie de la symphonie; il finit; il ne finit jamais; il ne finit guère.

13. il se lave; il ne se lave pas; il ne se lave jamais; il ne se lave que° la figure.

14. Aucune habitation ne m'a rendu si heureux que celle-ci.

15. Aucun homme n'a reçu de la nature le droit de commander aux autres. La puissance acquise par la force n'est qu'une usurpation.

16. La probabilité est cherchée; la probabilité n'est pas cherchée.

17. elle est finie; elle n'est pas finie; elle n'est jamais finie; il a fini l'expérience.

18. Il y a une méthode; il n'y a pas de méthode; il n'y a qu'une° méthode.

19. Il s'agit d'une hypothèse; il ne s'agit pas d'une hypothèse; il ne s'agit que° d'une hypothèse.

20. Il paraît que Jean arrive; il ne paraît pas que Jean arrive; Jean n'est jamais arrivé.

21. Il reste une complication; il ne reste qu'une° complication.

22. Il se peut que Robert arrive; il ne se peut pas qu'il arrive en retard.

23. Il signale un certain cas; il ne signale qu'un° certain cas.

24. il tient; il ne tient pas; il ne tient jamais; il ne tient que° son livre; il tient à examiner ce livre; il ne tient pas à examiner ce livre.

25. il obtient; il maintient; ils retiennent; nous retenons; nous obtenons; obtenons; retenons; elle contient.

26. il entretient; il n'entretient pas; il n'entretient guère.

27. ils tiendront; il tiendra; il ne tiendra pas; ils ne tiendront pas.

II. **Recopy the following sentences.** Underline verbs with two lines, negations (both parts) with one line. Place parentheses around noun-adjective groups and prepositional phrases, like this:

   (Dans l'algèbre) il ne s'agit jamais (de l'étude) (de la variation) (des fonctions).

6. **ressembl/er à** *v.* to resemble   9. **d'habitude** usually   14. **celle-ci** this one (cf. page 71)
15. **commander à** to command [*requires* **à**]; **puissance** *nf.* power; **acquis** *pp.* acquired   16.
cherch/er *v.* to seek   23. **signal/er** *v.* to point out, to indicate.

This will make the structure of the sentence clearer. Then translate into a rough translation if necessary, and finally into polished English.

28. Il n'y a pas (de substance radioactive) (dans cette matière.)

29. Il n'y a rien d'important dans cette matière.

30. Il s'agit d'une nouvelle théorie économique; il ne s'agit pas d'une bombe atomique.

31. Il ne reste qu'un° cas simple mais intéressant.

32. Quelquefois la mer du Nord est complètement calme et unie; il n'y a donc pas de vagues alors.

33. Nous n'avons constaté aucune différence de structure.

34. Son expérience ne comprend que° deux parties.

35. Il n'y a que° deux parties qu'il faut étudier au commencement.

36. On ne loue d'ordinaire que° pour être loué.

37. La clémence des princes n'est souvent qu'une° politique pour gagner l'affection des peuples.

38. L'amour de la justice n'est que° la crainte de souffrir de l'injustice.

39. L'amour de la justice n'est, en la plupart des hommes, que° la crainte de souffrir de l'injustice.

40. Il ne demande que° la faveur dont il a parlé.

41. L'homme ne s'occupe plus de l'essence impénétrable des choses.

42. Mais ce n'est qu'au° dix-septième siècle que la révolution est accomplie et triomphe avec Képler, Bacon et Descartes.

43. Pierre Fermat, qui était le plus puissant esprit mathématique de ce temps, n'a rien publié.

44. Il admet que l'instinct puisse être un guide en cette matière, mais il ne suffit pas.

45. On ne construit pas de bonnes salles de théâtre; on n'arrive à faire cela que° par une étude très sérieuse de l'acoustique.

46. Haydn a écrit cent dix-huit symphonies; la collection complète, en copies très correctes, est à la bibliothèque de notre Conservatoire.

47. Beaucoup d'entre elles ne sont que° de simples divertissements, écrits au jour le jour pour les petits concerts du prince Esterhazy.

---

32. **quelquefois** sometimes; **mer** *nf.* sea; **donc** therefore; **alors** then 33. **constat/er** *v.* to establish 34. **comprend/re*** *v.* to include 36. **lou/er** *v.* to praise; **d'ordinaire** ordinarily 37. **clémence** *nf.* clemency, mercy; **souvent** often; **gagn/er** *v.* to gain, to win; **peuple** *nm.* people 38. **amour** *nm.* love; **crainte** *nf.* fear; **souffr/ir*** *v.* to suffer 41. **homme** *nm.* man; **s'occup/er de** *v.* to be occupied with; **chose** *nf.* thing 42. **C'est** (*in historical context*) It was; **accompl/ir** *v.* to accomplish, to be completed 43. **puissant, -e** *adj.* powerful; **esprit** *nm.* mind; **temps** *nm.* time; **publier** *v.* to publish 44. **admet** (*Pres. of* **admett/re***, to admit); **puisse** (*fr.* **pouvoir*** to be able) may; **suffit** (*Pres. of* **suffire***) suffice 45. **construi/re*** *v.* to construct; **salle de théâtre** *nf.* auditorium 46. **Haydn** (**Franz-Joseph**) *célèbre compositeur autrichien, qui a définitivement fixé les lois de la symphonie classique.   Né à Rohrau en 1732, mort à Vienne en 1809.* **cent dix-huit** (*118*).   *Only 104 are generally listed now.*   **bibliothèque** *nf.* library; **notre** our   47. **d'entre elles** among them; **au jour le jour** day by day

READINGS

A. L'Air

[48] L'air est un mélange de gaz dont les principaux sont: l'oxygène et l'azote. [49] L'oxygène est un corps simple qui forme la partie active de l'air atmosphérique. [50] Ce gaz, désigné par le symbole chimique «O», entretient les combustions et, par conséquent, la respiration. [51] L'azote, au contraire, modère l'action de l'oxygène et n'entretient ni° la combustion ni° la respiration, quoiqu'il entre pour 78,03 pour cent dans la composition de l'air. [52] Le poids atomique d'oxygène est de 16,000; celui d'azote est de 14,008.

[53] L'air est indispensable aux êtres vivants. [54] En outre il est le véhicule du son. [55] Parmi les autres éléments qui se trouvent dans l'air sont néon, krypton, hélium et des traces d'un certain nombre d'autres gaz. [56] On y trouve aussi du gaz carbonique et de la vapeur de l'eau.

[57] — d'après J. DUTILLEUR ET E. RAMÉ. *Sciences physiques et naturelles*
(Larousse éditeurs)

B. Les Mathématiques

[58] Cette science a pour objet les propriétés de la grandeur en tant qu'elle est mesurable ou calculable. [59] Les mathématiques élémentaires, c'est la partie des mathématiques qui comprend l'arithmétique ou d'autres premières notions de cette science. [60] L'algèbre, la haute algèbre, et la géométrie sont classées parmi les *mathématiques pures,* c.-à-d. qui traitent de la grandeur d'une manière abstraite.

[61] La science des mathématiques appliquées comprend la mécanique et l'astronomie, qui considèrent les propriétés de la grandeur dans certains corps ou sujets.

[62] On appelle *quantité* ou *grandeur* tout ce qui est susceptible d'augmentation ou de diminution. Les longueurs, les superficies, les volumes des corps, etc., sont des quantités.

---

48. **mélange** *nm.* mixture 49. **corps simple** *nm.* element (*Chem.*) 50. **désign/er** *v.* to designate 51. **modér/er** *v.* to moderate, to retard; **ne . . . ni . . . ni . . .** neither . . . nor . . . nor . . .; **quoique** although; **il entre pour** it makes up; **78,03** *Remember that the French and German system is to use a comma (,) as a decimal point. This is therefore read 78.03 in English.* **pour cent** ("per hundred" =) per cent 52. **poids** *nm.* weight; **celui de** that of   53. **être** *nm.* being; **vivant, -e** *adj.* living 54. **en outre** furthermore 56. **aussi** also; **gaz carbonique** carbon dioxide gas; **vapeur** *nf.* vapor 57. **d'après** adapted from, according to; **éditeur**† *nm.* publisher 58. **grandeur** *nf.* size; **en tant que** insofar as 59. **premières notions** ("first notions" =) basic ideas 60. **c.-à-d.** (*Abbreviation for* **c'est-à-dire,** "that is to say" =) i.e., that is; **trait/er de** *v.* to deal with; **abstrait, -e** *adj.* abstract 61. **corps** *nm.* body; **ou** or 62. **tout** everything; **ce qui** which; **superficie** *nf.* area

[63] L'ARITHMÉTIQUE est la science des nombres, tandis que l'ALGÈBRE a pour but de généraliser et d'abréger la résolution des questions relatives aux quantités en général. [64] La GÉOMÉTRIE est une science qui a pour but de mesurer l'étendue, dont les trois dimensions sont la longueur, la largeur, et la profondeur. [65] Enfin il y a le CALCUL INFINITÉSIMAL (le calcul intégral et le calcul différentiel) qui sert à étudier la variation des fonctions.

C. Lohengrin*

[66] Le drame de *Lohengrin* porte le caractère sacré, mystérieux et pourtant universellement intelligible de la légende. [67] Une jeune princesse, accusée d'un crime abominable — du meurtre de son frère — ne possède aucun moyen de prouver son innocence. [68] Sa cause sera jugée par le jugement de Dieu. [69] Aucun chevalier présent ne descend pour elle sur le terrain; mais elle a confiance dans une vision singulière; un guerrier inconnu est venu la visiter en rêve. [70] C'est ce chevalier-ci qui va prendre sa défense. [71] En effet, au moment suprême et comme chacun la juge coupable, une nacelle paraît tirée par un cygne attelé d'une chaîne d'or. [72] Lohengrin, chevalier du Saint-Graal, protecteur des innocents, défenseur des faibles, a entendu l'invocation du fond de la retraite merveilleuse où est précisément conservée cette coupe divine. [73] Lohengrin, fils de Parcival, descend de la nacelle, revêtu d'une armure d'argent, le casque en tête, le bouclier sur l'épaule, appuyé sur son épée. [74] Il est évident que Lohengrin aime la princesse, et qu'elle est amoureuse de lui.

[75] L'innocence d'Elsa est proclamée par la victoire de Lohengrin. [76] La magicienne Ortrude et Frédéric, deux méchants intéressés à la condamnation d'Elsa, parviennent à exciter en elle la curiosité féminine, à flétrir sa joie par le doute, et l'obsèdent maintenant jusqu'à ce qu'elle viole le serment qu'elle a fait à Lohengrin de ne jamais demander son nom ni son origine. [77] Le doute a

---

63. **tandis que** whereas; **abrég/er** *v.* to shorten   64. **étendue** *nf.* extent; **largeur** *nf.* breadth, width; **profondeur** *nf.* depth   65. **enfin** finally; **servir*** à *v.* to serve to C. **Lohengrin.** *Un célèbre opéra en trois actes par Richard Wagner, composé vers 1850.*   66. **port/er** *v.* to carry, to bear; **sacré** *adj.* sacred; **pourtant** yet   67. **meurtre** *nm.* murder; **frère** *nm.* brother   68. **sera** (*Future of* **être***) will be; **Dieu** God   69. **chevalier** *nm.* knight; **terrain** *nm.* (*here*) the jousting-ground. *Medieval justice provided this means of trial: a knight would volunteer on behalf of the accused to join battle against another representing the accuser. If the knight representing the defendant was victorious, the defendant was deemed innocent, as God protects the innocent; if the knight was killed, it was a sign that the defendant was guilty, as God had not protected him.* **guerrier** *nm.* warrior; **inconnu** unknown; **venu** (*pp. of* **venir*** to come); **rêve** *nm.* dream   70. **Ce . . . -ci** this   71. **En effet**† in fact; **chacun** everybody; **la** her; **coupable** culpable, guilty; **nacelle** *nf.* nacelle (*a small boat*); **tir/er** *v.* to pull; **cygne** *nm.* swan; **attelé** harnessed; **or** (§24)   72. **Saint-Graal** Holy Grail; **faible** *nm.* weak person; **entendu** (*pp. of* **entend/re**, to hear); **fond** *nm.* depth; **retraite** *nf.* retreat, sanctuary; **coupe** *nf.* cup   73. **revêtu** *pp.* dressed; **argent** silver; **casque** *nm.* helmet; **épaule** *nf.* shoulder; **appuyé sur** leaning on; **épée** sword   74. **aim/er** *v.* to love; **amoureuse** *adj.* in love with   76. **méchant** *nm.* wicked person; **parviennent** (*fr.* **parvenir***) succeed; **flétr/ir** *v.* to dull; **doute** *nm.* doubt; **obséd/er** *v.* to obsess; **l'** her; **jusqu'à ce que** until; **viol/er** *v.* to violate, to break (*a promise*)

tué la foi, et la foi disparue emporte avec elle le bonheur. [78] Devant le roi, les guerriers et le peuple assemblés, il découvre enfin sa véritable origine: il leur déclare qu'il est Lohengrin, chevalier du Graal. [79] Malheureusement, il y a une règle qui interdit aux chevaliers du Graal de révéler leur nom. [80] Or, la question interdite ayant été posée, il faut que Lohengrin parte. [81] Le cygne reparaît sur la rive pour ramener le chevalier vers sa miraculeuse patrie. [82] La magicienne, dans l'infatuation de sa haine, dévoile que le cygne n'est autre que° le frère d'Elsa, emprisonné par elle dans un enchantement. [83] Lohengrin monte dans la nacelle après avoir adressé au Saint-Graal une fervente prière. [84] Une colombe prend la place du cygne, et Godefroi, duc de Brabant, reparaît. [85] Elsa qui a douté, Elsa qui a voulu savoir, examiner, contrôler, Elsa a perdu son bonheur. [86] L'idéal est envolé.

—d'après CHARLES BAUDELAIRE. *L'Art romantique*

77. **foi** *nf.* faith; **disparu** *pp.* vanished; **emport/er** *v.* to carry away; **bonheur** *nm.* happiness 78. **roi** *nm.* king; **découvr/ir*** *v.* to reveal   79. **malheureusement** unfortunately; **règle** *nf.* rule; **interdire*** *v.* to forbid   80. **Or** now; **ayant** (*fr.* **avoir***) having; **part/ir*** *v.* to depart 81. **rive** *nf.* river bank; **ramen/er*** *v.* to take back...again; **patrie** *nf.* homeland   82. infatuation *nf.* obsession; **haine** *nf.* hate; **dévoil/er** *v.* to reveal; **ne...que** (*here*) is none other than; **enchantement** *nm.* spell   84. **colombe** *nf.* dove   85. **voulu** (*pp. of* **vouloir***) wanted; **savoir*** *v.* to know; **perdu** (*pp. of* **perd/re** to lose) lost   86. **envol/er** *v.* to fly away; to disappear

Chapter VI

Personal Pronouns Used as Subjects

Present Tense of Regular Verbs

Recognition of Future and Conditional

System

38. Personal Pronouns Used as Subjects

Just as English verbs have first-, second-, and third-person forms with corresponding subject pronouns (*I, you, he,* etc.), French verbs have three persons in the singular and three in the plural for each tense **, with corresponding personal pronouns.

a. *Subject Pronouns.* Learn the following pronouns:

	SINGULAR		PLURAL	
FIRST PERSON	je	I	nous	we
SECOND PERSON	tu	you	vous	you
THIRD PERSON	il elle on	he, it she, it one (§26)	ils elles	} they

It should be noted that the third person has more than one subject form (il, elle, ce, on, l'on, etc.), but that there is only *one verb form* for the singular, and one for the plural of the third person.

b. *Meanings of Subject Pronouns.* Note the following special uses:

(1) **tu** is used only in speaking directly to *one* other person who is an intimate acquaintance — a member of the family, a close friend — a fellow "sufferer" such as another member of the military service to which the speaker belongs (but not one *officer* to another), or a fellow student — or to any small children and to animals.

** A *tense* is a group of (usually) six verb forms of a given verb. There are twelve commonly used tenses for each verb, and these tenses fall roughly into the three main time-divisions: past, **present**, and **future**. The time significance of each tense should be learned as presented. For example, the Present tense, which we are about to examine, has three uses (just as the English Present tense does): (1) to indicate action **going on at the very moment**, (2) to indicate action which **habitually** occurs, and (3) to indicate action in the **future** (as a kind of extension of the present):

(1) Il **examine** ce cas.   He **is examining** this case.
(2) Il **examine** ce cas tous les jours.   He **examines** this case every day.
(3) Il **examine** ce cas demain.   He **will examine** (**examines**) this case tomorrow.

In addition, it is sometimes used to address another person who does not fall into any of the "familiar" categories, but who is in a definitely lower social stratum (*e.g.*, in speaking to servants before the advent of democracy). It is also used to insult people who should *not* be thus addressed.

(2) **vous** is used for *you* in all applications not mentioned above, and is called the "polite" form, as opposed to the intimate or "familiar" form **tu.** It is used in speaking to **one** or to **several** persons; it is always used in speaking to *more than one* person.

(3) **il, ils** refer to masculine nouns. The form **il** may refer to a person, in which case it is translated *he,* or to a masculine thing like **le livre,** in which case **il** means *it.* The plural **ils** is always *they,* as this word may refer to persons *or* things.

(4) **elle, elles** refer to feminine nouns. In reference to a person **elle** means *she,* to a thing, *it.* The plural **elles** always is *they.*

(5) **on** *one, they* (general), *people* (general). Used as the subject of a third-person singular verb form for an unspecified general subject (§26):

On parle français en France. ⎰ One speaks French in France.
They speak French in France.
People speak French in France.

BETTER:
French is spoken in France.

The form **l'on** is sometimes seen, but there is no change or difference in translation.

39. Present Tense of Regular Verbs

The present tense of regular verbs may be recognized by the presence of the familiar *stem* which comes from the infinitive learned (§25). To this stem are added distinctive **endings** depending on the type of verb. The endings are represented in the following table:

INFINITIVES ENDING IN →	*-er*	*-re*	*-ir*	REMEMBER:	
je	-e	-s	-is	e	s
tu	-es	-s	-is	es	s
il	-e	none	-it	e	(t)
nous	-ons	-ons	-ISSons	ons	
vous	-ez	-ez	-ISSez	ez	
ils	-ent	-ent	-ISSent	ent	

EXAMPLE: Present tense of regular **-er** verb **arriv/er** *to arrive, to happen*

(1)   j'   **arrive**   I arrive, I am arriving [**je** becomes **j'** before vowels]
(2)   tu   **arrives**   you arrive, you are arriving

(3)   il ⎫
      elle ⎬ **arrive**
      on ⎭

he *or* it arrives, is arriving ⎫ it happens, it is happening
she *or* it arrives, is arriving ⎬
one arrives, one is arriving, *etc.* [see §38 (5) above]

(4) nous **arrivons**   we arrive, we are arriving
(5) vous **arrivez**   you arrive, you are arriving
(6)   ils ⎱
       elles ⎰ **arrivent**   they arrive, they are arriving

EXAMPLE: Present tense of regular -re verb **vend/re** *to sell*

je	vends	nous	vendons
tu	vends	vous	vendez
il	vend	ils	vendent

Elle **vend** sa maison.   She is selling her house.

EXAMPLE: Present tense of regular -ir verb **fin/ir** *to finish*

je	finis	nous	finISSons
tu	finis	vous	finISSez
il	finit	ils	finISSent

Je **finis** la leçon maintenant.   I am finishing the lesson now.

40. Future and Conditional Tenses of Regular Verbs

The **future** tense indicates an action which has not yet occurred, but which is expected to happen: it is translated with the word WILL [*do something*].

The **conditional** tense is translated with the word WOULD [*do something*].

a. *Recognition.* A verb may be recognized as being either **future** or **conditional** by the presence of the *entire infinitive* (up to and including the last -**r**) before the ending:

COMPARE

il arrive   (no -**r** before the ending, so no infinitive can be present. *Not* future or conditional, but present tense: *he is arriving* or *it is happening,* etc.)

il arrivera   (the presence of the -**r** near the end calls for a check. See if the whole infinitive is present, thus:

arriveR/a

As the verb before the line is the infinitive, we are dealing with a future or a conditional: either *WILL arrive* or *WOULD arrive* — but which?

To find out, examine the ending which follows the -**r**. There are two sets of endings, and it is this which determines the tense.

b. *Ending Systems*

	FUTURE	CONDITIONAL
	➤ will ...	➤ would ...
R+	-ai	-ais
	-as	-ais [All have 3 letters]
	-a	-ait
	-ons	-*i*ons
	-ez	-*i*ez [All include *i*]
	-ont	-a*i*ent

If the infinitive is followed by an ending on the left, translate with *will* . . . ; otherwise with *would*. . . . In the example used above, the form

il arriveR/a

contains an ending from the future tense system, and is therefore *he will arrive* or *it will happen*.

Remember that if the ending in the singular has *three* letters, (-ais, -ais, -ait) it is the longer word (*would*) that is used to translate. In the plural, the conditional endings all include the letter -i- before the regular ending. Associate the -i- with the "i's" in "conditional."

EXAMPLES:	nous finissons	(PRESENT) we are finishing
	nous finirions	(CONDITIONAL) we would finish
	nous finirons	(FUTURE) we will finish
	ils vendent	(PRESENT) they are selling
	ils vendront	(FUTURE) they will sell
	ils vendraient	(CONDITIONAL) they would sell

[NOTE: The portion **vendr** is the entire infinitive of **vendre** up to the -**r**. This is typical of all -**re** verbs, in which the final -**e** of the infinitive must be absent from the future and conditional.]

**General Rule for Identification
of Future or Conditional**

1. If there is an -**r**- before the ending, check to see if every-thing up to the -**r**- is a complete infinitive.
2. If **entire infinitive** is present, determine tense by the ending.
3. If FUTURE, translate **WILL** (*do something*)
   If CONDITIONAL, translate **WOULD** (*do something*)

EXERCISES

I. **Translate into English.** Verbs are given in the infinitive form, and in the present, future, and conditional tenses — first a few in that order, then in random order.

1. pour préparer; nous préparons; vous préparerez; elle préparerait.
2. il faut donner; il donne; ils donneront; ils donneraient.
3. sans étudier; j'étudie; vous étudierez; il étudierait.
4. à chercher; tu cherches; il cherchera; nous chercherions.
5. de trouver; vous trouvez; nous trouverons; ils trouveraient.
6. pour expliquer; elle explique; elles expliqueront; il expliquerait.
7. sans discuter; je discute; nous discuterons; nous discuterions.
8. il faut réfléchir; il réfléchit; elle réfléchira; ils réfléchiraient.
9. pour être*; il est; il sera; il serait.
10. sans avoir*; il a, il aura; il aurait.
11. pour arriver; j'arrive; il arrive; elle arriverait; nous arriverons.
12. il faut remarquer; nous remarquerions; vous remarquez; ils remarqueraient.
13. pour bâtir; vous bâtiriez; ils bâtissent; ils bâtiraient; ils bâtiront.
14. sans choisir; vous choisissez; il choisira; nous choisirions.
15. à tenir*; il tient; il tiendra; il tiendrait; il ne tient pas; je tiens.
16. tenir* à; je tiendrai à; il tiendrait à; nous tenons à; elle tiendra à.
17. pour obtenir*; nous obtiendrons; ils obtiennent; vous obtiendriez.
18. sans être*; je serai; je serais; je ne serai pas; il est; il n'est pas; nous serions; vous serez; ils seront; ils seraient; ils ne seraient jamais.
19. il faut avoir*; nous avons; nous aurons; nous aurions; vous avez.
20. s'agir de; il s'agit de; il s'agira de; il s'agirait de; il ne s'agira pas de.
21. se composer de; il se compose de; ils se composeront de; il ne se composerait pas de; elle ne se composera que° de.
22. il faut observer; ne jamais observer; j'observerai; il observerait; nous n'observerions plus; vous observez; observez; observons.
23. pour ralentir; sans ralentir; ne pas ralentir; nous ralentirons; il ralentit; ralentissons; ils ralentissent; ils ralentiraient.
24. pour découvrir*; sans découvrir*; nous découvrirons; ils découvrent; ils découvriront; je découvrirais; il ne découvrirait jamais.
25. il faut porter; pour porter; nous portons; ils porteront; elle porte; elle porterait; elle portera; elle ne portera que°.
26. gagner; ne pas gagner; il gagne; nous gagnons; ils gagneront.
27. admettre*; pour admettre*; il faut admettre*; nous admettrons; nous admettons; admettons; vous admettriez; j'admets.
28. examiner; pour examiner; d'examiner; j'examine; j'examinerai; je n'examinerais jamais; nous examinons; examinons; ne pas examiner.
29. il faut observer; observons; nous observons; il observera; elle observerait; elle observe; elle n'observe plus.
30. il est* possible; il sera possible; il serait possible; il ne sera plus possible.

---

1. **préparons** (*second item*). *Although there is an* **-r-** *before the ending, the test for the infinitive fails, as* **prépar** *is not the complete infinitive. This is therefore not future or conditional, but* **present** *tense.* 7. **discut/er** *v.* to discuss, to argue 9. **ser-** *Note that the future and conditional of this irregular verb (* **être*** *) uses a special stem (* **ser-** *) instead of the infinitive. This is true of many irregular verbs, and such stems must be learned.* 10. **aur-** *Special future and conditional stem of* **avoir*** 22. **observez** *Imperative Form of* **observer**, *i.e., a command:* observe! *This imperative is simply the 2nd person plural of the present tense, without the subject pronoun* **vous**; **observons** *Imperative:* let us observe. 23. **ralentissons** *Imperative* 26. **gagn/er** *v.* to gain, to win 27. **admettre*** *v.* to admit

II. Translate the following scrambled verb forms into English. All forms thus far studied are mixed in random order.

31. il a préparé; préparons; il faut préparer; il aura préparé.
32. nous donnons; nous avons donné; nous n'avons pas donné.
33. vous étudierez; il faut étudier; ils ont étudié; étudions.
34. il construit*; il a construit; il construira; nous construisons.
35. contenir*; il ne contiendrait que°; il contient; il ne contient pas.
36. ne pas produire*; il produira; elle ne produit pas; nous produisons.
37. comprendre*; il comprendra; nous comprenons; vous comprendrez.
38. descendre; je descends; il descendrait; elle ne descendra pas.
39. ne jamais demander; il demande; elle ne demanderait pas; il a demandé; il aura demandé; nous aurions demandé.
40. ne pas finir; il faut finir; nous finissons; tu ne finis pas; ils ont fini; ils finiront; ils ne finiraient pas; il est fini.

III. Translate the following sentences, rewriting or changing word order whenever *necessary* to achieve good English style.

41. Les trois frères se réuniront pour partager les biens de leur père.
42. Il sera impossible de diviser dix-sept chameaux par deux.
43. Les trois fils trouveront une solution. Il reste dix-sept chameaux.
44. Quand le derviche arrivera, il attachera son propre chameau à côté des autres.
45. Alors il y aura dix-huit chameaux qui seront rangés devant lui.
46. Quand les trois fils auront pris leurs chameaux, le derviche partira.
47. Lorsque le son rencontre un obstacle, il sera réfléchi et il produira l'écho.
48. Horatio Nelson, le célèbre amiral anglais, a dit que la flotte de Napoléon à Aboukir serait détruite.
49. Ces cas se diviseront en deux groupes très différents.
50. Nous examinerons un échantillon de l'air atmosphérique; nous trouverons dans cet échantillon un mélange de plusieurs gaz.
51. Le nouveau train dont la locomotive sera électrique portera des voyageurs mais pas de marchandises.
52. Il paraît que la plupart des substances minérales se présenteront sous des formes cristallines.
53. On préparera des plans pour la Cité de Refuge à Paris.
54. C'est les architectes, et surtout Monsieur Le Corbusier, qui prépareront les tracés du nouveau bâtiment.
55. Les données dont il examinera la valeur seront préparées par des physicien† aux États-Unis.
56. La nouvelle maison de ce millionnaire se trouvera à Houston (Texas).

36. **produire*** *v.* to produce   37. **comprendre*** *v.* to include, to understand   47. **lorsque** (or **quand**) *followed by present tense* whenever, every time that . . .   53. **Cité de Refuge** *nf.* City of Refuge, *a modernistic building in Paris housing the various services of the Salvation Army.   Designed by the architect Le Corbusier.   An article about this fine structure appears on pp. 149 ff.*   54. **tracé** *nm.* layout, plan (*Arch.*)   55. **physicien†** *nm.* physicist; **États-Unis** United States

57. Si nous avons le temps, nous étudierons le français.

58. Cette expérience aura pour but† de découvrir la composition de cette substance.

59. Cette voiture aurait trois roues, dont une à la fois directrice et motrice.

60. Nous ne ferons pas un parallèle entre les fusées engins [*rocket missiles*] soviétiques et les fusées engins américaines sol-air [*ground-to-air*].

61. Les premières applications des piles atomiques mobiles intéresseront certainement la propulsion des sous-marins.

62. Le sous-marin atomique dont la construction est commencée utilisera des neutrons lents et probablement de l'hélium pour le refroidissement de la pile.

63. L'installation d'un cyclotron comprendra trois parties.

64. Le soleil éteint, qu'en arrivera-t-il? Les plantes périront, les animaux périront, et voilà la terre solitaire et muette.

65. Le nez de Cléopâtre: s'il eût été plus court, toute la face de la terre aurait changé.

—PASCAL. *Pensées*, 162

66. Des institutions accéléreront les progrès de cette fraternité des nations, et les guerres entre les peuples, comme les assassinats, seront au nombre de ces atrocités extraordinaires qui humilient et révoltent la nature.

—CONDORCET. *Des Progrès de l'esprit humain.*

67. La perfection de l'humanité ne sera pas l'extinction, mais l'harmonie des nationalités.—RENAN. *L'Avenir de la science*

68. A l'avenir, un seul pouvoir gouvernera réellement le monde, ce sera la science, ce sera l'esprit. —RENAN. *Lettre à Berthelot*

69. Notre intelligence tient dans l'ordre des choses intelligibles le même rang que notre corps dans l'étendue de la nature. —PASCAL. *Pensées*, 72

57. **français** *nm.* French (*language*)   58. **découvrir*** *v.* to discover   59. **voiture** *nf.* vehicle; **aur/ait** *Note the use of the conditional in technical writing to indicate hypotheses or probability* — is said to have; **à la fois** at the same time; **directrice** *adj.* steering; **motrice** *adj.* power, drive; **roue** *nf.* wheel   60. **fer-** (*Fut. and Cond. stem of* **faire*** to make, to do)   61. **intéress/er** *v.* to concern, to involve (*Which fits best?*); **sous-marin** *nm.* submarine   62. **lent, -e** *adj.* slow; **refroidissement** *nm.* cooling (*related to* **froid**, cold);   64. **éteindre*** *v.* to extinguish [*pp. is* éteint]; **périr** *v.* to perish; **muet, -te** *adj.* mute   65. **eût** (*fr.* **avoir***) had; **Pensée** *nf.* thought   66. **guerre** *nf.* war; **assassinat** *nm.* assassination; **au nombre de** among; **esprit** *nm.* mind   67. **avenir** *nm.* future   68. **réellement** actually, really; **monde** *nm.* world   69. **rang** *nm.* rank, stature

R E A D I N G S

A. Calcul des probabilités

[71] La PROBABILITÉ d'un événement est le rapport qui existe entre le nombre des cas favorables à cet événement et le nombre total des cas possibles. [72] La probabilité est donc représentée par une fraction toujours moindre que l'unité. [73] L'unité est le symbole de la certitude.

[74] Un événement doit être considéré comme probable lorsque sa probabilité est plus grande que ½; car les chances favorables sont plus nombreuses que les chances défavorables.

[75] La somme des probabilités de tous les événements possibles est toujours égale à l'unité. [76] Ainsi, quand on a une urne qui contient *b* boules blanches, *n* boules noires et *r* boules rouges, la probabilité d'extraire une boule blanche est exprimée par la fraction

$$\frac{b}{b+n+r},$$

la probabilité d'extraire une boule noire est exprimée par

$$\frac{n}{b+n+r},$$

et la probabilité d'en tirer une boule de couleur rouge est

$$\frac{r}{b+n+r};$$

enfin la somme de ces trois fractions est égale à l'unité. [77] Cette évaluation suppose les cas également possibles.

[78] Si les cas ne sont pas également possibles, il faut déterminer d'abord leurs possibilités respectives; et la probabilité est alors la somme des *possibilités* de chaque cas favorable.

[79] Par exemple, au jeu bien connu de *pile ou face,* la probabilité d'amener pile au premier coup est évidemment ½; tandis que si l'on cherche *la probabilité*

---

71. rapport *nm.* connection, relation　**72. toujours** *adv.* always; **moindre** *adj.* smaller
74. doit (*fr.* **devoir***) should; **car** for, because; **défavorable** = pas favorable　**75. somme** *nf.*
sum; **tous** all; **égal, -e** *adj.* equal　**76. ainsi** thus; **urne** *nf.* urn; **boule** *nf.* ball; **blanc, -he** *adj.*
white; **noir, -e** *adj.* black; **rouge** *adj.* red; **extraire*** *v.* to extract; **exprim/er** *v.* to express; **en
tirer** to take from it; **enfin** finally　**77. également** *adv.* equally.　*The termination* **-ment** *often is
equivalent to the English* **-ly**.　　**78. Si** if; **d'abord** first of all; **chaque** each　**79. jeu** *nm.* game;
connu (*pp. of* **connaître*** to know); **pile ou face** heads [face] or tails [pile]; **amener*** *v.* to get;
coup *nm.* toss (*here*); **tandis que** *conj.* whereas

d'amener pile au moins une fois en deux coups, on peut ne compter que° trois cas différents, savoir: [80] pile au premier coup, ce qui dispense d'en jouer un second; face au premier coup et pile au second coup; enfin face au premier et au second coup:

[81] La probabilité d'amener pile au premier coup est toujours ½, mais celle des deux autres cas est ¼, en sorte que la probabilité cherchée est ½ + ¼ ou ¾. [82] On parvient au même résultat en considérant que les lettres A et B ne peuvent donner lieu qu'aux° quatre arrangements également possibles — AA AB BA BB — et que trois de ces arrangements sont favorables à l'événement dont on cherche la probabilité.

[83] Si les événements sont indépendants les uns des autres, la probabilité de l'existence de leur ensemble est le *produit* de leurs probabilités particulières. [84] On exprime cela d'ordinaire en disant que la *probabilité composée* est le produit des *probabilités simples.*

[85] Supposons par exemple que l'on ait assemblé dans un paquet les 13 cartes d'une même couleur qui se trouvent dans un jeu complet de 52 cartes, et qu'on demande la probabilité que les deux premières cartes du paquet soient un *as* et un *deux.* [86] La probabilité que l'as soit la première dans le paquet de 13 cartes est ⅟₁₃, cette carte ôtée, il en reste 12, et la probabilité que le deux soit la première du nouveau paquet est ⅟₁₂. [87] Ainsi la probabilité du concours de ces deux événements sera

$$\frac{1}{13} \times \frac{1}{12} \text{ ou } \frac{1}{156}.$$

[88] Quand deux événements dépendent l'un de l'autre, la probabilité de l'événement composé est encore le produit de la probabilité du premier événement par la probabilité que, cet événement étant arrivé, l'autre arrivera.

au moins at least; peut (*Pres. of* pouvoir* to be able); savoir (*before an enumeration*) namely   80. ce qui which; dispens/er *v.* to obviate; jou/er *v.* to play, (*here*) to toss   81. toujours *adv.* still; celle that; en sorte que so that   82. même same; en considérant que in considering that. *Note that the ending* -ant *corresponds to* -ing *in English;* peuvent (*Pres. of* pouvoir*) can; donn/er lieu to allow, to permit   83. les uns des autres from each other (*Literally* "the ones from the others"); ensemble *nm.* totality   84. cela that; disant *present participle of* dire* to say [*cf. note 82 above*]; composé *adj.* compound; produit *nm.* product   85. Supposons (*Imperative of* suppos/er) Let's suppose; ait (*fr.* avoir*) has; couleur *nf.* suit (*of cards*); jeu *nm.* deck; soient (*fr.* être*) be; as† *nm.* ace   86. ôt/er *v.* to remove   87. concours *nm.* co-existence   88. étant (*ps.p. of* être*) being; BUT étant arrivé having happened

[89] Ainsi soient trois urnes A, B, C, dont deux ne renferment que° des boules blanches, et dont une ne renferme que° des boules noires. [90] On demande la probabilité d'extraire à la fois des urnes B et C des boules blanches. [91] La probabilité d'extraire de C une boule blanche est ⅔; et si cette boule est réellement extraite, la probabilité d'extraire une boule blanche de B serait ½. [92] La probabilité d'extraire à la fois des boules blanches des urnes B et C est donc

$$\frac{2}{3} \times \frac{1}{2} \text{ ou } \frac{1}{3}$$

B. De l'Éducation selon Rousseau et Pestalozzi[×]

Madame de Staël

[93] Rousseau dit avec raison que les enfants ne comprennent pas ce qu'ils apprennent et il en conclut qu'ils ne doivent rien apprendre. [94] Pestalozzi a profondément étudié ce qui fait que les enfants ne comprennent pas, et sa méthode simplifie et gradue les idées de telle sorte qu'elles sont mises à la portée des enfants, et que l'esprit de cet âge arrive sans se fatiguer aux résultats les plus compliqués. [95] En passant avec exactitude par tous les degrés du raisonnement, Pestalozzi met l'enfant en état de découvrir lui-même ce qu'on veut lui enseigner.

[96] La méthode de Pestalozzi est exacte; il n'y a pas d'à peu près dans sa méthode. On comprend bien, ou l'on ne comprend pas: car toutes les propositions se touchent de si près, que le second raisonnement est toujours la conséquence immédiate du premier. [97] Rousseau a dit que l'on fatiguait la tête des enfants par les études que l'on exigeait d'eux; [98] Pestalozzi les conduit toujours par une route facile et positive. [99] Il ne leur en coûte pas plus de s'initier dans les sciences les plus abstraites que dans les occupations les plus simples. [100] Chaque pas dans ces sciences est aussi aisé (par rapport à l'antécédent) que la

89. **soient** (no subject before this verb: it is imperative) let there be; **renferm/er** v. to contain **B. Madame de Staël.** Célèbre romancière (novelist) française (1766–1817). Son œuvre inspira le romantisme. 93. **Rousseau (Jean-Jacques).** Philosophe et écrivain suisse (1712–1778). Ses goûts de la nature et de la solitude contribuèrent au romantisme du siècle suivant; **comprennent** (Pres. of **comprendre*** to understand); **ce qu'** (ce que) what; **apprennent** (Pres. of **apprendre*** to learn); **en** (cf. p. 90) from that; **conclut** (PD of **conclure**, to conclude); **doivent** (Pres. of **devoir***, p. 91) must; 94. **Pestalozzi (Jean-Henri).** Pédagogue suisse (1746–1827) qui s'intéressa surtout à l'instruction des enfants pauvres; **ce qui fait que** what causes [the fact that]; **gradue** (Pres. of **graduer,** to grade [i.e. in order of difficulty]); **mises à la portée de** put within the grasp of; **sans se fatiguer** (cf. §31c.); **aux** refers back to **arrive;** **les plus** [ADJECTIVE] superlative the most [ADJ.]; 95. **en passant** ps.p. (see p. 70) by going; **met** (Pres. of **mettre*** to put); **en état de** in a position to; **veut** (use table on p. 175 for practice.); 96. **pas d'à peu près** nothing approximate, nothing imprecise; **l'on** Do not translate the l', which carries no meaning and is used only to prevent a conjunction of two vowels; **de si près** so closely 97. **exigeait** (Imperf. of **exiger** to require) 98. **conduit** (Pres. of **conduire*** to lead) 99. **en** Do not translate. 101. **leur faire sauter** (Causative

conséquence la plus naturelle tirée des circonstances les plus ordinaires. [101] Ce qui fatigue les enfants, c'est de leur faire sauter les intermédiaires, de les faire avancer sans qu'ils sachent ce qu'ils croient avoir appris. [102] Il y a dans leur tête alors une sorte de confusion qui leur rend tout examen redoutable, et leur inspire un invincible dégoût pour le travail. [103] Il n'existe pas de trace de ces inconvénients chez Pestalozzi: les enfants s'amusent de leurs études.

[104] La méthode de Pestalozzi, comme tout ce qui est vraiment bon, n'est pas une découverte entièrement nouvelle, mais une application éclairée et persévérante de vérités déjà connues. [105] La patience, l'observation, et l'étude philosophique des procédés de l'esprit humain, lui ont fait connaître ce qu'il y a d'élémentaire dans les pensées, et de successif dans leur développement; [106] et il a poussé plus loin qu'un autre la théorie et la pratique de la gradation dans l'enseignement. [107] On a appliqué avec succès sa méthode à la grammaire, à la géographie, à la musique; mais il serait fort à désirer que les professeurs distingués qui ont adopté ses principes, les fissent servir à tous les genres de connaissances. . . .

— d'après MADAME DE STAËL, *De l'Allemagne,* chapitre XIX.

faire, *p. 80*) to have them skip; **les faire avancer** (*Causative* **faire**) to have them advance   102. **rendre** [NOUN] **redoutable** to make [NOUN] frightening, *or* makes (them) dread [NOUN]; **dégoût** *nm.* distaste (disgust)   103. **s'amuser de** to have a good time with   105. **de** (**successif**) *Refers back to* **ce qu'il y a,** *which is understood as though repeated here.*   106. **un autre** another (*i.e.* **tout autre personne**); **gradation dans l'enseignement** *It may be noticed that this is the basis of modern programmed instruction and machine teaching.*   107. **les fissent servir** (*Causative* **faire,** *p. 80*) (might) use them, *literally,* "cause them to serve."   *The form* **fissent** *is the imperfect subjunctive of* **faire***.

Adjective Comparisons: A Further Word

Notice the formation of the comparative (2) and superlative (3) forms of adjectives which follow the noun:

un problème **simple**	a *simple* problem	(1)
un problème **plus simple**	a *simpler* problem	(2)
le problème **le plus simple**	*the simplest* problem	(3)

When the adjective precedes the noun (cf. page 11, sec. 15) the comparison appears as follows:

les petits animaux	the small animals
les **plus petits** animaux	the smaller (smallest) animals

In the latter case, the context will tell you whether to use the comparative (for two objects) or superlative (for more than two objects).

There is one irregular comparison:

bon, bonne	un **bon** livre	a *good* book (1)
meilleur, -e	un **meilleur** livre	a *better* book (2)
le meilleur	**le meilleur** livre	*the best* book (3)
(**la meilleure**)	(**la meilleure** maison)	*the best* house

Test VI, pages 205–206

Chapter VII

Special Future and Conditional Stems of Irregular Verbs · Past Tenses

Translation of the Imperfect Tense · avoir*

---

41. Special Stems of Irregular Verbs for Future and Conditional

The General Rule stated at the end of the last chapter for the recognition of the Future-Conditional system still operates for *ir*regular verbs. However, after finding the characteristic -r- with which all Future-Conditional stems end, it will be noted that the *whole infinitive* is **not present** in some irregular verbs. Instead we will find one of the following characteristic special stems, which should be learned in association with the infinitive involved:

INFINITIVE	MEANING	FUTURE-CONDITIONAL STEM	
être*	to be	ser-	will be (*sometimes, with* a *past participle,* will have), would be
avoir*	to have	aur-	will have, would have
faire*	to make	fer-	will make, would make
aller*	to go	ir-	will go, would go
tenir*	to hold	tiendr-	will hold, would hold
venir*	to come	viendr-	will come, would come
pouvoir*	to be able	pourr-	will be able, would be able
vouloir*	to want	voudr-	will want, would like
valoir*	to be worth	il vaudr-	it will (would) be worth
(il faut)	it is necessary	il faudr-	it will (would) be necessary

EXAMPLES:

{ nous **serons** contents	we **will be** happy
{ nous **serions** contents	we **would be** happy
{ il **sera** arrivé	he **will have** arrived (it...happened)
{ il **serait** arrivé	he **would have** arrived (it...happened)
vous **obtiendriez**	you **would** obtain
ils **pourront**	they **will be able**
il **faudra** partir	it **will be necessary** to depart
elle **irait**	she (it) **would go**

42. Past Tenses

There are only three general areas of possible time: PRESENT, PAST, and FUTURE. Representing time as marching on in the direction of the arrow below, we can visualize these possibilities:

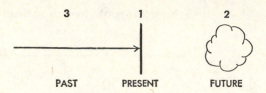

a. *Identification of Past Tenses by Elimination.* We can now recognize present tense verbs and future-conditional system verbs. If, therefore, we encounter a strange verb form, its tense can be deduced by the following steps:

1. Check to see if it is PRESENT (you should recognize it as such at once). If not, then
2. Check for the FUTURE:
    (a) Is there an -r- before the ending?
    (b) Is everything up through the -r- an infinitive—or a special irregular future stem?
3. If tests one and two fail, call it a PAST TENSE, and translate accordingly.

b. *Examples of Tense Elimination.* Remember the *order* of tense elimination, and follow it at all times.

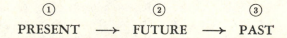

(1) PROBLEM 1:   Translate il représenta
    STEP 1.   Present Tense? No.
           This verb ends in -a, and the table of endings (§39) shows no such Present Tense ending for the subject **il,** or for any other subject.
           Present Tense is eliminated. Go on to second step.
    STEP 2.   Future or Conditional System? No.
           There is no -r before the ending, so that this possibility is immediately eliminated.
    STEP 3.   Steps 1 and 2 have failed to furnish a translation.
           As a result, this must be a past tense. Translate accordingly:
           he represented *or* it represented.

(2) PROBLEM 2:   Translate **ils entrèrent** [from **entr/er**]
    STEP 1:   Present Tense? No. (Present is **ils entrent.**) Eliminated.
    STEP 2:   Future Tense? It is possible because of the -r-.
           Examine more closely. After the -r- we find **-ent.** This is neither a Future nor Conditional ending (See table in §40b). Eliminated.

STEP 3:   Translate as a past tense: they entered.

(3) PROBLEM 3:   Translate **vous aurez examiné**

As the past participle is always translated the same way (here, examined), it is necessary only to inspect **aurez**. It is not the present tense of this irregular verb (that would be **vous avez**). The Future-Conditional test succeeds; the ending is Future: translate *you will have/examined.*

43. Translation of the Imperfect Tense

One of the past tenses has the same endings as the Conditional (§40b). This is the *Imperfect Tense,* and is translated

(1) WAS DOing something [in progress in the past]
(2) USED TO DO something [habitual in the past]
(3) DID something [*if* equivalent to (1) or (2) above]

For example the form **il examinait** is analyzed. It is not Present (**il examine**), and it is not Future (no -r-, no infinitive); it is therefore past: he examined. The three translations indicated above are possible, as the ending is -ait, same as the Conditional tense:

	(1) he examined [simple past]
il examinait	(2) he was examining [going on in the past]
	(3) he used to examine [habitual in the past]

The context of the reading will indicate the best selection. For instance, if the context were

Il examinait ce livre quand M. Dupont est entré.
He   this book when Mr. Dupont came in.

it would be clear that (2) would be best. (The examination of the book was *already in progress* when Dupont entered.)

Compare: il examinait   he examined, he was examining, *or* he used
                                          to examine (IMPERFECT)
          il examinerait   he would examine (CONDITIONAL)
          il examine   he examines (PRESENT)
                              he is examining
          il examina   he examined (a PAST tense)
          il examinera   he will examine (FUTURE)

44. Irregular Verb *avoir**

Learn the following forms for identification of the verb **avoir*** *to have:*

PRESENT TENSE

j'ai	I have	nous avons	we have
tu as	you have	vous avez	you have
il a	he (it) has	ils ont	they have

FUTURE and CONDITIONAL STEM   aur-
IMPERFECT: j'avais, tu avais, il avait; nous avions, vous aviez, ils avaient
PAST DEFINITE: j'eus, tu eus, il eut; nous eûmes, vous eûtes, ils eurent
     [A simple past tense: *I had, you had, he had,* etc. Recognize eu as part of **avoir***]
PAST PARTICIPLE: eu   *had*   e.g., **Il a eu** *He has had, He had.*
PRESENT PARTICIPLE: ayant *having*
DO NOT CONFUSE with **avant** *before* (in time)

REMEMBER ABOUT **AVOIR***

FULL PRESENT TENSE Stems **aur-** and **eu-**

EXERCISES

I. Translate the following verb structures:

1. arriver (two meanings); pour arriver; il arrive; il arrivera; il arriverait; ils arrivèrent; il arriva; il est arrivé; sans arriver; nous arrivons; nous sommes arrivés; cet événement n'arrive jamais; plusieurs autos arrivèrent; cela arrive souvent; cela n'est jamais arrivé.

2. être*; il faut être*; sans être*; ne pas être*; il est; il était; il serait; il sera; il a été; il aura été; il aurait été; nous serons; nous ne serons jamais; vous ne seriez guère; il fut; je fus; ils furent; il ne fut pas.

3. donner; il donnait; en donnant; sans donner; il donnera; nous donnerions; vous donnez; donnez-vous?; est-ce qu'il donne?; il donna; nous donnons; donnez-moi; je ne donne pas; j'ai donné; il a donné; il avait donné; il aura donné; il aurait donné; nous aurons donné; nous n'aurons pas donné.

4. avoir*; sans avoir; ne pas avoir; ayant; il a; il n'a pas; il avait; elle avait; elles avaient; ils avaient; il a eu; elle n'a pas eu; il eut; nous eûmes; ils eurent; nous aurons; vous n'auriez pas; il aura parlé; il aurait considéré; il n'aurait pas considéré cela; il a constaté; il avait constaté; il avait eu.

5. finir; sans finir; pour finir; finissant; fini; il a fini; il avait fini; il n'avait pas fini; il aura fini; il aurait fini; ils finissaient; ils finiraient; ils finiront; ils ont fini; Cette maison sera finie; elle ne serait pas finie.

6. il y a; il y aura; il y avait; il y aurait. il n'y a pas; il n'y aura pas; il n'y avait pas; il n'y aurait pas; il n'y a rien; il n'y avait rien; il n'y aura rien; il n'y a aucun livre; il n'y a guère; il n'y aurait plus.

7. se trouver; il se trouve; il se trouverait; ils se trouvent; ils se trouveront; il ne se trouve pas; il ne se trouvait pas; ils ne se trouveraient pas; il se trouva.

8. prendre* *to take;* sans prendre; prenant; ayant pris; je prends; il prend; il ne prend pas; il prenait; il prendrait; il prendra; il ne prenait pas; il ne prendrait

---

1. **plusieurs** *adv.* several; **souvent** *adv.* often; **cela** *pn.* that 2. **f-** (*fr.* **être***) *Special stem of the Past Definite tense was or were. Clearly not present nor future, by rule.* 3. **en — ant.** *The present participle is often preceded by* **en** *while;* **donnez-vous?** *Inverted form and question mark indicate the interrogative.* 4. **ayant** *ps. p. of* **avoir***   7. **il se trouverait** *it would be located, it would be* [found].   8. **pris** (*pp. of* **prendre***) [*Present tense of* **prendre*** = prends, prends, prend, prenons, prenez, prennent. Future stem is regular,* prendr-. *Other forms can now be deduced by rule*].

plus; il a pris; il avait pris; nous aurons pris; nous avions pris; nous n'avions pas pris; ils prirent; il prit.

9. remarquer; il remarque; il ne remarque pas; il remarquera; ils remarquèrent; ils remarqueront; ils remarqueraient; je remarquai; nous remarquions; il a remarqué; elle a remarqué; il avait remarqué; il n'avait pas remarqué; il aurait remarqué.

10. il contient; contenant; il contiendra; il ne contenait pas; il contiendrait; elle contint; il a contenu; il a obtenu; il a retenu; il avait contenu; il aura contenu; il aurait contenu; nous maintenons; nous maintiendrons; nous maintiendrions.

11. comprendre* *to include* or *to understand;* il comprend; nous comprenons; il a compris; il comprit; il avait compris; il aurait compris; ils comprirent; ils ont compris; ils comprennent; il comprendra; ils comprendront; nous comprendrons.

II. Translate the following sentences:

12. Au XVIIe siècle la France était au niveau du mouvement scientifique.

13. Alors on n'accusa plus l'esprit humain de témérité sacrilège, simplement parce qu'il cherchait à pénétrer les secrets de la création.

14. Descartes perfectionna la géométrie des courbes, ce qui lui permit de résoudre des problèmes qu'on croyait insolubles.

15. Pour Descartes comme pour Newton, le problème de l'univers physique était un problème de mécanique, et Descartes enseignera le premier, sinon la solution, du moins la vraie nature du problème.

16. Si nous n'avions point d'orgueil, nous ne nous plaindrions pas de celui des autres.

17. Il est plus facile de connaître l'homme en général que de connaître un homme en particulier.

18. Il y avait une fois un roi qui était superstitieux mais qui ne voulait pas l'avouer.

19. L'astrologue soupçonna que le roi ne l'aimait pas.

20. Nous prendrons en cet ouvrage le terme d'«opérations» dans un sens limité et bien défini.

21. De ce point de vue, nous prendrons le terme d'intuition, ou de pensée intuitive, dans un sens également limitatif: ce sera pour nous la pensée préopératoire — c'est-à-dire qui ne repose que° sur des configurations perceptives ou sur les tâtonnements empiriques de l'action. — JEAN PIAGET

22. Si cette théorie de la radioactivité était générale, il faudrait admettre que tous les corps radioactifs émettent de l'émanation. —MME CURIE

23. La dernière chose qu'on trouve en faisant un ouvrage, est de savoir celle qu'il faut mettre la première. — PASCAL

10. (*See §37 if necessary*)   11. **comprendre*** *is merely a compound of* **prendre***, *note 8 above.*   12. **siècle** *nm.* century; **niveau** *nm.* level; (*here*) forefront   13. **témérité** *nf.* presumptuous boldness; **parce que** because   14. **René Descartes** (1596–1650), *mathématicien et philosophe français.* **courbe** *nf.* curve; **ce qui** which; **lui** to him   15. **enseign/er** *v.* to teach; **sinon** if not   16. **orgueil** *nm.* (*le contraire de* modestie, humilité); **se plaindre*** to complain.   *Here the* **se** *has changed to an extra* **nous** (*before the verb*) *which need not be translated;* **celui** *pn.* that   17. **connaître*** *v.* to know, to understand (*here*)   18. **Il y avait une fois** Once upon a time there was . . .; **vouloir*** *v.* to want; **avou/er** *v.* to admit; **l'** *before verb* it   19. **soupçonn/er** *v.* to suspect   20. **ouvrage** *nm.* work (*literary*)   21. **préopératoire** *adj.* preoperational (*evidently a coined word, as the author goes on to explain what he means*); **reposer sur** *v.* to depend upon; **perceptif, -ve** *adj.* perceptual (*pertaining to perception*); **tâtonnement** *nm.* tentative action, groping about; **empirique** *adj.* empirical, experimental   22. **émett/re*** *v.* (*like* **mettre***) to emit, to give off; **émanation** *nf.* radiation   23. **chose** *nf.* thing; **dernier, dernière** *adj.* last; **celle** *pn.* the one (thing)

24. Si tous les hommes savaient ce qu'ils disent les uns des autres, il n'y aurait pas quatre amis dans le monde. — PASCAL. *Pensée* 101
25. Il n'aime plus cette personne qu'il aimait il y a dix ans. Je crois bien: elle n'est plus la même, ni lui non plus. Il était jeune et elle aussi; elle est tout autre. Il l'aimerait peut-être encore, telle qu'elle était alors. — PASCAL. *Pensée* 123
26. Mes lettres n'avaient pas accoutumé d'être si étendues. Le peu de temps que j'ai eu en a été cause. Je n'ai fait cette lettre si longue que° parce que je n'ai pas eu le loisir de la faire plus courte. — PASCAL. *Lettres provinciales*, XVI

READINGS

A. Le Promeneur solitaire: Rousseau chez lui

[27] De toutes les habitations où j'ai demeuré, aucune ne m'a rendu si véritablement heureux que l'Ile de Saint-Pierre au milieu du lac de Bienne. [28] Cette petite île, qu'on appelle à Neuchâtel l'île de la Motte, est bien peu connue, même en Suisse. [29] Aucun voyageur, que je sache, n'en fait mention. Cependant elle est très agréable, et singulièrement située pour le bonheur d'un homme qui aime à se circonscrire.

[30] Les rives du lac de Bienne sont plus sauvages et romantiques que celles du lac de Genève, parce que les rochers et les bois y bordent l'eau de plus près; [31] mais elles ne sont pas moins riantes. [32] S'il y a moins de culture de champs et de vignes, moins de villes et de maisons, il y a aussi plus de verdure naturelle, plus de prairies, d'asiles ombragés de bocages, des contrastes plus fréquents et des accidents plus rapprochés. [33] Comme il n'y a pas sur ces heureux bords de grandes routes commodes pour les voitures, le pays est peu

---

24. **disent** (*Pres. of* **dire** * to say*) say   25. **Il y a** [+ AMOUNT OF TIME] = [AMOUNT OF TIME] ago (*cf.* §67e); **crois** (*Pres. of* **croire** * to believe*); **bien** *emphasizes the verb it follows;* **lui** he (*emphatic*); **ne ... non plus** neither; **tout autre** quite different; **peut-être** perhaps; **encore** still, yet; **tel, -le** such   26. **accoutumé** been in the habit; **en** of it; **loisir** *nm.* leisure, free time A. **promeneur** *nm.* walker, rambler   27. **lac** *nm.* lake   28. **bien** *adv.* very; **même** *adv.* even 29. **aucun** [NOUN] (*Cf.* §34); **que je sache** as far as I know, **n'en** *The* n' *goes with* aucun. **en** of it (*cf.* §62); **cependant** however; **bonheur** *nm.* happiness; **se circonscrire** *v.* to remain aloof, to have privacy   30. **rive** *nf.* shore; **celles** *pn.* those (*cf.* §51); **y** there. *Place immediately after* **parce que** *in translation;* **bordent** (*fr.* **border**, to border)   31. **riant(es)** *adj.* pleasant, cheerful 32. **culture** *nf.* cultivation; **champ** *nm.* field; **vigne** *nf.* vineyard; **asile** *nm.* shelter; **ombragé (de)** *adj.* shaded (by); **bocage** *nm.* grove; **accident** *nm.* hills (*technically, folds or irregularities of the terrain*); **rapproché** *adj.* close together   33. **comme** since; **grande route** *nf.* highway; **fréquenté** *pp.* frequented, visited

fréquenté par les voyageurs; [34] mais il est intéressant pour les contemplatifs solitaires qui aiment à s'enivrer à loisir des charmes de la nature, et à se recueillir dans un silence que ne trouble aucun autre bruit que le cri des aigles, le ramage entrecoupé de quelques oiseaux, et le roulement des torrents qui tombent de la montagne. [35] Ce beau bassin, d'une forme presque ronde, enferme dans son milieu deux petites îles, l'une habitée et cultivée; l'autre plus petite, déserte et en friche.

> — d'après JEAN-JACQUES ROUSSEAU. *Les Rêveries d'un promeneur solitaire, Cinquième promenade.*

B. *Le Système solaire*

[37] La terre que nous habitons fait partie d'un système de corps dits *planètes* qui tourne autour d'une étoile que nous appelons le *soleil.* [38] Le soleil possède au moins neuf planètes; il occupe à peu près le centre du système. [39] Il y a d'ailleurs de nombreuses comètes et de satellites des planètes qui font partie du système solaire.

[40] La terre est la troisième des planètes dans l'ordre des distances du soleil. [41] C'est un globe à peu près sphérique, dont le circuit est de 40.000 kilomètres et le diamètre moyen de 12.732 kilomètres. [42] Elle tourne sur elle-même en 23 heures 56 minutes 4 secondes, et autour du soleil dans l'espace de 365 jours ¼, ou une année. [43] Le diamètre autour duquel la révolution diurne s'opère s'appelle l'*axe,* dont les extrémités sont les pôles. [44] La terre est légèrement aplatie aux pôles.

[45] La révolution annuelle s'effectue suivant une courbe plane; c'est en effet une ellipse que décrit la terre en tournant autour du soleil. [46] L'axe de la terre est incliné (d'une façon variable) d'environ 23° 27′ 37″ à celui de l'écliptique. [47] La distance moyenne du soleil à la terre est d'environ 150 millions de kilomètres.

[48] Outre les planètes il y a des satellites qui tournent autour d'une planète

---

34. **contemplatifs solitaires** *Which is the adjective that should be given first in English?* (*cf.* §11); **s'enivrer (de)** *v.* to become intoxicated (by); **à loisir** at leisure; **se recueillir** *v.* to commune with oneself, to collect one's thoughts; **bruit** *nm.* noise; **aigle** *nm.* eagle; **ramage** *nm.* song, warbling; **entrecoupé** *adj.* interrupted; **oiseau** *nm.* bird (*cf. p. 5 for formation of plural*); **roulement** *nm.* rumbling; **torrent** *nm.* mountain stream   35. **bassin** *nm.* lake (*here*); **enfermer** *v.* to contain, to close; **en friche** uncultivated, fallow   37. **autour de** *prep.* around; **étoile** *nf.* star; **soleil** *nm.* sun   38. **à peu près** approximately   39. **d'ailleurs** moreover; **faire* partie de** to be part of   41. **circuit** *nm.* circumference; **moyen, -ne** mean, average; **Kilomètres** *can be converted into miles by multiplying kilometers by .62137.*   42. **tourn/er sur (elle)-même** to turn on its own axis   43. **duquel** which   44. **légèrement** *adv.* slightly; **aplati** (*pp.* of aplatir to flatten)   45. **que décrit la terre** *After que, skip the verb and say the next noun, then return to the verb:* que (1) la terre (2) décrit.   47. **d'environ = à peu près**   48. **outre** in addition to

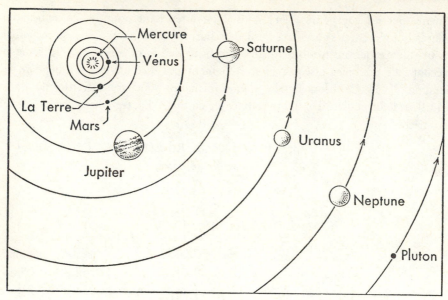

Les Planètes du soleil

principale. [49] Ainsi la terre est accompagnée, dans son mouvement de trans-
lation†, par la *lune,* qui tourne autour de la terre et sur elle-même. [50] La lune
est de 50 fois plus petite que la terre, dont elle est éloignée de 384.000 kilomètres. [51] Jupiter, la plus grande planète du soleil, a douze satellites; Saturne
en a neuf, et de plus trois anneaux; Uranus possède quatre satellites.

[52] Des *comètes* innombrables se meuvent aussi autour du soleil. [53] Elles
diffèrent essentiellement des planètes en ce qu'elles traversent l'espace dans tous
les sens, suivant des orbites très allongées, et qu'elles sont accompagnées d'une
traînée de lumière qu'on nomme la *queue* ou *chevelure.* [54] Il y a des comètes
qui disparaissent et reviennent périodiquement, comme la célèbre comète dit de
Halley qui reparaît tous les soixante-seize ans.

[55] **Attraction ou pesanteur universelle.** — De la première loi de Kepler
on peut déduire l'existence d'une force dirigée vers le centre du soleil. [56] La
loi du mouvement elliptique, ou l'expression de la vitesse qui se déduit de cette loi,
montre que l'intensité de cette force varie selon la distance au soleil. [57] L'intensité de la force qui s'appelle la *pesanteur universelle* varie en raison inverse
du carré de la distance au soleil. [58] Enfin la troisième loi dè Kepler montre
qu'à égalité de distance au centre du soleil, l'intensité de la force motrice est
proportionnelle à la masse de chaque planète et indépendante de la nature parti-

49. **translation** *nf. following its orbit*   50. **éloigné de** separated by   51. **douze** 12; **de plus** in
addition; **anneau** *nm.* ring   53. **sens** *nm.* direction; **traînée** *nf.* wake (*like that of a ship*); **queue**
nf. tail; **chevelure** *nf.* coma   54. **dit** called; **tous les soixante-seize ans** every seventy-six years
(*literally "every sixty-sixteen years"*).   It last appeared in 1910.   55. **pesanteur** *nf.* weight;
pesanteur universelle *nf.* gravity; **loi** *nf.* law; **dirig/er** *v.* to direct; **vers** *prep.* towards
56. **montr/er** *v.* to show; **selon** according to   57. **en raison** in proportion; **carré** *nm.* square

culière de cette planète. [59] Tous les corps de la nature s'attirent mutuellement en raison directe des masses et en raison inverse du carré de la distance. [60] Mais les corps célestes agissent les uns sur les autres et sur le soleil lui-même, et de ces attractions diverses il résulte des *perturbations*. [61] L'étude de ces forces s'appelle la *mécanique céleste,* une partie importante de l'astronomie; c'est l'étude de la théorie des mouvements des astres.

C. Quick Thinking*

[62] Il y avait une fois un roi qui était superstitieux, mais qui ne voulait pas l'avouer. [63] Il apprit qu'un certain homme dans son royaume prétendait† qu'il pouvait lire l'avenir dans les étoiles et prédire ce qui allait arriver.

[64] Le roi se croyait très habile et il se fâcha contre cet astrologue qui faisait ce que lui, le roi, ne pouvait faire. [65] Il le fit venir au palais royal, ayant résolu de le mettre à mort et, en même temps, de montrer à ses courtisans que ses prétentions étaient fausses.

[66] Suivant les ordres de leur maître deux soldats se tenaient prêts à jeter l'astrologue par la fenêtre, quand le roi leur donnerait le signal. [67] Se retournant† vers le pauvre homme qui venait d'entrer dans la grande salle du palais, le monarque lui dit:

[68] «Vous prétendez savoir ce qui va arriver dans l'avenir. [69] Eh bien, pouvez-vous prédire quand vous mourrez vous-même?»

[70] L'astrologue soupçonna ce que le roi avait l'intention de faire, et, après avoir réfléchi quelques moments, il répondit:

[71] «Sire, je ne puis pas prédire le jour de ma mort, mais je sais très bien que je mourrai exactement trois jours avant Votre Majesté.»

[72] Les deux soldats avaient beau attendre le signal. [73] Le roi se ravisa bien vite et, au lieu de tuer l'astrologue il le pria de rester† au palais, de se soigner et de ne courir aucun danger. [74] Il fallait prendre le plus grand soin d'une vie si précieuse.

—E. B. CRAMPTON. *All-In French Course* (Nelson)

59. **s'attir/er** *v.* to be attracted   60. **ag/ir** *v.* to act   61. **s'appel/er*** *v.* to be called   63. **apprit** (*Past of* **apprendre*** to learn); **royaume** *nm.* kingdom, realm; **prétend/re** *v. and false friend to* claim; **prédire*** *v.* to predict; **allait** (*Imperf. of* **aller*** to go)   64. **habile** *adj.* talented; **croyait** (*Imperf. of* **croire*** to believe); **se fâch/er** *v.* to become angry; **ne pouvait faire** *The* **pas** *of the negation is sometimes omitted (as here) with the verb* **pouvoir***.   65. **fit venir** *The verb* **faire*** *followed immediately by an infinitive means to cause.   Thus* **fit venir** *means* caused to come, *i.e.,* sent for. **mettre* à mort** to put to death; **fausse** *adj.* false   66. **Suivant** (*ps. p. of* **suivre*** to follow); **prêt, -e** *adj.* ready; **jet/er** *v.* to throw; **fenêtre** *nf.* window   67. **se retourn/er** *v.* to turn around; **venait d'entrer** *The verb* **venir*** *followed by* **de** [+ *infinitive*] *means* to have just [done something] had just entered.   69. **Eh bien** well; **mourr-** (*Future stem of* **mourir*** to die) 70. **quelques** a few   71. **avant** *prep.* before (*in time*)   72. **avoir* beau** [+ *infinitive*] to [do something] in vain **Ils avaient beau (attendre) le signal** They waited in vain for the signal. 73. **se ravis/er** *v.* to change one's mind; **au lieu de** instead of; **pri/er** *v.* to ask; **rest/er** *v.* to remain; **se soign/er** *v.* to take care of oneself; **cour/ir*** *v.* to run.   74. **Il fallait** (*Imperfect of* **il faut**); **soin** *nm.* care; **vie** *nf.* life

Chapter

VIII

Object Pronouns

être*

---

45. Object Pronouns

    a. *General.* A pronoun is a word which replaces a noun. It is usually used to improve style by eliminating unnecessary repetition of a noun already mentioned. Note the following English sentences, the second of which uses the pronoun *it* for this purpose:

                    1   2
   (1) There is **the new house.** Mr. Ducrot is selling **the new house.**

                    1
   (2) There is **the new house.** Mr. Ducrot is selling   **it.**

    b. *Position of French Pronouns.* As you observe in example (2) above, the English pronoun is positioned exactly where the noun would have been. This is not true of French, where we find the object pronoun *before the verb:*

                     1   2
   (1) Voilà **la nouvelle maison.** M. Ducrot vend **la nouvelle maison.**
   (2) Voilà la nouvelle maison.   M. Ducrot   **la**   vend.

Vend is the verb, and **la** (*it*) appears *before* the verb. In translating, therefore, read the verb first, *then* the pronoun in front of it:

            nous **les** observons   we observe **them**
             1   3   2   1   2   3

---

46. Direct and Indirect Object Pronouns

    As with the subject pronouns already learned (§38), the so-called object pronouns normally precede a verb form — in fact, they come *between the subject and the verb.*
    Learn the possible translations of these object pronouns, and note in the examples that the context (sense) of the sentence determines which translation to use for a given word.

SUBJECT		CORRESPONDING OBJECT PRONOUNS			
		DIRECT		INDIRECT = to ...	
je		me	me	=	me	to me
tu		te	you	=	te	to you
il		le	him, it	{	lui	to him, to it
elle		la	her, it	{	lui	to her, to it
nous	=	nous	us	=	nous	to us
vous	=	vous	you	=	vous	to you
ils		{ les	them	{	leur	to them
elles		{ les	them	{	leur	to them

All words in the INDIRECT column mean *to* [a PERSON].

me means *me* or *to me,* depending on the sentence.
  te means *you* or *to you*
nous means *us* or *to us*
vous means *you* or *to you*

and **le** means *him* or *it* }
    la means *her* or *it* }   DIRECT OBJECTS
    les means *them* }

    lui means *to him, to her,* or *to it* }   INDIRECT
    leur means *to them* }   OBJECTS

Both **le** and **la** are written **l'** before a vowel or *h*.

EXAMPLES: . . . **le cas.** Nous **le** signalons.   We point **it** out.
      . . . **le cas.** Nous **l'**examinons.   We examine **it.**
      . . . **la maison.** Il **la** vend.   He is selling **it.**
      . . . **la maison.** Elle **l'**aime.   She likes **it.**
      . . . **les cas.** Nous **les** examinons.   We are examining **them.**
      . . . **les maisons.** Vous **les** aimez.   You like **them.**
      . . . **le président.** On **l'**honore.   He is honored; One honors **him.**
      . . . **le président.** Je **lui** parle.   I speak **to him.**
      . . . **les soldats.** Nous **leur** parlons.   We are talking **to them.**
      M. Renault **vous** parle.   Mr. Renault is talking **to you.**
      Le professeur **me** regarde.   The teacher is looking at **me.**

How does one know whether **leur** means *their* (§17) or *to them?* As a possessive adjective, **leur** means *their:* **leur livre** *their book.* Remember that an adjective always modifies a noun, so that **leur** before a **noun** is *their,* before a **verb,** *to them.*

leur + NOUN   **leur + VERB**
their PERSON or THING   *to them* DOES SOMETHING

THIRD PERSON DIRECT OBJECT PRONOUN USES:

le	him, it	replaces a masculine singular noun already mentioned, like **le professeur, le cas.**
la	her, it	replaces a feminine singular noun, like **la maison, ma mère.**
l'	him, her, it	replaces **le** or **la** when the verb begins with a vowel or *h*.
les	them	replaces any plural noun regardless of gender, like **les professeurs, mes maisons.**

47. Two Object Pronouns Before a Single Verb

Often a verb is preceded by two object pronouns, one direct (D.O.) and one indirect (I.O.) (i.e., *to* someone or something). As before, translate the subject, skip the pronouns and read the verb, *then* read the pronouns skipped at first:

(1) Jean les lui *a donnés.*
    1   D.O. I.O.   2

John *gave* them to him (to her).
     1   2   D.O.   I.O.

(2) Je vous l'*ai déjà dit.*
    1   2

I *have already told* it to you.
  1   2

(3) Il la leur *a refusée.*
    1   2

He *refused* it (to) them.
   1   2

48. Irregular Verb *être** "to be"

Learn the following forms of être*:

PRESENT TENSE

je **suis**	*I am*	nous **sommes**	*we are*
tu **es**	*you are*	vous **êtes**	*you are*
il **est**	*he is, it is*	ils **sont**	*they are*

FUTURE and CONDITIONAL STEM: **ser-** (*endings* §40b)

IMPERFECT: stem: **ét-** (endings like Conditional, §40b.)
    j'*étais* I was, I used to be
    il *était* he was, he used to be, etc.

PAST DEFINITE: Stem: **f-** [+ us type endings (§66c)]

je *fus*	I was	nous *fûmes*	we were
tu *fus*	you were	vous *fûtes*	you were
il *fut*	he was, it was	ils *furent*	they were

PAST PARTICIPLE: **été** *been* (Used with various tenses of **avoir***)

il a été	he (it) has been, he was; it was
il avait été	he had been; it had been
il aura été	he will have been; it will have been
il aurait été	he would have been; it would have been

PRESENT PARTICIPLE: é*tant being;* (with verbs of motion) *having*

> étant riche   being rich
> étant arrivé   having happened; having arrived
> étant entré   having entered

REMEMBER

FULL PRESENT TENSE Stems: ser- ét- f(u)-
as parts of être*

EXERCISES

I. Translate into English:

1. M. Hervieu a une belle maison. Nous la regardons. Nous ne l'achetons pas. Il l'aime, et Mme Hervieu l'aime beaucoup aussi. On l'a construite il y a deux ans. La famille Hervieu l'habite maintenant. C'est une belle maison.

2. Le roi regardait un astrologue qui était dans la grande sàlle du palais royal. Il ne l'aimait pas, et il ne lui dit rien. Même les courtisans ne l'honoraient pas.

3. Les astrologues observent les étoiles; ils les observent très minutieusement. Je les observerai aussi, quand j'aurai le temps de le faire.

4. Cassini a imaginé des opérations pour mesurer la terre; et en effet† il l'a mesurée assez exactement.

5. Les personnes qui désireront voir une machine à calculer s'adresseront à Monsieur Roberval, qui la leur montrera, et en enseignera l'usage.

6. C'est en 1932 que Lawrence a perfectionné son modèle de cyclotron. Le prix Nobel de physique pour 1939 lui a été attribué pour cette réalisation.

7. L'ordre des opérations est le suivant: après avoir fermé la boîte, on la glisse entre les deux pièces polaires du cyclotron, et l'on y fait un vide très poussé, au moyen de pompes puissantes.

8. Un témoin du désastre de la flotte française à Aboukir nous le décrit.

9. Je vous vois, et je vous parle. Pourquoi ne me répondez-vous pas?

10. Voilà Marie; je lui parlerai. Voilà Pierre; je lui parlerai.

11. Un dictionnaire est utile, et une grammaire l'est aussi.

12. En voyant les professeurs, les élèves leur ont posé des questions.

13. Est-ce que cette machine est nécessaire? Oui, elle l'est.

14. Les conclusions tirées par M. Gage nous ont été signalées.

15. Richardson est un auteur qui vous ramène sans cesse aux objets importants de la vie. Plus on le lit, plus on se plaît à le lire.

---

1. achet/er *v.* to buy; **habit/er** *v.* to inhabit, to live in **2. même** *adv.* even **3. minutieusement** *adv.* minutely, in detail **4. imagin/er** *v.* to think of, to imagine **5. voir*** *v.* to see; **machine à calculer** see §23 **6. réalisation** *nf.* accomplishment **7. boîte** *nf.* case; **gliss/er** *v.* to slide; **pièces polaires** poles (*of a magnet*); **vide** *nm.* vacuum; **poussée** *adj.* high, advanced; **au moyen de** by means of; **puissant, -e** *adj.* powerful **8. décrire** (*3rd person present* **décrit**) *v.* to describe **10. voilà** there is, there are **11. utile** *adj.* useful **13. est-ce que** *placed before a statement makes it into a question. Do not attempt to translate this phrase.* **elle l'est** it is *The* **l'** *refers to the idea "necessary," but is not translated.* **14. tiré** *pp.* drawn **15. ramen/er** *v.* to bring back; **sans cesse** incessantly; **lit** (*fr.* **lire*** to read) *present tense;* **plaire*** **à** to enjoy *doing something.*

16. Il y avait une fois un roi qui était superstitieux, mais qui ne voulait pas l'avouer.

II. Translate (§48): Drill on forms of être*

17. Ce roi superstitieux était plutôt stupide.
18. Ces bâtiments furent construits de brique.
19. La cathédrale de Notre-Dame de Paris, dont l'architecture est gothique, fut construite en 1245.
20. Elle avait été commencée en 1163. On l'avait commencée en 1163.
21. C'est en 1831 que Victor Hugo, étant alors âgé de 29 ans, a composé son roman célèbre, *Notre-Dame de Paris.*
22. —Mais je tiens à voir la capitale, dit Candide, étant arrivé devant le roi.
23. Cet événement étant arrivé, l'autre arrivera.
24. Candide aurait été heureux s'il avait trouvé Cunégonde dans le pays d'Eldorado.
25. Candide avait été très heureux chez le baron de Thunder-ten-tronckh, et il le serait encore s'il n'avait pas été indiscret.
26. Aujourd'hui il sera question de Pierre-Augustin Caron de Beaumarchais; c'est l'auteur des comédies le *Barbier de Séville,* le *Mariage de Figaro,* et de l'opéra sans succès *Tarare.*

READINGS

A. *Sous-marins atomiques*

[27] Les premières applications des piles nucléaires mobiles intéresseront certainement la propulsion des navires, et tout d'abord celle des sous-marins.

[28] Le principal avantage escompté est un rayon d'action pratiquement illimité sans ravitaillement en combustible et sans consommation d'oxygène.

[29] Un sous-marin pourrait naviguer pendant très longtemps en plongée, sans jamais faire surface, à la seule condition de fournir à son équipage l'oxygène nécessaire à sa respiration et de fixer l'excès de gaz carbonique exhalé, problèmes résolus depuis longtemps.

[30] L'eau qui entoure la coque d'un sous-marin assure une protection naturelle très efficace contre les rayonnements. [31] Seule la face de séparation entre

17. **plutôt** *adv.* rather 21. **roman** *nm.* novel 22. **tenir*** à see §37b 24. **heureux** *adj.* happy; **pays** *nm.* country 25. **chez** *prep.* at the home of 27. **intéress/er** *v.* to concern; **navire** *nm.* ship; **tout d'abord** first of all; 28. **escompté** *adj.* anticipated; **rayon** *nm.* range, radius; **ravitaillement** *nm.* replenishment; **combustible** *nm.* fuel 29. **sans jamais** without ever; **à la seule condition** on the single condition; **équipage** *nm.* crew; **exhalé** *adj.* exhaled; **depuis longtemps** a long time ago 30. **entour/er** *v.* to surround; **coque** *nf.* hull, shell; **rayonnement** *nm.* radiation 31. **face de séparation** separating wall

la pile nucléaire et ses accessoires, d'une part, et le reste du bâtiment, d'autre part, devra recevoir un blindage convenable. [32] Au mouillage, le bâtiment devra disposer d'abris et de bassins spécialement aménagés.

[33] Le renouvellement du combustible partiellement brûlé sera facilité du fait qu'on pourra immerger les cylindres destinés à la purification soit dans des caissons dans les rades, soit en mer en certains points bien repérés où les services de récupération viendront les chercher.

[34] Deux prototypes d'installations motrices pour sous-marins sont à l'étude aux États-Unis, l'un par la General Electric au Knolls Laboratory, l'autre par la Société Westinghouse, en collaboration avec le Laboratoire d'Argonne au centre d'Arco dans l'Idaho. [35] Le premier doit utiliser une pile à neutrons intermédiaires avec refroidissement par un métal fondu.

[36] Le second, dont la construction est commencée, utilisera des neutrons lents et probablement de l'hélium pour le refroidissement de la pile. [37] On évalue les frais d'établissement de ce prototype à 26 millions de dollars.

— MAURICE E. NAHMIAS. *L'Énergie nucléaire* (Larousse)

B. La Mer

[38] La surface du globe se compose de grandes masses de terres appelées *continents,* et de grands bassins d'eau nommés *mers.* [39] A vrai dire il n'y a qu'une° seule mer qui s'étend d'un pôle à l'autre, en couvrant à peu près les trois quarts de la surface de la terre. [40] Pour plus de commodité on a divisé cette mer en plusieurs sections auxquelles on a donné des noms différents. [41] On distingue les mers extérieures, qui entourent les continents et les îles, des mers intérieures ou méditerranées, qui sont comprises entre les continents, mais qui pourtant communiquent avec la mer extérieure par une portion d'eau resserrée entre deux terres, et qui, suivant les pays, prend les noms de *détroit, pas* (e.g. le Pas de Calais), *canal, manche,* ou *bras.*

[42] La mer pénètre dans certaines terres et y forme des enfoncements qu'on nomme *golfes* ou *baies,* lorsqu'ils ont une certaine dimension; s'ils sont d'une

---

d'une part . . . d'autre part on the one hand . . . on the other hand; **bâtiment** *nm.* ship; **devra** (*Future of* **devoir***) must; **blindage** *nm.* armor; **convenable** *adj.* appropriate 32. **mouillage** *nm.* mooring; **disposer de** to have available; **abri** *nm.* shelter; **aménag/er** *v.* to arrange 33. **brûlé** *adj.* burned; **du fait** by the fact; **soit . . . soit** either . . . or; **destiné pour** designed for; **caisson** *nm.* receptacle; **rade** *nf.* port; **en mer** at sea; **repéré** *pp.* marked; **récupération** *nf.* salvage; **cherch/er** *v.* to get   34. **à l'étude** under study   35. **doit** is to; **fondu** *pp.* melted, molten   37. **frais** *n.pl.* costs   39. **à vrai dire** to tell the truth; **les trois quarts** three-quarters   40. **commodité** convenience; **auxquelles** to which   41. **compris** (*pp. of* **comprendre*** to include); **pourtant** *adv.* however; **resserré** *pp.* constricted; **suivant** depending upon; **prend** (*Pres. of* **prendre*** to take); **détroit** *nm.* narrows; **pas** strait; **Pas de Calais** Straits of Dover; **canal** channel; **manche** channel (*cf.* **La Manche,** The English Channel); **bras** arm 42. **y** there; **enfoncements** indentations; **golfe** gulf

étendue assez peu considérable pour offrir un abri aux vaisseaux, ils prennent le nom de *port, havre, anse* ou *rade.*

[43] L'eau de la mer contient du sel commun (chlorure de sodium), du sulfate de soude, du chlorure de calcium et du chlorure de magnésium.

[44] La couleur de la mer varie beaucoup; elle est vert-bouteille dans l'Atlantique qui baigne les côtes de France, de Hollande, et d'Allemagne; bleue dans la Méditerranée et dans les hautes latitudes, surtout quand elle est calme. [45] Dans le golfe de Guinée la mer est blanche; vermeille dans le golfe de Californie, et noire aux attérages des Maldives. [46] La mer Noire mérite bien son nom sur une partie des côtes de la Russie méridionale.

[47] Quand la mer est phosphorescente, sa surface tout entière paraît être au feu. [48] Ce phénomène, causé par la présence de divers protozoaires et noctiluques, se montre communément dans les mers des pays chauds, où on le voit dans toute sa beauté; cependant on l'observe aussi dans les hautes latitudes.

[49] La mer est sillonnée de toutes parts par des courants. [50] Dans l'Atlantique, le plus considérable est le gulf-stream, qui, partant du golfe du Mexique, s'avance jusqu'au cap Nord et au Spitzberg où il porte des fruits et les bois de l'Amérique tropicale. [51] Il se ramifie en diverses branches dont l'une, plus considérable que toutes les autres, redescend le long de la côte occidentale de l'Afrique.

[52] Quelquefois la mer est complètement calme et unie. [53] Quand le vent souffle, la longueur et la hauteur de ses vagues varient suivant la force du vent, la proximité et la forme des continents. [54] Les vagues les plus hautes que l'on ait observées ne paraissent pas avoir dépassé vingt mètres. [55] Cependant une vague géante dont la hauteur dépassa trente-quatre mètres a été observée en 1933.

C. Building Troubles

[56] Alphonse et Téléphone sont deux paysans qui habitent les bayous de la Louisiane. [57] Ils travaillent pendant la journée à la charpente d'une maison

assez peu considérable (*see* §22, Note) small enough; **havre** *nm.* harbor; **anse** bay 43. **sel** *nm.* salt; **chlorure** *nm.* chloride; **sulfate** *nm.* sulphate; **soude** *nf.* soda 44. **couleur** *nf.* color; **vert-bouteille** bottle-green; **baigne** (*Pres. of* **baign/er** to bathe, to wash); **côte** *nf.* coast; **Allemagne** Germany; **surtout** *adv.* especially 45. **Guinée** Guinea; **vermeille** vermillion; **attérage** *nm.* land approaches 46. **méridional, -e** *adj.* southern 47. **tout entière** entire; **au feu** on fire 48. **divers** various; **protozoaire** *nm.* protozoan; **noctiluques** *n.pl.* noctiluca (phosphorescent organisms); **se montr/er** *v.* to appear, to show itself; **chaud, -e** *adj.* warm; **où** where; **cependant** however 49. **sillonné** *pp.* furrowed; **courant** *nm.* current 50. **considérable** *adj.* big, important; **partant** (*ps.p. of* **partir*** to leave) starting; **jusqu'à** to, as far as; **cap** *nm.* cape; **nord** north; **Spitzberg** Spitzbergen 51. **se ramifi/er** *v.* to branch out; **redescend/re** *v.* to go back down; **le long de** along; **occidental, -e** *adj.* western 53. **vent** *nm.* wind; **souffl/er** *v.* to blow; **hauteur** *nf.* height 54. **les plus hautes** the highest; **dépass/er** *v.* to exceed; **vingt** twenty 55. **cependant** however; **géant, -e** *adj.* giant; **trente-quatre** thirty-four 56. **Téléphone** *is an uncommon name. His mother was so impressed by this invention that she named her child for it.* 57. **travaill/er** *v.* to work; **pendant** during; **journée** *nf.* day; **charpente** *nf.* carpentry work, framing

neuve. [58] Ils ont commencé par mettre quelques planches en place sur le mur de l'est, et maintenant Alphonse s'occupe d'une façon très assidue à enfoncer des clous à coups de marteau. [59] Téléphone, au lieu de l'aider comme il faut, fait tout autrement. [60] Il prend un clou dans la boîte qui se trouve par terre, il l'examine minutieusement, et puis il le rejette par terre. [61] Il continue ainsi l'examen des clous, un à un, en les rejetant tous sur la terre. [62] Enfin Alphonse s'impatiente, car c'est lui qui fait tout seul le travail destiné à tous les deux.

[63] — Hé Téléphone! s'écrie-t-il, qu'est-ce que tu fais là, par exemple? Qu'est-ce qui t'empêche de m'aider un tout petit peu?

[64] — Il s'agit de ces clous-ci, répond l'autre, d'un ton très sérieux. Ils sont tous défectueux; je ne puis pas les employer.

[65] — Et pourquoi diable pas? réplique le premier, très impatienté.

[66] — C'est que la tête se trouve à la fausse extrémité.

[67] — Idiot! s'écrie Alphonse. Ces clous-là sont réservés pour l'autre côté de la maison!

neuf, neuve *adj.* brand-new 58. mettre* *v.* to put; planche *nf.* plank, board; est east; s'occup/er à [+ *Infinitive*] to be busy at [*Doing something*]; d'une façon in a way; assidu, -e *adj.* industrious; enfonc/er *v.* to drive in, to sink; clou *nm.* nail; coup *nm.* blow; marteau *nm.* hammer 59. comme il faut as is proper; tout autrement quite otherwise 60. dans (*here*) from; par terre on the ground; puis *adv.* then; rejet/er* *v.* to throw down 61. ainsi thus; examen *nm.* examination; tous all 62. s'impatient/er *v.* to become impatient; car for; c'est lui it is he; tout seul all alone; tous les deux both 63. Hé hey!; s'écri/er *v.* to shout, to exclaim; qu'est-ce que what; par exemple (*mild ejaculation*) for Pete's sake!; empêch/er *v.* to prevent; un tout petit peu just a little 64. ces [*noun*] -ci these; d'un ton in a tone; défectueux *adj.* defective; puis (*Pres. of* pouvoir* to be able) can 65. diable *nm.* Devil; pas not; répliqu/er *v.* to reply 66. tête *nf.* head; fausse wrong; extrémité *nf.* end 67. ces [*noun*] -là those; côté *nm.* side (*Do not confuse with* la côte, coast)

Verb Exercise: Past Indefinite Tense

You have now seen many verbs composed of the present tense of *avoir* or *être*, followed by a past participle. For example:

> Lawrence **a perfectionné** le cyclotron.
> Paul **est arrivé** à Paris.

Up to this point we have translated each word of the verb separately. A preferred way (usually) is to use just *one* English word:

VERB	(LITERAL)	PREFERRED TRANSLATION
a perfectionné	(has/perfected)	perfected
est arrivé	(has/arrived)	arrived

If the verb *avoir* or *être* is negative, this does not pertain:

> Paul **n'est pas arrivé**. Paul **has not arrived**.

Test VIII, pages 209–210

Chapter

IX

Present Participles : Comparisons

celui : prendre* : faire*

---

49. Present Participles (*ps.p*)

Verb forms ending in -ant may usually be translated by the English equivalent ending in -ing. Often the present participle is preceded by **en** or **tout en** (*while, by means of, upon.*)

en examinant	while examining, by examining
tout en examinant	while examining
en finissant	upon, by finishing
en considérant	in considering
contenant	containing
criant	shouting
charmant	charming

The stems of these verbs are easily identified, but there are a few irregular verbs having unusual stems for the present participle. Learn the following:

FROM	*ps.p.*	MEANING
être to be	étant	being; (*before some verbs of motion*) having
avoir to have	ayant	having
connaître to know	connaissant	knowing, being acquainted with
paraître to appear	paraissant	appearing
faire to do	faisant	doing, making
savoir to know	sachant	knowing
voir to see	voyant	seeing
dire to say	disant	saying

REMEMBER: -ANT = -ING

50. Comparisons (*Review page 52 also.*)

a. *Things.* Quantities of things are compared using the following scheme:

+ plus de		more	
= autant de }	NOUN que	as much (many) }	THINGS than (as)
− moins de		less (fewer)	

Ils ont examiné **moins de** cas **que** nous. They examined **fewer** cases **than** we.
Nous examinerons **plus** d'échantillons **que vous.** We will examine **more** specimens **than** you.

70

b. *Characteristics (adjectives).*—The same general scheme, slightly modified, is used to compare qualities or characteristics:

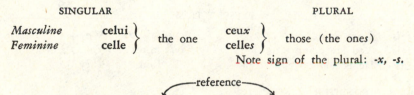

+ plus			more			
= aussi	ADJECTIVE	que	as	}	HOW?	than (as)
− moins			less			
si			so			

Il est **plus** intelligent **que** Jean.   He is **more** intelligent **than** John.
Il est **aussi** riche **qu'**intelligent.   He is **as** rich **as** (he is) intelligent.
Il est **moins** intéressant **que** cela.   It is **less** interesting **than** that.

c. *plus de* [+ NUMBER]. This expression is translated *more than:*

Nous avons examiné **plus de** neuf   We have examined **more than** nine
    échantillons.   samples.

51. *celui* "the one"

Learn the following translations, which will always fit the context of passages being translated:

	SINGULAR		PLURAL		
Masculine	celui	}	ceux	}	
Feminine	celle	the one	celles	those (the ones)	

Note sign of the plural: *-x, -s.*

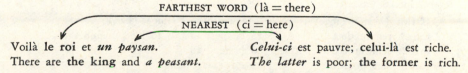

—————reference—————
Nous étudions les satellites de Jupiter et **ceux** de Saturne.
We are studying the satellites of Jupiter and **those** of Saturn.

NOTE: celui replaces a noun already mentioned, to avoid an awkward repetition of the noun. In the above example, the use of **ceux** avoided repetition of **les satellites**; the form **ceux** (masculine plural) was selected because it represented a masculine plural noun (**les satellites**).

SPECIAL CASE: When two nouns have previously been mentioned, the suffixes **-ci** (*the latter*) and **-là** (*the former*) are often appended to the appropriate form of **celui** for reference purposes:

FARTHEST WORD (là = there)
NEAREST (ci = here)

Voilà **le roi** et *un paysan.*   *Celui-ci* est pauvre; celui-là est riche.
There are **the king** and *a peasant.*   *The latter* is poor; the former is rich.

52. Irregular Verb *prendre** "to take"

Learn the forms of **prendre***; the same basic forms are used in several compounds of this verb, such as *apprendre** to learn, comprendre** to understand, entre-prendre** to undertake, se méprendre** to be mistaken, reprendre** to take back, to continue,* and *surprendre** to surprise.*

PRESENT TENSE

je **prends**	I take, am taking	nous **pren***ons*	We
tu **prends**	You take, are taking	vous **pren***ez*	You } take, are taking
il **prend**	He (it) takes, is taking	ils **prenn***ent*	They

[NOTE: The stem **pren-** is easily associated with the infinitive.]

FUTURE AND CONDITIONAL STEM (regular in formation): **prendr-**

PAST DEFINITE: Stem: **pr-** [+ **is** type endings (§66c)]

je pr*is*	I	nous pr*imes*	We
tu pr*is*	You } took	vous pr*îtes*	You } took
il pr*it*	He	ils pr*irent*	They

PAST PARTICIPLE: pris taken (*Used with auxiliary* avoir*)

PRESENT PARTICIPLE: **prenant** taking

53. Irregular Verb *faire** "to make," "to do"

PRESENT TENSE

je **fais**	I am doing, etc.	nous **fais***ons*	We
tu **fais**	You are doing	vous **faites**	You } are doing
il **fai***t*	He is doing	ils **font**	They

FUTURE AND CONDITIONAL STEM: **fer-**

PAST DEFINITE: Stem: **f-** [+ **is** type endings (§66c)]

je f*is*	I	nous f*îmes*	We
tu f*is*	You } did, made	vous f*îtes*	You } did, made
il f*it*	He	ils f*irent*	They

PAST PARTICIPLE: **fait** done, made (*Used with auxiliary* avoir*)

PRESENT PARTICIPLE: **faisant** doing, making

NOTE: Special Cases

Il fait (beau) (mauvais).	The weather is (fine) (bad).
faire* partie de...	to be part of...; to be a member of...
faire* semblant de...	to pretend to...
faire* son possible	to do (his) best
faire* remarquer que...	to point out that...

EXAMPLES:

Ce monsieur fera partie de la société.	This gentleman will be a member of the organization.
Cet animal a fait semblant de dormir.	This animal pretended to sleep.

EXERCISES

I. Present Participles. Translate:

1. en parlant français
2. en suivant les côtes
3. en abandonnant le projet
4. en obtenant des données utiles
5. en résistant à la pression extérieure
6. en naviguant sur la mer
7. en tombant par terre
8. en choisissant une méthode
9. en fournissant de l'oxygène
10. étant difficile à faire
11. étant arrivé (*two ways*)
12. l'événement étant arrivé
13. en considérant ce cas
14. en voyant le livre
15. sachant les faits
16. se reposant sur ce fait
17. paraissant peu profonde
18. ayant trouvé le pas
19. ayant eu assez de temps
20. faisant semblant d'étudier

II. Translate:

21. Chevenard, ayant développé ces appareils, a contribué à nos progrès dans cette étude.
22. Cette constatation étant faite, nous avons continué le procédé.
23. Cette planète ayant été observée, il a fallu calculer sa distance du soleil.
24. Suivant les ordres de leur maître, deux soldats se tenaient prêts à jeter l'astrologue par la fenêtre.
25. Livingston obtenait des protons d'une énergie correspondant à une tension de 80 000 volts, en n'appliquant que° 1 600 volts sur les électrodes d'accélération.
26. On obtient ainsi des monolithes n'exerçant qu'une° pression verticale.
27. Nous n'avons envisagé cette question épineuse de l'acoustique d'un théâtre qu'en° considérant les ressources dont nous pourrions disposer.

III. Comparisons, *celui*. Translate:

28. Mais ce fut en ce point que je rencontrai des obstacles *aussi* grands *que* ceux que je voulais éviter.   (Items 28–32: See page 154, Pascal's Machine.)
29. Voilà une invention que j'ai trouvée pour faire toutes sortes d'opérations mathématiques par une méthode *aussi* nouvelle *que* commode.
30. Les inventions qui ne sont pas connues ont toujours *plus de* censeurs *que* d'approbateurs.
31. On blâme ceux qui les ont trouvées, parce qu'on ne les comprend pas.

21. **appareil** *nm.* apparatus, instrument, equipment; **progrès** *n. pl.* progress 22. **constatation** *nf.* observation, verification; **procédé** *nm.* procedure 23. **il a fallu** (*Past Indefinite tense of* **il faut**) it was necessary 26. **monolithe** *nm.* monolith (*made of a single block of stone*) 27. **épineux, -se** *adj.* troublesome, spiny; **dispos/er de** *v.* to have at one's disposal. *In this sentence, the word* **dont** *replaces the* **de** *of* **disposer de.** 28. **évit/er** *v.* to avoid 29. **commode** *adj.* convenient 30. **connu** *pp. of* **connaître***; **censeur** *nm.* critic (*unfavorable*); **approbateur** *nm.* person who approves (*cf. Engl.* approbation) 31. **trouv/er** *v.* (*here*) to discover, to invent; **parce qu(e)** because

32. Cette machine facilite la calculation; et le plus ignorant y trouve *autant* d'avantage *que* le plus expérimenté†.   (See page 154)
33. Ce gaz est *moins* actif *que* l'oxygène.
34. Les vagues de la mer Méditerranée sont *aussi* hautes *que* celles de l'Atlantique.
35. Notre expérience† actuelle† est *aussi* difficile *que* celle de l'année passée.
36. La comète de Halley est *plus* célèbre *que* toute autre comète.
37. Le gaz carbonique est beaucoup *moins* actif *que* l'oxygène.
38. L'échantillon de fer choisi pour cet essai serait *aussi* libre de toute impureté *que* possible.
39. Ces conclusions se justifieront par ce résultat et celui de plusieurs autres physiciens†.
40. En examinant cet échantillon, on y trouve autant d'azote que dans l'autre cas.

READINGS

A. Les Étoiles de mer

[41] Les *Astéries* ou *Étoiles de mer* ont la forme étoilée; elles possèdent cinq bras soudés à une partie centrale appelée disque; leur corps est recouvert d'un épiderme coriace mais flexible qui sécrète un mucus venimeux. [42] La carapace est composée de plaques calcaires s'étendant depuis la bouche jusqu'à l'extrémité des bras; [43] elles sont unies entre elles par des articulations, et elles sont mobiles les unes sur les autres, grâce au jeu des muscles qui les unissent.

[44] Les plaques latérales et dorsales portent des piquants; les plaques ventrales portent des pédicellaires, organes de préhension, et des pieds ambulacraires garnis de ventouses qui leur permettent de progresser rapidement même sur les

32. **facilit/er** *v.* to facilitate, to make easier; **ignorant** *nm.* ignorant person. *Note that adjectives often become substantives*, as le petit the little [*person*], l'autre the other [*person*], etc. *The word* person *is usually understood in such cases*; **expérimenté** *nf.* (*as above,* person *is understood*) an experienced person
35. **année** *nf.* year (*remember* **annual**); **passé** *adj.* last, past 38. **fer** *nm.* iron (*remember* **ferrous**); **essai** *nm.* test; **libre** *adj.* free; **tout(e)** all 39. **se justifi/er** *v.* to be proved, to be supported; **physicien** † (*a false friend*) physicist
A. **Étoiles de mer** *n.pl.* Starfish 41. **Astérie** Asteroidea, *a zoological classification. Note the French word* **astre** "star," *related to this, and the English and French* "dis-aster" (**désastre**) *meaning* ill-starred, ill-fated. *Such terminology relates, of course, to ancient superstition and to astrology.* **étoilé** *adj.* (*fr.* **étoile**) star-shaped; **soudé** *pp.* fused, attached; **corps** *nm.* body; **recouvert** *pp.* (*fr.* **recouvrir***) covered (**de**) with; **coriace** *adj.* coriaceous (= tough, hard, leathery); *note both adjectives* (coriace mais flexible) *modify* épiderme. **venimeux** *adj.* venomous (= poisonous). 42. **carapace** *nf.* carapace (= bony hood); **plaque** *nf.* plate; **calcaire** *adj.* calcareous (= composed of calcite, lime, or calcium carbonate); **s'étend/re** *v.* to extend; **depuis** *adv.* from; **bouche** *nf.* mouth; **jusqu'à** to, as far as
43. **uni** *pp.* joined (*also* smooth *in some contexts, as seen in Chapter VIII, exercise sentence 52.* **les un(e)s sur les autres** across each other; **jeu** *nm.* action (*Other meanings encountered are* game, play, deck [of cards]). **un/ir** *v.* to unite, to join   44. **port/er** *v.* to carry, to bear; **piquant** *nm.* stinger; **ventral, -e** *adj.* ventral (= stomach-side); **pédicellaire** *nf.* pedicel (= a rudimentary kind of foot); **pied** *nm.* foot; **ambulacraire** *adj.* ambulacral (**pied ambulacraire** = tube foot); **garni** *pp.* equipped (**de**) with; **ventouse** *nf.* suction cup; **même** even

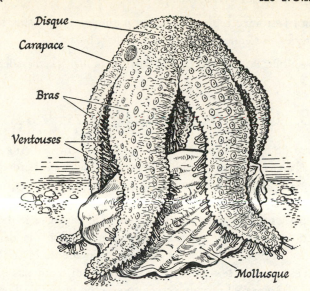

Disque

Carapace

Bras

Ventouses

Mollusque

Étoile de mer en train d'ouvrir un mollusque

surfaces verticales. [45] Les bras terminés en pointe sont très mobiles, très souples; leurs extrémités sont munies d'organes qui fonctionnent comme des palpes sensibles au toucher et à l'odorat. [46] Il y a un tentacule tactile qui porte un œil à sa base.

[47] Ces bras se régénèrent très facilement; si l'un d'eux se trouve pris, l'animal se libère en l'abandonnant. [48] Ce phénomène se nomme l'*autotomie*. Non seulement un bras coupé peut se régénérer, mais un seul bras peut reconstituer l'animal dans son entier: le disque et ensuite les quatre autres bras. [49] Cette régénération en voie de réalisation s'appelle la forme «comète.»

[50] Les Étoiles de mer sont des animaux très voraces. Leur nourriture consiste en poissons, crustacées, oursins, et Mollusques bivalves qu'elles capturent au moyen de leurs pieds ambulacraires. [51] Pour dévorer un Mollusque bivalve qui est assez grand, les Astéries se dressent sur l'extrémité de leurs bras et appliquent perpendiculairement leurs pieds ambulacraires sur sa coquille; [52] à ce moment l'estomac de l'Étoile de mer sort par sa bouche et s'insinue peu à peu entre les deux valves; [53] les sucs digestifs, exerçant une action paralysante sur les muscles, rendent bientôt la victime à sa merci.

[54] L'estomac très dilatable se moule sur la chair† du Mollusque qui se trouve

45. **souple** *adj.* supple, flexible; **muni** (= garni, *above*); **comme** as; **palpe** *nf.* feeler; **sensible** *adj.* sensitive; **toucher** *nm.* (sense of) touch; **odorat** *nm.* (sense of) smell   46. **tactile** *adj.* tactile (*sensitive to touch*)   47. **régénér/er** *v.* to regenerate; **se trouv/er** *v.* to happen (to be); **pris** (*pp. of* **prendre***) caught (*here*).   48. **seul, -e** *adj.* single; **entier** *nm.* entirety; **ensuite** *adv.* next   49. **en voie de** in the process of   50. **vorace** *adj.* voracious; **nourriture** *nf.* nourishment, food; **poisson** *nm.* fish; **crustacées** *n.pl.* Crustacea (= shellfish); **oursins** *nm.* sea-urchins; **au moyen de** by means of   51. **dévor/er** *v.* to devour; **se dress/er sur** *v.* to rise on; **coquille** *nf.* shell   52. **sort** (*fr.* **sortir***, to go out) leaves; **s'insinu/er** *v.* to creep in; **peu à peu** *adv.* little by little, gradually; **entre** *prep.* between   53. **suc** *nm.* juice; **rend/re** *v.* to render, (*here*) to bring; **merci** *nf.* mercy   54. **se moul/er sur** *v.* to be molded over

digéré, après quoi l'estomac reprend sa place normale. [55] Dans leur position normale les Astéries se tiennent la bouche vers le sol.

—NOËL BOUDAREL. *Les Richesses de la Mer* (Lechevailer, Editeur)

B. *La Guerre d'Amérique* (1775–1783)

[56] La guerre de Sept ans, si favorable, politiquement, à l'Angleterre, avait ruiné ses finances en portant sa dette à la somme de deux milliards et demi, qui exigeaient un intérêt annuel de 88 millions de francs. [57] La métropole pensa à se décharger sur ses colonies d'une partie de ce pesant fardeau. [58] Elle mit un impôt sur le papier timbré, plus tard sur le verre, le papier et le thé. [59] Des émeutes forcèrent de supprimer ces taxes: on ne garda que° la dernière. [60] Mais les habitants de Boston, invoquant le grand principe de la constitution anglaise que nul n'est tenu de se soumettre aux impôts qui n'ont pas été votés par ses représentants, jetèrent à la mer une cargaison de thé venue de Londres, plutôt que de payer le droit, et la guerre éclata (1775). [61] L'insurrection gagna toutes les provinces; l'année suivante, leurs députés, réunis en congrès général à Philadelphie, publièrent la déclaration d'indépendance où se remarquaient les principes suivants, qui semblaient sortir du sein de la philosophie française: [62] «Tous les hommes ont été créés égaux; ils ont été doués, par le Créateur, de certains droits inaliénables; pour s'assurer la jouissance de ces droits, les hommes ont établi parmi eux des gouvernements dont la juste autorité émane du consentement des gouvernés; [63] toutes les fois qu'une forme de gouvernement quelconque devient destructive des fins pour lesquelles elle a été établie, le peuple a le droit de la changer et de l'abolir.»

[64] La France accueillit avec enthousiasme une révolution où elle se reconnaissait. [65] Les trois députés américains, Arthur Lee, Silas Deane, surtout le vieux Franklin, si célèbre déjà comme physicien†, furent, pendant leur séjour à

---

digéré *pp.* digested; **après quoi** after which   55. **sol** *nm.* soil   56. **dette** *nf.* debt; **milliard** *nm.* billion; **exig/er*** *v.* to require   57. **métropole** *nf.* mother country; **pens/er** *v.* to think, to consider; **décharg/er** *v.* (*fr.* **dé** *"un"* + **charger** *"to load"*); **pesant** (*ps.p* of **pes/er** to weigh) weighty, heavy; **fardeau** *nm.* burden, load   58. **mit** (*Past Definite of* **mettre*** to put); **impôt** *nm.* tax; **papier timbré** *nm.* legal documents.   *In France, legal documents must be written upon special paper, bought from a government office, and bearing a stamp* (**timbre**) *or seal indicating that the tax on this paper has been paid.   This is done merely as a source of revenue, and is a government monopoly.   The British were applying the same system here.* **plus tard** later; **verre** *nm.* glass; **thé** *nm.* tea   59. **émeute** *nf.* riot; **forcèrent** (*fr.* **forc/er**)   *The ending* -ent *makes it impossible for it to be future tense; it is the past definite* forced; **supprim/er** *v.* to suppress, to cancel; **gard/er** *v.* to retain   60. **habitant** *nm.* (*fr.* **habit/er** to live in) = **une personne qui habite**; **nul n'est** (*cf.* §34) nobody is; **tenu** *pp.* bound, required; **cargaison** *nf.* cargo; **droit** *nm.* tax; **la guerre éclata** *Translate* "war (did something)".   *What is the probable English meaning of* **éclata**?   61. **suivant** (*ps.p. fr.* **suivre*** to follow); **où** *adv.* where, in which; **sein** *nm.* (bosom) heart; **doué** *pp.* endowed; **droit** *nm.* right (*What other meaning do you know for this?*)   62. **jouissance** *nf.* enjoyment; **parmi eux** among themselves   63. **quelconque** any; **devient** becomes; **fin** *nf.* = le but; **lesquelles** which   64. **accueillir** *v.* to welcome; se herself; **déjà** *adv.* already (*basic vocabulary*); **séjour** *nm.* stay, visit

Paris, l'objet d'une ovation perpétuelle. [66] Le marquis de la Fayette, à peine âgé de vingt ans, quitta sa jeune femme enceinte et fréta lui-même un vaisseau qu'il chargea d'armes.

[67] Le gouvernement redoutait cependant une rupture avec l'Angleterre. Turgot avait demandé qu'on restât neutre, croyant que l'Angleterre gagnerait plus à reconnaître l'indépendance de ses colonies qu'à les tenir frémissantes sous le joug. [68] De Vergennes se contenta d'envoyer d'abord des secours indirects en armes, argent et munitions, que Beaumarchais se chargea de faire arriver.

[69] Louis XVI n'aimait pas la guerre; il ne voulait point surtout passer pour l'agresseur, et peut-être se faisait-il à lui-même, au fond de l'âme, les mêmes raisonnements que lui adressa une brochure anglaise:

«[70] Vous armez, imprudent . . . vous armez pour soutenir l'indépendance de l'Amérique et les maximes du congrès. Il est une puissance qui s'élève aujourd'hui au-dessus des lois, c'est celle des raisonnements ambitieux; [71] elle conduit une révolution en Amérique, peut-être elle en prépare une [*révolution*] en France. Les législateurs de l'Amérique s'annoncent en disciples des philosophes français; [72] ils exécutent ce que ceux-ci ont rêvé. [73] Les philosophes français n'aspirent-ils point à être législateurs dans leur propre pays? . . . [74] Vous vous inquiéterez, mais trop tard, quand vous entendrez répéter dans votre cour des axiomes vagues et spécieux que vos officiers auront médités dans les forêts d'Amérique. [75] D'où vous vient cette sécurité quand on brise en Amérique la statue du roi de la Grande-Bretagne? [76] L'Angleterre ne sera que° trop vengée de vos desseins hostiles, quand votre gouvernement sera examiné, jugé, condamné, d'après les principes qu'on professe à Philadelphie, et qu'on applaudit dans votre capitale.»

[77] Prophétiques avertissements! Pourtant Louis XVI signa avec les États-Unis un traité de commerce, corroboré d'une alliance offensive et défensive, si l'Angleterre déclarait la guerre à la France. [78] L'ambassadeur anglais fut aussitôt rappelé.

66. **à peine** scarcely; **femme** *nf.* wife, woman; **enceinte** *adj.* pregnant, "expecting"; **frét/er** *v.* to charter (a ship); **charg/er** *v.* (*see note 57 above*)   67. **redout/er** *v.* to fear; **l'Angleterre** England.   **Turgot, Robert-Jacques,** *économiste français et plus tard contrôleur des Finances sous Louis XVI.* **restât** remained; **croyant** *ps. p.* (*of* **croire***) to believe; **frémissant, -e** *adj.* trembling; **joug** *nm.* yoke   68. **Vergennes, Charles, comte de,** *ministre des Affaires étrangères sous Louis XVI, après avoir été ambassadeur à Constantinople et à Stockholm. Un des plus habiles diplomates du roi.* **envoyer*** to send; **argent** money; **se charg/er de** *v.* to undertake, to take the responsibility for; **faire arriver** *idiomatic construction:* "to cause/ to arrive" = to deliver. 69. **se faisait-il à lui-même . . . les mêmes raisonnements** he was telling himself the same arguments; **au fond de l'âme** "at the bottom of his soul" = in his heart   70. **maximes** *n. pl.* maxims, dicta; **il est . . .** there is (*impersonal*); **puissance** *nf.* power   71. **elle** *refers to* **puissance**   73. **propre** (*before a noun*) own   74. **s'inquiét/er** *v.* to be worried (*here in the future*); **répét/er** *Translate here as if it were a past participle.* **cour** *nm.* court; **spécieux** *adj.* plausible but fallacious, specious; **médit/er** *v.* to meditate   75. **bris/er** *v.* to break; **Grande-Bretagne** Great Britain   76. **veng/er de** *v.* to avenge for; **dessein** *nm.* plan; **sera** *When a future tense comes after the word* **quand**, *it may often be translated as if it were present (cf. sentence 74,* **entendrez***); **profess/er** *v.* to set forth, profess 77. **Prophétiques avertissements!** *The adjective is here displaced from normal position for emphasis* (§14). **avertissement** *nm.* warning; **pourtant** however; **traité** *nm.* treaty; **corroboré** *pp.* strengthened. 78. **aussitôt** *adv.* immediately

[79] L'année 1781 fut pour la France la plus heureuse de cette guerre. Le comte de Grasse remporta une série de brillants succès. [80] Ses victoires contribuèrent à celles que Washington, Rochambeau et la Fayette remportèrent sur le continent américain. [81] Le 11 octobre 1781, ils forcèrent le général Cornwallis à capituler dans York-Town, avec 7000 hommes, 6 vaisseaux de guerre et 50 bâtiments marchands. [82] Ce fait d'armes fut décisif pour l'indépendance américaine. [83] Les Anglais, qui occupaient encore New-York, Savannah, Charlestown, ne firent plus que° s'y défendre.

—Extrait de VICTOR DURUY. *Histoire de France* (Librairie Hachette, Éditeur)

C. L'Encyclopédie: L'Autorité politique*

[84] Aucun homme n'a reçu de la nature le droit de commander aux autres. [85] La liberté est un présent du ciel, et chaque individu a le droit d'en jouir aussitôt qu'il jouit de la raison. [86] Si la nature a établi quelque autorité, c'est la puissance paternelle. Mais la puissance paternelle a ses bornes; et dans l'état de nature elle finirait aussitôt que les enfants seraient en état de se conduire. [87] Toute autre autorité vient d'une autre origine que la nature. [88] Si l'on examine bien, on la fera toujours remonter à l'une de ces deux sources: ou la force et la violence de celui qui s'en est emparé; ou le consentement de ceux qui se sont soumis par un contrat fait ou supposé entre eux et la personne à qui ils ont cédé l'autorité.

[89] La puissance acquise par la violence n'est qu'une usurpation. Elle ne dure qu'autant que la force de celui qui commande l'emporte sur celle de ceux qui obéissent, [90] de sorte que si ces derniers deviennent à leur tour les plus forts, et qu'ils secouent le joug, ils le font avec justice. [91] La même loi qui a fait l'autorité la défait alors: c'est la loi du plus fort. . . .

—d'après DENIS DIDEROT. *L'Encyclopédie*

Test IX, pages 211–212

79. **comte** *nm.* Count; **remport/er** *v.* to win, achieve   80. **Rochambeau, J.-B. Donatien,** *commandant des troupes envoyées au secours des Américains; plus tard maréchal de France.*   81. **le 11 octobre** *Note the manner of stating dates.   Translate by prefacing the unexpressed words* "On the . . ."; **bâtiment** *nm.* ship; **marchand, -e** *adj.* merchant   82. **fait d'armes** *nm.* military action C. **L'Encyclopédie.** *Ouvrage énorme (publié de 1751 à 1772) qui, tout en voulant faire connaître les progrès de la science et de la pensée dans tous les domaines, a tenté de remettre en question les principes jusqu'alors inviolables du pouvoir absolu du roi et de l'Eglise.*   84. **aux** *Required by* commander à. *Do not translate* **aux**   85. **jouir de** [N] *v.* to enjoy [N]; **aussitôt que** *conj.* as soon as   86. **borne** *nf.* limit; **se conduire** *v.* to lead one's own life, make one's own decisions   88. **la fera . . . remonter** trace it back (*cf. p. 80,* **faire faire** *construction*); **l'une** *Disregard* l', *placed here merely for stylistic reasons;* **ou . . . ou** either . . . or; **s'en est emparé** has seized it; **consentement** *nm.* consent; **se sont soumis** (*fr.* **soumettre***, *cf.* §56) have submitted; **eux** *pn.* them (*cf.* §78)   89. **autant que** *conj.* as long as; **l'emporter** (**sur**) *v.* to prevail (over)   90. **de sorte que** *conj.* in such a way that, so that; **derniers** latter; **et qu'** (*here*) and if; **secouer le joug** to shake off the yoke; **avec justice** *Use an adverb ending in* **-ly** *for these words.*   91. **défait** (*pp. of* **défaire***) to undo, to destroy

Chapter

X

Inverted Word Order

faire faire **Construction**

mettre * · **savoir** *

voir * · **pouvoir** *

54. Inverted Word Order

a. *Normal Word Order.* By normal word order we mean that the subject precedes the verb, just as in English:

Nous	examinons	ces données.
SUBJECT	VERB	
1	2	= NORMAL WORD ORDER

b. *Inversion.* When the order of subject and verb is reversed, we call the order "inverted":

Examinons - nous   ce cas?   IN A QUESTION
  2   1
Are we examining   this case?

Peut-être *examinerons-nous*   ce cas.   AFTER CERTAIN ADVERBS
         2   1
Perhaps we will examine   this case.

"Nous examinerons ce cas,"   *dit-il.*   EXPLANATORY VERBS WITH
                       2   1   DIRECT QUOTATIONS
"We will examine this case,"   said he.
                [*or*]   he said.

It may be noted that in English, regular order may be used for translation of inverted French verbs in every case except in *questions*. In the case of questions, the English subject and verb are also inverted. As a general rule, then, translate all inverted French verbs in regular normal order in English, except in questions.

c. *Inversion After* **que** (**qu'**), *"that."* One case of inversion in French is likely to cause difficulty unless mastered; it is inversion after **que** (or the elided form **qu'** before a vowel).

When a clause is introduced by **que** *followed immediately by a verb, then a noun-group,* it is this noun-group which is the subject of the verb — *not* **que**. In translating, say "that" for **que**, skip over the verb to the next noun and translate it, then return to translate the verb:

79

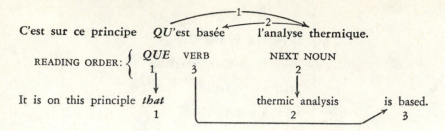

C'est sur ce principe   QU'est basée   l'analyse thermique.

READING ORDER: *QUE*   VERB   NEXT NOUN
                   1   3   2

It is on this principle *that*   thermic analysis   is based.
                    1   2   3

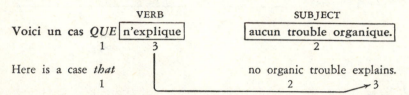

                    VERB   SUBJECT
Voici un cas *QUE* |n'explique| |aucun trouble organique.|
          1   3   2

Here is a case *that*   no organic trouble explains.
         1   2   3

In the event that *que* is followed immediately by a noun, read directly in the French order, paying no attention to the above rule:

Cette étude montre que l'hypothèse de   This study shows that Maxwell's hypothesis
   Maxwell n'est qu'une approximation.   is only an approximation.

GENERAL RULE: After the word **que**, normal word order must be used in an English translation. Translate (1) **que** (*that*), (2) the first NOUN after **que**, and (3) the first VERB after **que**, in that order. [*cf.* **dont**, §28, page 24]

55. *faire** [+ INFINITIVE] "to cause (something) TO BE DONE"

When an inflected form of **faire** is followed immediately by an INFINITIVE, translate **faire** as a form of *to cause,* then translate the first noun following the infinitive, and finally translate the infinitive itself, usually in the form of *"to be* + PAST PARTICIPLE," or simply *"to —":*

EXAMPLE 1

Le commandant   fait PLONGER   *le sous-marin.*
           1   3   2

   1. **faire,** inflected, Present tense: "causes"
   2. First noun after infinitive: "the submarine"
   3. Infinitive: "to dive"

The commander   causes   *the submarine*   TO DIVE.
        1   2   3

EXAMPLE 2

Le professeur   FERA   BATIR   *une maison.*
          1   3   2

The teacher will cause   *a house*   TO BE BUILT.   ROUGH TRANSLATION
         1   2   3

The teacher will have a house built.   FINISHED TRANSLATION

EXAMPLE 3

Il FERAIT VOIR *l'appareil* aux physiciens.
He would CAUSE the *apparatus* TO BE SEEN by the physicists.   ROUGH
He would show the apparatus to the physicists.   FINISHED

SOME COMMON COMBINATIONS:

faire remarquer	to point out ("to cause to be noticed")
faire voir	to show ("to cause to be seen")
faire venir	to send for ("to cause to come")
faire savoir	to inform ("to cause to be known")
faire intervenir	to involve
faire arriver	to deliver
faire semblant	to pretend

56. Irregular Verb *mettre** "to put"

There are many compounds of **mettre*** whose forms are identical with it, except for the prefixes: **ad**mettre *to admit;* **commettre*** *to commit;* **émettre*** *to emit;* **o**mettre* *to omit;* **permettre*** *to permit;* **promettre*** *to promise;* **sou**mettre* *to submit;* **trans**mettre* *to transmit;* and some others.

PRESENT TENSE

je mets	I am putting	nous mettons	We	
tu mets	You are putting	vous mettez	You	are putting
il met	He is putting	ils mettent	They	

FUTURE AND CONDITIONAL STEM: Regular (mettr-)

PAST DEFINITE STEM: m- [+ is type endings: see chart on page 101, §66c]
    mis, mis, mit; mîmes, mîtes; mirent   put (*past*)

PAST PARTICIPLE: mis put;   j'ai mis I put;   j'avais mis I had put, etc.

PRESENT PARTICIPLE: Regular (**mettant,** putting)

57. Irregular Verb *savoir** "to know" [a fact]; "to know how to" [VERB]

This verb also means *to know how* [to do something], and *to be able* [to do something]. (Do not confuse with **connaître,** *to be acquainted with,* page 168.)

PRESENT TENSE

SAI-	je sais	I know	nous savons	We know
	tu sais	You know	vous savez	You know
	il sait	He knows	ils savent	They know

FUTURE AND CONDITIONAL STEM: saur-

PAST DEFINITE STEM: s- [+ us type endings]
    sus, sus, sut; sûmes, sûtes, surent.

PAST PARTICIPLE: su found out
    Example: il a su   he found out

PRESENT PARTICIPLE: sachant knowing

58. Irregular Verb *voir** "to see"

Other verbs based on this one are *prévoir* to foresee, to predict* (in which the Future and Conditional stem deviates from **voir**: **prévoir-**), and *revoir* to see again.*

PRESENT TENSE

VOI-	je vois	I see	nous **voyons**	We see
	tu **vois**	You see	vous **voyez**	You see
	il **voit**	He sees	ils **voient**	They see

FUTURE AND CONDITIONAL STEM: **verr-**   e.g., **je verrai** I will see

PAST DEFINITE STEM: **v-** [+ is type endings]
   vis, vis, vit; vîmes, vîtes, virent.

PAST PARTICIPLE: **vu** (*similar to* savoir [su])

PRESENT PARTICIPLE: **voyant** seeing

59. Irregular Verb *pouvoir** "to be able" [physical ability or permission]

PRESENT TENSE

PEU-	je peux (puis)	I can	nous **pouvons**	We can
	tu **peux**	You can	vous **pouvez**	You can
	il **peut**	He can	ils **peuvent**	They can

FUTURE AND CONDITIONAL STEM: **pourr-**   (Fut.) **il pourra** He (it) will be able
                                                    (Cond.) **il pourrait** He (it) would be able; he (it) could

PAST DEFINITE STEM: **p-** (+ us type endings)
   pus, pus, put; pûmes, pûtes, purent

PAST PARTICIPLE: **pu** (been able)   NOTE: **il a pu** he was able *or* he succeeded in

PRESENT PARTICIPLE: **pouvant** being able

REMEMBER

STEMS   **peu-** (Pres.)   **pourr-** (Fut.)   **p(u)-**
          as parts of **pouvoir***

EXERCISES

I. Translate: Obtain a rough translation by using "to cause" for **faire**; then provide an excellent English equivalent.

1. Monsieur Gage fera voir l'appareil aux physiciens.

2. Il le fera voir aux physiciens.

3. Il leur fera voir l'appareil.

4. Il le leur fera voir immédiatement.

5. Le commandant fait plonger le sous-marin en laissant pénétrer l'eau de mer dans les ballasts.

6. Le professeur fait lire un roman par les étudiants.

7. L'institutrice fait chanter les enfants.

8. Elle fait chanter une chanson aux enfants.

9. J'ai fait porter ma lettre par la concierge.

10. On fait étudier les sciences naturelles à tous les étudiants.

11. Mon ancien professeur a fait construire une maison par un architecte.

12. On a fait réparer ces vieux bâtiments.

13. Il ne faut pas faire avancer trop vite les enfants.

14. Il n'est pas bon de leur faire sauter les intermédiaires.

15. Le roi fit venir l'astrologue au palais royal.

16. Descartes fit faire un pas énorme à l'algèbre en inventant la notation des puissances par exposants numériques.

17. Un jour le hasard fit pénétrer une lumière pour révéler l'âme de l'Empereur.

II. Review: dont (§28). Isolate the **dont**-phrase in parentheses, to separate its meaning from that of the main clause, and translate into polished English:

18. La planète dont le satellite est la lune s'appelle la terre.

19. Le périscope d'un sous-marin est un tube **dont** la longueur dépasse souvent 12 mètres.

20. Tous les êtres vivants sont susceptibles de variations **dont** nous avons vu les évidences.

21. La trapèze est une forme géométrique quadrilatère **dont** deux des côtés sont inégaux et parallèles.

22. Le crime abominable **dont** Elsa fut accusée était le meurtre de son frère.

23. Les animaux **dont** la mer est peuplée ne sont pas répartis uniformément sur la surface du globe.

24. Les gaz principaux **dont** l'air atmosphérique est composé sont l'oxygène et l'azote.

---

2. **le** *replaces* l'appareil *of the first sentence.*   3. **leur** *replaces* aux physiciens   5. **l'eau de mer** sea water   6. **roman** *nm.* novel   7. **institutrice** *nf.* teacher (*elementary school*)   8. **chanson** *nf.* song   9. **concierge** *nm/f* concierge   11. **ancien, -ne** *adj.* former (*See Sec. 74, page 117*)   16. **pas** *nm.* step (forward); **puissance** *nf.* power; **exposant** *nm.* exponent   17. **hasard** *nm.* fate, chance   19. **dépass/er** *v.* to exceed; **souvent** *adv.* often   23. **répartir** *v.* to distribute

25. Autrefois il y avait des gens qui avaient l'idée que la terre **dont** nous sommes les habitants était plate!

26. La locomotive **dont** le train est remorqué est un Diesel.

27. L'hypothèse **dont** il s'agit dans ce livre ne nous regarde pas.

28. La théorie économique **dont** nous avons examiné la structure ne paraît guère solide.

29. Les trois fils **dont** le père est mort s'occupaient à partager les dix-sept chameaux entre eux.

III. Inverted Word Order: Translate:

30. C'est sur ce principe **qu'**est basée l'analyse thermique.

31. Il est intéressant de comparer ces résultats avec ceux **que** fournissent les méthodes classiques.

32. Les philosophes français n'aspirent-ils pas à être législateurs dans leur propre pays?

33. C'est alors que sont élevées ces cathédrales de Paris, de Rouen, de Chartres.

34. De là cette impression vague et lointaine **que** produisent dans les grandes salles les orchestres les meilleurs et les plus nombreux.

35. Ainsi l'engin est-il beaucoup plus solide **que** ne l'était son devancier.

36. **Combien** un avocat bien payé par avance trouve-t-il plus juste la cause qu'il plaide! — PASCAL. *Pensée* 82

IV. Translate:

37. Pour bien savoir les choses, il **en** faut savoir le détail, et comme il est presque infini, nos connaissances sont toujours superficielles et imparfaites.
                                                    — LA ROCHEFOUCAULD. *Maximes,* 106

38. On ne donne rien si libéralement que° ses conseils. — *Maximes,* 110

39. Alors Micromégas prononça ces paroles: «Je vois plus que jamais qu'il **ne** faut juger de **rien** sur sa grandeur apparente.» — VOLTAIRE

40. La plupart des lois semblent arbitraires: elles dépendent des intérêts, des passions, et des opinions de ceux qui les ont inventées, et de la nature du climat où les hommes se sont assemblés en société.
                                                    — VOLTAIRE. *Traité de la métaphysique,* Chapitre IX

41. Cela nous **ferait** voir les lois physiques qui ont opéré pendant cette expérience.

42. Les échantillons seront retirés du four dans une heure; ils sont alors transmis aux autres appareils de mesure.

---

27. **regard/er** *v.* to concern   31. **tenseur** *nm.* tensor, vector; **polarisabilité** *nm.* polarizability, susceptibility to polarization   33. **alors** *adv.* then   34. **De là** hence; **lointain, -e** *adj.* distant; **nombreux, -se** *adj.* having a large personnel = large   35. **ne** *need not be translated, as the second half of the negation is not present.* **devancier** *nm.* predecessor   36. **avocat** *nm.* lawyer; **plaide** pleads   37. **en** of them; **presque** *adv.* almost   38. **conseil**(s) *nm.* advice   39. **parole** *nf.* word; **plus que jamais** more than ever   40. **passions** enthusiasms   41. **ferait voir** *This combination should now evoke the word "show" (in the appropriate tense) so that the rough translation is not necessary (i.e., "cause — to see").*   42. **de mesure** (see §23)

43. La première mise en évidence directe des moments magnétiques nucléaires est la célèbre expérience de RABI, que nous allons brièvement décrire.

44. Supposons qu'il y a deux gaz auxquels il faut ajouter un troisième.

45. Cela constitue une sorte de film cinématographique qui nous ferait VOIR la généalogie de chaque espèce.

46. On ne saurait DÉTERMINER précisément la provenance de la grande majorité des animaux.   (See Sec. 85, page 144 for omission of *pas*.)

47. Après avoir pris naissance dans le golfe du Mexique, le Gulf-Stream traverse l'Atlantique nord.

48. On voit que les résultats obtenus par les chercheurs à Yale nous permettront de modifier notre procédé.

R E A D I N G S

A. French Impressions of Developing America

[51] Il n'y a pas de peuple sur la terre qui ait fait des progrès aussi rapides que les Américains dans le commerce et l'industrie. Ils forment aujourd'hui la seconde nation maritime du monde; et, bien que leurs manufactures aient à lutter contre les obstacles naturels presque insurmontables, elles ne laissent pas de prendre chaque jour de nouveaux développements. [52] Mais ce qui me frappe le plus aux États-Unis, ce n'est pas la grandeur extraordinaire de quelques entreprises industrielles, c'est la multitude innombrable des petites entreprises.

[53] Presque tous les agriculteurs des États-Unis ont joint quelque commerce à l'agriculture; la plupart ont fait de l'agriculture un commerce.

[54] Il est rare qu'un cultivateur américain se fixe pour toujours sur le sol qu'il occupe. Dans les nouvelles provinces de l'Ouest principalement, on défriche un champ pour le revendre et non pour le récolter; [55] on bâtit une ferme dans la prévision que, l'état du pays venant bientôt à changer par suite de l'accroissement de ses habitants, on pourra en obtenir un bon prix.

43. **mise en évidence** *nf.* demonstration; **décrire*** *v.* to describe   44. **auxquels** to which   45. **espèce** *nf.* species   46. **provenance** *nf.* origin   47. **prendre*** **naissance** to originate   48. **chercheur** *nm.* (*fr.* chercher) = une personne qui cherche, researcher A. **oeuvre** *nm.* work; Lavoisier, Antoine-Laurent de (1743–94). *Il a inventé la nomenclature chimique, découvert la composition de l'air, énoncé le rôle de l'oxygène dans les combustions. En physique c'est lui qui a effectué les premières mesures calorimétriques. Lavoisier fut exécuté pendant la révolution avec les fermiers généraux* [tax collectors], *dont il faisait partie.*   51. **peuple** *nm.* people, nation; **manufacture** *nf.* factory; **lutter** to struggle; **ne laisser pas de** do not fail to   52. **ce qui** what; **ce it** (*redundant; omit in translation*); **des petites entreprises** small businesses   53. **agriculteur** *nm.* farmer; **joint** *pp.* of **joindre*** to join   54. **se fixer** to settle down; **défricher** to clear [land]; **revendre** *The prefix* re- *means "again".* In translation, place the word "again" at the end of the clause or sentence; **récolter** to harvest   55. **prévision** *nf.* anticipation; **en** for it

[56] Tous les ans un essaim d'habitants du Nord descend vers le Midi et vient
s'établir dans les contrées où croissent le coton et la canne à sucre. [57] Ces hommes
cultivent la terre dans le but de lui faire produire en peu d'années de quoi les
enrichir, et ils entrevoient déjà le moment où ils pourront retourner dans leur patrie
jouir de l'aisance ainsi acquise. [58] Les Américains transportent donc dans l'agriculture l'esprit du négoce, et leurs passions industrielles se montrent là, comme
ailleurs.

[59] Les Américains font d'immenses progrès en industrie, parce qu'ils s'occupent
tous à la fois d'industrie; et pour cette même cause ils sont sujets à des crises industrielles très inattendues et très formidables.

[60] Comme ils font tous du commerce, le commerce est soumis chez eux à des
influences tellement nombreuses et si compliquées, qu'il est impossible de prévoir à
l'avance les embarras qui peuvent naître. [61] Comme chacun d'eux se mêle plus
ou moins d'industrie, au moindre choc que les affaires y éprouvent, toutes les for-
tunes particulières trébuchent en même temps, et l'État chancelle.

[62] Je crois que le retour des crises industrielles est une maladie endémique
chez les nations démocratiques de nos jours. [63] On peut la rendre moins dangereuse, mais non la guérir, parce qu'elle ne tient pas à un accident, mais au tempéra-
ment même de ces peuples.

—Professions industrielles
De la Démocratie en Amérique
Alexis de Tocqueville (1805–1859)

B. Finding a Seat

[64] Un voyageur qui avait passé toute la journée sous la pluie arriva un soir
à une auberge dans une petite ville. [65] Il espérait se sécher en attendant son

56. essaim *nm.* swarm, throng; le Midi the South; où croissent (*The verb* croissent *should have
the next noun group placed in front of it as a subject*); croître to grow; sucre *nm.* sugar   57. de
quoi enough; entrevoir* to see; jouir de to enjoy; aisance *nf.* ease   58. donc therefore (*place
first in sentence*); transportent *should be followed by the next independent noun group*, then
the prepositional phrase; négoce *nm.* business; passion *nf.* enthusiasm; se montrer to be revealed
59. s'occuper de to be busy with   60. embarras *nm.* difficulty; naître* to arise   61. affaires,
les business; particulier, particulière *adj.* private; trébucher totter; chanceller totter   63. ne
tient pas à does not depend upon   64. journée *nf.* day; pluie *nf.* rain; auberge *nf.* inn; ville
nf. city (*What would a* petite ville *be?*).   65. espér/er *v.* to hope; se séch/er *v.* to dry oneself;
attend/re *v.* to wait for

dîner, mais quand il entra dans la salle à manger il y vit sept autres voyageurs qui s'étaient déjà installés autour de la cheminée.

[66] Appelant l'aubergiste il lui dit: «Portez vite une douzaine d'huîtres à mon cheval.

— Comment, monsieur! A votre cheval!?

— Peut-être que cela vous semble un peu étrange, mais faites quand même ce que je vous dis.»

[67] L'aubergiste alla dans la cuisine chercher des huîtres. Après les avoir ouvertes il sortit à l'écurie, suivi de tous les voyageurs, qui avaient grande envie de voir manger des huîtres à un cheval.

[68] Quelques minutes plus tard ils rentrèrent tous.

[69] «Monsieur, dit l'aubergiste, votre cheval ne désire pas d'huîtres.

[70] — N'importe, répondit le voyageur, mettez-les sur la table. Je les mangerai moi-même.»

[71] Pendant l'absence des autres, il avait pris une bonne place près du feu.

—E. B. CRAMPTON. *All-In French Course* (Nelson)

C. *Superficies des figures planes*

[72] Par la *hauteur* d'un triangle on entend la perpendiculaire abaissée d'un de ses sommets sur le côté opposé pris pour *base*. [73] Le *pied* de la hauteur peut tomber dedans ou dehors le triangle. [74] La *surface* d'un triangle est égale au produit de la base par la moitié de la hauteur.

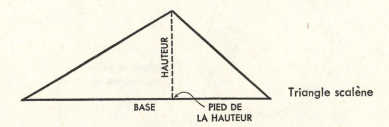

[75] Un triangle *isocèle* est celui qui a deux côtés égaux; un triangle *équila-téral* a les trois côtés égaux; un triangle *scalène* est celui dont les trois côtés sont

salle à manger *nf.* dining room; cheminée *nf.* fireplace   66. aubergiste *nm.* le propriétaire de l'auberge; vite *adv. le contraire de* lentement; douzaine *nf.* approximately 12, a dozen; huîtres oysters; cheval *nm.* horse; comment! what!; quand même anyway, all the same   67. cuisine *nf.* kitchen; chercher *v.* to get; écurie *nf.* un bâtiment destiné à loger les animaux, surtout les chevaux; suivi (de) *pp.* followed (by); envie *nf.* desire; à (un cheval) by (. . .)   68. rentr/er *v.* (= re encore + entrer)   70. n'importe (pas) (*fr.* import/er *to* matter); moi-même myself   72. hauteur *nf.* altitude, height; entend/re *v.* to understand; abaiss/er *v.* to drop, to lower; pris pour taken as   73. dedans inside; dehors le contraire de *dedans*   74. surface *nf.* area

inégaux. [76] Un triangle *rectangle* est un triangle qui a un angle droit (c.-à-d. de 90 degrés).

[77] La hauteur d'un parallélogramme est la perpendiculaire qui mesure la distance entre deux côtés parallèles. [78] L'*aire* d'un parallélogramme quelconque est égale au produit de la base par la hauteur.

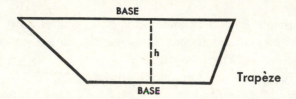

BASE

h

BASE

Trapèze

[79] Un trapèze est un quadrilatère dont deux des côtés sont inégaux et parallèles. [80] Les deux côtés parallèles forment les *bases;* la distance entre eux est la *hauteur.* [81] L'aire d'un trapèze s'obtient en multipliant la somme des bases par la moitié de la hauteur. [82] On peut aussi exprimer cela par la formule

$$Aire\ du\ trapèze = \frac{h}{2}\,(b + b')$$

[83] Un *polygone régulier* est celui dont tous les angles et tous les côtés sont égaux entre eux. [84] Tout polygone régulier peut être inscrit dans un cercle. Ce cercle peut être considéré comme un polygone régulier d'une infinité de côtés.

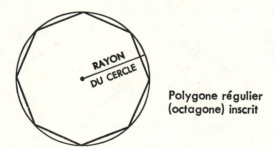

RAYON DU CERCLE

**Polygone régulier
(octagone) inscrit**

[85] Or un polygone régulier a pour mesure la moitié du produit de son périmètre par le rayon du cercle circonscrit:

$$Aire\ du\ polygone = \frac{1}{2}\,a\,n\,r$$

lorsque *a* est le côté, *n* le nombre des côtés, et *r* le rayon du cercle circonscrit.

78. **quelconque** any; ordinary   84. **tout** every; **peut être** can be. *Do not confuse with* peut-être, *"perhaps"*; **inscrit** *pp.* (*fr.* **inscrire**, to inscribe)   85. **rayon** *nm.* radius; **circonscrit** *pp.* circumscribed

Chapter XI

Supplemental Auxiliary Verbs

lequel · en

60. Supplemental Auxiliary Verbs

a. In addition to the auxiliary verbs **avoir*** and **être***, which are used with past participles of all other verbs to form the compound tenses of those verbs, there are certain other "helping" verbs which we shall refer to as "supplemental auxiliary verbs."

b. *Use.* These auxiliary verbs, unlike **avoir*** and **être***, are followed by an INFINITIVE. As an example, we have studied the verb **pouvoir*** *to be able.* Used as an auxiliary to aid in the meaning of a following infinitive, it might appear in

Nous **pouvons** ACCEPTER les résultats de cette expérience.

We $\begin{Bmatrix} \text{can} & \text{ACCEPT} \\ \text{are able} & \text{TO ACCEPT} \end{Bmatrix}$ the results of this experiment.

c. *Translation.* The translation of these auxiliary verbs offers no special difficulty. The proper tense must be selected, of course, but the following INFINITIVE can usually be translated in the normal infinitive form ("to *do something*"), as indicated in the second alternate translation of the example in **b.** above.

d. *List of Supplemental Auxiliary Verbs to be Learned.* Learn the following verbs which may be used with a following infinitive:

savoir*		(to be) able	
pouvoir*		(to be) able	
vouloir*	+ INFINITIVE	(to) want	[TO DO SOMETHING]
devoir*		(to be) obliged	
aller*		(to be) going	
laisser		(to) allow	[SOMETHING TO BE DONE]

EXAMPLES:

savoir* (§57) to be able, to know how
   Nous *ne* **saurions** *pas* SOUTENIR votre prétention.
   We **would** *not* **be able** TO SUPPORT your claim.

pouvoir* (§59) to be able

Nous pouvons DÉSINTÉGRER plusieurs millions d'atomes.

We $\begin{cases} \text{are able} & \text{TO DISINTEGRATE} \\ \text{can} & \text{DISINTEGRATE} \end{cases}$ several million atoms.

vouloir* (§63) to want
Einstein **voulait** PROUVER que l'espace et le temps sont identiques.
Einstein **wanted** TO PROVE that space and time are identical.

devoir* (§64) to be obliged, to be required
Le reste du bâtiment **devra** RECEVOIR un blindage convenable.
The rest of the ship **will be obliged** TO RECEIVE an appropriate armor.
The rest of the ship **must** BE PROVIDED WITH appropriate shielding.

aller* (§65) to go; to be going [TO DO SOMETHING]
Nous **allons** EXAMINER les données.
We **are going** TO EXAMINE the data.

laisser (Regular) to allow, to leave
L'électron périphérique est arraché, **laissant** SUBSISTER des protons.

The peripheral electron is stripped off, $\begin{cases} \text{leaving} \\ \text{allowing TO REMAIN} \end{cases}$ protons.

Monsieur Dupuis *va nous* **laisser** PASSER.   DOUBLE AUXILIARY
Mr. Dupuis *is going* to allow *us* TO PASS.   (**aller** and **laisser**)

Laissons de côté l'hypothèse de Maxwell.   [Not used as an auxiliary]
Let's disregard Maxwell's hypothesis.

61. *lequel* "which"

The word **lequel** has four basic forms, all of which are translated "which":

	SINGULAR	PLURAL	
Masculine	lequel	lesquels	WHICH
Feminine	laquelle	lesquelles	

The contractions listed in §19 apply to this word, the first half of which is simply the definite article **le**:

WITH *à*: *au*quel, à laquelle, *aux*quels, *aux*quelles   *TO* WHICH

WITH *de*: *du*quel, de laquelle, *des*quels, *des*quelles   *OF* WHICH
(All replaceable by dont, § 28)   *FROM* WHICH

62. *en* "some," "of it," "of them," "from there"

The word **en** is used to replace a prepositional phrase beginning with **de**, and not referring to a person. It is always found before the verb (except in positive commands):

Il a beaucoup *de livres.*   Il EN a beaucoup.
He has many *books*   He has many OF THEM.

Avez-vous *de l'argent?*	EN avez-vous?
Have you *some money?*	Have you SOME?

Nous avons examiné *des cas intéressants.*   Nous EN avons examiné.
We have examined *some interesting cases.*   We have examined SOME.

Elles arrivent *de Paris* aujourd'hui.   Elles EN arrivent aujourd'hui.
They are arriving *from Paris* today.   They are arriving FROM THERE *today.*

63. Irregular Verb *vouloir** "to want"

This is used as an auxiliary, or alone. In the present tense it indicates a very strong desire — insistence; in the conditional (**je voudrais**) it indicates a *polite* desire.

PRESENT TENSE

VEU-	je **veux**	I want	nous **voulons**	We want
	tu **veux**	You want	vous **voulez**	You want
	il **veut**	He wants	ils **veulent**	They want

FUTURE AND CONDITIONAL STEM: **voudr-**

PAST DEFINITE STEM: **voul-** (+ us type endings)
    voulus, voulus, voulut; voulûmes, voulûtes, voulurent   wanted

PAST PARTICIPLE: **voulu** wanted; j'avais voulu   I had wanted

PRESENT PARTICIPLE: **voulant** (regular)   wanting

REMEMBER

STEMS: **veu-** (*Pres.*)   **voudr-** (*Fut. and Cond.*)
as parts of **vouloir***

64. Irregular Verb *devoir** "to be obliged," "to be required," "to owe"

PRESENT TENSE *must; owe*

DOI-	je **dois**	I must, I owe	nous **devons**	We must, we owe
	tu **dois**	You must, you owe	vous **devez**	You must, you owe
	il **doit**	He must, he owes	ils **doivent**	They must, they owe

EXAMPLES: Je **dois** partir.   [Used as an auxiliary]
        I **must** leave.   *or*   I **am to** leave. (obligation)
        Nous lui **devons** cinq dollars.
        We **owe** him five dollars.

IMPERFECT MEANING: Je **devais** partir.   I was to leave.

FUTURE AND CONDITIONAL STEM: **devr-**

    Meanings: FUTURE   will have to   Il **devra** partir.
                                    He will have to leave

CONDITIONAL: ought to, should

Nous **devrions** partir.
We ought to leave.

PAST DEFINITE STEM: d- [+ us type endings]
dus, dus, dut; dûmes, dûtes, durent   had to, must have

Il **dut** partir hier.   =   Il a **dû** partir hier.
He **had** to leave yesterday. *or* He **must have** left yesterday.
(obligation)   (probability)

PAST PARTICIPLE: **dû** Ex. **il a dû**   he had to, he must have

PRESENT PARTICIPLE: **devant**   being obligated to, owing

REMEMBER

STEMS   **doi-** (Pres.)   **devr-** (Fut.)   **du-**
as parts of **devoir***

65. Irregular Verb *aller** "to go"

PRESENT TENSE

VA-	je vais	I am going		nous **allons**	We are going
	tu vas	You are going		vous **allez**	You are going
	il va	He is going		ils **vont**	They are going

FUTURE AND CONDITIONAL STEM: **ir-**   F. will go   **C.** would go

PAST DEFINITE STEM: **all-** [+ ai type endings]
allai, allas, alla; allâmes, allâtes, allèrent   went

PAST PARTICIPLE: **allé**   gone   AUXILIARY   **être**
il *est* **allé**   he *has* gone, he went
il *était* **allé**   he *had* gone
il *sera* **allé**   he *will have* gone
il *serait* **allé**   he *would have* gone

PRESENT PARTICIPLE: **allant**   *going*

REMEMBER

STEMS   **va- vo-** (Present)   **ir-** (Fut.)
as parts of the verb **aller***

EXERCISES

I. Verb Drill. Translate the following verb forms:

1. nous tenons; ils tiennent à partir; maintenons!; ils obtiendront; il avait obtenu;
   elle a obtenu; elle est obtenue; retenez bien cela; il n'obtint pas; a-t-il
   obtenu?

2. prendre; pour prendre; sans prendre; apprendre; pour apprendre; il prend;
   il prit; il prendrait; nous avons pris; nous prîmes; comprenez-vous?; en
   prenant; ils prennent; elles prenaient; vous ne preniez pas; ils prirent; on
   prend; on le prend.

3. faire; pour faire; il fait; il fera; il ferait; il fit; nous ferions; il fait semblant
   de dormir; il a fait semblant d'étudier; elle nous fait remarquer que . . . ;
   il fait beau aujourd'hui; il fait partie de la société; il fait bâtir une maison;
   nous ferons voir l'appareil aux physiciens.

4. en mettant; sans émettre; il met; il ne mettait jamais; il mettra; nous avons
   mis; elle ne nous promet rien; nous ne lui promettons rien; il transmit les
   renseignements; il transmet les renseignements; ils promirent de le faire;
   ils ont promis de le faire; n'omettez rien.

5. il fait voir la machine aux professeurs; il leur fera voir la machine; il la
   leur fait voir; il ne la leur fera pas voir; nous vous ferons remarquer
   que . . . ; il a fait venir le médecin; il nous a fait savoir ce qui était
   arrivé.

6. il sut; il saura; il ne savait pas; ils surent; il a su; savez-vous?; sachant les
   faits; il sait parler français; nous ne saurons éviter ce danger; je ne saurais
   vous l'expliquer; vous savez ce qu'il faut faire.

7. voir; pour voir; il faut voir; en voyant; ne pas voir; il vit; il voit; ils
   virent; ils verront; il verra; nous ne voyons pas; il voyait; nous voyions;
   nous voyons; nous verrons; il avait vu; elle était vue; elle a vu; il n'aura
   pas vu; je vois; j'ai vu; j'aurais vu; je prévois.

8. pouvoir; pouvant; il se peut; il put; il a pu; nous pourrons; vous ne pouvez
   pas; pouvez-vous?; est-ce que vous pouvez? est-ce qu'ils pouvaient? il
   pouvait; il aura pu.

1. a obtenu *Use of the auxiliary* **avoir*** *with the past participle indicates that this is the Past Indefinite
tense. On the other hand, the next form,* **est obtenue,** *cannot be a past tense, as* **être*** *is used as an auxiliary
only with certain verbs of motion, all intransitive:* (See pages 142–143)

aller* to go	**venir*** [venu] to come		
retourner to return	**devenir*** [devenu] to become		
	revenir* [revenu] to come back		
arriver to arrive	**partir*** to depart		
entrer to enter	**sortir*** to go out		
monter to go up	**descendre*** to descend		
rester to remain	**tomber** to fall		

All Reflexive Verbs (§27) *and* **naître*** [né] *to be born* **mourir*** [mort] *to die*

a-t-il *Inverted forms of third-person verbs often have an additional* -t- *inserted for reasons of pronunciation.
No translation is needed for this letter, which merely keeps two vowels from coming into juxtaposition.*

9. vouloir; voulant; je veux; je voudrais; j'ai voulu; j'avais voulu; il a voulu; il ne veut pas; il ne voudrait pas; il veut parler; il voudrait parler.

10. devoir; je dois partir; devant; j'ai dû partir hier; je devais partir; je devrais partir; il a dû apprendre le français; je dois faire mes devoirs; nous devons profiter de leur exemple; les élèves doivent s'inscrire aux cours.

11. aller; il va; il est allé; elle est allée; il était allé; il serait allé; il ira; il irait; en allant; il alla; ils allèrent; ils iront; il n'est pas allé; nous ne sommes jamais allés; vous allez souvent; ils vont étudier; je vais vous le donner; elle va l'examiner.

II. Sentence Drill. Translate into good English:

12. Cette organisation nous a **fait** RÉALISER† de beaux progrès dans la science biologique.
13. Le rôle de l'ingénieur se généralise de plus en plus et s'insère dans tous les domaines.
14. Avant de cultiver le tabac dans une région quelconque, on doit, en effet, déterminer d'une façon aussi exacte que possible l'alternance des saisons.
15. Il reste† deux ans. Il ne reste que° deux ans. Il *ne* reste *plus* que° deux ans pour la médecine proprement dite.
16. On ne **saurait** DIRE en tout cas que ce personnel soit défavorable à l'instruction des élèves.
17. Ces réacteurs doivent utiliser du combustible nucléaire à haute teneur en matière fissile, donc cher.
18. L' ordinateur utilise de minuscules éléments de ferrite qui peuvent être aimantés par l'action d'un courant électrique.
19. Les techniques objectives ne **doivent** REPRÉSENTER qu'une° portion de la méthode médicale.
20. Il ne faut pas oublier que Conrad tenait à transcrire ses expériences.
21. Les personnes qui ne connaissent pas l'œuvre de Haydn ne **sauraient** SE METTRE à un juste point de vue pour juger les œuvres actuelles.
22. Le sous-marin **devra** DISPOSER d'abris et de bassins spécialement aménagés.
23. **Pouvez**-vous PRÉDIRE quand vous mourrez vous-même?
24. Je ne **puis** pas PRÉDIRE le jour de ma mort, mais je sais très bien que je mourrai exactement trois jours avant votre Majesté.
25. Le roi ne **voulait** pas AVOUER qu'il était superstitieux.
26. Il n'y a point de théorie qui ne **doive** SE MODIFIER constamment.
27. Le but qu'on **doit** POURSUIVRE est de la perfectionner.
28. L'hypothèse en question **peut** EXPLIQUER les nouveaux faits.
29. Les lettres A et B ne **peuvent** DONNER LIEU qu'aux° quatre arrangements également possibles.

---

10. **s'inscri/re** *v.* to register (*Acad.*)   14. **quelconque** any   15. **proprement** dit(e) per se
17. **teneur** content; **fissile** fissionable; **cher** expensive   18. **ordinateur** *nm.* computer; **minuscule** *adj.* tiny; **aimantés** magnetized   19. **objectif, -ve** *adj.* objective (*modifies the preceding word*)
20. **transcrire*** to transcribe   21. **ne sauraient, ne doive** *Note that some verbs may omit the second term* (See §85 page 144)   29. **donner lieu à** to give rise to, to permit of

30. Elsa a **voulu** SAVOIR, EXAMINER, CONTRÔLER.
31. Vouloir c'est pouvoir. — PROVERBE FRANÇAIS.
32. Les personnes faibles ne **peuvent** ÊTRE sincères. — LA ROCHEFOUCAULD.

READINGS

A. Haydn

PAR CAMILLE SAINT-SAËNS

[33] Haydn a écrit cent dix-huit symphonies; la collection complète, en copies très correctes, est à la bibliothèque de notre Conservatoire. [34] Beaucoup d'entre elles ne sont que° de simples divertissements, écrits au jour le jour, pour les petits concerts quotidiens du prince Esterhazy; mettons que le quart mérite d'être exécuté †: cela fait encore un joli chiffre. [35] En tout cas, les magnifiques et célèbres symphonies qu'Haydn écrivit à Londres, pour les concerts de Salomon, ont un droit incontestable à la lumière du jour. [36] Haydn est le père de la musique instrumentale moderne; qui ne connaît pas son œuvre ne saurait se mettre à un juste point de vue pour juger les œuvres actuelles; [37] dans ses deux oratorios, *la Création, les Saisons,* il a déployé une fertilité d'invention, une richesse de coloris qui tiennent du prodige; et tels effets **dont** nos amateurs attribuent l'invention à Mendelssohn ou à Schumann, existent déjà dans ces œuvres merveilleuses. [38] Haydn possède un atticisme étonnant, analogue à celui de nos écrivains français du temps passé. [39] Il sait toujours s'arrêter à temps, et sa musique n'engendre jamais l'ennui. [40] Elle n'est ni shakespearienne, ni byronnienne, c'est évident; Haydn n'était pas un agité, son style reflète la sérénité de sa belle âme. [41] Est-ce une raison pour écarter ses œuvres? [42] Une galerie de tableaux se couvrirait de ridicule, si elle remisait au grenier un Pérugin, sous prétexte qu'on n'y trouve pas les effets troublants d'un Ruysdaël ou d'un Delacroix. [43] Il en est d'un répertoire de concert comme d'une galerie

---

31. *Aside from the literal translation, what English proverb conveys the same idea?* **A. Haydn** *See note 46, p. 38* **34. quotidien, -ne** *adj.* daily; **mettons** *v.* (*Imperative*) Let's say that, Let's postulate that . . .; **quart** *nm.* quarter; **execut/er** *v.* to perform; **chiffre** *nm.* number **35. Salomon** *Impresario who arranged for Haydn's visit to England, and who commissioned the last six symphonies* **36. qui** who*ever* **37. tenir*** de *v.* to derive from; **prodige** *nm.* genius; **invention** *nf. Use in translation before the word* **dont**. *In case of confusion, enclose the* **dont**-*phrase in parentheses:* (**dont . . . Schumann**) **38. atticisme** *nm.* Atticism, classicism; **étonn/er** *v.* to astonish **39. ennui** *nm.* boredom **40. agité** *nm.* a troubled person; **âme** *nf.* soul, mind **41. écart/er** *v.* to push aside **42. tableau** *nm.* picture; **elle** *pn. Refers to the management;* **remis/er** *v.* to relegate; **grenier** *nm.* attic; **Pérugin** *Peintre italien (vers 1445–1523), un des maîtres du célèbre peintre Raphaël. C'est surtout des tableaux religieux qu'il a peints.* **y** in them; **Ruysdaël, Jacob Isaac,** *peintre hollandais dont les tableaux étaient des paysages, pleins de couleur.* **Delacroix, Eugène,** *peintre français (1798–1863) et chef de l'école romantique, dont le tableau le plus célèbre est "la Barque de Dante."* **43. (en être*)** Il en est de . . . **comme** It is the same with . . . as

de peinture: tout ce qui est bon doit y trouver place. [44] Le public, mesurant volontiers la valeur des œuvres à l'intensité des sensations qu'elles lui font éprouver°, se trompe du tout au tout: [45] c'est l'élévation des idées, leur originalité, la profondeur du sentiment et la beauté du style qui font la valeur des œuvres, non le trouble plus ou moins grand que leur audition amène dans le système nerveux. [46] La recherche de la sensation, lorsqu'elle devient le but de la musique, la tue à bref délai, amenant en peu de temps une monotonie insupportable et une exagération mortelle.

— SAINT-SAËNS. *Portraits et souvenirs*

B. *An Interview between Napoleon and the Pope*

[47] En effet, dit le capitaine Renard en reprenant la lettre de mes mains, je venais d'être nommé page de l'Empereur en 1804. On avait osé créer des pages, mais nous portions l'uniforme d'officiers, en attendant la livrée verte à culottes rouges que nous devions prendre au sacre. [48] Déjà le maître se plaisait à peupler ses antichambres; et comme le besoin de dominer le suivait partout, il ne pouvait s'empêcher de l'exercer dans les plus petites choses et tourmentait ceux qui l'entouraient. [49] Il s'amusait de ma timidité; il jouait avec mes terreurs et mon respect. Quand il était hors de la chambre, je pouvais respirer, le sang commençait à circuler dans mes veines, la mémoire me revenait et avec elle une honte inexprimable; la rage me prenait, j'écrivais ce que j'aurais dû lui répondre; puis je me roulais sur le tapis, je pleurais, j'avais envie de me tuer.

[50] « Son attitude, sa voix, son geste, ne sont qu'une pantomine d'acteur, » me disais-je, « une misérable parade de souveraineté dont il doit savoir la vanité. Il n'est pas possible qu'il croie en lui-même aussi sincèrement! » Cependant je ne savais comment voir le fond de cette âme déguisée. Le pouvoir et la gloire la défendaient sur tous les points.

---

44. **volontiers** *adv.* willingly; **elles** *Refers to* œuvres; **éprouv/er** *v.* to experience, to feel; **se tromp/er** *v.* to be mistaken; **du tout au tout** completely   45. **audition** *nf.* hearing; **amen/er*** *v.* to bring to   46. **recherche** *nf.* seeking; **à bref délai** in a short time; Saint-Saëns, Camille (1835–1921) *compositeur de nombreux concertos, plusieurs morceaux de musique de chambre, une symphonie avec orgue, et auteur de "Samson et Dalila," "Danse macabre," et "Le Rouet d'Omphale," entre autres. Né à Paris, c'est un organiste dont la musique est marquée par la perfection de la forme.*   47. **venais de** had just; **oser** to dare; **porter** to wear; **livrée** *nf.* livery; **vert, verte** *adj.* green; **culotte** *nf.* breeches; **devions prendre** were to wear; **sacre** *nm.* coronation *Refers to the ceremony by which Napoleon became Emperor in 1804.*   48. **maître** *nm.* master (*here, Napoleon is thus referred to.*); **se plaire à** to take pleasure in; **s'empêcher de** to prevent [himself] from; **tourmenter** to torment   49. **s'amuser** to make fun of; **honte** *nf.* shame; **prenait** overcame; **j'aurais dû** I should have; **tapis** *nm.* carpet   50. **parade** *nf.* display; **croie** [**croire***] believes; **aussi** so; **fond** *nm.* [bottom] essence; **déguiser** to disguise

[51]—Un jour, pourtant, le hasard, notre maître à tous, fit pénétrer une lumière d'un moment.—Un jour, ce fut peut-être le seul de sa vie, il rencontra plus fort que lui et recula un instant devant un ascendant plus grand que le sien.—J'en fus témoin, et me sentis vengé. Voici comment cela m'arriva:

[52] Nous étions à Fontainebleau. Le Pape venait d'arriver. L'Empereur l'avait attendu impatiemment pour le sacre, et l'avait reçu en voiture. Il revenait au château. J'avais laissé plusieurs officiers dans la chambre qui précédait celle de l'Empereur, et j'étais resté seul dans la sienne. Je considérais une longue table couverte d'un amas de lettres que Napoléon ne lisait jamais—des implorations inutiles des veuves et des orphelins. [53] Je considérais ces lettres abandonnées: des cris de douleur inentendus, et les prenant pour les lire, les rejetant ensuite, moi-même je me faisais juge entre ces malheureux et le maître qu'ils s'étaient donné, et qui allait aujourd'hui s'asseoir plus solidement que jamais sur leurs têtes. [54] Je tenais dans ma main l'une de ces pétitions méprisées, lorsque le bruit des tambours qui battaient *aux champs* m'apprit l'arrivée subite de l'Empereur. J'eus le temps à peine de me jeter dans une alcôve fermée par des rideaux.

[55] L'Empereur était fort agité. Il marcha seul dans la chambre comme quelqu'un qui attend avec impatience. Il s'avança vers la fenêtre et se mit à y tambouriner une marche avec les ongles. Une voiture roula dans la cour. Il cessa de battre, frappa des pieds comme impatienté de la vue de quelque chose qui se faisait avec lenteur, puis il alla brusquement à la porte et l'ouvrit au Pape.

[56] Pie VII entra seul. Bonaparte se hâta de refermer la porte derrière lui, avec une promptitude de geôlier. Je sentis une grande terreur, je l'avoue, en me voyant en tiers avec de telles gens. Cependant je restai sans voix et sans mouvement, regardant et écoutant de toute la puissance de mon esprit.

[57] Le Pape était d'une taille élevée; il avait un visage allongé, jaune, souffrant, mais pleine d'une noblesse sainte et d'une bonté sans bornes. Il entra lentement, avec la démarche calme et prudente d'une femme agée. Il vint s'asseoir, les yeux baissés, sur un des grands fauteuils romains dorés et chargés d'aigles, et attendit ce que lui allait dire l'autre Italien.

---

51. **fit pénétrer** *See. Sec. 55, page 80, for word order*; **rencontra** met [a man *is understood*]; **reculer** to fall back; **ascendant** *nm.* influence; **J'en fus témoin** I was a witness of it; **vengé** avenged 52. **venait de** had just *See Sec. 68, page 102 and page 183, for the other forms of* venir; **la sienne** his; **amas** *nm.* pile; **imploration** *nf.* plea; **veuve** *nf.* widow; **orphelin** *nm.* orphan 53. **douleur** *nf.* grief; **inentendu** unheard (*The prefix* **in-** *often indicates the English prefix* **un-**); **rejeter** to throw down; **moi-même** myself; **malheureux** *nm. pl.* unfortunates 54. **méprisé** scorned; **tambour** *nm.* drum; **aux champs** official salute; **subite** *adj.* sudden; **rideau** *nm.* curtain 55. **fort** = très; **avec impatience** impatiently *See page 184 for this use of* avec + *noun*; **se mit à** began to *Review Sec. 56, page 81 and page 183*; **tambouriner** to drum; **ongle** *nm.* [finger]-nail; **cour** *nf.* courtyard; **frapper des pieds** to stamp [feet]; **qui se faisait** that was taking place 56. **Pie VII** Pope Pius VII, *pope from 1800–1823, held captive at Fontainebleau until 1814*; **se hâter de** to hasten to; **geôlier** *nm.* jailer; **en tiers** as a third party; **de telles gens** such people 57. **taille** *nf.* stature; **borne** *nf.* limit; **fauteuil** *nm.* armchair; **doré** *adj.* gilded; **chargés d'aigles** decorated with [imperial] eagles; **ce que** what (*followed by the next noun group, then the verbal group*)

[58] Napoléon ne cessa pas de marcher dans la chambre quand le Pape fut entré; il se mit à rôder autour du fauteuil comme un chasseur prudent. Il se mit alors à parler, en marchant circulairement et jetant des regards perçants dans les glaces de l'appartement où se réfléchissait la figure grave du Saint-Père, et le regardant en profil quand il passait près de lui, mais jamais en face, de peur de sembler trop inquiet de l'impression de ses paroles:

[59] « Il y a quelque chose, » dit-il, « qui me reste sur le cœur, Saint-Père, c'est que vous consentez au sacre de la même manière que l'autre fois au concordat, comme si vous y étiez forcé. Vous avez un air de martyr devant moi, vous êtes là comme résigné, comme offrant au ciel vos douleurs. Mais, en vérité, ce n'est pas là votre situation, vous n'êtes pas prisonnier, par Dieu! vous êtes libre comme l'air. »

[60] Pie VII sourit avec tristesse et le regarda en face.

« Oui, » reprit Bonaparte avec plus de force, « vous êtes parfaitement libre; vous pouvez vous en retourner à Rome, la route vous est ouverte, personne ne vous retient. »

Le Pape soupira et leva sa main droite et ses yeux au ciel sans répondre; ensuite il laissa retomber très lentement son front ridé et se mit à considérer la croix d'or suspendue à son cou.

[61] « Moi, je ne sais pas, » reprit Napoléon, « pourquoi vous auriez de la répugnance à siéger à Paris pour toujours. Je vous laisserais, ma foi, les Tuileries, si vous vouliez. Ne voyez-vous pas bien, *Padre*, que c'est là la vraie capitale du monde? Moi, je ferais tout ce que vous voudriez; je vous mettrais ensuite dans la main les vraies clefs du monde, et comme Notre-Seigneur a dit: "Je suis venu avec l'épée," je garderais l'épée, moi; je vous la rapporterais seulement à bénir après chaque succès de nos armes. »

[62] Il s'inclina légèrement en disant ces dernières paroles.

Le Pape, qui jusque-là n'avait cessé de demeurer sans mouvement, comme une statue égyptienne, releva lentement sa tête, sourit avec mélancholie, leva ses yeux en haut et dit, avec un soupir paisible, comme s'il eût confié sa pensée à son ange gardien invisible:

« *Commediante!* »

[63] Bonaparte sauta de sa chaise et bondit comme un léopard blessé. Une vraie colère le prit. Il me semblait qu'il allait arriver quelque terrible et grande chose.

---

58. **rôder** to prowl; **chasseur** *nm.* hunter; **jetant** casting; **perçants** piercing; **glace** *nf.* mirror; **où** (*to be followed by the first complete noun group, then the verb*); **inquiet, inquiète** *adj.* worried about, concerned about   59. **qui me reste sur le cœur** which hurts me; **Concordat** *Agreement between the Pope and Napoleon in 1801*: y into it; **douleur** *nf.* grief   60. **soupirer** to sigh; **laissa retomber** (*Place next noun group before* **retomber**); **front** *nm.* forehead; **croix** *nf.* cross, crucifix; **cou** *nm.* neck   61. **siéger** to have your headquarters; **ma foi!** My goodness!; **Tuileries** *A palace adjoining the Louvre, erected by Catherine de Médicis in 1564, destroyed by fire in 1874. Only a park remain on the site.*; **dans la main** in your hands; **clef** *nf.* key; **épée** *nf.* sword; **bénir** to bless   62. **s'incliner** to bow; **là** then; **soupir** *nm.* sigh; **paisible** *adj.* peaceful; **pensée** *nf.* thought; **Commediante** [*Italian*] comedian   63. **bondir** to leap, to bound; **il allait** [*The word* **il** *is impersonal here, and should be replaced by the first noun group* (**quelque ... chose**) *which is the true subject of* **allait**]

La bombe éclata tout à coup.

« Comédien! Moi! Ah! je vous donnerai des comédies à vous faire tous pleurer comme des femmes et des enfants. Mon théâtre, c'est le monde; le rôle que j'y joue, c'est celui de maître et d'auteur; pour comédiens, j'ai vous tous, Pape, Rois, Peuples! Comédien! Ah! Il faudrait être d'une autre taille que la vôtre pour m'oser applaudir ou siffler, *signor Chiaramonti*! Savez-vous bien que vous ne seriez qu'un pauvre curé, si je le voulais? Vous et votre tiare, la France vous rirait au nez, si ne je gardais mon air sérieux en vous saluant. »

[64] Il se tut. Je n'osais pas respirer. J'avançai la tête pour voir si le pauvre vieillard était mort d'effroi. Le même calme dans l'attitude, le même calme sur le visage. Il leva une seconde fois les yeux au ciel et, après avoir encore jeté un profond soupir, il sourit avec amertume et dit:

« *Tragediante.* »

Bonaparte, en ce moment, était au bout de la chambre, appuyé sur la cheminée de marbre aussi haute que lui. Il partit comme un trait, courant sur le vieillard; je crus qu'il allait le tuer. Mais il s'arrêta court, prit, sur la table, un vase de porcelaine de Sèvres, et le jetant sur le plancher, le broya sous ses pieds. Puis, tout d'un coup, il s'assit et demeura dans un silence profond et une immobilité formidable. Il devint triste, sa voix fut sourde et mélancholique et, dès sa première parole, je compris que ce Protée, dompté par deux mots, se montrait lui-même.

[65] « C'est vrai! Tragédien ou Comédien.—Tout est rôle, tout est costume pour moi depuis longtemps et pour toujours. Quelle fatigue! quelle petitesse! Poser! Toujours poser! ... »

—d'après Alfred de Vigny, *La Canne de Jonc*

éclater to explode; **tout à coup** suddenly; **la vôtre** yours; **siffler** to hiss; **curé** *nm.* priest; **tiare** Pope's tiara; **au nez** in your [face]   64. **se tut** fell silent; **vieillard** *nm.* old man; **effroi** *nm.* fright; **amertume** *nf.* bitterness; **Tragediante** [*Italian*] tragedian; **appuyé** leaning; **cheminée** *nf.* fireplace; **trait** *nm.* arrow; **je crus** [**croire***] I believed; **plancher** *nm.* floor; **broyer** to grind; **devint** [**devenir***] became; **sourd, sourde** *adj.* hollow [voice]; **dès** from; **Protée** Proteus *in Greek mythology, a sea-god son of Poseidon (Neptune) who would assume various shapes and forms when captured*; **dompté** subdued   65. **petitesse** *nf.* pettiness

Test XI, pages 215–216

Chapter XII

66. Past Definite Tense

a. *Identification.* In following the rule for tense identification by elimination (§42), our procedure has been (1) to check for the PRESENT TENSE, (2) for the FUTURE or CONDITIONAL, and then, if both of these tests fail, to call the verb under examination a PAST TENSE. It is to this last step that we now turn our attention in more detail.

A verb which is identified under the above rule as a past tense will probably be either the IMPERFECT (§43) or the PAST DEFINITE. If the ending is -ais, -ait, -ions, -iez, or -aient (same as the endings for the Conditional), we know that the verb is Imperfect. Otherwise a simple verb is to be considered PAST DEFINITE.

b. *Translation.* The Past Definite tense is "just plain past," with no subtle distinctions as are found in the Imperfect. A good translation should show that the action indicated by the verb is something that happened, is over and done:

PAST DEFINITE FORM	TRANSLATION	FROM:
il examin*a*	he examined	(examiner)
ils remarqu*èrent*	they noticed	(remarquer)
nous vend*îmes*	we sold	(vendre)
vous fin*îtes*	you finished	(finir)
il all*a*	he went	(aller*)
il *eut*	he had	(avoir*)

c. *Ending System of the Past Definite.* The following endings are added to the stem of regular verbs; and to the special stems learned for irregular verbs, as indicated beneath the endings:

100

VERB TYPE (Infinitive)		Regular		Some IRREGULAR -oir*
		-er	-ir and -re	
ENDING SYSTEMS	je	-ai	-is	-us
	tu	-as	-is	-us
	il	-a	-it	-ut
	nous	-âmes	-îmes	-ûmes
	vous	-âtes	-îtes	-ûtes
	ils	-èrent	-irent	-urent
IRREGULAR VERBS USING ENDINGS		all- (aller*)	d- (dire*) f- (faire*) m- (mettre*) pr- (prendre*) v- (voir*)	d- (devoir*) e- (avoir*) p- (pouvoir*) s- (savoir*) voul- (vouloir*) AND f- (être*)

d. *Comparison of Past Definite and Imperfect.*

Whereas the Imperfect has three translations, the Past Definite has only one:

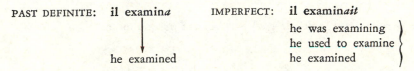

PAST DEFINITE: **il examin*a***   IMPERFECT: **il examin*ait***

|
he examined

he was examining)
he used to examine }
he examined)

The context determines which translation of the Imperfect to use, and the best choice is one of the first two, usually. No choice has to be made with the Past Definite.

67. Expressions of Time

a. Certain adverbs indicating time are essential to know as an aid to tense identification. The list following this paragraph contains some adverbs of time which we have already seen, and some new ones. Memorize them all very carefully.

b. *Adverbs of time*

alors	then	aujourd'hui	today
bientôt	soon	demain	tomorrow
d'abord	at first; first of all	hier	yesterday
ensuite	next	le lendemain	the next day
longtemps	for a long time	désormais	henceforth
maintenant	now	quelquefois	sometimes
souvent	often	toujours	always, still
déjà	already	dès . . .	from . . . on

c. *depuis* [+ TIME]. When the word **depuis** is followed immediately by a quantity of time, translate **depuis** as *for*. The verb tense in the sentence must also be changed to make sense in English:

> Nous examinons ce cas **depuis** TROIS JOURS.
> We (   ) this case **for** THREE DAYS.

The verb is in the Present Tense in French [reason: the action is *still* in progress], but this sounds rather peculiar in English. The English would be **have been** (doing something) **for** [TIME]. Hence we translate the above example as

> We *have been examining* this case for THREE DAYS.

The depuis-Construction and the **il y a** [+ TIME]-Construction below are the only structures in which a translator may normally change a verb tense.

d. *il y a* [TIME] *que.* This construction parallels that indicated above for depuis. Translate **il y a** as *for,* and invert order:

> Il y a TROIS JOURS que nous examinons ce cas.
> We **have been examining** this case for THREE DAYS.

The inversion of order is simple, as we merely begin the sentence as usual, with the **subject** (nous) and **verb** (examinons), remembering to change the verb to *have been —ing.*

e. *il y a* [TIME] "ago." *Il y a* [+ TIME] and *no* que means "ago."

> il y a DIX ANS   TEN YEARS **ago**

68. Irregular Verb *venir** "to come"

There is a close resemblance betwen **venir** and **tenir** (§37). **Venir** has a number of compounds which follow the same conjugation system: *convenir** to suit, to agree; devenir** to become; prévenir** to inform, to warn; parvenir** to attain; provenir** de to stem from; se souvenir** de to remember;* and others.

PRESENT TENSE

je **viens**	I am coming	nous ven**ons**	We are coming
tu **viens**	You are coming	vous ven**ez**	You are coming
il vien**t**	He is coming	ils vien**nent**	They are coming

FUTURE AND CONDITIONAL STEM: viendr-

IMPERFECT: (*fr. Present* venons) je venais, etc. I was coming, used to come

PAST DEFINITE: vins, vins, vint, vînmes, vîntes, vinrent came

PAST PARTICIPLE: venu come   (*Uses auxiliary* être**)
>   EX.: **il** *est* **venu**   he came;   **il** *était* **devenu**   he *had* become

PRESENT PARTICIPLE: venant coming

REMEMBER

STEMS vien- (*Pres.*)   viendr- (*Fut.*)   vin- (*Past Def.*)   venu (*pp.*)
as parts of **venir***

NOTE: Il **vient** nous voir.   He comes to see us.
         Il **vient** à nous voir.   He **happens** to see us.

69. *venir* de [+ INFINITIVE] "to have just [DONE SOMETHING]."

The special construction including a form of **venir*** followed immediately by de plus an INFINITIVE is translated as follows:

TENSE OF venir*	TRANSLATION
Present (il vient de . . .)	*has* just . . .
Imperfect (il venait de . . .)	*had* just . . .

EXAMPLES: Nous **venons** d'examiner ce cas.
                   We *have just* examined this case.

                   Nous **venions** d'examiner ce cas.
                   We *had just* examined this case.

EXERCISES

I. **Verb Drill.** Translate the following verbs into their English equivalents. When several translations are possible, as with verbs in the Present and Imperfect tenses, give all possible translations.

1. faire*; il fait; nous ferons; nous faisions; nous fîmes; ils firent; je ne fais pas; elle n'a pas fait; ils ne firent jamais; nous avons fait bâtir une maison; il nous fit voir l'appareil.

2. venir*; il venait; il vint; ils vinrent; ils ne vinrent pas; il vient de partir; il venait de partir; elle était venue; elle est venue; elle sera venue; venant; pour venir.

3. convenir*; il convient; cela me convient; nous convenons.

4. examiner; pour examiner; sans examiner; il faut examiner; j'examinais; il examinerait; nous examinions; examinons; il avait examiné; elle aura examiné.

5. pouvoir*; sans pouvoir; il a pu; il pouvait; nous avons pu; il put; ils purent; je ne pus pas; il ne pouvait jamais; il pourra.

6. voir*; je vois; il voit; il vit; il verra; nous verrons; vous verrez; voyons!; nous avons vu; il avait vu; nous aurons vu; sans voir.

7. obtenir*; il obtenait; il a obtenu; il avait obtenu; il aura obtenu; il obtint; nous obtenons; nous aurons obtenu; ils obtinrent.

8. apprendre*; il a appris; il apprit; nous apprîmes; elle avait appris; sans apprendre; il faut apprendre; j'appris; j'apprends; j'apprenais.

II. Sentence Drill. Translate:

9. Descartes découvrit la loi de la réfraction.

10. Il crut, avec Galilée, au mouvement de la terre autour du soleil.

11. Pascal créa le calcul des probabilités pour aider son ami, le chevalier de Méré, à réussir aux jeux de chance.

12. Pierre Fermat fut peut-être le plus puissant esprit mathématique de son siècle.

13. Deux physiciens *mirent au point* un modèle de cyclotron en 1932. [mettre* au point = perfectionn/er]

14. Il n'aime plus cette personne qu'il aimait il y a dix ans.

15. Il y a trois ans qu'il déteste cette personne malhonnête.

16. Un jour la belle demoiselle Cunégonde rencontra Candide en revenant au château, et elle rougit. [rougir = devenir* rouge]

17. Candide rougit aussi; elle lui dit bonjour d'une voix entrecoupée, et Candide lui parla sans savoir ce qu'il disait.

18. Le lendemain, après le dîner, comme on sortait de table, Cunégonde et Candide se trouvèrent derrière un paravent.

19. Cunégonde laissa tomber son mouchoir, et Candide le ramassa.

20. Elle lui prit innocemment la main, le jeune homme baisa innocemment la main de la jeune demoiselle avec une vivacité, une sensibilité, une grâce toute particulière. Leurs bouches se rencontrèrent, leurs yeux s'enflammèrent, leurs genoux tremblèrent, leurs mains s'égarèrent.

21. M. le baron de Thunder-ten-tronckh passa auprès du paravent, et, voyant cette cause et cet effet, chassa Candide du château à grands coups de pied dans le derrière.

22. Candide, chassé du paradis terrestre, marcha longtemps sans savoir où, pleurant, levant les yeux au ciel, les tournant souvent vers le plus beau des châteaux, qui renfermait la plus belle des baronnettes.

　　　—VOLTAIRE. *Candide ou l'optimisme.* Chapitre I (sentences 16–22)

23. *Il y a* deux mois *que* nous examinons ces données.

24. Nous examinons les données *depuis* deux mois.

25. *Il y avait* une semaine *que* Winkler employait cet appareil.

26. Voilà un fait que nous savons *depuis* longtemps.

27. *Il y a* deux mois nous examinions cet échantillon de fer.

28. Nous voyageons en Europe depuis six semaines; nous étions à Marseille il y a huit jours. [une semaine = huit jours]

---

10. **crut** (*fr.* **croire*** to believe); **Galilée** (*1564–1642*) *Astronome et physicien italien qui fut un des fondateurs de la méthode expérimentale. Il formula les lois gouvernant la chute des corps, construisit le premier téléscope, et énonça le principe d'inertie.* [Galileo] 15. **malhonnête = qui n'est pas honnête**
16. **demoiselle** *nf.* young lady 17. **entrecoupé** *adj.* broken 18. **paravent** *nm.* folding screen
19. **mouchoir** *nm.* handkerchief; **ramass/er** *v.* to pick up 20. **bais/er (la main)** *v.* to kiss (the hand); **sensibilité** *nf.* feeling; **particulière** *adj.* unusual; **genou** *nm.* knee; **s'égar/er** *v.* to wander, to stray 21. **auprès de** *adv.* very close to; **coup de pied** *nm.* kick 22. **pleur/er** *v.* to weep, to cry; **ciel** *nm.* sky; **baronnette** *nf.* little baroness

29. Quand le général Wellington gagna la bataille de Waterloo le 18 juin 1815, Napoléon était de retour sur le continent depuis cent jours.

30. MM. Lawrence et Livingston ont mis au point leur appareil, le cyclotron, il y a plus de trente-cinq ans.

READINGS

A. Les Sciences au 17ᵉ siècle

[31] Dans les sciences, la France était au niveau du mouvement scientifique, mais non à la tête. [32] Car, si elle avait Descartes et Pascal, à d'autres pays appartenaient Kepler, Galilée, Newton et Leibnitz.

[33] L'antiquité et le moyen âge avaient pu cultiver avec succès les sciences de raisonnement; mais l'étude du monde physique était frappée de stérilité, tant que les vraies méthodes d'expérimentation n'étaient pas trouvées. [34] Et elles ne pouvaient l'être qu'après° qu'on eut acquis la confiance que l'univers est gouverné par des lois immuables, et non par les volontés arbitraires de puissances capricieuses. [35] Alors seulement on n'accusa plus l'esprit humain de témérité sacrilège, parce qu'il cherchait à pénétrer les secrets de la création. [36] L'alchimie, la magie, l'astrologie, toutes ces folies du moyen âge devinrent des sciences, du moment que l'homme ne s'occupa plus de l'essence impénétrable des choses, et, au lieu de s'arrêter aux phénomènes isolés, s'efforça de saisir les lois qui les produisent. [37] Ce temps commence avec Copernic, au seizième siècle; mais ce n'est qu'au° dix-septième que la révolution est accomplie et triomphe avec Kepler, Bacon et Descartes.

[38] **Descartes** fit faire° un pas immense à l'algèbre en inventant la notation des puissances par exposants numériques, et à la géométrie des courbes, ce qui lui permit de résoudre des problèmes qu'on croyait insolubles. [39] Il découvrit la loi de réfraction; il crut, avec Galilée, au mouvement de la terre autour du soleil, et, comme les erreurs mêmes du génie sont fécondes, son chimérique *système des tourbillons* (suivant lequel le soleil et les étoiles fixes sont le centre d'autant de tourbillons de matière subtile, qui font° circuler les planètes autour d'eux), a été le germe de la célèbre *hypothèse newtonienne de l'attraction.* [40] Pour Descartes comme pour Newton, le problème de l'univers physique est un problème de mécanique et Descartes enseignera le premier, sinon la solution, du moins la vraie nature du problème.

---

33. **frapp/er** *v.* to strike, (*pp.*) stricken; **tant que** as long as 34. **acquis** *pp.* acquired 35. **témérité** *nf.* temerity, boldness; **sacrilège** *adj.* sacrilegious 36. **moyen âge** *nm.* the Middle Ages; **chose** *nf.* thing; **s'efforc/er (de)** *v.* to strive (to); **sais/ir** *v.* to grasp 37. **Copernic** Copernicus; **seize** 16; **dix-sept** 17 38. **pas** *nm.* step; **exposant** *nm.* exponent; **courbe** *nf.* curve 39. **même** *adj. after a noun* very; **chimérique** *adj.* fanciful; **tourbillon** *nm.* eddy, whirlpool; **subtil, -e** *adj.* thin, rarefied; **attraction** *nf.* attraction, gravitation

[41] **Pascal,** à douze ans, lisait en cachette de son père les *Éléments* d'Euclide; à seize ans, il composa son traité *Des sections coniques.* Un peu plus tard il créa le calcul des probabilités, démontra la pesanteur de l'air par la fameuse expérience du Puy-de-Dôme, imagina le haquet et peut-être la presse hydraulique. Il a certainement inventé la machine à calculer.   (See page 154)

[42] **Pierre Fermat** (1601–1665), conseiller au parlement de Toulouse, n'a rien imprimé, mais fut peut-être le plus puissant esprit mathématique de ce temps. [43] Il partagea avec Descartes la gloire d'avoir appliqué l'algèbre à la géométrie, et imagina la méthode de *maximis et de minimis,* en même temps que Pascal créa le calcul des probabilités.

[44] **L'abbé Mariotte** (1620–1665) reconnut que le volume d'un gaz, à une température constante, varie en raison inverse de la pression qu'il supporte.

[45] **Denis Patin,** né à Blois en 1647, créa ou perfectionna plusieurs machines et pensa le premier à employer la vapeur condensée comme force motrice. [46] En Allemagne, sur la Fulda [*a river*] il fit des expériences avec un *bateau à vapeur* qui remontait le courant. [47] De stupides mariniers brisèrent la machine du grand physicien, qui mourut à Londres dans la misère.

[48] Trois étrangers que Colbert invita en France justifièrent par leurs travaux les faveurs du roi. [49] Le Danois **Rœmer** détermina la vitesse des rayons solaires; le Hollandais **Huygens** découvrit l'anneau et un des satellites de Saturne; l'Italien Dominique **Cassini** en vit quatre autres. [50] On doit encore à Huygens l'invention des horloges à pendule, et à Cassini les premières opérations qui devaient servir à mesurer la terre; [51] il les exécuta avec l'abbé Picard, professeur d'astronomie au Collège de France, et tous deux commencèrent en 1669 la méridienne qui fut prolongée plus tard jusqu'au Roussillon. [52] C'est d'après la mesure du degré donnée par Picard, que Newton put enfin calculer la force qui retient la lune dans son orbite.

— VICTOR DURUY. *Histoire de France* (Librairie Hachette, Éditeur)

41. **en cachette** secretly (de) in hiding from; **traité** *nm.* article, treatise; **pesanteur** *nf.* weight; **Puy-de-Dôme** *a mountain near Clermont-Ferrand in central France, where Pascal's experiment took place. A mercury column was carried from the base to the summit (4806 feet); the change in the level of the mercury demonstrated the effect of atmospheric pressure.* **haquet** *nm.* dray (*two-wheeled cart for carrying heavy loads*) 42. **conseiller** *nm.* councillor (*representative*); **imprim/er** *v.* to print. 43. **maximis et de minimis** maximums and minimums (*a determination which is part of calculus*) 44. **en raison inverse** in inverse proportion (ratio) 45. **force motrice** motive power 46. **Allemagne** Germany; **remont/er*** **le courant** to go upstream 47. **marinier** *nm.* sailor; **bris/er** *v.* to break; **mourut** (*fr.* **mour/ir*** to die); **Londres** London; **misère** *nf.* poverty 48. **étranger** *nm.* foreigner; **Colbert, Jean-Baptiste** (*1619–1683*) *un des plus grands ministres de la France, contrôleur général des finances sous Louis XIV.* 49. **Danois** *une personne originaire du Danemark* 50. **encore** (*here*) moreover, in addition; **horloge** *nf.* clock; **devaient** (*Imperfect of* **devoir***) were to 51. **abbé** (*form of address for a Catholic Priest*) Father; **tous deux** both

B. *Thorium et uranium* 233

[53] Découvert en 1829 par Berzélius, le thorium est probablement une matière première de grand avenir pour l'industrie atomique, car il permet de fabriquer un isotope fissible d'uranium, l'uranium 233.

[54] Le thorium existe en quantités importantes dans la nature. [55] Il est trois fois plus abondant que l'uranium dans l'écorce terrestre, et il présente sur l'uranium l'avantage d'avoir été concentré par l'érosion naturelle en gisements facilement exploitables et bien distribués géographiquement.

[56] Les principaux minerais de thorium sont la thorite (silicate de thorium et d'uranium) et la thorianite (oxydes de thorium et d'uranium), que l'on trouve dans l'île de Ceylan, dans le Texas, en Norvège et à Madagascar.

[57] L'extraction du minerai s'effectue par des méthodes primitives, la main-d'œuvre indigène le chargeant dans des paniers et le transportant ainsi à l'usine de traitement, qui opère par séparation magnétique, après tamisage et enrichissement.

[58] Les monazites sont les seules sources de terres rares actuellement exploitées. [59] Certaines ont des applications industrielles, comme le cérium, le lanthane, le néodyme et le praséodyme. D'autres, comme le samarium, l'europium, le terbium et l'erbium, ne servent qu'à° des recherches de laboratoire. [60] Les terres rares sont utilisées dans la fabrication des noyaux d'électrodes en charbon pour arcs électriques. [61] Leurs oxydes peuvent servir au polissage des verres d'optique. [62] Avec le lanthane, on fabrique certains verres spéciaux et des filtres pour la photographie aérienne.

[63] Le thorium naturel se compose de 7 isotopes, dont le plus abondant est le thorium 232. [64] Ce dernier, en absorbant un neutron, donne du thorium 233, radio-actif, qui, par émission β, avec une période de 23 minutes, se transforme en protactinium 233. [65] Une deuxième émission β, avec une période de 27 jours, donne l'isotope fissible 233 de l'uranium. [66] Ces opérations peuvent s'effectuer à l'échelle industrielle dans les piles avec irradiation du thorium, sous forme de carbonate ou de tétrafluorure, par des neutrons.

[67] L'uranium 233 peut être extrait par des solvants organiques, après une période d'attente de 4 à 6 mois, nécessaire pour que la presque totalité du pro-

---

B. Thorium, Uranium. *Throughout this article, it will be noted that names of many chemical elements are identical in French and English.*   53. **matière première** *nf.* raw material; **de** with; **fissible** fissionable (*able to be split*)   55. **écorce terrestre** Earth's crust; **gisement** *nm.* stratum, layer; **exploitable** *adj.* workable   56. **minerai** *nm.* ore   57. **main-d'œuvre** labor, manpower; **indigène** *adj.* native, indigenous; **panier** *nm.* basket; **usine** *nf.* plant, factory; **tamisage** *nm.* sifting, screening; **enrichissement** *nm.* enrichment   58. **monazite** (*Cognate*); **terre rare** *nf.* rare-earth (*oxides of metals*)   59. **lanthane** *nm.* lanthanum; **néodyme** *nm.* neodymium; **praséodyme** *nm.* praseodymium.   60. **noyau** *nm.* nucleus, core; **charbon** *nm.* carbon; **arc** (*Cognate*).   61. **verre** *nm.* glass   63. **isotopes** (*Cognate*) (*nuclei of the same chemical element having the same number of protons, but a variable number of neutrons*)   64. **période** *nf.* half-life   66. **échelle** *nf.* scale; **irradiation** *nf.* irradiation, bombardment   67. **attente** *nf.* waiting; **mois** *nm.* month; **pour que** *conj.* so that

tactinium ait eu le temps de se désintégrer (ce délai correspond à cinq à six fois la période de désintégration du protactinium); on assure ainsi la disparition des produits de fission les plus gênants, dont la période est courte.

[68] Néanmoins, toutes les opérations de traitement doivent être conduites à distance et avec de grandes précautions, l'intégralité de ces produits étant fortement radio-active.   — MAURICE E. NAHAMIAS. *L'Énérgie nucléaire* (Larousse)

période de désintégration = période (*note 64*); **disparition** *nf.* (*fr.* disparaître*); **gênant, -e** *adj.* troublesome   68. **intégralité** *nf.* entire collection

Use of the Irregular Stem Index

The Irregular Stem Index on page 172 provides you with quick access to verb meanings for reading in books and journals. Practice using it now. The method is as follows:

1. Locate as much of the verb form as possible on the stem list, pages 172–175. (With a verb like **dirent,** you would have to drop all the way to just **d-** on this list.)

2. Observe the tense symbol in italics after the form you have found on the list. If there is only one such symbol (like *PDi*), use the meaning shown in English without further search. The *exact* meaning is shown.

3. If there are *two* or more italic tense symbols of the listing, you must find out which applies by looking for the remainder of the verb on the ending table on page 172. To do this, locate the horizontal line having the tense symbol in front of it. Look across the line to find the ending that completes the form you are seeking, i.e. the beginning from the list, and the ending from the table. The line on which you find the ending determines the translation that applies (as shown on the list).

EXAMPLE 1: Translate **ils mirent**
1. Find **m-** on the list, page 173. This is as close as you can come alphabetically. (Note that **mis** is a complete word, as it does not have a dash after it, and cannot be used for any other form except **mis.**)

2. Only *one* italic symbol appears on the listing; therefore the translation is *they put.*

EXAMPLE 2: Translate **elle irait**
1. Find **ir-** on the list.
2. There are *two* italic symbols (*F* and *C*) on the list: therefore you must find the completion of the verb on the ending table, page 172.
3. On the table, look along line *F*. The ending you seek would be in vertical column (3), which is for the subjects *il* and *elle*. In any case, there is no **-ait** anywhere in the line, and the translation in the list after *F* does *not pertain.*
4. Since the only remaining possibility is *C,* translate using the English on the list after the symbol *C: she* (*it*) *would go.* (You may also check by referring to the table of endings on the line *C*; in column (3) you find **-ait,** confirming that this is the Conditional tense. It completes the form: **ir-** from the list, **-ait** from the ending table.

In a few cases endings appear right in the listings. If you sought **il dut,** for example, you find **d-** and have a clue to the next letter from the **u** in the symbol *PDu*. A full ending is given for **nous eûmes** on the same line in the listing on page 173, so that in such cases you do not need to refer to the ending table.

Test XII, pages 217–218

Chapter
XIII

Relative Pronouns

Importance of Gender for Meanings

tout · ouvrir*

---

70. Relative Pronouns

a. *General.* The term *relative pronoun* is used to designate certain words which link two simple sentences together by pointing out the bond, or relationship, between them. As a simple example, take the two sentences below:

Haydn a composé cent quatre symphonies.   (1)

Haydn était autrichien.   (2)

The repetition of the name Haydn characterizes poor — or at least juvenile — style. These two sentences can be related in two ways, depending upon which sentence is considered the more important thought. If we take (1) as the main thought (*main clause*), we may insert (2) by replacing Haydn with **qui** *who:*

Haydn,   a composé cent quatre symphonies.   (1)

qui était autrichien,   (2)

or, inverting the situation to make (2) the main clause:

qui a composé cent quatre symphonies,   (1)

Haydn,   était autrichien.   (2)

In each case the word **qui** was the link used to relate the clauses: hence the name *relative pronoun.*

b. *Uses.* The link between two clauses may be effected by a relative pronoun used (1) as the subject of a verb, (2) as the direct object of a verb, or (3) as the object of a preposition. The following table shows which pronouns apply to the various uses; it will be noted that, in the third case, it makes a difference whether the antecedent is a person or a thing:

USE	Referring to a	
	PERSON	THING
Subject	QUI	
	(who)	(which)
Direct Object	QUE**	
	(whom)	(which)
Object of Preposition	QUI	LEQUEL [§61]
	(whom)	(which)

('that' bracket spanning Subject, Direct Object, and Object of Preposition THING column)

**qu' must always be the *direct object,* as *qui* does not elide.

TRANSLATION: (1) If the antecedent of a relative pronoun is a **thing**, always translate
it as *which* (last column above).

(2) If the antecedent is a **person,** try *who* or *whom;* (the proper choice
between these two is within your own competence in English).

EXAMPLES:

PERSON
(1) Il y avait une fois un **roi** / **qui** était superstitieux.
       Antecedent = roi
         (person)   **who**

There was once a king / **who** was superstitious. [PERSON, SUBJECT]

THING
(2) Il y avait une fois un **bateau** / **qui** n'avait jamais navigué.
       Antecedent (a thing) **which**
There was once a boat / **which** had never sailed. [THING, SUBJECT]

PERSON
(3) Voilà le **médecin** / **que** nous avons rencontré. [PERSON, DIRECT OBJECT]
There is the doctor / **whom** we met.

THING
(4) Voilà la **table** / **que** nous avons achetée. [THING, DIRECT OBJECT]
There is the table / **which** we bought.

PERSON
(5) Le **roi** / avec **qui** l'astrologue parlait / était superstitieux. [PERSON, OBJECT OF
                                   PREPOSITION]
The king / with **whom** the astrologer was talking / was superstitious.

THING
(6) Le **stylo** / avec **lequel** j'écrivais / était mauvais. ['THING, OBJECT OF
                                   PREPOSITION]
The pen / with **which** I was writing / was bad.

71. Gender as It Affects Meaning

It has been stated (§5) that the learning of the gender of nouns is not necessary
for a reading knowledge of French. Exception must now be made, however, for a
few pairs of nouns, otherwise identical, which have opposite genders and different
meanings depending upon the gender. Study the following pairs:

MASCULINE		FEMININE	
un **aide**	assistant	une **aide**	aid, assistance
le **critique**	critic	la **critique**	criticism
le **livre**	book	la **livre**	pound (*weight*)
le **manche**	handle	la **manche**	sleeve
		La Manche	English Channel

le mémoire	bill, memoir, memorandum	la mémoire	memory
le mode	manner, mood	la mode	fashion
le moule	model, mould	la moule	mussel
un œuvre	work (e.g., literary)	une œuvre	a piece of work
le page	page-boy	la page	page (of a book)
le pendule	pendulum	la pendule	clock
le poêle	stove	la poêle	frying-pan
le politique	politician	la politique	politics; policy
le poste	post, situation, (employment)	la poste	post-office
le somme	nap, sleep	la somme	sum (*Math.*)
le tour	turn (to do something)	la tour	tower
le vapeur	steamboat	la vapeur	steam; vapor
le vase	vase	la vase	mud; slime
le voile	veil	la voile	sail (of a ship)

Thus in such a sentence as

> Nous examinions le pendule.

it becomes important to note the gender of the noun to determine whether it is the *pendulum* (masculine) or the *clock* (feminine) which we were examining. Ordinarily the context will already have made it clear which to expect.

72. *tout* "all"

Like most other adjectives, **tout** has four forms, so that it may be made to agree with any noun. It normally precedes the noun it modifies.

	MASCULINE	FEMININE	MEANING
SINGULAR	tout tout le	toute toute la	each, every the whole
PLURAL	tous les	toutes les	all (of) the

EXAMPLES:

tout livre	every book, each book	toute la maison	the whole house
tout le livre	the whole book	tous les livres	all the books
toute maison	every house, each house	toutes les maisons	all the houses

b. *Idioms Using* **tout**. Learn the following fixed expressions as vocabulary items:

tous deux	both	tout à fait	completely
tout à coup	suddenly	tout le monde	everybody
tout d'un coup	at one go	tout [évident]	quite [evident]

tout autre	quite otherwise	pas du tout	not at all
tout de suite	immediately	tout au plus (moins)	at the very most
tout à l'heure	just now;		(least)
	soon, right away	à toute [vitesse]	at full [speed]

73. Irregular Verb ouvrir* "to open"

Verbs which follow the same pattern as **ouvrir*** are **couvrir*** *to cover,* **découvrir*** *to discover,* **offrir*** *to offer,* and some others.

PRESENT TENSE

j'ouvre	I am opening	nous ouvrons	We are opening
tu ouvres	You are opening	vous ouvrez	You are opening
il ouvre	He is opening	ils ouvrent	They are opening

NOTE: In the present tense, this verb uses the regular stem (ouvr-) plus the endings for -er verbs, rather than the -ir endings which might have been expected. (§39) Given this information, all other tenses are regularly formed, using normal -ir endings for the rest of the tenses. One other irregular form is the past participle **ouvert** *opened.*

FUTURE AND CONDITIONAL: (Regular)   **ouvrir-**

IMPERFECT: (Regular)   il **ouvr**ait   he was opening, used to open

PAST DEFINITE: (Regular)   **ouvr-** [+ **ir** type endings]

PRESENT PARTICIPLE: (Regular)   **ouvr**ant   opening

PAST PARTICIPLE: **ouvert**   opened
                   couvert   covered
                   découvert   discovered
                   offert   offered

EXERCISES

I. Relative Pronouns (§70). **ce qui** and **ce que** *what.* Isolate the subordinate clause in parentheses; translate the sentence; state whether the relative pronoun in **boldface** type is used as a subject, direct object, or object of a preposition:

1. C'est Lohengrin **qui** aimait la belle princesse.
2. Elsa, **qui** a douté, a perdu son bonheur.
3. La probabilité est le rapport **qui** existe entre le nombre des cas favorables à cet événement et le nombre total des cas possibles.
4. On a une urne **qui** contient plusieurs boules de couleur rouge.
5. Voilà une boîte dans **laquelle** se trouvent des clous.
6. Il n'aime plus cette personne **qu'**il aimait il y a dix ans.
7. «Vouloir c'est pouvoir» est un proverbe français **que** j'ai souvent entendu répéter.

7. **entendu répéter** heard repeated = heard to be repeated

8. Le cyclotron est une invention sans **laquelle** nos connaissances de la structure atomique seraient beaucoup plus limitées qu'elles ne le sont.

9. Je sais **ce que** vous désirez; c'est une Cadillac neuve.

10. L'astrologue soupçonna **ce que** le roi avait l'intention de faire.

11. Vous prétendez savoir **ce qui** va arriver dans l'avenir.

12. Le roi se fâcha contre cet astrologue **qui** faisait **ce que** lui, le roi, ne pouvait faire.

II. *tout* and *ouvrir** (§§72, 73). Treat these sentences as you did those above:

13. Toutes les expériences physiques demandent des appareils coûteux.

14. Toute expérience physique demande des appareils coûteux.

15. Tous les poissons que nous avons étudiés ne sont pas de la même espèce.

16. Voilà la sardine dont nous avons étudié la rétine; toute la rétine a été examinée minutieusement.

17. Tout le monde qui arrive à Paris se précipite tout de suite vers la tour Eiffel.

18. C'est en juin 1833 que Musset a fait la connaissance de George Sand; ils sont descendus tous deux à l'Hôtel Danieli à Venise.

19. Tout à coup Alfred de Musset devint malade; il a dû partir de Venise pour regagner sa patrie.

20. Toutes les histoires d'amitié ne sont pas si intéressantes que celle-là.

21. Toute l'histoire est romantique et un peu triste.

22. Tout le monde connaît l'histoire de Candide, qui était amoureux de la belle Cunégonde.

23. Le livre sur la table est ouvert; je l'ai ouvert ce matin.

24. C'est le professeur Einstein qui a découvert la formule $E = mc^2$.

25. Il est surtout célèbre pour sa création de la théorie de relativité, qui a profondément marqué la science moderne.

R E A D I N G S

A. Vitamines dans le développment végétal

[26] *La Provitamine A* existe en abondance dans la grande majorité des cellules; elle semble avoir une action dans les rapports entre noyau et protoplasme et activer les divisions.

---

13. **coûteux, -se** *adj.* costly, expensive   15. **espèce** *nf.* species, kind   16. **rétine** *nf.* retina (of the eye); **dont** whose + [NOUN]   17. **se précipit / er** *v.* to rush   18. **descend / re** à un hôtel to stay at a hotel; **Venise** Venice   19. **regagn / er** *v.* to regain, to get back to; **patrie** *nf.* homeland, native country   20. **amitié** *nf.* friendship   21. **triste** *adj.* sad   22. **histoire** *nf.* story; **amoureux de** in love with   23. **matin** *nm.* morning   24. $E = mc^2$ *The "mass-energy equation" which indicates that large amounts of energy may be released by the conversion of mass.* 26. **provitamine** (cognate)

[27] Le groupe des *Vitamines B* a été trouvé dans les feuilles, les tiges, les racines, les fruits, les graines. La *Vitamine B₁* des cotylédons disparaît au cours de la germination et doit être considérée comme un facteur de croissance. [28] La *Vitamine C* (acide ascorbique) est synthétisée dans les tissus en liaison également avec la croissance; son apparition dans les graines est une des premières indications de la germination.

[29] Cependant la démonstration de l'action des vitamines sur les tissus végétaux en voie de croissance et sur les cultures d'organismes n'est pas nécessairement établie par la simple constatation de la présence de ces substances. [30] Il faut prouver que tissus et cultures réagissent favorablement lorsqu'ils sont mis en contact avec celles-ci. [31] Mais généralement les cellules possédant leurs vitamines de manière adéquate ne répondent pas à l'expérience tout au moins après un temps court. [32] On a réussi cependant à démontrer que les vitamines appliquées dans certaines conditions ont un effet activant sur la croissance d'organes déterminés.

[33] La plupart des plantes sont autotrophes en matière de vitamines, c'est-à-dire qu'elles en font la synthèse, mais certaines dépendent du milieu, au même titre que les animaux, pour éviter les avitaminoses.

—Raymond Bouillenne *Phytobiologie*.
(Paris: Masson & Cie., 1946)

B. *Candide ou l'optimisme*[×]

PAR VOLTAIRE

Comment Candide fut élevé dans un beau château, et comment il fut chassé de là

[34] Il y avait en Westphalie, dans le château de M. le baron de Thunder-ten-tronckh, un jeune garçon à qui la nature avait donné les mœurs les plus douces. [35] Sa physionomie annonçait son âme. [36] Il avait le jugement assez droit avec l'esprit le plus simple: c'est, je crois, pour cette raison qu'on le nommait Candide. [37] Les anciens domestiques de la maison soupçonnaient qu'il était fils de la sœur de monsieur le baron et d'un bon et honnête gentilhomme du voisinage, que cette demoiselle ne voulut jamais épouser parce qu'il n'avait pu

---

27. graine *nf.* seed; cotylédon (*cognate*); croissance *nf.* growth   33. autotrophe autotrophic; synthèse (*a near cognate*); milieu *nm.* environment; au même titre in the same way as; avitaminose *nf.* vitamin deficiency   34. Westphalie Westphalia (*province of Germany*); Thunder-ten-Tronckh *is as difficult a name to pronounce in French as Voltaire could invent — he wanted to satirize the peculiar-sounding, lengthy, hyphenated German names.* mœurs *n.pl.* manners; doux, -ce *adj.* gentle   37. ancien, -ne *adj.* former (See Sec. 74); voisinage *nm.* neighborhood; épous/er *v.* to marry

prouver que° soixante et onze quartiers, et que le reste de son arbre généalo-
gique avait été perdu par l'injure du temps.

[38] Monsieur le baron était un des plus puissants seigneurs de la Westphalie,
car son château avait une porte et des fenêtres. [39] Sa grande salle même était
ornée d'une tapisserie. [40] Tous les chiens de ses basses-cours composaient une
meute dans le besoin; ses palefreniers étaient ses piqueurs; le vicaire du village
était son grand aumônier. [41] Ils l'appelaient tous Monseigneur, et ils riaient
quand il faisait des contes.

[42] Madame la baronne, qui pesait environ trois cent cinquante livres, s'at-
tirait par là une très grande considération, et faisait les honneurs de la maison
avec une dignité qui la rendait encore plus respectable. [43] Sa fille Cunégonde,
âgée de dix-sept ans, était haute en couleur, fraîche, grasse, appétissante. [44]
Le fils du baron paraissait en tout digne de son père. [45] Le précepteur Pangloss
était l'oracle de la maison, et le petit Candide écoutait ses leçons avec toute la
bonne foi de son âge et de son caractère.

[46] Pangloss enseignait la métaphysico-théologico-cosmolo-nigologie. [47]
Il prouvait admirablement qu'il n'y a point d'effet sans cause, et que, dans ce
meilleur des mondes possibles, le château de monseigneur le baron était le plus
beau des châteaux et madame la meilleure des baronnes possibles.

[48] «Il est démontré, disait-il, que les choses ne peuvent être autrement: car,
tout étant fait pour une fin, tout est nécessairement pour la meilleure fin. Remarquez bien que les nez ont été faits pour porter des lunettes; aussi avons-nous
des lunettes. [49] Les jambes sont visiblement instituées pour être chaussées,
et nous avons des chausses. [50] Les pierres ont été formées pour être taillées et
pour en faire des châteaux; aussi monseigneur a un très beau château; le plus
grand baron de la province doit être le mieux logé; et, les cochons étant faits
pour être mangés, nous mangeons du porc toute l'année: [51] par conséquent,
ceux qui ont avancé que tout est bien ont dit une sottise; il fallait dire que tout
est au mieux.»

[52] Candide écoutait attentivement, et croyait innocemment: car il trouvait
Mlle Cunégonde extrêmement belle, quoiqu'il ne prît jamais la hardiesse de le

---

soixante et onze [60 + 11]; **quartiers** quarter(ing)s (*Heraldry*) *This is already quite a lot of
quarterings for a coat of arms — Voltaire implies a most inordinate insistence on the importance of "social
background," which he ironically satirizes here.* **injure** ravages   38. **seigneur** *nm.* lord
39. **tapisserie** *nf.* tapestry   40. **basse-cour** *nf.* farmyard; **meute** *nf.* pack; **besoin** *nm.* [in case
of] need; **palefrenier** *nm.* stable-boy; **piqueur** *nm.* huntsman; **aumônier** *nm.* chaplain
41. **Monseigneur** Milord; **ri/re** *v.* to laugh; **faire* des contes** to tell stories   42. **cinquante**
fifty; **s'attir/er** *v.* to attract (to oneself); **par là** because of that   43. **fille** *nf.* daughter; **fraîche**
[with a] fresh [complexion]; **grasse** *adj.* plump; **appétissante** *adj.* tempting   44. **digne** *adj.*
worthy   45. **précepteur** *nm.* tutor; **Pangloss** *represents a theory of systematic optimism which Voltaire
ridicules in this story.*   46. **nigologie** stupidity (*fr.* **nigaud**, *stupid*)   48. **lunette** *nf.* glasses,
spectacles; **aussi** therefore (§80a)   49. **jambe** *nf.* leg; **chaussé** *pp.* shod; **chausse** *nf.* shoe
50. **pierre** *nf.* stone; **taillé** *pp.* cut, trimmed; **logé** *pp.* lodged; **le mieux** *adv.* the best; **cochon**
nm. pig; **mang/er** *v.* to eat   51. **sottise** *nf.* stupid thing; **il fallait dire** they should have said;
au mieux at its best   52. **Mlle** *abbreviation for* **Mademoiselle** Miss; **quoiqu(e)** *conj.* although

lui dire. [53] Il concluait qu'après le bonheur d'être né baron de Thunder-ten-tronckh, le second degré de bonheur était d'être Mlle Cunégonde; le troisième, de la voir tous les jours; et le quatrième, d'entendre maître Pangloss, le plus grand philosophe de la province, et par conséquent de toute la terre.

[54] Un jour, Cunégonde, en se promenant auprès du château, dans le petit bois qu'on appelait parc, vit entre des broussailles le docteur Pangloss qui donnait une leçon de physique expérimentale à la femme de chambre de sa mère, petite brune très jolie et très docile. [55] Comme Mlle Cunégonde avait beaucoup de disposition pour les sciences, elle observa sans souffler les expériences réitérées dont elle fut témoin; elle vit clairement la raison suffisante du docteur, les effets et les causes, et s'en retourna tout agitée, toute pensive, toute remplie du désir d'être savante, songeant qu'elle pourrait bien être la raison suffisante du jeune Candide, qui pouvait aussi être la sienne.

[56] Elle rencontra Candide en revenant au château, et rougit; Candide rougit aussi; elle lui dit bonjour d'une voix entrecoupée, et Candide lui parla sans savoir ce qu'il disait. [57] Le lendemain, après le dîner, comme on sortait de table, Cunégonde et Candide se trouvèrent derrière un paravent; Cunégonde laissa tomber son mouchoir, Candide le ramassa; elle lui prit innocemment la main, le jeune homme baisa innocemment la main de la jeune demoiselle avec une vivacité, une sensibilité, une grâce toute particulière; leurs bouches se rencontrèrent, leurs yeux s'enflammèrent, leurs genoux tremblèrent, leurs mains s'égarèrent. [58] M. le baron de Thunder-ten-tronckh passa auprès du paravent, et, voyant cette cause et cet effet, chassa Candide du château à grands coups de pied dans le derrière; [59] Cunégonde s'évanouit; elle fut souffletée par madame la baronne dès qu'elle fut revenue à elle-même; et tout fut consterné dans le plus beau et le plus agréable des châteaux possibles.

—VOLTAIRE. *Candide ou l'optimisme*, Chapitre I

53. **né** *pp.* (*fr.* **naître***) born   54. **se promen/er*** *v.* to walk; **vit** (*Past Definite of* **voir***); **broussailles**. *nf. pl.* brushwood; **femme de chambre** *nf.* chambermaid; **brune** *nf.* brunette 55. **disposition** *nf.* inclination; **souffl/er** *v.* to breathe; **raison suffisante** *nf.* sufficient reason *a technical philosophical term which Voltaire satirizes.*   **tout**(e) *is here used as an adverb meaning* very; **rempli** *pp.* filled; **savante** *adj.* learnèd; **song/er** *v.* to reflect 59. **s'évanou/ir** *v.* to faint; **soufflet/er** *v.* to slap; **dès que** as soon as

Test **XIII**, pages 219–220

Chapter
XIV

Adjectives with Variable Meanings

Possessive Adjectives

y · Conjunctions

74. Adjectives with Variable Meanings According to Position

There are a few adjectives whose meaning depends upon their position in relation to the noun modified. The five most important are listed below:

	BEFORE THE NOUN	AFTER THE NOUN (*or as* PREDICATE ADJECTIVE)
ancien -ne	former	ancient, old
propre	own	clean, neat
seul -e	only, single	alone
même	same	very, itself
certain -e	certain (particular)	sure, indisputable

EXAMPLES:

mon **ancien** professeur	my **former** professor
l'histoire **ancienne**	**ancient** history
L'église est **ancienne**.	The church is **old**.
ma **propre** chambre	my **own** room
ma chambre **propre**	my **clean** room
La chambre est **propre**.	The room is **clean**.
la **même** histoire	the **same** story
l'histoire **même**	the story **itself**; the **very** story
un **certain** homme	a **certain** (*particular*) man
un fait **certain**	an indisputable fact

75. Possessive Adjectives

The following table shows all the possessive adjectives normally used before nouns. They do not have any other forms (i.e., no -e is added to construct the feminine forms):

NOTE: son, sa, and ses all mean *his, her,* or *its.* The context of the passage is the only way of telling which applies. For example:

> Voilà **Henri**. J'aime beaucoup **sa** sœur.
> There is **Henry.** I like **his** sister very much.

117

BEFORE A SINGULAR NOUN which is			BEFORE A PLURAL NOUN	
*Masculine**	*Feminine*	*Either*		
mon my (**ton** your)† son {his her its	ma my (**ta** your)† sa {his her its	notre our votre your leur their	mes my (**tes** your)† ses {his her its	nos our vos your leurs their
†familiar form (used when subject is *tu*) see §38b (1)		↑ OUR, YOUR, THEIR	↑ ALL END IN PLURAL SIGN -s	

EXAMPLES: mon   livre (*m. sing.*)   my book.
             ma   table (*f. sing.*)   my table
             mes   livres et **mes** tables   my books and my tables

             son   livre (*m. sing.*)   his book, her book, its (?) book
             sa   table (*f. sing.*)   his table, her table, its table
             ses   tables (*f. pl.*)   his tables, her tables, its tables

             leur livre (*m. sing.*)   their book
             leurs livres (*m. pl.*)   their books

76. *y* "there"

The word *y* may be translated as *there* in most instances. It replaces a prepositional phrase beginning with *à* (*au, aux*) and not referring to persons:

┌──────── REPLACING ────────┐
Nous **y** allons.   Nous allons (**à Paris**).
We are going **there**.   We are going (**to Paris**).

However there are certain verbal constructions which require the preposition
à in which the meaning, as translated, may be other than *to*. For example

         Nous pensons (à ce problème).   Nous **y** pensons.
         We are thinking (**about** this problem).   We are thinking **about it**.

In such cases the word *y* retains the meaning of the phrase it replaces.

The expression **il y a** *there is, there are* need not be analyzed, as it is a fixed
expression.

77. Conjunctions

Learn the following important conjunctions normally used to join two clauses:

et	and	cependant }		jusqu'à ce que	until	
mais	but	pourtant }	however	à moins que (ne)	unless	
ou	or	néanmoins	nevertheless	de sorte que)	in such	
que	that	parce que	because	de manière que }	a way	
si	if	alors que)		de façon que)	that	
comme	as	tandis que }	whereas	et . . . et	both . . . and	
quand	when	afin que)		ou . . . ou	either . . . or	
quoique	although	pour que }	in order that	soit . . . soit	either . . . or	

*Also used with feminine singular nouns which begin with a vowel sound: **mon école** my school
son université his (her) university

EXERCISES

I. Adjectives with Variable Meanings (§74); **Possessive Adjectives** (§75).
Translate:

1. ma maison; ma propre maison; mon ancienne maison; ma maison ancienne.
2. une auto; mon auto; ma seule auto; mon ancienne auto; mon auto ancienne.
3. un cas; un certain cas; un cas certain; le cas seul; le seul cas.
4. une salle; ma propre salle; une salle propre; une salle ancienne.
5. un fait; le même fait; le fait même; un certain fait; un fait certain.
6. leur expérience; leurs expériences; ses expériences; son expérience.
7. Voilà monsieur Dupont. Nous avons lu son livre.
8. Voilá madame Curie. Nous avons lu son livre.
9. Vos expériences m'intéressent; votre livre les décrit bien.
10. Nos expériences ne sont pas achevées; notre rapport en donnera les détails.

II. _y_ (§76)

11. Les comptes-rendus de la société se trouvent à la bibliothèque; il faut y aller pour les consulter.
12. Les lois de la nature sont immuables; tous les corps y obéissent.
13. Ce problème est d'une extrême complexité; nous y pensons depuis longtemps.
14. Il y a plusieurs musées célèbres situés à Paris; le Louvre en est un qu'il faut visiter; on y voit le portrait de Mona Lisa (par Léonard de Vinci) qui s'appelle _la Joconde._
15. Après avoir fermé la boîte, on y fait un vide très poussé au moyen de pompes puissantes.

READINGS

A. Le Cyclotron

[16] C'est en 1932 que Lawrence et Livingston ont mis définitivement au point leur modèle de cyclotron. [17] Le prix Nobel de physique pour 1939 a été attribué à E. O. Lawrence pour cette réalisation. [18] Lawrence et Livingston obtenaient en 1932 des protons d'une énergie correspondant à une tension de 80 000 volts en n'appliquant que° 1 600 volts sur les électrodes d'accélération.

[19] Dès avant la guerre, en 1939, le professeur Lawrence et ses collabora-

---

7. **lu** _pp._ (_fr._ **lire*** to read)   9. **décrit** (_Pres. of_ **décrire*** to describe)   10. **achev/er** _v._ to complete   11. **compte-rendu** _nm._ report; minutes   15. **vide** _nm._ vacuum; **poussé** high   17. **réalisation** _nf._ accomplishment

teurs ont obtenu, à Berkeley (Californie), un faisceau de deutons de 22 millions de volts.

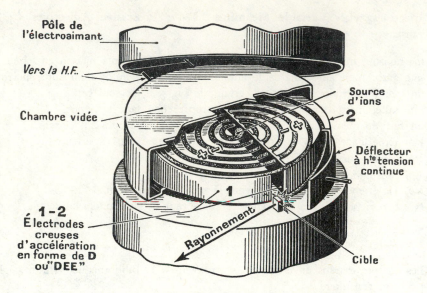

Pôle de l'électroaimant

Vers la H.F.

Chambre vidée

Source d'ions

2

Déflecteur à h^{te} tension continue

1

1-2 Électrodes creuses d'accélération en forme de D ou"DEE"

Rayonnement

Cible

Fig. 42. — Coupe et schéma d'un cyclotron

[20] En 1935, il n'existait encore au monde qu'un° seul cyclotron; on en compterait aujourd'hui une cinquantaine. [21] Le premier cyclotron de Lawrence et Livingston ne coûta pas plus de 1 000 dollars; le dernier modèle de Berkeley est revenu à 3 000 000 de dollars.

[22] L'installation d'un cyclotron comprend trois parties principales: un électro-aimant, un poste de haute fréquence, et enfin la boîte du cyclotron proprement dit, où les ions sont accélérés. (*fig. 42*)

[23] L'électro-aimant peut être plus ou moins puissant. Le premier, qu'ont utilisé, en 1930, Lawrence et Edlefsen, donnait un champ maximum de 5 000 gauss dans un entrefer de 20 centimètres, sur un diamètre de 30 centimètres. [24] Il en existe actuellement une douzaine de tailles différentes. [25] Celui du laboratoire de chimie nucléaire du Collège de France donne un champ maximum de 21 000 gauss dans un entrefer de 9 centimètres sur un diamètre de 80 centimètres.

[26] Le poste de haute fréquence est identique à un poste émetteur de

19. **faisceau** *nm.* beam   20. **compterait** *Note the use of the Conditional in reporting what is alleged to be the case, although the writer does not wish to take responsibility for the accuracy of the information. A possible translation is* there are said to be . . . (of them).   21. **revenu à** came to   22. **aimant** *nf.* magnet; **poste** *nm.* source   23. **champ** *nm.* field; **gauss** *Unit of intensity of a magnetic field;* **entrefer** *nm.* (**entre** = between; **fer** = iron) gap (*of a magnet*)   24. **taille** *nf.* size   26. **émetteur** *adj.* broadcasting

T.S.F. [27] Il peut être d'une puissance de quelques centaines de watts pour les petits cyclotrons et atteindre plusieurs dizaines de kilowatts pour les grands cyclotrons.

[28] La figure 43 représente schématiquement la boîte du cyclotron. On voit en bas une coupe verticale de l'appareil sur laquelle T_1 et T_2 sont les pièces polaires, et 1 et 2 les deux électrodes creuses ou «dees» qui accélèrent les ions et auxquelles on applique la haute fréquence.

[29] L'ordre des opérations est le suivant: après avoir fermé la boîte à l'aide de ses deux couvercles, on la glisse entre les deux pièces polaires et l'on y fait un vide très poussé, par l'orifice V, au moyen de pompes puissantes. [30] Dès que l'on atteint une pression de l'ordre du millionième de millimètre de mercure, on introduit une toute petite quantité d'un gaz déterminé, de l'hydrogène, par exemple. [31] Au centre du cyclotron, il existe un filament F de tungstène, que l'on porte au rouge vif au moyen d'un courant électrique. [32] Ce filament émet un nombre considérable d'électrons, que l'on accélère par une électrode placée juste au-dessous et à laquelle on applique une tension positive de l'ordre de 1 000 volts. [33] Il y a intérêt à alimenter le filament par un courant alternatif de grande fréquence, et non par du courant continu, afin d'éviter que sa déformation dans le champ magnétique rende sa vie très courte.

[34] Les electrons ainsi accélérés vont bombarder les molécules d'hydrogène introduites dans la boîte et leur arracher leur électron périphérique, laissant subsister des ions d'hydrogène ou protons. [35] Comme les protons portent une charge électrique positive, ils décrivent sous l'action du champ magnétique vertical des cercles dans un plan horizontal. [36] Dans leur course circulaire, ils passent alternativement dans les électrodes creuses 1 et 2. [37] Entre ces électrodes, on applique une chute de tension de l'ordre de 50 000 volts. [38] En alternant le sens de cette tension un million de fois par seconde, par exemple, on imprime ainsi, à chaque demi-tour, une accélération électrostatique de 50 000 volts à tous les ions, qui mettent un millionième de seconde pour traverser entièrement l'une des deux électrodes. [39] Prenons, en effet,† un ion qui vient de° parcourir un demi-cercle de rayon r_1 dans l'électrode 1, en un millionième de seconde. [40] Lorsqu'il entre en 2, la tension entre 1 et 2 ayant justement changé de polarité, l'ion subit une accélération qui lui fait décrire en 2 un demi-cercle, de rayon r_2 légèrement supérieur, d'environ 1 millimètre, à r_1. [41] Son trajet va se trouver augmenté; mais sa vitesse s'étant également accrue, il arrive à la sortie de 2 encore une fois au bout d'un millionième de seconde.

T.S.F. (*abbreviation for* **télégraphie sans fil**) radio; **atteind/re*** *v.* to attain   28. **coupe verticale** *nf.* cross-section; **creuse** *adj.* hollow; **dee** *shaped like the letter* D   29. **gliss/er** *v.* to slide   31. **rouge vif** red-hot   32. **au-dessous** below   33. **Il y a intérêt à** It is advisable to   34. **arrach/er** *v.* to strip off   35. **plan** *nm.* plane   38 **sens** *nm.* direction; **demi-** half-; **à** *is part of* **imprim/er à** to impart to; **mett/re*** [*time*] *v.* to take   39. **en effet** in fact; **vient de** (*See section 69, page 103*)   40. **sub/ir** *v.* to undergo; **d'environ** *by* about   41. **trajet** *nm.* travel; **sortie** *nf.* exit; **encore une fois** once again; **au bout de** at the end of

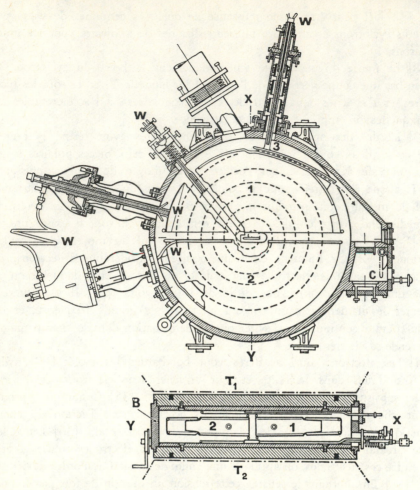

Fig. 43. — Coupe horizontale et verticale d'un cyclotron
W. Eau de refroidissement; C. Cible

[42] A ce moment-là, la polarité des électrodes s'inverse et atteint un maximum. [43] L'ion subit une nouvelle accélération et décrit un demi-cercle de
rayon r_3, légèrement supérieur à r_2 . . ., et ainsi de suite. [44] De la sorte,
l'ion décrit une spirale, dont quelques boucles sont représentées sur la figure 43.
[45] Arrivé en 3 avec une énergie correspondant au nombre de fois qu'il a
subi la tension accélératrice des électrodes (100 fois 50 000 volts, soit 5 millions de volts, par exemple), l'ion est finalement dévié de la route circulaire,
que lui impose constamment le champ magnétique, par l'électrode 3 portée
à un potentiel statique négatif de l'ordre de 70 000 volts. [46] La porte P

44. **boucle** *nf.* turn

étant ouverte, l'ion tombe alors sur la cible C et désintègre ou non un atome. [47] Si nous faisons arriver° des milliards et des milliards de projectiles en C, nous pourrons désintégrer plusieurs millions d'atomes de la substance placée en C.

—MAURICE E. NAHMIAS. *L'Énergie nucléaire* (Larousse)

B. *Alphonse et Téléphone vont à la pêche*

[48] Alphonse et Téléphone ne travaillent jamais le samedi*. [49] D'ordinaire ils ne font que flâner, mais un beau jour d'été Alphonse était en train de réfléchir. [50] Une idée magnifique lui vient, tout inattendue.

[51] — Hé Téléphone! dit-il. J'ai une idée. Allons au Bayou Lafourche pêcher à la ligne! Peut-être attraperons-nous quelques beaux poissons.

[52] —Formidable! répliqua Téléphone avec enthousiasme, en se levant et en se dirigeant sur-le-champ vers sa canne à pêche.

[53] Ils sortirent de la maison, montèrent dans leur vieux tacot, et se mirent en route vers le bayou Lafourche. [54] Ils voyageaient depuis une heure lorsqu'ils arrivèrent au bord de la rivière, stationnèrent la voiture, et allèrent louer un canot. [55] Ils en choisirent un bon d'entre ceux qui étaient offerts à louer par un vieil indigène. [56] S'étant installés dans le canot avec leur attirail de pêche, ils s'éloignèrent du rivage, et commencèrent leur aventure.

[57] Bientôt ils étaient loin de toute habitation; on n'entendait que les cris des oiseaux et le faible son de l'eau qui murmurait contre le rebord. [58] Ils entrèrent ensuite dans un bayou très étroit, presque caché sous les grands arbres luxuriants qui traînaient leurs branches sur la surface de l'eau tiède. [59] Sous peu ils débouchèrent dans un grand lac isolé. [60] Vers le milieu de ce lac ils trouvèrent un certain endroit où ils eurent beaucoup de chance: ils commencèrent à prendre des poissons l'un après l'autre. [61] Ils faisaient tout leur possible pour accommoder tous les poissons qui avaient apparemment envie de prendre passage avec eux dans le canot, et qui ne demandaient pas mieux que de garnir l'intérieur de leur poêle à frire à la fin de la journée.†
[62] Mais il faut dire que les deux jeunes hommes évitèrent d'accepter les invitations d'un alligator amical qui leur souriait en aiguisant ses dents sur le bois de leur canot.

46. **cible** *nf.* target; **désintègre ou non** may or may not disintegrate 47. **milliard** *nm.* billion B. **pêche** *nf.* fishing 48. **samedi** Saturday 49. **flân/er** *v.* to loaf; **été** summer 51. **Bayou** *a creek or small river (here, in Louisiana)* 52. **formidable** swell! **sur-le-champ = tout de suite;** **canne** *nf.* rod 53. **tacot** *nm.* jalopy; **se mettre* en route** to set out 54. **canot** *nm.* boat 55. **lou/er** *v.* to rent; **indigène** *nm.* native 56. **s'éloign/er** *v.* to move away *(related to* **loin**) 57. **oiseau** *nm.* bird; **rebord** *nm.* side (of the boat) 58. **cach/er** *v.* to hide; **traîn/er** *v.* to drag; **tiède** *adj.* tepid (lukewarm) 59. **Sous peu = bientôt;** **débouch/er** *v.* to emerge 60. **endroit** *nm.* place 61. **garn/ir** *v.* to decorate; **poêle à frire** *nf.* frying-pan; **journée** *nf.* day 62. **évit/er** *v.* to avoid; **souri/re*** *v.* to smile; **aiguis/er** *v.* to sharpen

---

***le samedi** Saturday, every Saturday, Saturdays. *When the article* le *precedes the name of a* day of the week, *the word* every *is indicated.* Otherwise it implies "next" or "last," depending on the verb tense.

[63] Ils pêchaient ainsi depuis trois heures lorsque Téléphone eut faim et voulut rentrer. [64] Se retournant vers son ami, il lui dit:

[65] — Hé Alphonse! Nous avons assez de poissons. Si nous rentrions maintenant!

[66] — Ça va, répliqua l'autre, qui, lui aussi, était un peu las de ce travail. [67] Mais avant de partir, marque bien cet endroit. La prochaine fois que nous venons à la pêche, nous le retrouverons.

[68] Alors ils se remirent en route; ils firent le voyage de retour en suivant les mêmes bayous toujours mystérieux et déserts. [69] En arrivant à l'endroit où ils avaient loué le canot, Alphonse demanda à Téléphone:

[70] — Dis, est-ce que tu as bien marqué l'endroit où nous avons pris tous ces poissons?

[71] — Bien sûr, pardi! exclama Téléphone. J'ai marqué un gros «X» juste là sur le rebord du canot. Regarde-le!

[72] — Idiot! s'écria Alphonse, qui comprit tout de suite la bêtise qu'a commise Téléphone. A quoi penses-tu donc? Et si nous ne pouvons pas louer le même canot la prochaine fois?

63. **avoir* faim** to be hungry; **rentr/er** *v.* to go home   64. **se retourn/er** *v.* to turn around
65. **si** suppose   66. **las** *adj.* tired   67. **prochain, -e** *adj.* next   71. **bien sûr, pardi** Heck, yes!
72. **bêtise** *nf.* stupid action; **commis** *pp. of* **commettre***; **si** suppose

Circumflex Accent (^): A Cue to Past Tenses

The circumflex accent in the *ending* of a verb form (always over the vowel **a, i,** or **u**) indicates either the **simple past** (Past Definite, pages 100–101) or the **imperfect subjunctive:**

1. **â, î, û** plus **-mes** or **-tes** is the past definite tense. Translate it as a simple past tense.

> nous fin**î**mes   we finished
> vous all**â**tes   you went

2. **â, î, û** plus **-t** only. This is the imperfect subjunctive, and may be translated as a simple past tense also. It is a literary form for formal writing, and sometimes may be translated as *would* or *might* [*do something*]:

> Je doutais qu'il **vendît** sa maison.
> I doubted that he *sold* (or *would sell*) his house.

NOTE the following exceptions: *present* tense of irregular verbs:
   a. **il paraît** (**paraître***) it seems; he seems
   b. **il connaît** (**connaître***) he knows (is acquainted with)
   c. **il plaît** (**plaire***) it pleases; he pleases
   d. **il croît** (**croître***) it grows
      [il croit (**croire***) he believes]

Test XIV, pages 221–222

Chapter XV

Disjunctive Pronouns

Imperatives

aussi

78. Disjunctive Pronouns

These pronouns are used (1) after all prepositions, (2) alone, or isolated from the main sentence, or (3) as a part of a compound subject. The word disjunctive [dis- *not* + junct(ure) *joined*] indicates that this type of pronoun is separated from the verb, whereas most other pronouns come immediately before the verb.

The disjunctive pronoun **moi**, corresponding to the subject pronoun **je**, is shown below in the three uses enumerated:

Alain a étudié ce cas avec **moi**.
Alain studied this case with **me**.

(1) AFTER A PREPOSITION

Qui est là? **Moi.**
Who is there? **Me.**

(2) ALONE

Je ne suis pas allé à Lyon, **moi**.
I didn't go to Lyon.

ISOLATED, FOR EMPHASIS

Alain et **moi**, nous avons étudié ce cas.
Alain and I [we] studied this case.

(3) PART OF COMPOUND SUBJECT
Note that in French the pronoun **nous** summarizes the compound subject. It is not translated.

NOTE: An additional use of disjunctive pronouns is after **C'est** or **Ce sont** *it is:*

C'est moi qui vous parle.
C'est lui qui arrive.

It is *I* who am speaking to you.
He's arriving.

They are also used with -**même**: **moi-même** myself.

TABLE OF DISJUNCTIVE PRONOUNS

Subject	*Disjunctive*	
je	moi	me
tu	(toi)	you
il	lui	him, it
elle	elle	her, it
nous	nous	us
vous	vous	you
ils	eux	them
elles	elles	them

125

79. Imperative Verb Forms

a. General. Imperative forms of verbs are used to give orders or make suggestions. There are two very common sources for these forms, which we have been using all along: the Present tense **nous-** and **vous-**forms, minus these subject pronouns.

PRESENT		IMPERATIVE	
nous finissons	we are finishing.	**finissons!**	let's finish!
vous finissez	you are finishing	**finissez!**	finish!
nous parlons	we are speaking	**parlons!**	let's speak!
vous parlez	you are speaking	**parlez!**	speak!

b. Special Imperatives of avoir* and être*. Learn the imperatives of these three irregular verbs: (These are based upon the subjunctive, page 134.)

avoir*	**ayons**	let's have	**ayez**	have
être*	**soyons**	let's be	**soyez**	be
savoir*	**sachons**	let's know	**sachez**	know

c. *Third Person Imperatives.* In giving orders to another person about what a *third* person should do, the commands are prefaced by **qu'.** The verb form is not taken directly from the Present tense which we have studied, but the stem resembles the third person plural of the regular Present tense, so that it can readily be identified. (Also based upon the subjunctive forms.)

Qu'il finisse sa leçon!	Have him (Let him) finish his lesson!
Qu'elle parle français!	Have her speak French!
Qu'il vienne! (venir*)	Have him come!
Qu'ils prennent...!	Have them take...
(prendre*)	

d. Familiar Imperative. In giving orders to another person who is a member of the family, a close friend, or other person who is usually addressed by using **tu** [§38b(1)], the imperative form is derived from the **tu-**form of the Present tense, minus the subject pronoun **tu.** Note that the final **-s** is dropped after **-e** or **-a:**

finis!	Finish!	**Finis** ta leçon.	Finish your lesson.
parle!	Speak!	**Parle** français!	Speak French!
sois*!	Be!	**Sois** sage!	Be good!
aie*!	Have!	**N'aie** pas peur!	Don't be afraid!
			(Don't have fear)

80. *aussi, aussi bien . . . que*

a. aussi "also." Usually the word **aussi** may be translated as *also,* unless it appears at the beginning of a clause. In such a case it means *therefore:*

Nous avons étudié ce cas aussi.	We studied this case also.
Aussi avons-nous étudié ce cas.	Therefore we studied this case.

Note the inverted word-order when *aussi* appears at the beginning of a clause or sentence (cf. §54).

b. *aussi bien . . . que* "both . . . and." Note the use of this construction in the following examples:

L'air atmosphérique contient **aussi bien** l'azote **que** l'oxygène.
Atmospheric air contains **both** nitrogen **and** oxygen.   OR
Atmospheric air contains nitrogen **as well as** oxygen.

Ce poisson chasse **aussi bien** en pleine eau **qu'**en surface.
This fish hunts **both** in deep water **and** near the surface.   OR
This fish hunts in deep water **as well as** near the surface.

NOTE: In using the translation *as well as,* nothing is said (or written) for **aussi bien**; the phrase *as well as* is given when the word **que** is reached:

L'air atmosphérique contient **aussi bien** l'azote **que** l'oxygène.
Atmospheric air contains (   ) nitrogen **as well as** oxygen.

EXERCISES

I. Imperative Forms (§79). Translate:

1. Examinez; examinons; ne l'examinez pas; examine; qu'ils examinent.
2. Vendez; vendons; qu'il vende; qu'ils vendent; vends.
3. Finissez; finis; finissons; qu'ils finissent.
4. Apprenez; apprenons; qu'ils apprennent; qu'elle apprenne.
5. Mettons; mettez; qu'il mette; ne le mettez pas.
6. Soyez; soyons; qu'il soit; qu'ils soient; sois.
7. Ayons; ayez; qu'il ait; n'ayez pas peur; n'aie pas peur.
8. Tenez; tenons; qu'ils tiennent; ne retenons pas.

II. Disjunctive Pronouns (§78). Translate:

9. avec moi; avec eux; avec elles; avec vous; avec lui; avec elle.
10. sans elle; sans lui; sans vous; sans nous; sans eux; sans moi.
11. Je n'ai pas examiné ce livre; Pierre l'a examiné, lui.
12. Voilà Jean et Marie; voici son livre à lui.
13. Voilà Jean et Marie; voici son livre à elle.
14. Moi, je parle français; Henri parle allemand, lui.
15. Henri et moi, nous parlons anglais tous les deux.
16. C'est moi qui vous parle; ce n'est pas votre sœur.
17. Cet auteur vous ramène sans cesse aux objets importants de la vie. C'est lui qui porte le flambeau au fond de la caverne.

12–13. **à lui, à elle** *is redundant, but is necessary to explain whether* son livre *is* his *or* hers 17. **flambeau** *nm.* torch

III. *aussi* (§80). Translate:

18. Les nez sont faits pour porter des lunettes; aussi avons-nous des lunettes.
19. Nos élèves étudient aussi bien les mathématiques que la physique.
20. La géologie est une science qui a pour but l'étude aussi bien des minéraux que de la forme extérieure de notre globe.
21. La nature chimique des minéraux est leur caractère le plus facile à reconnaître: aussi leur classification est-elle actuellement basée sur cela.

IV. General Drill: Sentences. Translate into idiomatic English:

22. A force d'étudier les vieilles choses, on comprend les nouvelles.
23. L'avenir commence à l'instant.
24. Si tous les hommes savaient ce qu'ils disent les uns des autres, il n'y aurait pas quatre amis dans le monde. — PASCAL. *Pensées,* 101

25.
>   L'autre jour, au fond d'un vallon,
>   Un serpent piqua Jean Fréron.
>   Que pensez-vous qu'il arriva?
>   Ce fut le serpent qui creva.
>
>   — VOLTAIRE

26. Notre intelligence tient dans l'ordre des choses intelligibles le même rang que notre corps dans l'étendue de la nature. — PASCAL. *Pensées,* 72
27. La puissance des mouches: elles gagnent des batailles, empêchent notre âme d'agir, mangent notre corps. — *Ibid.,* 367
28. Tous les chats sont gris, la nuit.
29. Effrayer un oiseau n'est pas le moyen de le prendre.
30. Ne dis pas: «va,» mais vas-y toi-même.
31. Celui qui a un grand nez croit que tout le monde en parle.
32. Le temps perdu ne se retrouve jamais.
33. Vous regardiez la lune et êtes tombé dans un puits.
34. Ne montrez jamais les dents à moins que vous ne puissiez mordre.
35. On ne connaît pas le prix de l'eau jusqu'à ce que le puits (ne) soit à sec.

READINGS

A. L'Entrée de Napoléon à Moscou*

PAR CHATEAUBRIAND

[36] La débâcle avait commencé à Moscou; les routes de Cazan étaient couvertes de fugitifs à pied, en voiture, isolés ou accompagnés de serviteurs. [37]

23. **à l'instant** = **tout de suite**   25. **vallon** *nm.* valley; **piqu/er** *v.* to bite; **Fréron, Elie,** *poète français que Voltaire détestait;* **arriv/er** *v.* to happen; **crev/er** *v.* to die   29. **effray/er** *v.* to frighten   32. **perd/re** *v.* to lose   33. **puits** *nm.* well   34. **à moins que** *conj.* unless; **puissiez** (*fr.* **pouvoir***) can; **mord/re** *v.* to bite   35. **à sec** dry   36. **débâcle** *nf.* catastrophe

A l'approche des longs convois de blessés† russes qui se présentaient aux portes, toute espérance s'évanouit. [38] Kutuzoff avait flatté Rostopschine de défendre la ville avec quatre-vingt-onze mille hommes qui lui restaient. Rostopschine demeura seul.

[39] La nuit déscend: des émissaires vont frapper mystérieusement aux portes, annoncent qu'il faut partir et que Ninive est condamnée. [40] Des matières inflammables sont introduites dans les édifices publics et les Bazars, dans les boutiques et les maisons particulières†; les pompes sont enlevées. [41] Alors Rostopschine ordonne d'ouvrir les prisons: du milieu d'une troupe immonde on fait sortir un Russe et un Français; le Russe, appartenant à une secte d'illuminés allemands, est accusé d'avoir voulu livrer sa patrie et d'avoir traduit la proclamation des Français; son père accourt; le gouverneur lui accorde un moment pour bénir son fils: «Moi, bénir un traître!» s'écrie le vieux Moscovite, et il le maudit. [42] Le prisonnier est livré à la populace et abattu. . . .

[43] Les autres malfaiteurs relâchés reçoivent, avec leur grâce, les instructions pour procéder à l'incendie, quand le moment sera venu. [44] Rostopschine sort le dernier de Moscou, comme un capitaine de vaisseau quitte le dernier son bord dans un naufrage.

[45] Napoléon, monté à cheval, avait rejoint son avant-garde. [46] Moscou *aux coupoles dorées,* disent les poètes slaves,† resplendissait à la lumière du jour, avec ses deux cent quatre-vingt-quinze églises, ses quinze cents châteaux, ses maisons ciselées, colorées en jaune, en vert, en rose: il n'y manquait que les cyprès et le Bosphore. [47] Le Kremlin faisait partie de cette masse couverte de fer poli ou peinturé. [48] Au milieu d'élégantes villas de briques et de marbre, la Moskowa coulait parmi des parcs ornés de bois de sapins, palmiers de ce ciel. [49] Ce fut le 14 septembre [1812], à deux heures de l'après-midi, que Bonaparte aperçut sa nouvelle conquête.

[50] Une acclamation s'élève: «Moscou! Moscou!» s'écrient nos soldats. En apercevant Moscou, les régiments entiers se jetèrent à genoux et remercièrent le Dieu des armées de les avoir conduits par la victoire dans la capitale de leur ennemi le plus acharné.

[51] Les acclamations cessent; on descend muets vers la ville; aucune députation ne sort des portes pour présenter les clefs dans un bassin d'argent. [52] Le mouvement de la vie était suspendu dans la grande cité. [53] Quelques-uns de

---

37. **blessé** *nm.* wounded (person); **russe** *adj.* Russian; **espérance** *nf.* hope 38. **Kutuzoff, Michaïl,** *prince et maréchal russe, vainqueur à la bataille de Smolensk. Plus tard général en chef de l'armée russe.* **Rostopschine, Fedor,** *homme politique russe. Il était gouverneur de Moscou en 1812.* 39. **Ninive,** *ville, capitale de l'Assyrie* 40. **boutique** *nf.* shop; **particulier** *adj.* private; **enlev/er*** *v.* to remove, to take away 41. **immonde** *adj.* filthy; **traduit** *pp.* translated; **accour/ir*** *v.* to hasten to (*a place or person*); **bén/ir** *v.* to bless; **maudi/re*** *v.* to curse 42. **abatt/re** *v.* to kill, to strike down 44. **bord** *nm.* ship; **naufrage** *nm.* shipwreck 45. **doré** *adj.* gilt [or = gold]; **slave** *adj.* Slavic; **église** *nf.* church; **ciselé** *adj.* covered with carvings; **jaune** yellow; **vert** green; **rose** pink 48. **coul/er** *v.* to flow; **sapin** *nm.* fir-tree; **ciel** *nm.* sky [*i.e.,* country] 50. **genou** *nm.* knee; **remerci/er** *v.* to thank [**merci** = thank you]; **acharné** *adj.* relentless 51. **clef** *nf.* key (*to the city*)

nos officiers pénètrent dans la ville; ils reviennent et disent à Napoléon: «Moscou est déserte! — Moscou est déserte? c'est invraisemblable! Qu'on m'amène les boyards.» [54] Point de boyards, il n'est resté que des pauvres qui se cachent. [55] Rues abandonnées, fenêtres fermées: aucune fumée ne s'élève des foyers d'où s'en échapperont bientôt des torrents. [56] Pas le plus léger bruit. Bonaparte hausse les épaules.

[57] Murat, s'étant avancé jusqu'au Kremlin, y est reçu par les hurlements des prisonniers devenus libres pour délivrer leur patrie: on est contraint d'enfoncer les portes à coups de canon.

[58] Napoléon fit une course le long de la Moskowa, ne rencontra personne. [59] Il revint à son logement, nomma le maréchal Mortier gouverneur de Moscou. [60] La garde impériale et les troupes étaient en grande tenue pour paraître devant un peuple absent. [61] Bonaparte apprit bientôt avec certitude que la ville était menacée de quelque événement. [62] A deux heures du matin on lui vient dire que le feu commence. Le vainqueur quitte le faubourg de Dorogomilow et vient s'abriter au Kremlin: c'était dans la matinée du 15. [63] Il éprouva un moment de joie en pénétrant dans le palais de Pierre le Grand.

[64] On contient d'abord l'incendie; mais dans la seconde nuit il éclate de toutes parts; des globes lancés par des artifices crèvent, retombent en gerbes lumineuses sur les palais et les églises. [65] Une bise violente pousse les étincelles et lance les flammèches sur le Kremlin: il renfermait un magasin à poudre; un parc d'artillerie avait été laissé sous les fenêtres mêmes de Bonaparte. [66] De quartier en quartier nos soldats sont chassés par les effluves du volcan.

[67] Le bruit se répand que le Kremlin est miné: des serviteurs se trouvent mal, des militaires se résignent. La tour de l'Arsenal, comme un haut cierge, brûle au milieu d'un sanctuaire embrasé. [68] Comment fuir? En cherchant de tous les côtés, on découvre une poterne qui donnait sur le Moskowa. [69] Le vainqueur avec sa garde se dérobe par ce guichet de salut. [70] Autour de lui dans la ville, des voûtes se fondent en mugissant, des clochers d'où découlaient des torrents de métal liquéfié se penchent, se détachent et tombent. [71] Des charpentes, des poutres, des toits craquant, pétillant, s'abîment dans un Phlégéthon

---

53. **invraisemblable**: [semblable = seeming, **vrai** = true; **in** = not] incredible; **boyards** *nm. pl. les anciens nobles de Russie*   54. **point de** = pas de   55. **fumée** *nf.* smoke; **aucun(e) . . . ne** (§34); **foyer** *nm.* hearth, fireplace   56. **bruit** *nm.* noise, rumor; **hauss/er les épaules** to shrug the shoulders   57. **Murat, Joachim** *maréchal de France, roi de Naples de 1808 à 1815, beau-frère de Napoléon. On le força à renoncer à son royaume. En essayant de le reconquérir il fut pris et fusillé (1815).* **hurlement** *nm.* shout   58. **course** *nf.* walk (*or* ride)   60. **en grande tenue** in dress uniform   62. **faubourg** *nm.* suburb; **s'abrit/er** *v.* to take shelter [**abri** = shelter]   64. **globe** *nm.* fireball; **artifice** *nm.* fireworks; **crev/er** *v.* to burst; **gerbe** *nf.* shower of sparks   65. **bise** *nf.* wind; **étincelle** *nf.* spark; **flammèche** *nf.* flake (*of fire*)   66. **effluves** *nm. or f.* effluvium   67. **se trouv/er mal** to be sick; **cierge** *nm.* candle; **embrasé** *adj.* burning   68. **fuir** *v.* to flee; **poterne** *nf.* postern (= back door); **donn/er sur** to open upon, to give access to   69. **se dérob/er** *v.* to slip out; **guichet de salut** *nm.* safety hatch   70. **se fond/re** *v.* to collapse; **mug/ir** *v.* to roar; **clocher** *nm.* bell-tower; **découl/er** *v.* = **couler**; **se pench/er** *v.* to lean over   71. **poutre** *nf.* beam; **toit** *nm.* roof; **pétill/er** *v.* to crackle; **s'abîm/er** *v.* to be ruined; **Phlégéthon** *une des rivières des Enfers* [Hell], *où coulaient des flammes au lieu d'eau.*

dont ils font rejaillir la lame ardente et des millions de paillettes d'or. [72] Bonaparte ne s'échappe que sur les charbons refroidis d'un quartier déjà réduit en cendres: il gagna Petrowski, villa du czar.

[73] Du rivage de Sainte-Hélène, Napoléon revoyait brûler la ville des Scythes: «Jamais» dit-il, «en dépit de la poésie, toutes les fictions de l'incendie de Troie n'égaleront la réalité de celui de Moscou.»

— CHATEAUBRIAND. *Mémoires d'Outre-tombe.* Livre XXI, Chapitre 4

B. Aspect des océans — Physique terrestre

[74] Dans l'hémisphère nord la plupart des icebergs proviennent des glaciers de la côte occidentale du Groenland. [75] Cette région est parfois couverte d'une carapace de glace pouvant atteindre 1.000 mètres d'épaisseur. [76] De ces glaciers se détachent des icebergs pouvant dépasser une hauteur de 50 mètres au-dessus du niveau de l'eau. [77] Ils flottent ainsi pendant huit à dix mois, entraînés par les courants jusqu'au voisinage sud de Terre-Neuve où ils deviennent très dangereux pour la navigation. [78] Les icebergs que l'on rencontre dans l'hémisphère sud atteignent des dimensions colossales: 80 à 90 kilomètres de longueur sur 250 mètres de hauteur. [79] Ces glaciers sont généralement plats et dérivent très loin en mer. [80] Heureusement, ils se trouvent rarement sur les routes fréquentées par les navires. [81] La glace de terre est de couleur bleu verdâtre, plus poreuse, moins transparente que la glace d'eau salée; celle-ci est plus incolore.

[82] *La Plaine abyssale.* — A la suite du plateau continental s'étend la plaine abyssale, immense, aux reliefs peu marqués, recouverte d'une vase à grains d'autant plus fins qu'elle est plus éloignée de la côte. [83] Elle commence vers une profondeur de 1.000 mètres avec une légère pente qui atteint au milieu de l'océan à des fonds de 4.000 mètres avec quelques rares fosses de 5 à 6.000 mètres sans que rien ne soit changé à l'aspect général si ce n'est que° de temps à autre quelques roches sont apportées par les icebergs ou rejetées par les volcans sous-marins. [84] Dans l'océan Pacifique on rencontre quelques dépressions de 7 à 8.000 mètres. [85] A ces endroits seulement la pente devient plus raide. La plaine abyssale de l'océan Atlantique n'est pas absolument unie: elle est de place en place hérissée de volcans dont les sommets forment les îles Bermudes, les Açores, Madère, les Canaries, qui occupent l'emplacement d'un ancien continent effondré appelé l'Atlantide que recouvrent aujourd'hui plusieurs milliers

---

rejaill/ir v. to spurt up; **ardent, -e** adj. fiery; **paillette** nf. spangle   72. **quartier** nm. section (*of a city*)   73. **en dépit de** in spite of   77. **entraîn/er** v. to carry along; **Terre-Neuve** Newfoundland   79. **dériv/er** v. to drift   81. **verdâtre** greenish. *The suffix -âtre with names of colors means* -ish; **salé** adj. salt   82. **d'autant ... que** proportionately ... as   83. **fosse** nf. hole; **de temps à autre** = de temps en temps; **pente** nf. slope; **si ce n'est que°** except for   85. **raide** adj. steep; **hérissé** adj. bristling; **effondré** pp. submerged

de mètres d'eau. [86] Cet effondrement qui atteint maintenant 4.000 mètres a commencé du côté américain; il s'est effectué en trois fois. [87] Seules les algues, «les Sargasses» qui recouvrent son littoral y flottent depuis ces temps lointains, elles se sont adaptées à ce genre de vie ainsi que quelques animaux littoraux qui s'y reproduisent périodiquement. [88] De même les anguilles viennent chaque année d'Europe faisant 6.000 kilomètres pour frayer à l'endroit où vivaient leurs ancêtres.

— Extrait de NOËL BOUDAREL. *Les Richesses de la mer* (Paul Lechevalier, Éditeur)

C. Généralités sur la perception du son

[89] Le son, formé par la propagation de variations périodiques ou irrégulières de la pression atmosphérique se caractérise par sa fréquence et par son intensité.

La fréquence d'un son—en cycles ou en hertz—correspond au nombre de vibrations par seconde émises par la source sonore.

L'oreille humaine ne perçoit que les ondes de la bande sonore dont les fréquences sont comprises entre 30 et 20.000 hertz: en déçà, il s'agit d'infrasons et au-delà, il s'agit d'ultrasons.

[90] Aux fréquences faibles, correspondent les sonorités graves et aux fréquences élevées correspondent les sonorités aiguës. Les bruits ne sont généralement pas formés de sons purs, mais de combinaisons de sons émis sur des fréquences différentes et apparaissant au même instant («spectre sonore»).

Le spectre couvre une bande de fréquences et donne ainsi la structure du bruit qui peut avoir en même temps des composantes graves, moyennes et aiguës. De plus, pour un même bruit, les nivaux d'intensité sonore varient d'une bande de fréquences à l'autre. Il est donc nécessaire d'expliquer brièvement en quoi consiste le niveau d'intensité sonore.

[91] Schématiquement, *l'intensité* correspond à la quantité de bruit que nous percevons, alors que la fréquence correspond à sa qualité. Pour mesurer les niveaux d'intensité acoustique, on utilise une unité logarithmique—*le* décibel (dB)—parce que l'échelle des variations de pression auxquelles l'oreille normale réagit est énorme: de 0,0002 microbar à 1.000 microbars. [92] La sensation sonore varie, en effet, comme le logarithme de l'excitation physique exercée sur le tympan: le rapport entre le son le plus faible perçu et le son le plus fort qui provoque la douleur est de mille milliards.

—Ariel Alexandre. *Prévision de la Gêne due au bruit autour des aéroports*

86. **effondrement** *nm.* sinking; **fois** *nf.* phase   88. **anguille** *nf.* eel; **fray/er** *v.* to spawn
89. **oreille** *nf.* ear; **perçoit** (percevoir) perceives; **en déça** below that; **infrason** *nm.* infrasonics;
au-delà beyond that; **ultrason** *nm.* ultrasonics   90. **faible** *adj.* low, weak; **aiguë** *adj.* sharp,
acute, high   91. **réagir** to react   92. **rapport** *nm.* ratio, relationship; **douleur** *nf.* pain;
mille milliards 1000 billions [**un milliard** is 1000 million]

Test XV, pages 223–224

Chapter XVI

Present Subjunctive

*servir**

81. Present Subjunctive

The so-called Subjunctive Mood is a group of four tenses (two of which are rarely used) which occur (1) after **il faut que** *it is necessary that;* (2) after certain conjunctions such as **jusqu'à ce que** *until* and **à moins que** *unless;* (3) after main clauses implying doubt, possibility, desirability, or emotion; and (4) in certain commands and exclamations which really fall into the preceding class. In almost every case the Subjunctive forms appear after the conjunction **que.**

a. *Present Subjunctive: Meaning.* The Present tense of the Subjunctive Mood is used either for **present** or **future** time. The determination of this is simplified by observing the adverb of time (§67b) which accompanies the verb in most cases:

Je doute que Robert **vienne** DEMAIN.   [DEMAIN *is the key to the time.*]
I doubt that Robert **will come** TOMORROW.   [FUTURE]

Je doute que Robert **vienne** AUJOURD'HUI.
I doubt that Robert **is coming** TODAY.   [PRESENT]

In these examples, the writer used the Present Subjunctive after **que** in the subordinate clause, because the main clause (**Je doute**) expressed doubt. The reader does not have to make a decision such as this; he has merely to identify the verb form for meaning, observe the adverb of time, and translate accordingly.

b. *Formation of Present Subjunctive.* The Present Subjunctive is formed by adding fixed endings to a stem, as with other tenses. The endings are:

     -e   -es   -e   -ions   -iez   -ent.

The *stem* to which these endings are added is taken from the Present Tense (Indicative) which we studied at the beginning of this text (§§25, 39). The form from which the stem comes is the 3rd person plural (**ils**-form):

VERB	3RD PERSON PLURAL PRESENT INDICATIVE	STEM DERIVED FOR SUBJUNCTIVE	PRESENT SUBJUNCTIVE
parl/er	ils parlent	parl-	que je parle que tu parles qu'il parle

VERB	3RD PERSON PLURAL PRESENT INDICATIVE	STEM DERIVED FOR SUBJUNCTIVE	PRESENT SUBJUNCTIVE
			que nous parlions
			que vous parliez
			qu'ils parlent
vend/re	ils vendent	vend-	que je vende, *etc.*
fin/ir	ils finissent	finiss-	que je finisse, *etc.*

It will be seen that the stem is derived from the 3rd person plural of the Present Indicative merely by omitting the ending -ent.

c. *Present Subjunctive of Irregular Verbs.* The verbs *avoir* * and *être,* * the auxiliary verbs, have completely irregular forms:

avoir*	aie, aies, ait, ayons, ayez, aient	have, will have
être*	sois, sois, soit, soyons, soyez, soient	be, will be;
		have, will have (+ past participle)

Other irregular verbs use the regular set of endings, appended to an irregular stem:

faire*	Stem: fass/-	[+ regular endings]	make, do; will make, will do
savoir*	sach/-	[+ regular endings]	know, will know; be able
pouvoir*	puiss/-	[+ regular endings]	be able, will be able

Still other irregular verbs use one stem for *nous* and *vous* forms, and another for all the rest; regular endings are used for all forms:

	All forms except nous *and* vous		nous *and* vous *stem*
aller*	aill/		all/
tenir*	tienn/		ten/
prendre*	prenn/		pren/
voir*	voi/	} -e, -es, -e, -ent	voy/ } -ions, -iez
vouloir*	veuill/		voul/
devoir*	doiv/		dev/
venir*	vienn/		ven/

NOTE: Imperfect Subjunctive is sometimes used. The most frequent form is 3rd person singular, and can be distinguished by the circumflex accent. Translate the same as the Imperfect Indicative (§43):

Quoiqu'il ne fût pas large des épaules . . .
Although he was not broad in the shoulders . . .

82. Irregular Verb *servir* * "to serve"

Other verbs which follow the same pattern are *sentir* * *to feel, partir* * *to depart, sortir* * to leave, to go out, courir* * to run,* and *dormir* * to sleep.*
These verbs are irregular only in the Present Indicative. The stem for the 1st,

2nd, and 3rd persons singular is italicized in the infinitives above; and the plural forms lack the -iss increment typical of regular -ir verbs (e.g., ils finissent).

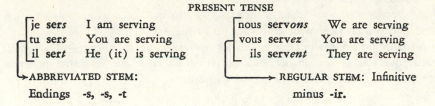

PRESENT TENSE

je **ser**s	I am serving	nous **serv**ons	We are serving
tu **ser**s	You are serving	vous **serv**ez	You are serving
il **ser**t	He (it) is serving	ils **serv**ent	They are serving

ABBREVIATED STEM:
Endings -s, -s, -t

REGULAR STEM: Infinitive
minus -ir.

EXERCISES

I. Sentence Drill: Subjunctive forms. Translate:

1. Ne montrez jamais les dents à moins *que* vous ne **puissiez** mordre.
2. Il se peut *que* les moteurs à réaction **soient** très efficaces.
3. Pour rendre le mouvement de ma machine à calculer plus simple, il a fallu *que* la machine **ait été** construite d'un mouvement plus composé.
4. Il faut *que* l'art **soit** aidé par la théorie jusqu'à ce *que* l'usage **ait** rendu les règles de la théorie si communes *qu*'il les **ait** enfin réduites en art.
5. M. Micromégas, habitant du pays de Sirius, était un géant; quant à son esprit, c'est un des plus cultivés *que* nous **ayons.**
6. Il se peut très bien *qu*'il y **ait** un grand nombre de ces substances.
7. S'il est possible *qu*'il y **ait** des êtres plus petits que ceux-ci, ils peuvent encore avoir un esprit supérieur à ceux de ces superbes animaux que j'ai vus dans le ciel, dont le pied seul couvrirait le globe où je suis descendu.
8. On ne connaît pas le prix de l'eau jusqu'à ce *que* le puits **soit** à sec.
9. Nous cherchons une auto *qui* **puisse** marcher très vite.
10. Il est possible *que* Pierre **vienne** demain; mais je doute *qu*'il **prenne** le bateau aujourd'hui.
11. Nous voulons *que* vous **alliez** en ville; il faut *que* nous **obtenions** un échantillon de cette matière.
12. Il vaut mieux *que* ces professeurs **fassent** voir les résultats de leur expérience.
13. Je suis bien content *que* vous le **sachiez;** maintenant il faut *que* je **voie** le médecin.

II. Translate:

14. Pour bien savoir les choses, il faut en savoir le détail; et comme il est presque infini, nos connaissances sont toujours superficielles et imparfaites.
    —d'après LA ROCHEFOUCAULD. *Maximes,* 106.
15. Les vieillards aiment à donner de bons préceptes, pour se consoler de n'être plus en état de donner de mauvais exemples. —*Ibid.,* 93.

1. **à moins que . . . ne** See §85b, page 145   12. **il vaut mieux** it is preferable   15. **vieillard** *nm.* old man

16. Nous avons tous assez de force pour supporter les maux d'autrui. — *Ibid.*, 19.

17. La dernière chose qu'on trouve en faisant un ouvrage, est de savoir celle qu'il faut mettre la première. PASCAL. *Pensées,* 19.

18. Nous courons sans souci dans le précipice, après que nous avons mis quelque chose devant nous pour nous empêcher de voir. — *Ibid.,* 183.

19. La mémoire est nécessaire pour toutes les opérations de la raison. — *Ibid.,* 369.

20. Quelle que soit sa provenance, chaque rétine est bâtie sur le même plan: la réception est assurée par les cônes ou les bâtonnets.

READINGS

A. Les Noyaux lourds primaires du rayonnement cosmique

[21] L'existence de noyaux lourds dans le rayonnement cosmique primaire a été découverte pour la première fois par les deux groupes de physiciens de Minnesota et Rochester. [22] Ils ont envoyé au moyen de ballons des émulsions photographiques et, en même temps, une chambre de Wilson jusqu'à une altitude de 31 km. au-dessus du niveau de la mer avec une durée de plafonnement de trois heures. [23] Ils ont observé dans les émulsions photographiques, aussi bien que sur quelques clichés de chambre Wilson, des trajectoires très ionisantes et de grand parcours. [24] L'estimation de la charge faite sur ces traces a montré qu'il s'agissait de noyaux dont la charge était très supérieure à celle des particules α; l'énergie de ces noyaux était très élevée, de l'ordre de 5×10^8 électron-volts par nucléon.

[25] Au moyen de l'écran de plomb de leur chambre de Wilson, les auteurs ont étudié l'absorption des noyaux lourds par la matière. [26] Ils ont placé des paquets photographiques au-dessus et au-dessous de la chambre et ont trouvé que tous les noyaux lourds avaient été absorbés par 25 cm. de plomb. [27] Leur forte absorption par la matière explique le fait que les noyaux lourds du rayonnement cosmique primaire ont un parcours très faible dans l'atmosphère et que l'on ne les observe pratiquement pas à des altitudes inférieures à 20 km.

[28] D'autre part, ils ont étudié la distribution angulaire des noyaux lourds observés dans l'émulsion photographique, et ont trouvé que les trois quarts de

16. **force** *nf.* strength; **maux** *pl.* (*fr.* mal) troubles; **autrui** other people   18. **sans souci** carefree [= without a care]; **dans = vers**   20. **quel(le) que soit** [x] whatever [x] may be; *also* for each [x] (*in math*); **provenance** *nf.* source, origin; **bâtonnet** *nm.* [un petit bâton] rod   22. **chambre de Wilson** *nf.* cloud chamber (*a small instrument which makes visible the paths followed by ionizing particles*); **plafonnement** *nm.* maximum altitude   23. **cliché** *nm.* photograph; **parcours** *nm.* travel   24. **trace** *nf.* track   25. **écran** *nm.* screen; **plomb** *nm.* lead (*metal*)   26. **au-dessus de** above

ces noyaux proviennent de la direction du zénith, l'angle d'incidence avec la verticale étant inférieur à 30°.

[29] L'ensemble des faits observés par ces auteurs indique de façon très solide qu'il s'agit de noyaux lourds venant de l'extérieur plutôt que de particules créés au sein de l'atmosphère. [30] Les recherches poursuivies ultérieurement par ces deux groupes de physiciens ont fourni des renseignements très précieux *tant pour* la connaissance des noyaux lourds à grande énergie *que* pour l'origine du rayonnement cosmique. [31] Leurs travaux ont fait l'objet de remarquables mémoires publiés dans *Physical Review* (FRIER, LOFGREN et OPPENHEIMER, Phys. Rev. 1948, 1828) auxquels nous allons constamment référer. . . .

> —Extrait de TCHANG-FONG HOANG. "Les Noyaux lourds primaires
> du Rayonnement cosmique." *Annales de Physique,* 1950

B. *Architecture ogivale:* XIII° *siècle*

[32] Tous les éléments de l'art sont dans la nature; l'art lui-même n'est que° dans la pensée de l'homme, comme tous les phénomènes que la chimie constate se trouvent dans la matière, tandis que la science chimique n'est que° dans l'âme humaine. [33] Suivant les temps, l'esprit dégage l'un ou l'autre de ces éléments. [34] Ainsi, à l'inverse du paganisme qui mettait la beauté au-dessus de l'expression, le christianisme a mis l'expression au-dessus de la beauté. [35] C'est le caractère de l'art au moyen âge, et le treizième siècle le porte à sa plus grande hauteur. [36] Le triomphe de l'architecture ogivale est enfin assuré. L'arc se brise, s'effile et s'élance, afin de porter plus haut, plus près du ciel, la voûte du temple et la prière des peuples. [37] C'est alors que sont élevées ces montagnes de pierre ciselée à jour — ces cathédrales de Paris, de Rouen, d'Amiens, de Chartres, de Reims, de Bourges, de Strasbourg et la Sainte-Chapelle de Saint Louis, à Paris — qui remplacent l'architecture romane, lourde encore et massive, par des temples où se montrent toutes les hardiesses de la pensée, toute l'élévation, toute la ferveur du sentiment religieux. [38] Le nouveau style, né au nord de la Loire, passe la Manche, le Rhin, et les Alpes: et des colonies d'artistes français vont le porter à Cantorbéry, à Utrecht, à Milan, jusqu'en Suède. [39] Une statuaire grossière, mais naïve, décore les portails, les galeries, les cloîtres; et la peinture sur verre a, pour produire de magiques effets dans les vitrages, des secrets que nous venons à peine de retrouver.

> —Extrait de VICTOR DURUY. *Histoire de France* (Librairie Hachette, Editeur)

---

29. **au sein de** in the . . . itself   30. **ultérieurement** *adv.* subsequently; **renseignements** *n.pl.* information; **tant pour . . . que** for . . . as well as for   B. **ogivale** Gothic   35. **moyen âge** *nm.* Middle Ages   36. **s'effil/er** *v.* to become tapered; **s'élanc/er** *v.* to thrust upward   37. **à jour** in openwork; **Saint Louis,** *c'est Louis IX (1214-1270)*   39. **grossière** *adj.* crude; **venons . . . de** See §69

La Cathédrale de Reims[1]

[1] The drawing of Reims Cathedral by Joseph Pennell is reproduced from *French Cathedrals*, by Elizabeth R. Pennell (New York: Appleton-Century-Crofts, Inc., 1909) by kind permission of the publisher.

C. L'Exécution de Louis XVI

[40] La guillotine était dressée ce jour-là au milieu de la place de la Révolution, devant la grande allée du jardin des Tuileries, en face et comme en dérision du palais des rois, non loin de l'endroit où la fontaine jaillissante la plus rapprochée de la Seine semble aujourd'hui laver éternellement le pavé.

[41] Depuis l'aube, les abords de l'échafaud, le pont Louis XVI, les terrasses des Tuileries, les parapets du fleuve, les toits des maisons de la rue Royale, les branches dépouillées des arbres des Champs-Elysées, étaient chargés d'une innombrable multitude qui attendait l'événement dans l'agitation, dans le tumulte et dans le bruit d'une ruche d'hommes, comme si cette foule n'eût pu croire au supplice d'un roi avant de l'avoir vu de ses yeux. [42] Les abords immédiats de l'échafaud avaient été envahis, grâce aux faveurs de la commune et à la connivence des commandants des troupes, par des hommes incapables d'hésitation ou de pitié. Se posant autour de l'échafaud comme les témoins de la république, ils voulaient que le supplice fût consommé et applaudi.

[43] A l'approche de la voiture du roi, une immobilité solennelle surprit cependant tout à coup cette foule et ces hommes eux-mêmes. La voiture s'arrêta à quelques pas de l'échafaud. Le trajet avait duré deux heures.

[44] Le roi, en s'apercevant que la voiture avait cessé de rouler, leva les yeux, qu'il tenait attachés au livre, et, comme un homme qui interrompt sa lecture pour un moment, il se pencha à l'oreille de son confesseur et lui dit à voix basse et d'un ton d'interrogation : «Nous voilà arrivés, je crois?» Le prêtre ne lui répondit que par un signe silencieux. [45] Un des trois frères Sanson, bourreaux de Paris, ouvrit la portière. Les gendarmes descendirent. Mais le roi, refermant la portière et plaçant sa main droite sur le genou de son confesseur d'un geste de protection: «Messieurs, dit-il aux autorités et aux bourreaux, aux gendarmes et aux officiers qui se pressaient autour des roues, je vous recommande monsieur que voilà. [46] Ayez soin qu'après ma mort il ne lui soit fait aucune insulte. Je vous charge d'y veiller.» Personne ne répondit. Le roi voulut répéter avec plus de force cette recommandation aux exécuteurs. L'un d'eux lui coupa la parole. «Oui, oui, lui dit-il avec un accent sinistre, sois tranquille, nous en aurons soin, laisse-nous faire.» [47] Louis

---

40. **dressée** erected; **place** *nf.* square; **place de la Révolution** *is today the* place de la Concorde; **allée** *nf.* path; **fontaine** *nf.* fountain; **jaillir** to gush; **rapprochée de** close to; **pavé** *nm.* pavement, paving stones   41. **aube** *nf.* dawn; **abords** *nm. pl.* area surrounding; **échafaud** *nm.* scaffold; **dépouillé** stripped; **chargé** packed, full of; **ruche** *nf.* beehive; **supplice** *nm.* execution, punishment   42. **envahir** to invade; **commune** *nf.* militia; **pitié** *nf.* mercy, pity; **fût** (*from* être) be   43. **solennel, -le** *adj.* solemn; **surprendre*** to take by surprise; **foule** *nf.* crowd, mob; **eux-mêmes** themselves; **pas** pace, step   44. **s'apercevant** perceiving, noticing; **interrompt** (*fr.* **interrompre**) interrupts; **oreille** *nf.* ear; **confesseur** *nm.* [father-] confessor   45. **bourreau** *nm.* executioner; **portière** *nf.* door (*of a vehicle*); **d'un geste** in a gesture; **roue** *nf.* wheel   46. **veiller** to see to it, to attend to it; **couper la parole** to cut off (*a speech*), interrupt

descendit. Trois valets du bourreau l'entourèrent et voulurent le déshabiller au pied de l'échafaud. Il les repoussa avec majesté, ôta lui-même son habit, sa cravate, et dépouilla sa chemise jusqu'à la ceinture. Les exécuteurs se jetèrent alors de nouveau sur lui. «Que voulez-vous faire? murmura-t-il avec indignation.—Vous lier» lui répondirent-ils; et ils lui tenaient déjà les mains pour les nouer avec leurs cordes. [48] «Me lier! répliqua le roi avec un accent où toute la gloire de son sang se révoltait contre l'ignominie. Non! non! je n'y consentirai jamais! Faites votre métier, mais vous ne me lierez pas, renoncez-y!» Les exécuteurs insistaient, élevaient la voix, appelaient à leur aide, levaient la main, préparaient la violence. Une lutte corps à corps allait souiller la victime au pied de l'échafaud. [49] Le roi, par respect pour la dignité de sa mort et pour le calme de sa dernière pensée, regarda le prêtre comme pour lui demander conseil. «Sire, dit le conseiller divin, subissez sans résistance ce nouvel outrage comme un dernier trait de ressemblance entre vous et le Dieu qui va être votre récompense.» Le roi leva les yeux au ciel avec une expression du regard qui semblait reprocher et accepter à la fois. [50] «Assurément, dit-il, il ne faut rien moins que l'exemple d'un Dieu pour que je me soumette à un pareil affront!» Puis se tournant en tendant lui-même les mains vers les exécuteurs: «Faites ce que vous voudrez, leur dit-il, je boirai le calice jusqu'à la lie!»

[51] Il monta, soutenu par le bras du prêtre, les marches hautes et glissantes de l'échafaud. Le poids de son corps semblait indiquer un affaissement de son âme; mais, parvenu à la dernière marche, il s'élança des mains de son confesseur, traversa d'un pas ferme toute la largeur de l'échafaud, regarda en passant l'instrument et la hache, et se tournant tout à coup à gauche, en face de son palais et du côte où la plus grande masse de peuple pouvait le voir et l'entendre, il fit aux tambours un geste de silence. [52] Les tambours obéirent machinalement. «Peuple! dit Louis XVI d'une voix qui retentit dans le silence et qui fut entendue distinctement de l'autre extrémité de la place, peuple! je meurs innocent de tous les crimes qu'on m'impute! Je pardonne aux auteurs de ma mort, et je prie Dieu que le sang que vous allez répandre ne retombe jamais sur la France ... »

[53] Il allait continuer; un frémissement parcourait la foule. Le chef d'état-major du camp sous Paris, le comte Beaufranchet d'Ayat, ordonna aux tambours de battre. Un roulement immense et prolongé couvrit la voix du roi et le murmure de la multitude. Le condamné revint à pas lents vers la guillotine et se livra aux exécuteurs. [54] Au moment où on l'attachait à la planche, il jeta encore un regard sur le prêtre qui priait à genoux au bord de l'échafaud. Il vécut, il posséda son âme tout

---

47. **valet** *nm.* servant; **déshabiller** to undress; **ôter** to remove; **dépouiller** to strip off; **chemise** *nf.* shirt; **ceinture** *nf.* belt, waist; **lier** to tie up; **nouer** to tie a knot   48. **sang** *nm.* blood, lineage; **métier** *nm.* job, work; **renoncer** to renounce, to give up; **souiller** to disgrace, shame   49. **subir** to submit to; **trait** *nm.* mark   50. **tendre les mains** to hold out his hands; **boire le calice jusqu'à la lie** to suffer in silence to the end   51. **glissant** slippery; **affaissement** *nm.* weakening; **parvenu** [having] arrived; **s'élancer** to spring forward; **hache** *nf.* the blade [of the guillotine]; **tambour** *nm.* drum   52. **retentir** to resound; **meurs** *See table on page 173 if you cannot deduce the meaning.*   53. **fréissement** *nm.* shudder   54. **planche** *nf.* plank [*to which the victims were attached at the guillotine to support their bodies*]; **vécut** lived;

entière jusqu'au moment où il la remit à son Créateur par les mains du bourreau. La planche chavira, la hache glissa, la tête tomba.

[55] Un des exécuteurs, prenant la tête du supplicié par les cheveux, la montra au peuple et aspergea de sang les bords de l'échafaud. Des fédérés et des républicains fanatiques montèrent sur les planches, trempèrent les pointes de leurs sabres et les lances de leurs piques dans le sang, et les brandirent vers le ciel en poussant le cri de : «Vive la République!» [56] L'horreur de cet acte étouffa le même cri sur les lèvres du peuple. L'acclamation ressembla plutôt à un immense sanglot. Les salves de l'artillerie allèrent apprendre aux faubourgs les plus lointains que la royauté était suppliciée avec le roi. La foule s'écoula en silence. [57] On emporta les restes de Louis XVI, dans un tombereau couvert, au cimetière de la Madeleine, et on jeta de la chaux dans la fosse, pour que les ossements consumés de la victime de la Révolution ne devinssent un jour les reliques du royalisme. [58] Les rues se vidèrent. Des bandes de fédérés armés parcoururent les quartiers de Paris en annonçant la mort du *tyran* et en chantant le sanguinaire refrain de la *Marseillaise*. Aucun enthousiasme ne leur répondit, la ville resta muette. Le peuple ne confondait pas un supplice avec une victoire.

—Alphonse de Lamartine
Histoire des Girondins, Livre 35ᵉ

chavirer to pivot forward   55. supplicié *nm.* the victim; asperger to sprinkle; fédéré Federate; tremper to dip; lance *nf.* point; pique *nf.* pike (*weapon*); brandir to brandish   56. étouffer to stifle; lèvre *nf.* lip; sanglot *nm.* sob; salve *nf.* salvo; faubourg *nm.* suburb; supplicier to execute; s'écouler to drift away   57. tombereau *nm.* tumbrel, tipcart; chaux *nf.* lime; fosse *nf.* pit, grave; ossements *nm. pl.* bones, remains; devinssent (*fr.* devenir) become

Test XVI, pages 225–226

Chapter

XVII

Compound Tenses
Interrogatives · *ne*

83. Compound Tenses

Compound tenses were introduced into the exercises soon after the formation of the past participle was explained (§21). As the word *compound* implies, there are two parts to a verb in a compound tense (like **nous avons parlé**), in contrast with

verbs in *simple* tenses, which have only one part (like **nous parlons**). Here are

the parts of a compound verb: (1) the auxiliary **avoir*** or **être,*** adjusted to the appropriate person and tense, and (2) the past participle of the verb in question:

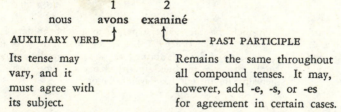

Its tense may vary, and it must agree with its subject.	Remains the same throughout all compound tenses. It may, however, add **-e**, **-s**, or **-es** for agreement in certain cases.

a. *Formation.* There are five commonly used compound tenses. The auxiliary verb **avoir*** is used for all verbs except (1) those listed in section *c* below, and (2) *reflexive* verbs, which use **être***. In all cases, the English translation of an auxiliary verb is a form of *to have,* regardless of which French auxiliary is used.

The table following shows the formation of the compound tenses of a regular **-er** verb, **examin/er.** The past participle is **examiné,** and the auxiliary is **avoir*** (since **examin/er** is not on the special list).

NAME OF TENSE	TENSE OF AUXILIARY	EXAMPLE	MEANING	
1. PAST INDEFINITE	Present	j'ai / examiné	I have /	
2. PLUPERFECT	Imperfect	j'avais / examiné	I had /	
3. FUTURE PERFECT	Future	j'aurai / examiné	I will have /	examined
4. PAST CONDITIONAL	Conditional	j'aurais / examiné	I would have /	
5. PAST SUBJUNCTIVE (Equivalent to Past Indefinite)	Present Subjunctive	j'aie / examiné	I have /	

b. *Translation.* Since the past participle is translated invariably (in the above example it is always *examined*), it is merely necessary to look at the auxiliary verb, determine the tense of "to have," and translate. This is what we have been doing in the exercises.

c. *Verbs Using être* as an Auxiliary.* The translation of être* with past participles of these verbs is always in a form of *to have:*

je suis	allé	I **have** / gone = I went	(1)
j'étais	allé	I **had** / gone	(2)
je serai	allé	I **will have** / gone	(3)
je serais	allé	I **would have** / gone	(4)
je sois	allé	I **have** / gone = I went	(5)

NOTE: The "House of être" may help recall the verbs which use this auxiliary:

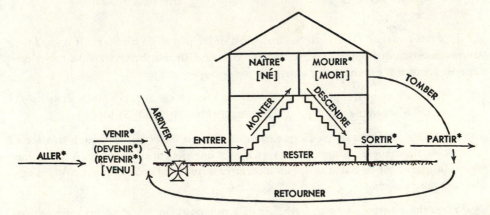

84. Interrogation

Questions are generally introduced by special interrogative words; and furthermore the subject-verb order may be inverted. Questions can always be identified by the interrogation point placed at the end of the question.

a. *Vocabulary of Interrogation.* Learn the following commonly used words found at the beginning of questions:

qui	who, whom	pourquoi	why
que, qu'	what	combien de	how much, how many
quand	when	comment	how
où	where	quel(le) [NOUN]	which [NOUN]

EXAMPLES:

Qui arrive?	Who is arriving?
Qu'entendez-vous?	What do you hear?
Quand arrive-t-il?	When is he arriving?
Combien de temps a-t-il?	How much time does he have?
Quelle revue désirez-vous?	Which magazine do you want?

b. *Questions beginning with* **est-ce que** (**est-ce qu'**). Disregard these expressions in translating; they merely signal the beginning of a question and permit normal (not inverted) French word order.

Est-ce qu'il a fini?	Has he finished?
Est-ce que **vous** comprenez?	Do you understand?

c. *Questions containing* **est-ce que, est-ce qu'**, *and* **est-ce qui** after the initial interrogative word. Disregard these expressions, and base the translation on the initial word (*a* above).

Qui est-ce qui parle?	Who is speaking?
Qu' est-ce que **vous** entendez?	What do you hear?
Quelle revue est-ce qu'il a?	What magazine does he have?

d. *Word Order in Questions.* Normal word order is used in questions if one of the forms of **est-ce que** appears. Nevertheless, your English translation should convert the remainder of the sentence from statement form to question form.

Où est-ce que vous allez?	[NORMAL ORDER OF SUBJECT AND VERB]
Où allez-vous?	[INVERTED ORDER: VERB–SUBJECT]

Notice that with forms of **est-ce que**, normal order is expected. Although this form resembles a statement, it must be converted to a question in translation. Without the question-signal **est-ce que**, the question form is in inverted order, similar to the English *are you? do you?*

When the subject is a noun (rather than a pronoun), inversion occurs only with a supplied redundant pronoun in the inverted position. Do *not* repeat the pronoun in translation:

Où le laboratoire se trouve-t-**il**?	Where is the laboratory?
Quand Georges finit-**il** son travail?	When does George finish his work?

e. **n'est-ce pas?** This expression appears at the end of a statement to elicit agreement. Translate according to the context:

Vous comprenez, n'est-ce pas?	You understand, **don't** you?
La lecture est longue, n'est-ce pas?	The reading is long, **isn't** it?
Vous pouvez l'ouvrir, n'est-ce pas?	You can open it, **can't** you?

85. *ne* in the Absence of *pas* ["COPS"]

a. Ne retains negative force with supplemental auxiliaries **cesser** *to cease*, **oser** *to dare*, **pouvoir*** *to be able*, and **savoir*** *to know* (*how*). When these verbs are followed by an expressed or understood infinitive, and preceded by **ne,** the negation is in force even though *pas* is omitted. [COPS = first letter of each verb]

Les personnes faibles **ne** peuvent être sincères.   Weak persons **cannot** be sincere.
Lui parler? Je **ne** saurais.   **Talk** to him? I couldn't.

b. *Ineffective ne.* **Ne** is entirely without negative force (1) after expressions of fear, (2) in the second part of a comparison of *in*equality, (3) after à **moins que** and **avant que,** and in certain other cases. The general rule is that (except for the supplemental auxiliaries above) there is *no negation* unless **ne** precedes the verb, and a *second negative term* (like **pas**) *follows it:*

Je crains que vous **ne** tombiez.   I am afraid that you **will fall.**   (1)
Il est plus intelligent qu'il **ne** le paraît.   He is more intelligent than he **appears.**   (2)
Nous partons à moins qu'il **n'**arrive.   We are leaving unless he **arrives.**   (3)

EXERCISES

I. Verb Drill. Translate the following verb forms and identify the tense by name:

1. Ils avaient fini l'expérience
2. Nous aurions parlé
3. Il est allé à Londres
4. Il était tombé
5. Elle sera devenue riche
6. Ils eurent rempli les verres
7. Nous fûmes étonnés
8. Vous retiendrez les billets
9. Ils se sont levés tout à coup
10. Il dit (*present* and *past definite*)
11. ils étaient venus nous voir
12. Je doute qu'ils aient leurs appareils.
13. Je doute qu'ils aient parlé de cela.
14. Pensez-vous que je puisse partir?
15. Il faut que le vide soit parfait.
16. Ils doutent qu'elle soit restée.
17. Un crayon: il sert à écrire.
18. ils avaient ouvert la porte
19. nous aurions admis
20. supposons (supposer *to assume*)

II. Interrogatives (§84). Translate:

21. Combien de filles est-ce que le baron avait?
22. Qui est sorti du château? Qui est-ce qui est sorti du château?
23. Qui est arrivé? Qu'est-ce qui est arrivé?
24. Comment Napoléon trouvait-il les pyramides d'Égypte?
25. Comment trouvez-vous l'histoire de Charles Bovary?
26. Pourquoi le baron était-il fâché contre Candide?
27. Où est-ce que Candide est allé après avoir été mis à la porte?
28. Et la belle Cunégonde, qu'est-ce qu'elle est devenue?
29. Qui devait marquer l'endroit où il y avait beaucoup de poissons?
30. Quelle sorte de marque est-ce que Téléphone a faite sur le canot?

23. **arriver** *is used in two senses here:* to arrive *and* to happen. *Which is which?* 24. **Comment trouv/er** *has the sense of* "How do (you) like . . . ?" 26. **fâché** *adj.* angry 27. **être* mis à la porte** to be kicked out 28. **devenir*** *sometimes means* "to become of"

31. Que voulez-vous faire ce soir après avoir étudié le français?
32. Pasteur effectua de remarquables travaux sur les maladies contagieuses, n'est-ce pas?
33. Eisenhower est né à Abilene (Kansas) en 1890, n'est-ce pas?
34. Nous apprenons à lire le français, n'est-ce pas?
35. La semaine prochaine nous irons à Paris, n'est-ce pas?

III. Uses of *ne* (§85). Translate:

36. Est-ce que Voltaire a dit «Je ne suis pas d'accord avec ce que vous dites, mais je défendrai jusqu'à la mort votre droit de le dire»? Je ne sais.
37. On croit généralement que c'est Voltaire qui l'a dit, mais en vérité c'était Madame E. B. Hall qui a composé cette maxime en anglais. Contredire le grand public? Je n'oserais.
38. Je crains que vous ne tombiez. Prenez donc garde!
39. Je n'affirme rien; je me contente de croire qu'il y a plus de choses possibles qu'on ne pense.
40. Ne partez pas avant que l'heure ne sonne.

READINGS

A. *Température et constitution du Soleil*

[41] Examinons, maintenant, les caractères intimes du foyer solaire. [42] Au point de vue chimique, il est constitué des mêmes éléments que le globe terrestre, mais ils se trouvent là dans des conditions totalement différentes. [43] En effet, la température du Soleil, d'après les plus sûres déterminations ayant pu être effectuées, est de 6 000° environ; du moins, s'agit-il de la température de la surface visible dont nous recevons le rayonnement, car elle croît de plus en plus vers le centre, où elle doit atteindre, d'après les calculs des astrophysiciens, plusieurs millions de degrés.

[44] De notre point de vue donc, tout doit être volatilisé. Mais, d'autre part, en raison de la dimension et de la masse du Soleil, des pressions formidables entrent en jeu, qui atteignent, à l'intérieur, plusieurs milliards d'atmosphères. [45] Aussi° éprouve-t-on quelque mal à concevoir vraiment ce qu'il en est de substances soumises à de telles conditions. [46] Les termes de solide, de liquide et de gaz concernent des propriétés relatives au domaine terrestre. [47] Sans

---

35. **semaine** *nf.* week 36. **être* d'accord** to be in agreement 38. **prendre* garde** to be careful 43. **croît** (*fr.* **croît/re*** to increase) increases 44. **volatilis/er** *v.* to volatilize (= to turn into vapor); **atmosphère** *nf.* atmosphere, *in Physics, a standard pressure of about 14.7 pounds per square inch, representing the pressure of atmospheric air at sea level* 45. **mal** difficulty; **ce qu'il en est** how things are with

doute, pour définir correctement l'état de la matière solaire, de nouveaux mots seraient-ils à créer! [48] Faute de mieux, et pour notre compréhension, il reste malgré tout suggestif de parler d'état gazeux car ce sont les lois connues de la physique relatives à l'état gazeux qui lui conviennent. [49] Notons pourtant que sous l'effet des pressions considérables, ces éléments gazeux acquièrent une densité et des propriétés qui les rendent plutôt comparables à ce que nous désignons communément sous le nom de liquide, et peut-être de solide, dans l'intérieur du globe.

[50] En fait, les couches superficielles du Soleil, décrites plus loin, sont seules accessibles à l'investigation directe. [51] Ce qu'on peut supposer, quant à la constitution des régions profondes de la masse, découle de vues théoriques, et l'on admet généralement une température centrale extraordinairement élevée — 20 à 25 millions de degrés, peut-être — avec une densité fortement croissante, dépassant largement celle des métaux les plus lourds.

[52] En définitive nous retiendrons que la quasi-totalité de la masse est dans un état gazeux. Nous allons voir comment peuvent s'expliquer alors les apparences du globe aussi nettement délimité que semble être le Soleil.

[53] En vérité, on ne distingue pas une surface bien définie (comme pourrait l'être celle d'un corps solide ou liquide), mais un niveau se dessinant au sein d'un ensemble très vaste et que nous étudierons plus loin. [54] Pour l'instant, disons qu'en vertu de la valeur élevée de la pesanteur, la pression s'accroît très rapidement à mesure qu'on s'enfonce davantage dans la masse gazeuse. [55] Le calcul permet d'estimer qu'à un niveau considéré, il suffit d'une différence de quelques dizaines de kilomètres pour que la pression devienne décuple. [56] Il est donc facile de concevoir qu'on passe bien vite d'un milieu transparent à un autre acquérant une densité suffisante pour que, à nos yeux, il se comporte comme une couche opaque. [57] Ainsi se trouve réalisée l'apparence d'une surface brillante à laquelle on donne le nom de *photosphère*.

[58] L'épaisseur gazeuse, mise ici en cause, est infime relativement au rayon du globe solaire; et en raison de l'éloignement qui, déjà, réduit considérablement celui-ci, cette zone de transition est vue sous une largeur apparente pratiquement inappréciable. [59] Par suite, la masse la plus condensée du Soleil paraît avoir un contour nettement délimité. [60] Cependant, à partir de là, et sans solution de continuité se développe en hauteur la matière gazeuse de plus en plus raréfiée. [61] Dans cette disposition, on peut voir, de façon imagée, comme une immense atmosphère environnant le globe solaire.

48. **faute de mieux** for lack of something better   50. **plus loin** later on [in the book]; 51. **fortement** sharply; **croissant** (*ps.p.* of **croître***)   52. **quasi-** almost-; **peuvent s'expliquer** *The subject of this verbal construction is* les apparences du globe.   53. **au sein de** in the midst of 54. **davantage** *adv.* still more   55. **considéré** under consideration; **décuple** *adj.* tenfold, ten times as great   56. **acquérant** *ps.p.* acquiring; **couche** *nf.* layer, stratum   58. **mis(e) en cause** under consideration; **infime** *adj.* lowest, very small, at the lowest level; **rayon** radius; **en raison de** = à **cause de**; **sous** (*here*) "as having"   59. **par suite** = **par conséquent**   60. **solution** *nf.* break 61. **disposition** *nf.* arrangement; **imagé** vivid; **comme** [something] like; **environn/er** *v.* to surround

[62] Ces couches extérieures échappent à la contemplation ordinaire, et la raison en est facile à comprendre. [63] En raison de leur transparence, nous distinguerons librement à travers elles l'éblouissante surface du disque solaire; au bord de celui-ci, où elles devraient se laisser apercevoir concentriquement disposées avec une luminosité relativement faible, elles sont alors dérobées à nos yeux par la clarté intense du voile aérien terrestre, diffusant la lumière de la photosphère. [64] Leur vision est seulement réservée aux rares instants pendant lesquels le disque solaire est totalement éclipsé par la Lune, cas auquel il devient loisible d'apercevoir ce qui l'environne, tandis que notre enveloppe aérienne cesse de se comporter fâcheusement. [65] Cependant, la physique est venue au secours des astronomes, en leur procurant les moyens d'éliminer notablement l'obstacle atmosphérique, de manière qu'au moins les portions les plus brillantes surmontant la photosphère, ainsi que les phénomènes dont elles sont le siège, peuvent être enregistrés maintenant sans l'intervention d'une éclipse. [66] Ces possibilités d'observation constante ont fait faire un grand pas à la connaissance générale de l'astre du jour.

[67] La base de l'enveloppe extérieure au globe apparent constitue une

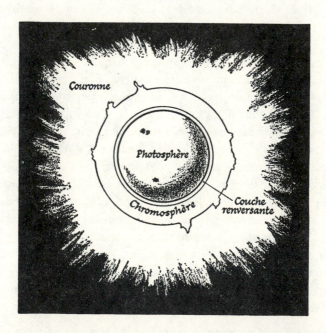

63. **à travers** through; **éblouissant, -e** *adj.* dazzling; **dérob/er** *v.* to hide; **clarté** *nf.* = brilliance; **voile aérien terrestre** Earth's atmosphere [literally "Earth's aerial veil"]   64. **leur vision** "their visibility" — *rearrange the English to suit the sense;* **loisible** *adj.* possible, convenient; **se com-porter** *v.* to behave; **fâcheusement** *adv.* in an annoying way   65. **surmontant** *ps.p.* surmounting- **siège** *nm.* source, seat; **enregistr/er** *v.* to record   66. **astre du jour** = le Soleil

couche appelée la *chromosphère*. [68]   Le passage de celle-ci à la photosphère s'effectue par une mince zone intermédiaire, dite *couche renversante*. [69] Enfin, au-dessus de la chromosphère, et avec une considérable, mais variable extension, s'étend la partie qui forme la *Couronne,* dont le spectacle est si remarquable pendant les éclipses totales du Soleil.

[70] Photosphère, Chromosphère et Couronne sont les trois grandes divisions de l'ensemble observable du Soleil. [71] Elles jouissent chacune de propriétés particulières, et nous les examinerons en détail successivement. [72] Cependant, soulignons dès maintenant qu'elles ne sont pas indépendantes: les phénomènes qui s'y produisent se rattachent plus ou moins intimement les uns aux autres et procèdent tous de l'activité variable du fantastique foyer solaire.

—Extrait de RUDAUX et VAUCOULEURS. *Astronomie.* (Librairie Larousse, Éditeurs)

B. *Recherches sur la Phytase*

[73] La phytase est un enzyme peu répandu et irrégulièrement distribué. Très rarement signalé chez les animaux, il a été retrouvé plus fréquemment chez les végétaux supérieurs; l'activité des feuilles est minime, celle des graines assez variable, certains (Blé, Seigle, Moutarde-blanche) représentent les sources de phytase les plus actives actuellement décrites.

[74] Des phytases furent également décelées chez les Aspergillacées et certaines levures mais, à notre connaissance, la présence de phytases n'a jamais encore été signalée chez des Bactéries.

[75] Courtois et Perez purent observer que les matières fécales humaines manifestaient à pH 5,2 une appréciable activité phytasique; cette phytase se comporte comme un desmoenzyme et paraît être d'origine bactérienne. En effet la phytase fait défaut dans les secrétions digestives des animaux supérieurs à l'exception du rat.

[76] D'autre part, il semble difficile d'attribuer à cette phytase fécale une origine alimentaire; l'adjonction de phytase du Blé à la ration n'améliore pas l'assimilation du phosphore de l'acide inositohexaphosphorique (acide phytique) chez le rat comme si la phytase d'origine végétale était inactivée dans le tube digestif.

from; **foyer solaire** *nm.* Sun's atmosphere B. **colibacille** coliforms; *here,* E. coli   73. **phytase** phytase; **feuille** *nf.* leaf, leafy plant; **blé** *nm.* corn; **seigle** *nm.* rye   74. **déceler** to discover, to reveal; **aspergillacées** Aspergillus; **levure** *nf.* yeast   75. **se comporter** to behave; **faire défaut** to be absent   76. **adjonction** *nf.* addition; **améliorer** to improve; **phytique** (*See page 2, Sec. 2e*); **végétal** *pertaining to plants;* **tube digestif** *nm.* digestive tract

[77] La proportion d'acide phytique ingéré dans les aliments et susceptible d'être éliminé inaltéré varie d'une espèce animale à une autre; on peut même noter d'assez grosses variations dans le cadre d'une même espèce.

[78] Ces faits avaient dès lors permis d'envisager que l'utilisation partielle et très variable du phosphore phytique alimentaire était en relation avec son hydrolyse plus ou moins accentuée par d'éventuelles phytases bactériennes. [79] D'autres chercheurs ont obtenu des résultats qui ne paraissent pouvoir s'interpréter que par l'intervention de phytases bactériennes: l'acide phytique est en effet presque totalement hydrolysé au cours des processus digestifs chez les Ruminants; c'est-à-dire dans les conditions où les bactéries intestinales ont à la fois le nombre et le temps pour intervenir. [80] Nous nous sommes donc proposé de rechercher ces phytases bactériennes; dès nos premiers essais avec le Colibacille, élément caractéristique de la flore intestinale, nous avons pu mettre en évidence une appréciable activité phytasique. Nous avons ainsi été conduits à préciser quelques caractères de ces phytases et à les comparer à ceux des phosphomonoestérases associées.

[81] Divers auteurs avaient déjà caractérisé des phosphomonoestérases chez les Colibacilles, comme CAPPELLATO; mais l'étude la plus complète est celle de PAGET et VITTU qui mirent en évidence au moins deux monoestérases distinctes qui paraissent appartenir aux groupes III et IV de la classification des phosphatases proposée par FOLLEY et KAY, puis ROCHE et COURTOIS.

[82] PROTOCOLE EXPÉRIMENTAL

A) *Substrats.*—Nous avons utilisé le β-glycérophosphate et l'inositohexaphosphate de sodium.

B) *Souches bactériennes.*—Nous avons eu recours à trois souches distinctes que nous désignerons dans la suite de ce mémoire par un numéro indicatif. Les deux premières provenaient des collections du Laboratoire de Microbiologie de la Faculté de Pharmacie de Paris: souche Samet = C_I et souche Benoist = C_{II}. La troisième, souche Monod = C_{III} nous a été procurée par l'Institut Pasteur de Paris.

[83] 1) *Culture.*

Nous avons utilisé tout d'abord des cultures de Colibacilles développées sur eau peptonée-glucosée avec addition au milieu de phosphate monopotassique. Après 16 à 20 heures à 37° nous collectons les bactéries par centrifugation, les lavons avec une solution de ClNₐ à 10 p. 1.000 et les desséchons dans le vide à la température du laboratoire.

---

77. **ingérer** to ingest; **aliment** *nm.* food; **cadre** *nm.* limits, bounds   78. **hydrolyse** *nf.* hydrolysis; **éventuel, -le** *adj.* possible   79. **hydrolysé** hydrolyzed; **nombre** *nm.* [critical] number; **temps** *nm.* time; *(here)* age   80. **se proposer de** to decide to; **Colibacille** E. coli; **flore** *nf.* flora   81. **chez les Colibacilles** in the family of E. coli   82. **substrat** *nm.* substrate, substratum; **glycérophosphate** glycerol; **inositohexaphosphate** inositol hexaphosphate; **souche** *nf.* strain; **mémoire** *nm.* paper *(contrast with the feminine* **mémoire,** memory); **provenir*** to originate   83. **peptonée-glucosée** peptone glucose; **milieu** *nm.* medium; **37°** 37° C *(All degree measurements are Centigrade unless otherwise stated.);* **ClNa** NaCl (sodium chloride) **10 p. 1.000** 10 parts per 1000; **dessécher** to dry

[84] Par la suite, sur les conseils de J. Monod, nous avons eu recours à un protocole opératoire légèrement différent qui nous a permis d'obtenir à la fois un meilleur rendement pondéral et des préparations microbiennes à caractères plus constants.

[85] Le milieu de culture dit M 57 présentait la composition suivante: phosphate monopotassique 27,2 g, sulfate d'ammonium 4 g, sulfate de magnésium à $7 \cdot OH_2$ 0,4 g, chlorure de calcium hydraté 0,01 g, citrate de fer ammoniacal 0,00066 g, glucose 8 g, potasse pure q.s. pour amener le milieu à un pH de 7,4 (soit 95 à 100 cm³ de potasse à 36° Bé), eau distillée q.s. pour 1 litre.

[86] Les bactéries prélevées à partir d'une culture sur gélose conservée à la glacière, sont tout d'abord accoutumées au milieu par cultures successives sur des tubes d'eau peptonée glucosée, puis des tubes contenant 10 ml de milieu M 57.

[87] Dans une fiole Fourneau renfermant 100 ml du milieu M 57 nous ensemençons le dernier de ces tubes. Nous plaçons 7 à 8 heures à 37° et transvasons dans 3 litres de milieu M 57 contenus dans un ballon de 6 litres de capacité; nous conservons à l'étude à 37° en agitant le milieu et en faisant barboter dans la culture un courant d'air stérile.

[88] Toutes ces opérations sont réalisées avec des récipients et solutions stérilisés dans des conditions d'asepsie complète.

[89] 2) *Récolte des bactéries*

Après 7 à 8 heures de culture nous collectons les bacilles par une centrifugation de 30 à 40 minutes à 3.800 tours minute. Le culot est suspendu dans une solution stérile de C1Na à 10 p. 1.000 et centrifugé à nouveau. Selon les cas nous avons desséché directement le culot dans le vide sur anhydride phosphorique ou nous avons procédé à un lavage par l'acétone refroidie à −20° avant de soumettre à la dessiccation. Les bactéries desséchées sont conservées à la glacière.

[90] 3) *Mise en suspension des bactéries pour l'essai ensymatique*

Les bactéries desséchées sont pesées, broyées dans un mortier stérile avec du sable de Fontainebleau lavé plusieurs fois par les acides et calciné; nous ajoutons alors de l'eau bistillée stérile, agitons puis recueillons après décantation du sable la fraction surnageante; cette opération est répétée plusieurs fois et les fractions surnageantes sont réunies.

[91] La suspension bactérienne ainsi obtenue est homogène comme l'ont montré d'une part des numérations sous le microscope, d'autre part la détermination de l'activité phytasique ou phosphomonoestérasique; diverses prises d'essai identiques de la même suspension ont toujours manifesté pratiquement la même activité;

84. **par la suite** next, afterward; **conseils** *nm.* advice; **rendement** *nm.* yield; **pondéral** *adj.* weight 85. **chlorure** *nm.* chloride; **citrate de fer ammoniacal** ferrous ammonium sulfate; **potasse** potash (potassium chlorate); **q.s.** = quantité suffisante; **Bé** Baumé 86. **prélevé** set apart; **gélose** agar-agar; **glacière** *nf.* refrigerator 87. **fiole** *nf.* flask; **ensemer** to innoculate; **placer** to incubate (*in this case*); **transvaser** to decant; **ballon** *nm.* carboy; **agiter** to stir; **barboter** to bubble; **courant** *nm.* stream 88. **asepsie** aseptic, sterile 89. **récolte** *nf.* collecting, harvest; **bacille** *nm.* bacteria; **culot** *nm.* precipitate; **refroidi** chilled 90. **broyer** to grind; **calciné** calcined; **bistillé** double distilled; **surnager** to float; **réunies** combined; **fraction surnageante** *f.* supernatant 91. **prise d'essai** test sampling; **sensiblement** appreciably; **essai** assay

d'autre part des suspensions obtenues au cours d'opérations distinctes à partir de la même préparation bactérienne permettaient d'obtenir des résultats sensiblement identiques. La suspension est toujours utilisée immédiatement pour une série d'essais.

J.E. COURTOIS et L. MANET. Recherches sur la Phytase. Les Phytases du Colibacille. *Bulletin de la Société de Chimie Biologique*

C. *Les Aptitudes musicales*

[92] Les tests d'aptitudes musicales, qui ne sont pas nombreux, sont présentés sur des disques. Le test du Talent Musical de Seashore, par exemple, sert à examiner la discrimination de la hauteur, de l'intensité, du rythme, du timbre, du temps et de la mémoire du son. [93] Le sujet doit également différencier deux sons qui se suivent de près. On calcule les percentiles pour chaque test.

[94] Il est compréhensible qu'un individu puisse avoir un score élevé aux tests de Seashore, mais être un mauvais pianiste ou violoniste n'ayant pas l'habileté des doigts requise. [95] Mais même étant très habile une personne ne peut pas réussir dans le domaine musical si elle ne sait pas discriminer les hauteurs, l'intensité et les temps.

[96] Les tests de Seashore et d'autres dans ce genre sont utilisés dans les écoles pour la sélection pour la carrière musicale. Un psychologue qui applique ces tests à un groupe d'élèves, tombe parfois sur quelqu'un qui, bien que n'ayant reçu aucune formation musicale, fait preuve d'un grand talent musical et qui peut être ainsi dirigé vers la carrière musicale, tandis que ceux qui se révèlent comme n'ayant aucun don, doivent être déconseillés au cas où ils voudraient poursuivre dans cette voie.

ORIENTATION ET SÉLECTION PROFESSIONNELLES

[97] Comment utilise-t-on actuellement† les résultats des tests en orientation et en sélection?

Lorsqu'un individu vient demander des conseils d'orientation à un spécialiste, celui-ci peut se servir de quelques tests appropriés à son cas. [98] Après avoir comparé les résultats de son sujet avec ceux d'autres sujets ayant servi pour la validation des tests, le conseiller d'orientation peut dire: «Vous êtes suffisamment intelligent pour réussir dans un des domaines qui vous intéressent, mais voici ce qui me paraît vous intéresser le plus. Ce domaine exige une très grande aptitude

---

92. disque [pour la reproduction phonographique]   94. habileté *nf*. skill, agility   95. elle refers to une personne, which may be either a male or a female   96. tom/ber [sur] *v*. to happen [upon]; formation *nf*. training; se révèlent *fr*. se révél/er = se montrer; don nm. talent, gift; déconseill/er *v*. to discourage, to advise against something   97. conseils d'orientation guidance   appropriés = convenables

mécanique et vos résultats montrent que vous l'avez. [99] Il y a donc des chances que si vous vous appliquez, vous réussirez très bien.» Par ailleurs, il peut être obligé de dire: «Vos réponses à certaines questions de ce test (d'intelligence) ne permettent pas de croire que vous pourrez avoir le diplôme de médecin, mais les autres tests (aptitudes mécaniques) indiquent que vous êtes exceptionnellement doué pour la technique et que vous réussirez probablement très bien dans une industrie qui exige ces dons.»

[100] Le conseiller d'orientation ne dit pas à l'individu qu'il réussira ou ne réussira pas dans un certain domaine car il y a bien d'autres conditions qui contribuent au succès ou à l'échec dans chaque travail, en plus de celles que° mesurent les tests.

[101] Le prognostic est plus facile lorsqu'il s'agit de sélection que d'orientation professionnelle. Le psychologue peut dire par exemple avec beaucoup de certitude que parmi les individus ayant donné de mauvais résultats aux tests d'aptitudes, il n'y aura pas plus de 20% de réussite s'ils suivent la formation de pilote et que 90% environ seront pilotes lorsqu'il s'agira d'individus ayant très bien réussi à ces tests.

[102] Ce que° doivent faire ceux qui se servent des tests de sélection, c'est de déterminer quel est le score critique (le score au-dessous duquel un individu ne peut pas être admis à exercer le métier donné), qui élimine le plus grand nombre d'échecs potentiels, tout en éliminant le moins possible d'individus qui paraissent pouvoir réussir.

—Norman L. Munn. *Traité de Psychologie* (Payot, Paris)

99. **doué** *pp.* gifted   100. **échec** *nm.* failure; **que**° cf. §54c, page 79, concerning inversion of word-order after **que**   101. **réussite** *nf.* success   102. **ceux . . . sélection** is the subject of the verb **doivent faire**, and should be given first in English; **métier** *nm.* profession, trade, occupation; **tout en éliminant = en éliminant**

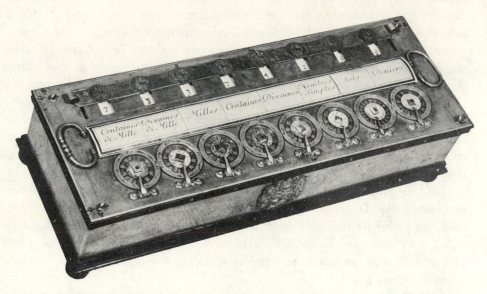

La Machine Arithmétique de Pascal

The first mechanical adding machine was invented by Blaise Pascal at the age of 19 to ease the long and complicated calculations of his father, a tax collector in Rouen. He spent ten years perfecting the calculator, building nearly fifty experimental models before achieving success in 1652 with an operative model. Hoping to gain honor and fortune through his invention, Pascal launched a commercial prospectus, *L'Avis nécessaire à ceux qui auront la curiosité de voir la Machine arithmétique et de s'en servir.*

The machine consists of a small case containing geared wheels which display the results of addition in the windows above the dials. Modern counterparts are still in use today. (Photograph courtesy of IBM).

1For references to Pascal's calculating machine, see pages 73 and 106.

A P P E N D I C E S

A GUIDE TO FURTHER READING IN FRENCH

Certainly you will wish to use your reading knowledge to do further reading for instruction and enjoyment. You may get some good recommendations not only from your French teacher, but from teachers of other subjects as well.

A brief list of books (marked with the symbol "B") and periodicals (P) in French is given below to help you get started. You will be able to find many of these in your library. For names of other books related to any given field, be sure to look in the Bibliography of books you do find; and in the Book Review section of periodicals.

In addition to the symbols (B) and (P) explained above, the symbol (T) indicates a book or periodical of a technical or advanced nature, and (G) indicates one of general interest.

Refer to the *Comptes Rendus de l'Académie de Science* (Paris) for current articles on a wide range of scientific subjects.

Automation

Automatisme (P) (T)

PRUDHOMME, R. *La Construction des machines automatiques.* Paris: Gauthier-Villars, 1964. (B) (T)

Architecture

Architecture Aujourd'hui (P)

LE CORBUSIER et PIERRE JEANNERET. *Œuvre complète.* Zürich: Editions Girsberger. Beautifully illustrated work of the foremost French architects of today. (B) (T and G)

VIOLLET-LE-DUC, E. *Dictionnaire raisonné de l'architecture.* Paris: Morel, 1875. Fully illustrated history of architecture, with historical emphasis. In several volumes. (B) (T,G)

Art

Gazette des Beaux-Arts (P)
L'Illustration (P) (G)
    Profusely illustrated in color.
Réalités (P) (G)
Revue d'Art

Biology, Biochemistry

Bulletin de la Société de Chimie Biologique (P) (T)

Comptes-rendus de la Société de Biologie (P) (T)

Société de Biologie de Marseille (P) (T)

Botany

Revue générale de Botanique (P) (T)

Chemistry

Annales de Chimie (P) (T)

Chimie et Industrie Génie Chimique (P) (T)

Journal de Chimie Physique (P) (T)

CHÊNE, H. and M. *Les méthodes de la chimie de la cellulose.* Paris: Dunot, 1949. (B) (T)

KARRER, PAUL. *Traité de chimie organique.* Neuchâtel: Griffon, 1948. (B) (T)

Economics

Revue Économique (P) (T) Six numbers per year.

FLAMANT and SINGER-KERL. *Crises et récessions économiques.* Paris: P.U.F., 2nd Ed., 1970.

GIDE, CHARLES and RIST, CHARLES. *Histoire des doctrines économiques.* Paris: Librairie de la Société du recueil Sirey. (B) (T)

Education

COMPAYRÉ, GABRIEL. *Histoire critique des doctrines de l'éducation en France.* Paris: Hachette, 1904. (B) (T,G)

ROUSSEAU, JEAN-JACQUES. *Émile, ou l'éducation.* (B) (G)

Engineering

Société des Ingénieurs civils de France (P) (T)

Acta Electronica (P) (T)

Forestry, Agronomy

Cahier des Ingénieurs agronomes (P) (T)

ROCHETTE, P. *Le Bois.* Paris: Dunod, 1964. (B) (T)

Revue forestière française (Nancy) (P) (T)

Genetics

BEISSON, J. *La Génétique.* Paris: P.U.F., 1971.

BLARINGHEM, L. *L'Hérédité mendélienne.* Paris: Gauthier-Villars, 1928. (B) (T)

History

BOULENGER, JACQUES. *Le Grand Siècle.* Paris: Hachette. (B) (G)

FUNCK-BRENTANO, F. *Le Moyen Âge.* Paris: Hachette. (B) (G)

STRYIENSKI, C. *Le XVIIIᵉ Siècle.* Paris: Hachette. (B) (G)

Literary Criticism and History

BRODIN, PIERRE. *Les écrivains américains de l'entre-deux-guerres.* New York: Brentano's, 1945. (B) (G)

CARRÉ, JEAN-MARIE. *La vie aventureuse de Jean-Arthur Rimbaud.* Paris: Plon, 1926. (B) (G)

COINDREAU, MAURICE EDGAR. *La farce est jouée.* New York: Éditions de la Maison Française, 1942. (B) (T).
     A study of the French theatre from 1900 to 1925.

LANSON, GUSTAVE et TUFFRAU, PAUL. *Manuel d'histoire de la littérature française.* Paris: Hachette, 1938; Boston: D. C. Heath, 1938. (B) (T,G)

MAUROIS, ANDRÉ. *Études littéraires.* New York: Éditions de la Maison Française, 1941. (B) (T,G)

Literature (Fiction)

CAMUS, ALBERT. *L'Étranger.*

FLAUBERT, GUSTAVE. *Madame Bovary.* (B) (G)

GIRAUDOUX, JEAN. *La folle de Chaillot.* (B) (G) [Play]

MAURIAC, FRANÇOIS. *Thérèse Desqueyroux.* (B) (G)

VOLTAIRE. *Candide.* (B) (G)
————— *Zadig.* (B) (G)
————— *Micromégas.* (Short story) (G)

Literature (General)

CHATEAUBRIAND, F. R. *Mémoires d'outre-tombe.*

LA ROCHEFOUCAULD. *Maximes.*

PASCAL, BLAISE. *Pensées.*

ROUSSEAU, JEAN-JACQUES. *Confessions.*

Literature (Comedy)

GIRAUDOUX, JEAN. *La Folle de Chaillot.*   (Play)
MOLIÈRE. *Le Médecin malgré lui.*   (Play)

Mathematics

GERMAIN, P. *Mécanique des milieux continus.* Paris: Masson, 1962. (B) (T)

POINCARÉ, HENRI. *Science et méthode.* Paris: Flammarion, 1908. (B) (G)
————— *Leçons sur la théorie mathématique.* Paris: Carré, 1889. (B) (T)

ROMAKINE, M.I. *Éléments d'Algèbre linéaire et de programmation linéaire.* Paris: Éditions d'Organisation, 1970.   (B)

Medicine

C. R. de l'Académie des Sciences (P) (T)

Microbiology

Annales de l'Institut Pasteur (P) (T)

Music

BERLIOZ, HECTOR. *Grand traité d'instrumentation et d'orchestration modernes.* Paris: Lemoine, 1952. (B) (T)

CORTOT, ALFRED. *La musique française du piano.* Paris: Presses universitaires, 1944. (B) (T,G)

DEBUSSY, CLAUDE. *Monsieur Croche antidilettante.* Paris: Gallimard, 1950. (B) (T) [Criticism]

DUPRÉ, MARCEL. *Traité d'improvisation à l'orgue.* Paris: Leduc, 1925. (B) (T)

GIDE, ANDRÉ. *Notes sur Chopin.* Paris: Éditions de l'Arche, 1948. (B) (G)

OFFENBACH, JACQUES. *Offenbach en Amérique, notes d'un musicien en voyage.* Paris: C. Lévy, 1877. (B) (G)

SCHWEITZER, ALBERT. *Jean-Sébastien Bach, le musicien-poète.* Lausanne, 1953.

Physics

Annales de Physique. (P) (T)

C. R. de l'Académie de Science (P) (T)

Journal de Physique (P) (T)

BRILLOUIN, LÉON. *Les Tenseurs en mécanique et en élasticité* Paris: Masson, 1949. (B) (T)

DE BROGLIE, LOUIS. *Éléments de la théorie des quanta et de mécanique ondulatoire.* Paris: Gauthier-Villars, 1953. (B) (T)

DE BROGLIE, MAURICE. *Les rayons-X.* Paris: Blanchard, 1922. (B) (T)

GUILLEN, ROBERT. *Physique nucléaire appliquée.* Paris: Ed. Eyrollés, 1963. (B) (T)

NAHMIAS, MAURICE E. *L'Énergie nucléaire.* Paris: Larousse, 1953. (B) (G)

DE PLUVINAGE. *Éléments de mécanique quantique.* (B) (G)

Politics

MONTESQUIEU, CHARLES. *L'Esprit des lois.* (B) (G)

Psychology

Psychologie française (P)

Revue de Psychologie appliquée (P) (T)

MUNN, NORMAN L. *Traité de psychologie.* Paris: Payot, 1956. An excellent introduction to the general field of psychology. (B) (G and T)

Sociology

Revue française sociologique (P) (T)

SAGNAC, PHILIPPE. *La formation de la société française moderne.* Paris: Presses universitaires, 1945. (B) (G)

Statistics

Revue de Statistique appliquée (P) (T)

Zoology

Société zoologique de France (P) (T)

General Reading

Mémento Larousse. An encyclopedia on a small scale. One small volume, containing articles on history, geography, physics, mathematics, grammar, music, and many other topics. (B) (G)

La Grande Encyclopédie (20 vol.)   Paris: Librarie Larousse.
Current articles on a wide range of general and technical subjects.

La Revue Scientifique. Serious semi-technical and technical articles. (P) (G)

Cahiers Français d'Information. Very interesting articles on all subjects of a current nature. Twice monthly. (P) (G)

L'Enfance. Deals with the psychology of children. (B) (T)

L'Année. Foremost journal in psychology. (P) (T)

La Presse médicale. Medical journal. (P) (G)

Les Temps modernes. Monthly journal on literary subjects, including new fiction and book reviews. Jean-Paul Sartre is its editor. (P) (G)

Les Nouvelles littéraires. Important reading for students of literature. Weekly issue in newspaper style. (P) (G)

Science et Vie. Much the same as the American *Popular Science.* (P) (G)

Réalités. Foremost beautifully printed and illustrated magazine of general interest, including travel, sports, geography, current events. (P) (G)

Paris-Match. Profusely illustrated news magazine. (P) (G)

Elle. Articles of interest to women. (P) (G)

MODEL REGULAR VERBS

1st Conjugation (-er)	2nd Conjugation (-ir)	3rd Conjugation (-re)
parl/er	fin/ir	vend/re

PRESENT	PRESENT	PRESENT
je parlE	je finIS	je vendS
tu parlES	tu finIS	tu vendS
il parlE	il finIT	il vend
nous parlONS	nous finISSons	nous vendONS
vous parlEZ	vous finISSez	vous vendEZ
ils parlENT	ils finISSent	ils vendENT

IMPERFECT	IMPERFECT	IMPERFECT
je parlAIS	je finissAIS	je vendAIS
tu parlAIS	tu finissAIS	tu vendAIS
il parlAIT	il finissAIT	il vendAIT
nous parlIONS	nous finissIONS	nous vendIONS
vous parlIEZ	vous finissIEZ	vous vendIEZ
ils parlAIENT	ils finissAIENT	ils vendAIENT

PAST DEFINITE	PAST DEFINITE	PAST DEFINITE
je parlAI	je finIS	je vendIS
tu parlAS	tu finIS	tu vendIS
il parlA	il finIT	il vendIT
nous parlÂMES	nous finÎMES	nous vendÎMES
vous parlÂTES	vous finÎTES	vous vendÎTES
ils parlÈRENT	ils finIRENT	ils vendIRENT

FUTURE	FUTURE	FUTURE
je parlerAI	je finirAI	je vendrAI
tu parlerAS	tu finirAS	tu vendrAS
il parlerA	il finirA	il vendrA
nous parlerONS	nous finirONS	nous vendrONS
vous parlerEZ	vous finirEZ	vous vendrEZ
ils parlerONT	ils finirONT	ils vendrONT

CONDITIONAL	CONDITIONAL	CONDITIONAL
je parlerAIS	je finirAIS	je vendrAIS
tu parlerAIS	tu finirAIS	tu vendrAIS
il parlerAIT	il finirAIT	il vendrAIT
nous parlerIONS	nous finirIONS	nous vendrIONS
vous parlerIEZ	vous finirIEZ	vous vendrIEZ
ils parlerAIENT	ils finirAIENT	ils vendrAIENT

PRESENT SUBJUNCTIVE	PRESENT SUBJUNCTIVE	PRESENT SUBJUNCTIVE
que je parlE	que je finISSe	que je vendE
que tu parlES	que tu finISSes	que tu vendES
qu'il parlE	qu'il finISSe	qu'il vendE
que nous parlIONS	que nous finISSions	que nous vendIONS
que vous parlIEZ	que vous finISSiez	que vous vendIEZ
qu'ils parlENT	qu'ils finISSent	qu'ils vendENT

(Other Subjunctive Tenses are omitted because of infrequency.)

Compound Tenses

PAST INDEFINITE	PAST INDEFINITE	PAST INDEFINITE
j' AI parlé	j' AI fini	j' AI vendu
tu AS parlé	tu AS fini	tu AS vendu
il A parlé	il A fini	il A vendu
nous AVONS parlé	nous AVONS fini	nous AVONS vendu
vous AVEZ parlé	vous AVEZ fini	vous AVEZ vendu
ils ONT parlé	ils ONT fini	ils ONT vendu

PLUPERFECT	PLUPERFECT	PLUPERFECT
j' AVAIS parlé	j' AVAIS fini	j' AVAIS vendu
tu AVAIS parlé	tu AVAIS fini	tu AVAIS vendu
il AVAIT parlé	il AVAIT fini	il AVAIT vendu
nous AVIONS parlé	nous AVIONS fini	nous AVIONS vendu
vous AVIEZ parlé	vous AVIEZ fini	vous AVIEZ vendu
ils AVAIENT parlé	ils AVAIENT fini	ils AVAIENT vendu

PAST ANTERIOR	PAST ANTERIOR	PAST ANTERIOR
j' EUS parlé	j' EUS fini	j' EUS vendu
tu EUS parlé	tu EUS fini	tu EUS vendu
il EUT parlé	il EUT fini	il EUT vendu
nous EÛMES parlé	nous EÛMES fini	nous EÛMES vendu
vous EÛTES parlé	vous EÛTES fini	vous EÛTES vendu
ils EURENT parlé	ils EURENT fini	ils EURENT vendu

FUTURE PERFECT	FUTURE PERFECT	FUTURE PERFECT
j' AURAI parlé	j' AURAI fini	j' AURAI vendu
tu AURAS parlé	tu AURAS fini	tu AURAS vendu
il AURA parlé	il AURA fini	il AURA vendu
nous AURONS parlé	nous AURONS fini	nous AURONS vendu
vous AUREZ parlé	vous AUREZ fini	vous AUREZ vendu
ils AURONT parlé	ils AURONT fini	ils AURONT vendu

PAST CONDITIONAL	PAST CONDITIONAL	PAST CONDITIONAL
j' AURAIS parlé	j' AURAIS fini	j' AURAIS vendu
tu AURAIS parlé	tu AURAIS fini	tu AURAIS vendu
il AURAIT parlé	il AURAIT fini	il AURAIT vendu
nous AURIONS parlé	nous AURIONS fini	nous AURIONS vendu
vous AURIEZ parlé	vous AURIEZ fini	vous AURIEZ vendu
ils AURAIENT parlé	ils AURAIENT fini	ils AURAIENT vendu

PAST SUBJUNCTIVE	PAST SUBJUNCTIVE	PAST SUBJUNCTIVE
que j' AIE parlé	que j' AIE fini	que j' AIE vendu
que tu AIES parlé	que tu AIES fini	que tu AIES vendu
qu'il AIT parlé	qu'il AIT fini	qu'il AIT vendu
que nous AYONS parlé	que nous AYONS fini	que nous AYONS vendu
que vous AYEZ parlé	que vous AYEZ fini	que vous AYEZ vendu
qu'ils AIENT parlé	qu'ils AIENT fini	qu'ils AIENT vendu

MODEL REGULAR REFLEXIVE VERB se laver

Summary in il-form

PRESENT	il se lave	he is washing [himself]*
IMPERFECT	il se lavait	he was washing
PAST DEFINITE	il se lava	he washed
FUTURE	il se lavera	he will wash
CONDITIONAL	il se laverait	he would wash
PRESENT SUBJUNCTIVE	qu'il se lave	he is washing; will wash
PAST INDEFINITE	il s'est lavé	he washed
PLUPERFECT	il s'était lavé	he had washed
PAST ANTERIOR	il se fut lavé	he had washed
FUTURE PERFECT	il se sera lavé	he will have washed
PAST CONDITIONAL	il se serait lavé	he would have washed
PAST SUBJUNCTIVE	qu'il se soit lavé	he has washed

---

himself is understood in all forms of the translations.

MODEL REGULAR VERB USING être AS AUXILIARY

Summary in il-form of entrer to enter

PRESENT	il entre	he is entering
IMPERFECT	il entrait	he was entering
PAST DEFINITE	il entra	he entered
FUTURE	il entrera	he will enter
CONDITIONAL	il entrerait	he would enter
PRESENT SUBJUNCTIVE	qu'il entre	he is entering, will enter
PAST INDEFINITE	il est entré	he entered
PLUPERFECT	il était entré	he had entered
PAST ANTERIOR	il fut entré	he had entered
FUTURE PERFECT	il sera entré	he will have entered
PAST CONDITIONAL	il serait entré	he would have entered
PAST SUBJUNCTIVE	qu'il soit entré	he has entered

IRREGULAR VERBS

General Remarks on Irregular Verbs

Pattern: Irregular verbs use the same verb endings as regular verbs, and in the present tense they follow the pattern for **-ir** verbs: the pattern **-s, -s, -t** is prevalent among irregular verbs.

Since the verb *endings* of irregular verbs are quite regular, the portion which causes the *IR*regularity is a vowel change in the STEM. This change takes place in all forms whose ending is silent (i.e., all but the **nous-** and **vous-** forms of the present tense). The 1st and 2nd persons plural of the present tense of irregular verbs tend to be regular — to conform to the stem form of the infinitive*:

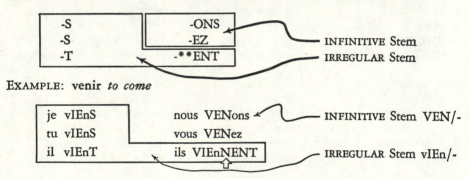

EXAMPLE: **venir** *to come*

** An additional consonant is often inserted here, as shown by the doubled *n* in *venir*.

Present Subjunctive: Most irregular verbs have a single stem throughout the six forms of the Present Subjunctive. However, some of them have *two* stems, which follow the plan indicated above. One stem is used for **nous-** and **vous-**forms, and another for all the rest. (§81c)

CONJUGATION OF ÊTRE*

Indicative Mood

PRESENT (*I am*, etc.)

je suis	nous sommes
tu es	vous êtes
il est	ils sont

PAST INDEFINITE (*I have been*, etc.)

j'ai été	nous avons été
tu as été	vous avez été
il a été	ils ont été

IMPERFECT (*I used to be, was*)

j' étais	nous étions
tu étais	vous étiez
il était	ils étaient

PLUPERFECT (*I HAD been*)

j'avais été	nous avions été
tu avais été	vous aviez été
il avait été	ils avaient été

PAST DEFINITE (*I was*)

je fus	nous fûmes
tu fus	vous fûtes
il fut	ils furent

PAST ANTERIOR (*I HAD been*)

j'eus été	nous eûmes été
tu eus été	vous eûtes été
il eut été	ils eurent été

FUTURE (*I WILL be*)

je serai	nous serons
tu seras	vous serez
il sera	ils seront

FUTURE PERFECT (*I WILL HAVE been*)

j'aurai été	nous aurons été
tu auras été	vous aurez été
il aura été	ils auront été

CONDITIONAL (*I WOULD be*)

je serais	nous serions
tu serais	vous seriez
il serait	ils seraient

PAST CONDITIONAL (*I WOULD HAVE been.*)

j'aurais été	nous aurions été
tu aurais été	vous auriez été
il aurait été	ils auraient été

Subjunctive

PRESENT (*I am*) (*I will be*)

que je sois	que nous soyons
que tu sois	que vous soyez
qu'il soit	qu'ils soient

PAST (*I have been, I was*)

que j'aie été	que nous ayons été
que tu aies été	que vous ayez été
qu'il ait été	qu'ils aient été

IMPERFECT (*I was*)

que je fusse	que nous fussions
que tu fusses	que vous fussiez
qu'il fût	qu'ils fussent

PLUPERFECT (*I had been*)

que j'eusse été	que nous eussions été
que tu eusses été	
qu'il eût été	que vous eussiez été
	qu'ils eussent été

PRINCIPAL PARTS: être, étant, été (avoir), je suis, je fus. FC: SER-
                   1   2   3   4   5

(1) Infinitive (2) Present Participle (3) Past Participle (for all Compound Tenses), (4) Present Tense, 1st Person Singular. (5) Past Definite, 1st Person Singular.

IMPERATIVES: **sois** (tu); **soyez** *be;* **soyons** *let's be;* **qu'il soit** *let him be*

CONJUGATION OF AVOIR*

Indicative Mood

PRESENT (*I have*, etc.)

j' ai	nous avons
tu as	vous avez
il a	ils ont

PAST INDEFINITE (*I have had*)

j' ai eu	nous avons eu
tu as eu	vous avez eu
il a eu	ils ont eu

IMPERFECT (*I USED TO have, I had*)

j' avais	nous avions
tu avais	vous aviez
il avait	ils avaient

PLUPERFECT (*I HAD had*)

j' avais eu	nous avions eu
tu avais eu	vous aviez eu
il avait eu	ils avaient eu

PAST DEFINITE (*I had*)

j' eus	nous eûmes
tu eus	vous eûtes
il eut	ils eurent

PAST ANTERIOR (*I HAD had*)

j' eus eu	nous eûmes eu
tu eus eu	vous eûtes eu
il eut eu	ils eurent eu

FUTURE (*I WILL have*)

j' aurai	nous aurons
tu auras	vous aurez
il aura	ils auront

FUTURE PERFECT (*I WILL HAVE had*)

j' aurai eu	nous aurons eu
tu auras eu	vous aurez eu
il aura eu	ils auront eu

CONDITIONAL (*I WOULD have*)

j' aurais	nous aurions
tu aurais	vous auriez
il aurait	ils auraient

PAST CONDITIONAL (*I WOULD HAVE had*)

j' aurais eu	nous aurions eu
tu aurais eu	vous auriez eu
il aurait eu	ils auraient eu

Subjunctive

PRESENT (*I have, I will have*)

que j' aie	que nous ayons
que tu aies	que vous ayez
qu'il ait	qu'ils aient

PAST (*I have had*)

que j' aie eu	que nous ayons eu
que tu aies eu	que vous ayez eu
qu'il ait eu	qu'ils aient eu

IMPERFECT (*I had*)

que j' eusse	que nous eussions
que tu eusses	que vous eussiez
qu'il eût	qu'ils eussent

PLUPERFECT (*I had had*)

que j'eusse eu	que nous eussions eu
que tu eusses eu	que vous eussiez eu
qu'il eût eu	qu'ils eussent eu

PRINCIPAL PARTS: avoir, ayant, eu (avoir), j'ai, j'eus

IMPERATIVES: aie, ayez, ayons, qu'il ait, qu'ils aient

TABLE OF IRREGULAR VERBS

The key recognition forms of the principal irregular verbs are given in the following table in the order used in the recognition rule (§42). Symbols are as follows:

Pr. **Present tense** in full. The first form is used with **je,** the second with **tu,** the third with **il** or **elle,** etc. Note that in form 4 (nous-form) the *italicized* portion is the stem of the Imperfect Tense.

Formation of the Imperfect: to the italicized stem indicated above (form Pr. 4), add the imperfect endings

-ais, -ais, -ait; -ions, -iez, -aient

Thus, for **aller,** the Imperfect forms would be (§43)

allais, allais, allait, allions, alliez, allaient

FC. **Future and Conditional** Stem. Note that this always ends in **-r.** (See §40b for distinctive endings; and §41)

PD. **Past Definite** Stem, followed by a dash and the first ending. This ending tells which of the three ending-systems to continue with for other forms. (§66c) See **aller** below for example.

PP. **Past Participle,** used for all compound tenses. (§83) The auxiliary verb is in parentheses. A sample compound tense form follows this.

PsP. **Present Participle** (English *-ing* form) (§49). Note that in most cases this is the Pr. 4 stem with **-ant** added.

Sj. **Present Subjunctive** Stem(s). The nous- and vous-forms may use a second stem. If so, it is indicated. (See *Remarks on Irregular Verbs,* p. 164) (§81)

INDEX TO TABLE OF IRREGULAR VERBS

Numbers refer to verb numbers in the Table of Irregular Verbs

1. ALLER *to go* §65

  Pr. vais, vas, va; *all*ons, allez, vont
  FC. ir-ai (-as, -a; -ons, -ez, -ont)
  PD. all-ai (-as, -a; -âmes, -âtes, -èrent)
  PP. allé (*être*)   elle est allée
  PsP. allant

  Sj. { qu'il aille
      { que nous all-ions

2. CONNAÎTRE *to know*

  Pr. connais, connais, connaît;
    *connaiss*ons, connaissez,
    connaissent
  FC. connaîtr-
  PD. conn-us
  PP. connu (*avoir*)   il avait connu
  PsP. connaissant
  Sj. qu'il connaiss-e
and apparaître *to appear;* disparaître *to
disappear;* paraître *to appear;* reconnaître
to recognize.

3. CONSTRUIRE *to construct*

  Pr. construis, construis, construit;
    *construis*ons, construisez,
    construisent
  FC. construir-
  PD. constru-is
  PP. construit (*avoir*) il a construit
  PsP. construisant
  Sj. qu'il construis-e
and reconstruire *to reconstruct.*

4. COURIR *to run*

  Pr. cours, cours, court; *cour*ons,
    courez, courent
  FC. courr-
  PD. cour-us
  PP. couru (*avoir*)   il a couru
  PsP. courant
  Sj. qu'il cour-e
and parcourir *to travel through.*

5. CROIRE *to believe*

  Pr. crois, crois, croit; *croy*ons,
    croyez, croient
  FC. croir-
  PD. cr-us
  PP. cru (*avoir*)   il a cru
  PsP. croyant

  Sj. { qu'il croi-e
      { que nous croyions
      { que vous croyiez
      { qu'ils croient

6. DÉCRIRE *to describe*

  Pr. décris, décris, décrit; *décriv*ons,
    décrivez, décrivent
  FC. décrir-
  PD. décr-is
  PP. décrit (*avoir*)   il a décrit
  PsP. décrivant
  Sj. qu'il décriv-e
and écrire *to write.*

7. DÉDUIRE *to deduce*

  Pr. déduis, déduis, déduit; *déduis*ons,
    déduisez, déduisent
  FC. déduir-
  PD. déduis-is
  PP. déduit (*avoir*)   il a déduit
  PsP. déduisant
  Sj. qu'il déduis-e

8. DEVOIR *owe, ought* §64

  Pr. dois, dois, doit; *dev*ons, devez,
    doivent
  FC. devr-
  PD. d-us
  PP. dû (*avoir*)   il a dû
  PsP. devant

  Sj. { qu'il doiv-e
      { que nous devions
      { que vous deviez
      { qu'ils doivent

9. DIRE *to say, to tell*

Pr. dis, dis, dit; *dis*ons, dites, disent
FC. dir-
PD. d-is
PP. dit (*avoir*)   il a dit
PsP. disant
Sj. qu'il dis-e
and contredire   *to contradict;* prédire
to predict.

13. FALLOIR *to be necessary* §31d

Pr. il faut (only form)
    il fallait (Imperfect)
FC. il faudr-a (F) -ait (C)
PD. il fallut
PP. il a fallu
Sj. qu'il faille

10. ENVOYER *to send*

Pr. envoie, envoies, envoie; *envoy-*
    ons, envoyez, envoient
FC. enverr-
PD. envoy-ai
PP. envoyé (*avoir*)   il a envoyé
PsP. envoyant

Sj. { qu'il envoi-e
     { que nous envoyions
     { que vous envoyiez

14. METTRE *to put* §56

Pr. mets, mets, met; *met*tons,
    mettez, mettent
FC. mettr-
PD. m-is
PP. mis (*avoir*)   il aura mis
PsP. mettant
Sj. qu'il mett-e
and admettre *to admit;* commettre *to
commit;* permettre *to permit;* remettre
to remit.

11. ÉTEINDRE *to extinguish*

Pr. éteins, éteins, éteint; *éteign*ons,
    éteignez, éteignent
FC. éteindr-
PD. éteign-is
PP. éteint (*avoir*)   ils avaient éteint
PsP. éteignant
Sj. qu'il éteign-e

15. MOURIR *to die*

Pr. meurs, meurs, meurt; *mour*ons,
    mourez, meurent
FC. mourr-
PD. mour-us
PP. mort (*être*)   il est mort
PsP. mourant

Sj. { qu'il meur-e
     { que nous mourions

12. FAIRE *to make, to do* §53

Pr. fais, fais, fait; *fais*ons, faites,
    font
FC. fer-
PD. f-is
PP. fait (*avoir*)   nous avons fait
PsP. faisant
Sj. qu'il fass-e

16. NAÎTRE *to be born*

Pr. nais, nais, naît; *nais*sons,
    naissez, naissent
FC. naîtr-
PD. naqu-is
PP. né (*être*)   elle est née
PsP. naissant
Sj. qu'il naiss-e
and renaître *to be reborn.*

17. OUVRIR *to open* §73

Pr. ouvre, ouvres, ouvre; *ouvr*ons,
  ouvrez, ouvrent
FC. ouvrir-
PD. ouvr-is
PP. ouvert (*avoir*) nous avons ouvert
PsP. ouvrant
  Sj. qu'il ouvr-e
and couvrir *to cover;* découvrir *to discover;* offrir *to offer;* souffrir *to suffer.*

18. PARAÎTRE *to appear*

Pr. parais, parais, paraît; *paraiss-
  ons,* paraissez, paraissent
FC. paraîtr-
PD. par-us
PP. paru (*avoir*)   il a paru
PsP. paraissant
  Sj. qu'il paraiss-e
and apparaître *to appear;* disparaître *to disappear;* reparaître *to reappear.*

19. PARTIR *to depart* §82

Pr. pars, pars, part; *part*ons,
  partez, partent
FC. partir-
PD. part-is
PP. parti (*être*) nous sommes partis
PsP. partant
  Sj. qu'il part-e
and repartir *to depart again.*

20. POUVOIR *to be able* §59

Pr. puis (peux), peux, peut;
  *pouv*ons, pouvez, peuvent
FC. pourr-
PD. p-us
PP. pu (*avoir*)   j'ai pu
PsP. pouvant
  Sj. qu'il puiss-e

21. PRENDRE *to take* §52

Pr. prends, prends, prend; *pren*ons,
  prenez, prennent
FC. prendr-
PD. pr-is
PP. pris (*avoir*)   il a pris
PsP. prenant
  Sj. qu'il prenn-e
    que nous prenions
and apprendre *to learn;* comprendre *to understand, to include;* entreprendre *to undertake;* reprendre *to take back;* surprendre *to surprise.*

22. PRODUIRE *to produce*

Pr. produis, produis, produit; *pro-
  duis*ons, produisez, produisent
FC. produir-
PD. produis -is
PP. produit (*avoir*)   ils ont produit
PsP. produisant
  Sj. qu'il produis-e
and conduire *to conduct;* construire *to construct;* déduire *to deduct;* détruire *to destroy;* introduire *to introduce;* reproduire *to reproduce;* traduire *to translate.*

23. RECEVOIR *to receive*

Pr. reçois, reçois, reçoit; *recev*ons,
  recevez, reçoivent
FC. recevr-
PD. reç-us
PP. reçu (*avoir*)   vous avez reçu
PsP. recevant

Sj. { qu'il reçoiv-e
     que nous recevions
     que vous receviez

and apercevoir *to perceive;* concevoir *to conceive;* devoir *to owe.*

24. SAVOIR *to know* §57

Pr. sais, sais, sait; *sav*ons, savez,
  savent
FC. saur-
PD. s-us
PP. su (*avoir*)   il avait su
PsP. sachant
  Sj. qu'il sach-e

25. SERVIR *to serve* §82

    Pr. sers, sers, sert; *serv*ons, servez,
       servent
    FC. servir-
    PD. serv-is
    PP. servi (*avoir*)   cela a servi
    PsP. servant
    Sj. qu'il **serv**-e

26. SORTIR *to go out* §82

    Pr. sors, sors, sort; *sort*ons, sortez,
       sortent
    FC. sortir-
    PD. sort-is
    PP. sorti (*être*)   elle est sortie
    PsP. sortant
    Sj. qu'il **sort**-e

27. SUIVRE *to follow*

    Pr. suis, suis, suit; *suiv*ons, suivez,
       suivent
    FC. suivr-
    PD. suiv-is
    PP. suivi (*avoir*)   il a suivi
    PsP. suivant
    Sj. qu'il **suiv**-e
and poursuivre *to pursue.*

28. TENIR *to hold* §37

    Pr. tiens, tiens, tient; *ten*ons, tenez,
       tiennent
    FC. tiendr-
    PD. tins, tins, tint; tînmes, tîntes,
       tinrent
    PP. tenu (*avoir*)   j'ai tenu
    PsP. tenant
    Sj. { qu'il **tienn**-e
       { que nous **ten**ions, etc.
and appartenir *to belong to;* contenir
to contain; entretenir *to maintain;*
maintenir *to maintain;* obtenir *to ob-*
tain; retenir *to retain, to remember;*
soutenir *to sustain.*

29. VALOIR *to be worth*

    Pr. vaux, vaux, vaut; *val*ons, valez,
       valent
    FC. vaudr-
    PD. val-us
    PP. valu (*avoir*)   il aurait valu
    PsP. valant
    Sj. { qu'il **vaill**-e
       { que nous **val**ions

30. VENIR *to come* §68

    Pr. viens, viens, vient; *ven*ons,
       venez, viennent
    FC. viendr-
    PD. vins, vins, vint; vînmes, vîntes,
       vinrent
    PP. venu (*être*)   elles sont venues
    PsP. venant
    Sj. { qu'il **vienn**-e
       { que nous **ven**ions
and convenir *to agree, to be appropri-*
ate; intervenir *to intervene;* prévenir
to warn; parvenir *to attain;* provenir
de *to stem from;* se souvenir de *to*
remember; revenir *to come back,* et al.

31. VOIR *to see* §58

    Pr. vois, vois, voit; *voy*ons, *voy*ez,
       voient
    FC. verr-
    PD. v-is
    PP. vu (*avoir*)   il a vu
    PsP. voyant

    Sj. { qu'il voi-e
         que nous voyions

and prévoir (except in FC: prévoir-),
to foresee.

32. VOULOIR *to want* §63

    Pr. veux,   veux,   veut;   *voul*ons,
       voulez, veulent
    FC. voudr-
    PD. voul-us
    PP. voulu (*avoir*)   il a voulu
    PsP. voulant

    Sj. { qu'il veuill-e
         que nous voulions

Special form: **veuillez** *Be so kind as
to . . .* (+ INFINITIVE)

IRREGULAR STEM INDEX

(For detailed instructions see page 108.)

This table can be used to identify irregular verbs even if the infinitive is not known. Symbols indicate the tenses for which each stem is used, as follows:

SYMBOL	TENSE	ENDINGS					
		je (1)	tu (2)	il (3)	nous (4)	vous (5)	ils (6)
Pr 1	Present	-s	-s	-t			
Pr 1x	Present	-x	-x	-t			
Pr 2	Present				-ons	-ez	
Pr 3	Present						-ent
Imperf.	Imperfect	-ais	-ais	-ait	-ions	-iez	-aient
C	Conditional	-ais	-ais	-ait	-ions	-iez	-aient
F	Future	-ai	-as	-a	-ons	-ez	-ont
PDi	Past Definite	-is	-is	-it	-îmes	-îtes	-irent
PDu	Past Definite	-us	-us	-ut	-ûmes	-ûtes	-urent
Sj 1	Present Subjunctive	-e	-es	-e			-ent
Sj 2	Present Subjunctive				-ions	-iez	
PP	Past Participle						

Where the word "Except" appears in parentheses, the exception is a spelling deviation within the tense indicated.

aill- (aller 1) *Sj 1* go(es), will go
aperçu (apercevoir 23) *PP* perceived, seen
connai- (connaître 2) *Pr 1* know(s)
connaiss- (connaître 2) *Pr 2, 3; Sj 1, 2* know; *Imperf.* knew
connaîtr- (connaître 2) *F* will know; *C* would know
connu (connaître 2) *PP* known
courr- (courir 4) *F* will run; *C* would run
couru (courir 4) *PP* run
cr- (croire 5) *PDu* believed

croi- (croire 5) *Pr 1, 3; Sj 1* believe(s)

croy- (croire 5) *Pr 2; Sj 2* believe; *Imperf.* believed, used to believe

cru (croire 5) *PP* believed

d- (dire 9) *PDi* said

d- (devoir 8) *PDu* had to, must have

décriv- (décrire 6) *Pr 2; Sj 1, 2* describe(s); *Imperf.* was describing

déduis- (déduire 7) *Pr 2; Sj1, 2* deduce(s); *PDi* deduced

dev- (devoir 8) *Pr 2; Sj 2* must, owe; *Imperf.* were to

devr- (devoir 8) *F* will have to; *C* would have to, ought to

dis- (dire 9) *Pr 2* (*Except* vous dites), *Pr 3* say; *Sj 1, 2* say, will say; *Imperf.* said, was saying, used to say

dit (dire 9) *PP* said

doi- (devoir 8) *Pr 1* must, owe

doiv- (devoir 8) *Pr 3; Sj 1* must, owe

dû (devoir 8) *PP* had to

e- (avoir) -us, -us, -ut, ûmes, -ûtes, -urent *PDu* had

écri- (écrire 6) *Pr 1* write(s)

écriv- (écrire 6) *Pr 2, 3; Sj 1, 2* write(s); *Imperf.* wrote, was writing; *PDi* wrote

enverr- (envoyer 10) *F* will send; *C* would send

envoi- (envoyer 10) *Pr 1, 3* (regular -er endings); *Sj 1* send(s), are sending

envoy- (envoyer 10) *Pr 2, Sj 2* send; *Imperf.* were sending, used to send

ét- (être) *Imperf.* was, were, used to be

f- (être) -us, -us, -ut, -ûmes, -ûtes, -urent *PDu* was (were)

f- (faire 12) -is, -is, -it, -îmes, -îtes, -irent *PDi* did, made, caused

fai- (faire 12) *Pr 1* do, make (§53)

fais- (faire 12) *Pr 2* (*Except* vous faites) make, are making, do, are doing; *Imperf.* used to make, used to do, were making, were doing.

fall- (falloir 13) il fallut *PD* it was necessary

fass- (faire 12) *Sj 1, 2* make, do; cause (sthg) to be done

faudr- (falloir 13) *F* il faudra it will be necessary; *C* il faudrait it would be necessary

fer- (faire 12) *F* will do, will make; *C* would do, would make

ir- (aller 1) *F* will go; *C* would go

m- (mettre 14) *PDi* put

met- (mettre 14) *Pr 1* (*Except* il met) put(s)

mett- (mettre 14) *Pr 2, 3; Sj 1, 2* put, are putting; *Imperf.* were putting, used to put

meur- (mourir) *Pr 1, 3; Sj 1* to be dying, dies

mis (mettre 14) *PP* put

mour- (mourir) *Pr 2; Sj 2* are dying; *Imperf.* was dying; *PDu* died

mourr- (mourir) *F* will die; *C* would die

nai- (naître 16) *Pr 1* (*Except* il naît) spring(s) from

naiss- (naître 16) *Pr 2, 3; Sj 1, 2* spring(s) from, is born; *Imperf.* was being born, was originating

naîtr- (naître 16) *F* will be born; *C* would be born

naqu- (naître 16) *PDi* was born

né (naître 16) *PP* born

offert (offrir 17) *PP* offered

ouvert (ouvrir 17) *PP* opened

p- (pouvoir 20) *PDu* was able, could

par- (paraître 18) *PDu* appeared

parai- (paraître 18) *Pr 1* (*except* il paraît) appear(s)

paraiss- (paraître 18) *Pr 2, 3; Sj 1, 2* appear(s); *Imperf.* were appearing, used to appear, appeared

peu- (pouvoir 20) *Pr 1x* can

peuv- (pouvoir 20) *Pr 3* can

pourr- (pouvoir 20) *F* will be able; *C* would be able, could

pouv- (pouvoir 20) *Pr 2* can; *Imperf.* used to be able, could

pr- (prendre 21) *PDi* took

pren- (prendre 21) *Pr 2; Sj 2* take, are taking; *Imperf.* were taking, used to take, took

prenn- (prendre 21) *Pr 3; Sj 1* take(s), are taking

pris (prendre 21) *PP* taken

produi- (produire 22) *Pr 1* produce(s)

produis- (produire 22) *Pr 2, 3; Sj 1, 2* produce(s); *Imperf.* were producing, used to produce, produced

pu (pouvoir 20) *PP* been able (§59)

pui- (pouvoir 20) *Pr 1* can (1st and 2nd pers. forms only)

puiss- (pouvoir 20) *Sj 1, 2* can, may be able, will be able

reç- (recevoir 23) *PDu* received

recev- (recevoir 23) *Pr 2; Sj 2* receive, are receiving; *Imperf.* were receiving, used to receive, received

recevr- (recevoir 23) *F* will receive; *C* would receive

reçoi- (recevoir 23) *Pr 1* receive(s)

reçoiv- (recevoir 23) *Pr 3; Sj 1* receive

s- (savoir 24) *PDu* knew

sach- (savoir 24) *Sj 1, 2* know(s), may know

sai- (savoir 24) *Pr 1* know(s); can (do sthg) [BEFORE INFINITIVE]

saur- (savoir 24) *F* will know, will be able; *C* would know, would be able

sav- (savoir 24) *Pr 2, 3* know(s), can; *Imperf.* used to know, knew, could

ser- (servir 25) *Pr 1* serve(s)

ser- (être) *F* will be; *C* would be

sor- (sortir 26) *Pr 1* leave(s), go(es) out; *with direct object* take(s) out

sort- (sortir 26) *Pr 2, 3* leave(s), go(es) out; *Imperf.*; *PDi; Sj 1, 2*

sui- (suivre 27) *Pr 1* follow(s)

suiv- (suivre 27) *Pr 2, 3; Sj 1, 2* follow(s); *Imperf.* used to follow etc.; *PDi* followed

ten- (tenir 28) *Pr 2; Sj 2* hold, are holding; *Imperf.* were holding, etc.

tenu (tenir 28) *PP* held

tien- (tenir 28) *Pr 1* hold(s), are holding

tiendr- (tenir 28) *F* will hold; *C* would hold

tienn- (tenir 28) *Pr 3; Sj 1* hold

tin- (tenir 28) -s, -s, -t, ^-mes, ^-tes, -rent *PD* held

v- (voir 31) *PDi* saw

vaill- (valoir 29) *Sj 1* is (are) worth

val- (valoir 29) *Pr 2, 3; Sj 2* are worth; *Imperf.* were worth; *PDu* were worth

vau- (valoir 29) *Pr 1x* is worth

vécu (vivre) *PP* lived

ven- (venir 30) *Pr 2; Sj 2* come, are coming; *Imperf.* were coming, used to come, came

venu (venir 30) *PP* (*with auxiliary* être) come

verr- (voir 31) *F* will see; *C* would see

veu- (vouloir 32) *Pr 1x* want(s)

veul- (vouloir 32) *Pr 3* want

veuill- (vouloir 32) *Sj 1* want(s), wish(es)

vien- (venir 30) *Pr 1* come(s); [*followed by* de + INF. have just]

viendr- (venir 30) *F* will come; *C* would come

vienn- (venir 30) *Pr 3; Sj 1* come, are coming

vin- (venir 30) -s, -s, -t,^ -mes,^ -tes, -rent *PD* came

voi- (voir 31) *Pr 1, 3; Sj 1* see(s)

voudr- (vouloir 32) *F* will want to; *C* would like to

voul- (vouloir 32) *Pr 2* want; *Imperf.* wanted; *PDu* wanted; *Sj 2* want

voy- (voir 31) *Pr 2; Sj 2* see; *Imperf.* saw

vu (voir 31) *PP* seen

NUMBERS

CARDINAL NUMBERS

1 un, une	15 quinze	70 soixante-dix
2 deux	16 seize	71 soixante et onze
3 trois	17 dix-sept	75 soixante-quinze
4 quatre	18 dix-huit	80 quatre-vingts
5 cinq	19 dix-neuf	81 quatre-vingt-un
6 six	20 vingt	90 quatre-vingt-dix
7 sept	21 vingt et un	91 quatre-vingt-onze
8 huit	22 vingt-deux	100 cent
9 neuf	30 trente	101 cent un
10 dix	31 trente et un	200 deux cents
11 onze	32 trente-deux	201 deux cent un
12 douze	40 quarante	1000 mille
13 treize	50 cinquante	1959 (*date*) mil neuf
14 quatorze	60 soixante	cent cinquante-neuf

Cardinal Numbers in Alphabetical Order

cent	100	mille	1000	quinze	15
cent un	101	mille un	1001	seize	16
cinq	5	milliard	billion	sept	7
cinquante	50	million	million	six	6
deux	2	neuf	9	soixante	60
deux cents	200	onze	11	soixante-dix	70
deux cent un	201	quarante	40	treize	13
dix	10	quatorze	14	trente	30
dix-huit	18	quatre	4	trois	3
dix-neuf	19	quatre-vingt-dix	90	un(e)	1
dix-sept	17	quatre-vingt-onze	91	vingt	20
douze	12	quatre-vingts	80	vingt et un	21
huit	8	quatre-vingt-un	81		

NOTES:

-aine added to a number indicates an approximate number:

une dizaine	about ten
une vingtaine	about twenty; a score

Decimals. In French the comma is used for a decimal:

$$3,1416 \qquad (\pi)$$

Period in Numbers. In numbers from 1,000 up, a period is used to separate thousand-groups:

15.000   fifteen thousand

A NOTE ON DICTIONARIES

Until you develop a wide personal vocabulary in French, a dictionary will be a necessary adjunct to your further reading. The selection of a dictionary to serve your purposes should be done with care, for dictionaries vary widely both in scope and preciseness of definitions. The first principle is to see that your dictionary is *large,* and that each word is not only defined, but used in several *examples.* Dictionaries which are short and which give only single word definitions are usually unsatisfactory to all but those having a good knowledge of the language already. *The less one knows of a language, the larger should be his dictionary.*

In addition to a French-English dictionary of large size and extensive definitions, it will be well to have a large English dictionary at hand. *Webster's International Dictionary,* unabridged, is recommended. Shorter editions do not contain a sufficient scope of technical words which are nearly identical in both French and English. However, a good desk dictionary may serve in the absence of an unabridged dictionary.

A good test for a dictionary is to open it to an entry requiring differentiation of meanings, and to examine the entry to determine whether adequate treatment is given that entry. In examining a dictionary for French, a good test word is *river.* Let us suppose we wanted to know the word to insert in the sentence, *"The Mississippi is a* **river.***"* Opening a typical small dictionary, we find:

> river   rivière   *n.f.*   fleuve   *n.m.*

Upon this basis we might select *rivière* because it *looks* like *"river,"* or because it is the first entry. In this case we would be quite wrong, and the dictionary is useless to the beginner, because it provides no basis for discerning that *fleuve* is correct for our problem.

Another dictionary gives the entry:

> river   rivière   *n.f.*; [large] fleuve   *n.m.*

This time we would be right in selecting *fleuve* for the Mississippi; but suppose we wanted to translate "Ohio River." Would *fleuve* be correct? Certainly the Ohio qualifies as "large." No, we would be wrong again, and this dictionary is eliminated.

A dictionary which may be considered adequate is *Mansion's Shorter French and English Dictionary* (D. C. Heath and Co., Boston), in which the entry for **river** is:

> river ['rivər] *s.* 1. Cours *m* d'eau; (*main r.*)
> fleuve *m;* (*small r.*) rivière *f.* **Down the**
> **river,** en aval. **Up the river,** en amont.
> **River port,** port fluvial. 2. Coulée *f.* (de
> lave, etc.); flot *m* (de sang.) 3. **Diamond**
> **of the finest river,** diamant de la plus belle

eau. **river-'bank,** *s.* Bord *m* de la rivière, du
fleuve; rive *f.* **river-'basin,** *s.* Bassin fluvial.
river-'bed, *s.* Lit *m* de rivière. **river-'head,**
s. source *f.*

This extensive article is an abridgment of the longer two-volume edition of the same work, which is recommended. Yet the differentiation between *rivière* and *fleuve* is still unsolved until we find in *Bellows' French Dictionary* the entry:

RIV'ER   *rivière;* [running into the sea] fleuve...

This distinction is what we needed: the Mississippi *runs into the sea:* it is **un fleuve,** whereas the Ohio is **une rivière,** since it does not run into the sea.

What is the basis for this distinction? French usage, determined (in a commonly accepted way) by reference to a standard French language dictionary such as LE NOUVEAU PETIT LAROUSSE ILLUSTRÉ (Librairie Larousse, Paris) in which this differentiation is immediately presented.

Technical Dictionaries. Dictionaries are often limited in scope, and must be selected for the type of reading contemplated. Thus *Mansion's,* upon examination, has a wide scope, and could be used for either literary or technical work; *Bellows',* an excellent dictionary for literary and conversational purposes, is not intended nor suitable for reading highly specialized scientific works. A list of specialized technical French-English dictionaries is appended to this chapter as a selected reference list.

Conclusions. (1) Use a large dictionary with explanations and examples, not one-word "equivalents"; (2) Use a dictionary suited to your subject in scope; (3) Have a large English dictionary at hand for technical terms which are cognates (words spelled identically, or nearly so, and having the same meaning in both languages).

A SELECTED LIST OF FRENCH DICTIONARIES

CUSSET, FRANCIS. *Vocabulaire technique.* Métallurgie, mines, électricité, mécanique, science. Paris: Editions Berger-Levrault, 1949.

DE VRIES, LOUIS. *French-English Science Dictionary.* New York: McGraw-Hill. (several editions).
   This dictionary is "for students in Agricultural, Biological, and Physical Sciences." Its definitions are of the one-word type. This is best suited to persons already conversant with grammatical material, and having a good knowledge of French. Its usefulness is limited to the fields indicated.

HOYER-KREUTER. *Dictionnaire Technologique.* New York: Ungar, 1944 (6th edition). 3 vols.
   A tri-lingual work in French, German, and English. Volume III is the French-English (and German) part which has the head-words in French. Complicated system.

KETTRIDGE, J. O. *French-English* (Vol. I), *English-French* (Vol. II) *Dictionary*. London: Routledge and Kegan Paul, Ltd., 1950. (2 vols.)

A superior, complete, and up-to-date technical dictionary. It covers the fields of Civil, Electrical, and Mining Engineering, Geology, Petrology, Mineralogy, Chemistry, Physics, and others. Volume I is French-English. If available in your library, this is an excellent reference work.

MANSION, J. E. *Harrap's Standard French and English Dictionary*. New York: Scribner; 1972. (2 vols.)

This dictionary is a definitive and current work, of reference value not only for technical and scientific subjects, but also for general reading in all fields, including literature. In two quarto volumes, of which Vol. I is the French-English part.

PATTERSON, A. M. *A French-English Dictionary for Chemists*. New York: John Wiley, 1921.

A small dictionary (about the same size as DE VRIES', *or about 7 x 5 x 1 inches) of limited scope, useful for chemistry and allied subjects.*

COMPREHENSION EXERCISES

Reading Comprehension Exercises: Answer the following questions.
Lohengrin, page 40

1. Identify the following:
   a. Elsa   b. Godefroi   c. Ortrude   d. Lohengrin
2. What specific crime was Elsa accused of?
3. What event at the end of the story proves her innocence?
4. Who was responsible, and in what way, for the disappearance of the alleged victim?
5. How was the trial of Elsa to be conducted?
6. Who appeared to assume Elsa's defense when nobody else would do so?
7. How did this defender arrive? How was he equipped?
8. Where had Elsa seen her defender before his actual appearance?
9. What promise was Elsa required to make to Lohengrin?
10. Whose influence caused her to break this promise?
11. What was the result of the breaking of this promise?
12. What is the importance of the swan which pulled the small boat?

De l'Éducation selon Rousseau et Pestalozzi, page 51
1. What did Pestalozzi study in depth?
2. How did a student learn under Pestalozzi's method?
3. In what way did Pestalozzi conduct his classes?
4. Why did students become restless under the old methods of instruction?
5. How did students respond under Pestalozzi's teaching?
6. Did Rousseau agree or disagree with Pestalozzi? Explain.

Quick Thinking, page 61
1. What unusual ability did the King pride himself upon?
2. What person in his kingdom appeared to be a rival in this ability?
3. How did the King intend to debunk this rival's claims?
4. What mechanism did the King arrange to disprove any prediction made by the astrologer?
5. When the astrologer answered the King's question, why did the King change his plans?
6. Was the King superstitious or not? Explain.

L'Encyclopédie: l'Autorité politique, page 78
1. Does authority of one individual over another exist in nature?
2. What other source of authority is there?
3. At what point does each type of authority surrender its power?

4. When is the overthrowing of authority justified on the part of the persons sub-
   jugated by it?
5. What was the political climate in 18th century France that would cause this article
   to appear subversive?

French Impressions of Developing America, page 85

1. According to de Tocqueville, how had Americans converted farming into an
   industry?
2. Did Americans, like Europeans, always settle down on a farm with the intention
   of keeping it and passing it on to their heirs? Explain.
3. What crops did de Tocqueville consider to be the most important in the South?
4. To what kind of crisis were Americans subject?

An Interview between Napoleon and the Pope, page 96

1. How did Napoleon treat this page boy, and what was the latter's reaction to the
   Emperor?
2. What does Renard say that shows his belief that Napoleon is merely "acting,"
   pretending to be a great man, and displaying ordinary vanity?
3. What evidence did Renard find on a table that proved the callousness and in-
   difference of the Emperor towards the common citizens?
4. Why did Renard hide, rather than leave the room where the interview was to
   take place?
5. How do Napoleon's physical actions contrast with those of the Pope?
6. What significance do you find in this contrast?
7. What evidently generous offer did Napoleon make the Pope?
8. What misstatement of fact caused the Pope to reply "Commediante!"?
9. In his rage, what disparaging remarks concerning the Pope's authority did Napoleon make?
10. What change in personality overtakes Napoleon when the Pope replies "Trage-
    diante!"?
11. In what way does Napoleon confirm Renard's opinion (Question 2) that the Em-
    peror is merely a vain and shallow actor?

Candide, page 114

1. Why was the name Candide appropriate for the main character of this selection?
2. What did the former servants suspect about Candide's origins?
3. Why had the Baron's sister refused to marry her suitor?
4. Describe the Baroness and her daughter, Cunégonde.
5. What humorous word does Voltaire invent to describe the academic field of
   Pangloss?
6. What evidence did Pangloss use to support his theory of "cause and effect"?
7. To whom was Candide attracted romantically?
8. What did Cunégonde happen upon one day? How did this encounter affect her
   relationship with Candide?
9. Why was Candid banished from the château of the Baron of Thunder-ten-tronckh?

10. What conclusions can be drawn about Voltaire's attitude towards:
    a. German petty nobility
    b. The German language
    c. New academic fields
    d. The theory of "cause and effect"
    e. The effect of ill-directed teaching

L'Entrée de Napoléon à Moscou, page 128

1. Who was Rostopschine, and what was his mission?
2. Before the imminent French occupation of Moscow, what did messengers tell the city's residents?
3. What measures were taken to prepare an unpleasant surprise for the French invaders?
4. Why did Rostophchine release all prisoners, and what instructions did he give them?
5. What did the French troops do when they came in sight of Moscow?
6. What reception did the Russian boyards give Napoleon at the gates?
7. When the French entered the city, what was the appearance of the streets?
8. What event caused Napoleon to leave the suburban residence and go to the Kremlin at two o'clock in the morning?
9. What made the Kremlin particularly unsafe at this time?
10. How did the French military personnel and servants react to the rumored mining of the Kremlin?
11. What escape route from the Kremlin was found to exist?
12. With the siege of what other city did Napoleon compare the burning of Moscow? Where was he when he made this retrospective comparison?

HINTS ON SIMPLIFYING TRANSLATION

1. **Idea Interrupters.** Such words as **d'abord, d'ailleurs, donc,** etc. occur in French sentences in places that may interrupt the main thought. In translation, place such words first in the sentence:

> L'ordre des opérations est **donc** le suivant:
> **Therefore** the order of operations is the following:

2. **Parenthetical Information.** Phrases set off by commas or parentheses may be skipped during the initial reading of the French in order not to lose the main thought. In the second reading, however, insert these phrases.

> La physique est essentiellement, **comme l'astronomie,** une science de mesures précises.
> (*First try*) Physics is essentially a science of precise measurements.
> (*Final*) Physics, **like astronomy,** is essentially a science of precise measurements.

Note also that in English translation, the word order is improved by placing *like astronomy* close to the subject.

3. **Missing Links.** In French, in a sentence with a prepositional phrase, you will often find that the direct object does not immediately follow its verb. In such cases, read your subject and verb, then move to the direct object, and finally to the prepositional phrase.

> Louis XVI **signa** avec les États-Unis un **traité de commerce.**
> Louis XVI **signed a trade agreement** with the United States.

When the verb *signed* is reached, you know that *something* had to be signed, and you must look ahead to find that direct object before continuing.

4. ***que* + Remote Noun Subject.** Remember to find the next independent noun structure when a clause begins with **qu'** or **que** followed by a verb. (Review Sec. 54c, page 79)

> Voilà le lion **qu'a tué M. Dubois.**
> There is the lion **that Mr. Dubois** killed.

If you fail to place a noun after **que** the meaning will be altered.

5. **ce qui** and **ce que** mean "what" most of the time.

6. **avec + NOUN** can sometimes be replaced by an adverb ending in -ly.

avec patience	patiently
avec bruit	noisily
avec enthousiasme	enthusiastically

7. **Idioms of High Frequency.** Be on the lookout for such idioms as:

venir de	(Sec. 69)	to have just
tenir à	(Sec. 37b)	to be eager to
se mettre à	(Sec. 56)	to begin to
avoir besoin de		to need
il y a		there is (are)
il y a [TIME]	(Sec. 67e)	[TIME] ago
il y a [TIME] que	(Sec. 67d)	for [TIME]

8. **Tricky Pairs**

ou / où	or / where, when
peut être / peut-être	can be / perhaps
a / à	has / to
soit ... soit	either ... or
ou ... ou	either ... or
d'une part ... d'autre part	on the one hand ... on the other hand
de ... à	from ... to

9. **même**

   (a) At the beginning of a sentence or clause: *Even*
      Même le roi...   *Even* the king...

   (b) Directly before a noun: *same*
      Le **même** professeur...The *same* teacher...

   (c) Directly after a noun: *very, itself, himself, herself*
      La théorie **même** est ridicule.   The theory *itself* is ridiculous.

   (d) Hyphenated to a disjunctive pronoun: *-self*
      Il l'a fait **lui-même.** He did it *himself.*

NAME .... SECTION .... DATE ....

    Print Last   *First*   *MI*

I. Translate the following vocabulary. After each item, indicate the gender and number by circling *m.* or *f.* (for masculine or feminine), and *s.* or *pl.* (for singular or plural). If the French noun is a false friend, place a dagger (†) after it.

		GENDER		NUMBER	
1.	la probabilité	*m.*	*f.*	*s.*	*pl.*
2.	le symbole	*m.*	*f.*	*s.*	*pl.*
3.	les lectures	*m.*	*f.*	*s.*	*pl.*
4.	le sentiment	*m.*	*f.*	*s.*	*pl.*
5.	la solidité	*m.*	*f.*	*s.*	*pl.*
6.	la densité	*m.*	*f.*	*s.*	*pl.*
7.	le tour	*m.*	*f.*	*s.*	*pl.*
8.	la théorie	*m.*	*f.*	*s.*	*pl.*
9.	les symboles	*m.*	*f.*	*s.*	*pl.*
10.	la réalité	*m.*	*f.*	*s.*	*pl.*

II. Translate the following phrases (noun-adjective groups), noting that the French word-order is (a) article, (b) noun, and (c) modifier. In translating, you must use the order (a)(c)(b) to achieve correct English order. Indicate gender and number in the parentheses.

1.	la théorie économique	( )
2.	les théories économiques	( )
3.	la bombe atomique	( )
4.	les collections complètes	( )
5.	le calcul différentiel	( )

6. .... le **mouvement** scientifique ( )

7. .... la **surface** verticale ( )

8. .... la **littérature** romantique ( )

9. .... la **côte** pacifique ( )

10. .... la **géographie** physique ( )

III. Use of Context for Determining Meaning. In the following exercise, translate the French words in boldface type. A *context* (meaning pattern) is given parenthetically in English to help you recall the appropriate meaning.

.... 1. (Our professor assigned us a long chapter as our) **lecture** (for tomorrow).

.... 2. (Houghton Mifflin is the) **éditeur** (of this book).

.... 3. (The study of weather is) **le but principal** (of the science of meteorology).

.... 4. (Pascal's principle can be demonstrated by a) **expérience simple.**

.... 5. (The Boulevard Saint-Michel is rather) **large.**

.... 6. (We are studying) **actuellement** (French vocabulary).

.... 7. (For greater) **commodité** (let's take our Cadillac).

.... 8. (I have to get to the campus early; I have a) **conférence** (in politics).

.... 9. (This situation has many) **inconvénients.**

.... 10. (I have a very small car) **car** (I am not rich).

IV. Discernment of English Style. While the definite article is generally written in French with each noun, it is not always necessary to use it in English. Read over your answers to question II above. In any cases in which the translation sounds better to you when *the* is omitted, put parentheses around this word.

NAME .... SECTION .... DATE ....
  Print Last   *First*   *MI*

I. Translate the following items, indicating number and gender by circling the appropriate symbols.

		GENDER		NUMBER	
1. .... le nez		*m.*	*f.*	*s.*	*pl.*
2. .... un journal		*m.*	*f.*	*s.*	*pl.*
3. .... des journaux		*m.*	*f.*	*s.*	*pl.*
4. .... le niveau		*m.*	*f.*	*s.*	*pl.*
5. .... le gaz		*m.*	*f.*	*s.*	*pl.*
6. .... des gaz		*m.*	*f.*	*s.*	*pl.*
7. .... le fils		*m.*	*f.*	*s.*	*pl.*
8. .... les nations		*m.*	*f.*	*s.*	*pl.*
9. .... des faits		*m.*	*f.*	*s.*	*pl.*
10. .... un animal		*m.*	*f.*	*s.*	*pl.*

II. Prepositional Phrase Drill. Underline the preposition in each phrase. Place parentheses around the entire phrase. Translate.

   Example: sous un poids énorme

   Answer: (<u>sous</u> un poids énorme) under an enormous weight

1. par l'action d'un courant électrique ....

2. sous des influences externes ....

3. sur un principe physique ....

4. à côté d'un hôpital important ....

5. derrière des autobus ....

6. dans des gaz dangereux ....

7. sous des poids cylindriques ....

III. Meaning in Context. Translate the French words in **boldface** type, taking into account the context given in English. Decide, as part of the problem, whether to include words like *the* and *some* in your final translation.

.... 1. (There must be) **des moyens** (of solving this problem).

.... 2. **Des moyens** (can always be found).

.... 3. (There are) **des raisons** (for our tremendous success).

.... 4. (Did Napoleon have) **des choix** (of strategy at Moscow)?

.... 5. (The farmer keeps) **des animaux** (in the barn).

.... 6. (I very much enjoy drinking) **le café.**

.... 7. (In New Orleans' French quarter) **les cafés** (stay open all night).

.... 8. (Oisette Murphée had) **des yeux** (of a beautiful blue).

.... 9. **Les yeux** (of Texas are upon you).

IV. Check the correct plural of the boldface word, and place the letter designating it in the space provided:

.... 1. **un animal**   (a) les animals   (b) des animaux   (c) les animaux

.... 2. **un gaz**   (a) des gaz   (b) les gaz   (c) des gazes

.... 3. **le fait**   (a) des faits   (b) le faits   (c) les faits

.... 4. **un œil**   (a) des œils   (b) les œix   (c) des yeux

.... 5. **une théorie** (a) les théories   (b) des théories   (c) unes théories

NAME .... SECTION .... DATE ....
    Print Last   *First*   *MI*

I. Adjective Identification, and Translation of noun-adjective groups

In each item (1) underline the adjective (2) place parentheses around the noun-adjective group (including the article), and (3) translate. Indicate gender and number as usual.

NOTE: Despite the general rule in §11, there are times when adjectives are placed before the noun — for emphasis usually. One or two of these have been included in this exercise. See if you can spot them.

		GENDER, NUMBER	
1.	une façade gothique	(	)
2.	l'opinion publique	(	)
3.	le rayonnement cosmique	(	)
4.	des émulsions photographiques	(	)
5.	la fameuse expérience	(	)
6.	une série géométrique	(	)
7.	des concepts fondamentaux	(	)
8.	les faits précis	(	)

II. Identification and Translation of Prepositional Phrases

A prepositional phrase is simply a noun-adjective group with a preposition prefixed. The following items have at least two prepositional phrases.

Instructions: (1) Underline each preposition, (2) place parentheses around the prepositional phrases, and (3) translate.

1. par un système simple de l'analyse chimique ....

....

2. des torrents de métal liquéfié ....

....

3. dans la capitale de l'ennemi mortel ....

....

4. par un courant alternatif de haute fréquence ....

....

5. sans un nombre important d'électrons ....

....

6. par la théorie de la réfraction ....

....

III. Identification of Noun-Adjective Groups and of Prepositional Phrases

Place parentheses around noun-adjective groups and around prepositional phrases. Underline prepositions. Translate.

1. avec la forme et [and] la proximité des continents ....

....

2. les bayous de la Louisiane ....

3. sur une partie des côtes de la Russie méridionale ....

....

4. de la théorie des mouvements des planètes ....

....

5. le centre exact d'un système planétaire ....

....

6. l'énorme talent d'un architecte célèbre ....

7. le plan de la façade de la cathédrale de Saint-Pierre à Rome ....

....

....

NAME .... SECTION .... DATE ....
     Print Last   *First*   *MI*

8. la science des nombres et des quantités en général ....

....

9. une conversation intéressante avec les officiers de l'armée de Napoléon ....

....

....

10. par la lecture incessante de la littérature politique et historique ....

....

....

NAME .... SECTION .... DATE ....
    Print Last   *First*   *MI*

I. Noun-Adjective Groups. Modifiers in both preceding and following positions. Translate into good English.

1. .... plusieurs grands **bâtiments**

2. .... beaucoup de **théories** intéressantes

3. .... assez de **pression** verticale

4. .... trop de longues **expériences**

5. .... la symphonie "fantastique" de Berlioz.

6. .... cinq mauvais **résultats**

7. .... Einstein: sa **théorie** de la relativité

II. Drill on *des, du, de la,* and *de l'*

All these forms may be (a) translated as *some,* (b) omitted, but with the word "some" understood, or (c) translated *of the.* Which of the possible meanings is correct in the contexts of the sentences below? Translate words in **boldface** type.

1. (The sides) **des maisons** (are constructed of glass). ....

2. (There are) **d'excellents musiciens** (on our faculty). ....

3. (The volume) **des gaz** (we studied is variable). ....

4. (We enjoyed hearing) **de la musique baroque.** ....

5. (Please give me) **du café.** ....

6. (We are speaking) **du but** (which we want to attain). ....

7. (We are concerned) **du but** (which we want to attain). ....

8. (We need) **du papier.** ....

9. (The surface) **du papier** (is rough). ....

10. (A measurement) de l'énergie (is being made). ....

11. (Future production of electricity will require) de l'énergie nucléaire. ....

III. Possessive Adjective Drill

Translate the words in boldface type:

1. Einstein: **sa** théorie de la conservation de l'énergie ....

....

2. Madame Curie: **sa** théorie de la radio-activité ....

....

3. Einstein et Curie: **leurs** théories scientifiques ....

....

4. Mozart: **ses opéras comiques** ....

....

5. Madame Curie: **ses contributions** à la science ....

....

6. Haydn: **sa symphonie «militaire»** ....

....

7. uranium: **son poids atomique** ....

....

8. les architectes: **leur dessein complet** ....

....

9. l'université: **ses bâtiments magnifiques** ....

....

10. le professeur: **ses recherches** ....

NAME .... SECTION .... DATE ....

    Print Last   *First*   *MI*

I. Past Participles used as Adjectives

Underline all past participles. Translate the entire phrase:

1. une particule accélérée ....

2. leur prisonnier condamné ....

3. son échantillon composé ....

4. des phénomènes isolés ....

5. moins de surfaces unies ....

6. des influences compliquées ....

7. une bonne bibliothèque est établie ....

NEXT: You have underlined past participles. Some of those you have underlined consist of a basic past participle, *plus* **-e, -s,** or **-es** for agreement. (§21b). Separate the *pp.* from the agreement letters by a diagonal: e.g., **finie > fini/e.**

II. Past Participles. Translate:

1. C'est une petite particule qui est accélérée. ....

....

2. Un miroir est une surface unie. ....

3. Une jeune princesse est accusée d'un crime. ....

....

4. La probabilité est représentée par une fraction. ....

....

5. Ravel a bien orchestré *Tableaux d'une exposition* de Moussorgski. ....

....

III. Sentence Analysis

Visualization of structure is very important. We will use the following drill to help identify the important parts of a sentence. Every sentence has a SUBJECT (main noun) and a VERB (predicate, indicating action). In the following sentences (1) underline the SUBJECT with one line, and the VERB with two lines, (2) place parentheses around all other noun-adjective groups and prepositional phrases. (Note that the VERB will not be within any set of parentheses. The SUBJECT cannot be in a prepositional phrase.)

Example: Ce bâtiment magnifique à Paris est bâti en béton armé.
(Ce bâtiment magnifique) (à Paris) est bâti (en béton armé).

1. La sociologie est une science moderne. [*Mark this line*]

.... [*Translation*]

2. L'oxygène existe dans l'air et dans la constitution des végétaux et des animaux.

.... [*Translation*]

....

3. Les mathématiciens classent l'algèbre avec les mathématiques pures.

.... [*Translation*]

....

4. La surface du globe est composée de grandes masses de terre et d'eau.

.... [*Translation*]

....

5. La cathédrale de Notre-Dame est située dans l'île de la Cité.

.... [*Translation*]

6. La capitale de la France est située sur la Seine.

.... [*Translation*]

7. Un son qui rencontre un obstacle est réfléchi en forme d'écho.

.... [*Translation*]

8. La mémoire est nécessaire pour les opérations de la raison.

.... [*Translation*]

NAME .... SECTION .... DATE ....
     Print Last   *First*   *MI*

I. Noun-Adjective Groups Including an Adverb

Translate into good English:

1. un globe à **peu près** sphérique ....

2. des orbites **très** allongées ....

3. des surfaces **plus ou moins** verticales ....

4. un animal **peu** féroce ....

5. une impression **assez** vague ....

6. une température **légèrement** réduite ....

7. une histoire **beaucoup trop** longue ....

8. une matière **fortement** radioactive ....

9. une petite blonde **très** intelligente ....

10. leur bibliothèque **partiellement** climatisée [*air-conditioned*] ....

....

II. Prepositional Phrases used as Attributes

Place parentheses around prepositional phrases; translate:

1. aux maisons en brique ....

2. des animaux à quatre pattes ....

3. un bateau à vapeur ....

4. cet homme à cheveux gris ....

5. la salle de lecture dans la bibliothèque ....

6. des planchers de béton armé ....

7. une Cadillac en or massif ....

III. Sentence Drill.

Translate.

1. Plusieurs gaz composent l'air atmosphériquè de la terre. ....

....

2. Des vibrations résultent de la compression de l'air. ....

....

3. Le fait le plus important dans ce cas est difficile à expliquer. ....

....

4. Le drame de l'opéra *Lohengrin* par Richard Wagner porte un caractère uni-

versellement intelligible. ....

....

....

5. La géométrie est une des diverses branches des mathématiques pures. ....

....

6. Le gouvernement des États-Unis d'Amérique a la forme démocratique. ....

....

7. Le personnage central de la trilogie *U.S.A.* de Dos Passos est un Américain

typique. ....

....

....

8. La machine à calculer inventée par Blaise Pascal facilite le travail [*work*]

mathématique. ....

....

....

9. Actuellement les architectes de Paris bâtissent des habitations très modernes. ....

....

NAME .... SECTION .... DATE ....
  Print Last   *First*   *MI*

I. Subject Pronoun Drill

Translate the words in boldface type, taking into account the antecedent of the subject pronoun as shown in lighter face type.

1. la lumière: **elle parcourt l'air** :...

2. la dame: **elle finit la lecture** ....

3. le général: **il présente son plan** ....

4. les généraux: **ils présentent leur plan** ....

5. les nations: **elles forment l'O.N.U.** [*U.N.*] ....

6. l'événement: **il est arrivé** ....

7. la structure: **elle est examinée** ....

8. **on exécute la musique** ....

II. Reflexive Verb Drill ($§27$)

Instructions: (1) place parentheses around noun-adjective groups and prepositional phrases, (2) underline the complete reflective verb, and (3) translate the sentences.

1. Ces règles se déduisent des données. ....

....

2. Le général en chef se trouve à Paris. ....

....

3. Ces phénomènes s'observent facilement. ....

....

í. Les rayons lumineux se réfractent. ....

....

5. Les livres se composent de pages imprimées. ....

....

6. Le chimiste s'occupe d'une nouvelle expérience. ....

7. Napoléon et son état-major se trouvent au Caire. ....

....

8. Le son se produit dans l'air. ....

9. L'extraction de l'or s'effectue par des méthodes primitives. ....

....

10. Le thorium 233 se transforme en protactinium 233. ....

....

III. Sentences Containing *dont*-phrases (§28)

Enclose the *dont*-phrase in parentheses. Translate the sentences into excellent English.

1. La planète **dont** le satellite est la lune s'appelle la Terre. ....

....

2. Le périscope d'un sous-marin est un tube **dont** la longueur est de 12 mètres.

....

....

3. La théorie économique **dont** on examine la structure ne paraît guère solide.

....

....

4. Les animaux **dont** nous parlons ne sont pas distribués uniformément sur la surface

du globe. ....

....

....

NAME .... SECTION .... DATE ....
        Print Last   *First*   *MI*

5. Les gaz principaux **dont** l'air se compose sont l'oxygène et l'azote. ....

....

6. Les données **dont** il examine la valeur ne sont pas exactes. ....

....

7. Les théories **dont** le professeur parle se trouvent dans ce livre. ....

....

8. Cette locomotive **dont** les moteurs sont électriques est énorme. ....

....

NAME .... SECTION .... DATE ....
      Print Last   *First*   *MI*

I. Larger Noun-Adjective Groups

Underline the noun, and translate the phrase.

1. une nouvelle théorie physique ....

2. un autre gaz combustible ....

3. la même surface brillante ....

4. la littérature américaine actuelle ....

5. une autre question difficile mais importante ....

6. leur nouvelle expérience partiellement complétée ....

7. d'autres jeunes officiers inexpérimentés ....

8. son université célèbre et respectée ....

II. Participle-Prepositional Phrase Linkage Drill

Place parentheses around noun-adjective groups and prepositional phrases. If there is a linkage required between a participle and a following prepositional phrase, mark the link with an arrow. Translate.

1. un grand bâtiment orienté au nord ....

....

2. le disque solaire éclipsé par la lune ....

....

3. la totalité des faits observés ....

4. la totalité des faits observés par ces physiciens ....

....

5. huit nouveaux échantillons examinés en détail par ces messieurs ....

....

6. trois opérations compliquées par des difficultés mécaniques ....

....

7. des cylindres destinés à la purification de l'eau ....

....

8. plusieurs lois promulguées par le corps législatif ....

....

9. quelques résultats intéressants obtenus par les chercheurs* à Yale ....

....

10. la limite fixée à un maximum de 100 ou 125 étudiants par année ....

....

III. Infinitives and Impersonal Verbs
Underline impersonal verbs. Translate the sentences.

1. Il faut étudier pour réussir à l'école.* ....

....

2. Charles commence à étudier sans regarder les autres. ....

....

3. Il est difficile d'expliquer cette nouvelle méthode. ....

....

4. Il faut commencer maintenant. ....

5. Après avoir observé ce fait, il faut préparer un nouveau plan. ....

....

6. Il est trop tard pour commencer à étudier après être arrivé à l'examen final.

....

*Vocabulary: **II 9. chercheur** researcher; **III 1. réussir** to succeed; **école** school

NAME .... SECTION .... DATE ....
    Print Last   *First*   *MI*

7. Il paraît que l'air se compose de plusieurs gaz. ....

....

8. Il importe qu'on exécute la musique avec une certaine précision. ....

....

9. La nuit se fait. ....

....

NAME .... SECTION .... DATE ....
　　　　Print Last　　　　*First*　　　*MI*

I. Negation Drill

Underline both negative elements (**ne** and **pas,** for example) in each sentence, and translate.

1. Ces vaisseaux ne contiennent pas d'eau. ....

....

2. Aucun professeur n'observe suffisamment la vraie intelligence des étudiants.

....

3. Les fils de l'Arabe n'ont que dix-sept chameaux. ....

....

4. L'aîné des trois fils ne retient que huit animaux. ....

....

5. Les derviches ne refusent jamais leurs services à personne. ....

....

6. Rien d'extraordinaire n'arrive maintenant. ....

....

7. Les trois jeunes hommes ne semblent plus mécontents. ....

....

8. Il n'y a pas encore d'hélicoptère atomique. ....

....

9. Il ne reste que sept expériences bio-chimiques à faire. ....

....

10. Ce jeune homme n'est guère responsable de cet accident. ....

....

II. Drill on *tenir** and its compounds

Underline the verb, place parentheses around structural groups, and translate.

1. Obtenons un échantillon de cette matière. ....

....

2. Nous tenons à visiter le Louvre à Paris. ....

....

3. Le professeur tient à parler français dans la classe. ....

....

4. Pendant la durée de l'expérience il faut maintenir une température constante.

....

....

5. L'azote n'entretient jamais la combustion. ....

....

III. Essential Vocabulary

Translate the word in **boldface** type.

.... 1. Les satellites accompagnent une planète. **Or,** la lune accompagne la Terre. La lune est donc un satellite.

.... 2. **D'après** la théorie de Bohr. . . .

.... 3. **En outre,** Voltaire détestait Rousseau.

.... 4. Candide aime la belle Cunégonde **à cause de** sa beauté.

.... 5. Il faut **surtout** éviter de répéter des fautes.

.... 6. **Enfin** Lohengrin monte dans la nacelle pour partir.

.... 7. Cette figure géométrique n'a que trois côtés; c'est **donc** un triangle.

NAME .... SECTION .... DATE ....
    Print Last   *First*   *MI*

I. Verb Recognition Drill

Examine the following verbs. Following the rule for identification, determine the tense and check whether Present, Future, or Conditional in the space provided. Then give appropriate translations. (In the case of the Present Tense, *two* translations are required.)

Pr   F   C   TRANSLATION

( ) ( ) ( )   1. nous étudions   ....

( ) ( ) ( )   2. elle réfléchirait   ....

( ) ( ) ( )   3. vous serez   ....

( ) ( ) ( )   4. ils obtiendront   ....

( ) ( ) ( )   5. j'arriverai   ....

( ) ( ) ( )   6. tu arrives   ....

( ) ( ) ( )   7. ils bâtissent   ....

( ) ( ) ( )   8. nous bâtirons   ....

( ) ( ) ( )   9. ils choisissent   ....

( ) ( ) ( ) 10. elles choisiraient   ....

( ) ( ) ( ) 11. ils vendent   ....

( ) ( ) ( ) 12. il maintiendra   ....

( ) ( ) ( ) 13. vous finiriez   ....

( ) ( ) ( ) 14. nous entrons   ....

( ) ( ) ( ) 15. nous entrerons   ....

IN THE FOLLOWING VERBS, ANALYZE THE AUXILIARY ONLY (NOT THE PAST PARTICIPLE) BUT TRANSLATE THE WHOLE VERB

( ) ( ) ( ) 16. nous avons navigué ....

( ) ( ) ( ) 17. il aura parlé ....

( ) ( ) ( ) 18. elle serait arrivée ....

( ) ( ) ( ) 19. il aurait examiné ....

( ) ( ) ( ) 20. vous auriez préparé ....

( ) ( ) ( ) 21. il sera allé ....

II. Sentence Analysis

Underline all verbs. Enclose structural groups in parentheses. Translate.

1. Nous examinerons le caractère des différents ordres de l'architecture. ....

....

2. Je terminerai ici mon explication des moyens employés pour la circulation de

l'air dans ce bâtiment. ....

....

3. Aucun homme mortel ne trouvera la solution du problème de l'univers. ....

....

4. Les deux soldats dans la grande salle du palais attendront le signal du roi. ....

....

5. Il y a un procédé qui donnera des résultats satisfaisants. ....

....

6. Je désire examiner les données et le rapport à la fois. ....

....

7. Le nouveau sous-marin utilisera une pile atomique à neutrons lents. ....

....

8. Quand nous visiterons le Louvre, nous chercherons le tableau qui s'appelle

La Joconde. ....

....

NAME .... SECTION .... DATE ....
     Print Last   *First*   *MI*

I. Imperfect Tense Drill (§43)

Give three translations in order of preference:

1. **il examinait** (a)........................ (b)........................ (c)........................

2. **il donnait** (a)........................ (b)........................ (c)........................

3. **nous préparions** (a)........................ (b)........................ (c)........................

4. **vous finissiez** (a)........................ (b)........................ (c)........................

5. **ils se composaient de** (a) ....

   (b) .... (c) ....

6. **elle obtenait** (a)........................ (b)........................ (c)........................

7. **on remarquait** (a)........................ (b)........................ (c)........................

8. **il était** (a)........................ (b)........................ (c)........................

9. **il se trouvait** (a)........................ (b)........................ (c)........................

10. **il arrivait** (a)........................ (b)........................ (c)........................

   [*second meaning*] (a)........................ (b)........................ (c)........................

11. **il se lavait** (a)........................ (b)........................ (c)........................

12. **je tenais à** (a)........................ (b)........................ (c)........................

NEXT: If any of the possible translations should be ruled out because they sound peculiar in English, strike them out with a single horizontal line.

II. Tense Elimination Drill (§42)

Using the three-step method of general identification of time indicated by a verb, examine the following forms. The three steps are represented by the three sets of parentheses in the left margin. If a step fails, mark that step "x"; if it succeeds, place a check mark (√) in the parentheses under the number of that step. Then translate into English.

211

PRESENT	FUTURE-COND.	PAST	
:-:	:-:	:-:	
1	2	3	

NOTE: If the form contains a past participle, underline it, but analyze *only the auxiliary verb* according to the steps.

( ) ( ) ( ) 1. nous **examinâmes** ....

( ) ( ) ( ) 2. ils **étaient** ....

( ) ( ) ( ) 3. il **aura** ....

( ) ( ) ( ) 4. vous **admettrez** ....

( ) ( ) ( ) 5. on **divisera** ....

( ) ( ) ( ) 6. elles **observèrent** ....

( ) ( ) ( ) 7. Napoléon **arriva** ....

( ) ( ) ( ) 8. il **était** ....

( ) ( ) ( ) 9. il **faudra** partir ....

( ) ( ) ( ) 10. nous **voudrions** ....

( ) ( ) ( ) 11. ils **préparent** ....

( ) ( ) ( ) 12. vous **finîtes** ....

( ) ( ) ( ) 13. il a **donné** ....

( ) ( ) ( ) 14. j'avais **parlé** ....

( ) ( ) ( ) 15. j'ai **parlé** ....

( ) ( ) ( ) 16. j'aurais **parlé** ....

( ) ( ) ( ) 17. il aura **obtenu** ....

( ) ( ) ( ) 18. il **obtiendrait** ....

( ) ( ) ( ) 19. il avait **obtenu** ....

( ) ( ) ( ) 20. il y **aura** ....

NAME .... SECTION .... DATE ....
    Print Last   *First*   *MI*

I. Object Pronoun Drill (§§45, 46)

Translate the following fragments containing object pronouns (shown in **boldface** type):

1. la maison: nous **l'**avons bâtie ....

2. le professeur: je **lui** parle ....

3. la dame: je **lui** parle ....

4. les tableaux: vous **les** regardez ....

5. l'expérience: il **l'**a terminée ....

6. les officiers: elle **leur** parlait ....

7. la table: nous **la** désirons ....

8. la leçon: nous **la** détestons ....

9. le livre: ils **le** regardaient ....

10. le colonel: vous **le** trouverez ....

II. Double Object Pronouns (§47)

Translate the entire phrase in each item. Underline the two object pronouns to show that you can identify them. (Do not translate the words in parentheses, which are there only to serve as *antecedents:* i.e., to show what the pronouns refer to.)

1. (le fils, le livre) **Je le lui donne.** ....

....

2. (la dame, le livre) **Je le lui donne.** ....

....

3. (les soldats, les livres) **Nous les leur donnerons.** ....

....

4. (les soldats, l'auto) **Nous la leur donnerons.** ....

....

5. (la dame, l'auto) **Nous la lui donnâmes.** ....

....

6. (le livre) **Nous vous le donnions.** ....

....

7. (les livres) **Vous nous les aviez donnés.** ....

....

8. (les résultats) **Ils me les rapporteront.** ....

....

9. (la conclusion) **Ne me la rapportez pas!** ....

....

10. (l'histoire) **Racontez-la-leur.** ....

....

III. Translation Exercise

Translate the following paragraph into English. Remember the principles upon which your translation will be judged: (1) it must **sound** like good, current English, with no peculiar word order or outlandish expressions; (2) it must **convey all the ideas** of the French passage, omitting nothing and adding nothing (3) it must **retain the verb tenses** of the French except when a change is absolutely necessary to make the English correct.

(Use a separate sheet, and double-space.)

La Méthode d'éducation de Pestalozzi

Pestalozzi explique ainsi l'idée fondamentale de son système: «La nature présente les objets sans ordre, au hasard; l'éducation doit tendre à régulariser l'influence de la nature, et à continuer les premières intuitions dans un enchaînement complet et gradué.» Il désire qu'on fixe toujours dans l'esprit tous les points élémentaires avant d'arriver à l'ensemble; et il tient à fortifier les facultés intellectuelles. Son système se place parmi les premiers qui combinent les lettres avec les sciences et les arts usuels; son but était de rendre à l'homme, dégradé par les travaux manuels ou par la misère, sa dignité native.

NAME .... SECTION .... DATE ....
    Print Last   *First*   *MI*

I. Comparisons (§50)

Each of the sentences in this exercise contains a comparison. Underline the two comparative terms (the second of which is always qu[e]), and translate the sentences.

1. Alphonse est aussi intelligent que Téléphone. ....

....

2. La pyramide de Chéops est beaucoup plus grande que celle du pharaon Mykérinos,

roi d'Égypte de la IVe dynastie. ....

....

3. L'eau contient plus d'hydrogène que d'oxygène. ....

....

4. La terre est une planète qui est moins grande que Saturne. ....

....

5. Aujourd'hui il y a plus de locomotives électriques que de locomotives à vapeur.

....

6. Il y a autant de grands bâtiments à Houston qu'à Dallas. ....

....

II. Present Participles and Infinitives (§49, 31)

Translate the words in **boldface** type, taking into account the context.

.... 1. Dupré s'est coupé au doigt **en préparant** cet appareil.

.... 2. **Sachant** les faits, le général abandonna le terrain.

.... 3. **En disant** bonjour, il s'inclina profondément.

.... 4. Il a appris le français **en étudiant** ses leçons.

.... 5. Le nouvel élève entra **sans parler.**

.... 6. Le professeur parlait français **en regardant** le pauvre Charles.

.... 7. **Tout en chantant** l'actrice expira; c'est comme ça qu'on agit dans les opéras.

.... 8. **En revenant pour hanter** les êtres vivants, l'esprit d'une personne morte gagne le nom de *revenant*.

.... 9. **En ne faisant rien** nous apprenons à **mal faire**.

III. *Celui* (§51)

Translate the words in **boldface** type.

.... 1. cette constatation et **celle de Bohr**.

.... 2. ce livre et **celui de Mallarmé**.

.... 3. ces événements et **ceux d'hier** [*yesterday*]

.... 4. le livre de Bohr et celui d'Oppenheimer; nous avons discuté **celui-là**.

IV. *Faire** and *Prendre**

Translate.

1. L'astrologue faisait semblant de réfléchir pendant quelques moments. ....

....

....

2. Il fait beau; le soleil brille. ....

....

3. Napoléon fit tout son possible pour vaincre les Russes. ....

....

4. Comprenez-vous l'importance du travail de Cuvier et de Lavoisier? ....

....

5. Le roi fut bien surpris quand il apprit ce que l'astrologue avait à lui dire.

....

NAME .... SECTION .... DATE ....
     Print Last   *First*   *MI*

I. Inverted Word Order (§54). Translate:

1. Voici la théorie qu'a présentée M. Darwin dans son livre *De l'origine des*

   espèces: . . . .

   ....

   ....

2. Ne comprenez-vous pas l'intention de Richardson en écrivant *Pamela?*

   ....

3. Le roi faisait-il semblant de dormir quand l'astrologue entra? ....

   ....

4. Peut-être pourrons-nous aller à Mars à l'avenir au moyen d'une fusée.

   ....

   ....

5. Comment l'astrologue a-t-il su que le roi avait l'intention de le tuer en le faisant
   jeter par la fenêtre?

   ....

   ....

6. Le corps simple qu'a trouvé Berzélius en 1829 s'appelle le *thorium.*

   ....

7. Les symphonies qu'ont composées Haydn et Mozart sont du style qu'on appelle
   aujourd'hui *classique.*

   ....

   ....

II. Faire (*faire*) Construction (§55)

Identify the **faire** (*faire*) construction by placing a heavy underline beneath the inflected form of faire and the following infinitive. Translate the sentences.

1. Pendant la réunion nous ferons voir le nouvel appareil aux physiciens.

   ....

   ....

2. Dans *Micromégas* Voltaire fait remarquer qu'il est très difficile pour un historien de ne rapporter que les faits.

   ....

   ....

3. J'ai besoin de cette machine; je la ferai transporter dans l'autre laboratoire cet après-midi.

   ....

   ....

4. En entrant dans la classe le professeur dit bonjour aux élèves; puis il leur fait traduire des phrases françaises en anglais.

   ....

   ....

5. Ce monsieur est malade; faites venir le médecin immédiatement!

   ....

III. Sentence Drill: *mettre*, savoir*, pouvoir*, voir**

1. Jacques sait danser, mais il ne peut pas; il lui faut rester à la maison.

   ....

2. Lawrence et Livingston mirent quelques années à perfectionner le cyclotron.

   ....

3. Les officiers de l'armée française ont vu la destruction de Moscou par le feu.

   ....

NAME .... SECTION .... DATE ....

     Print Last   *First*   *MI*

I. Write the appropriate translation for the word(s) in **boldface** type in the space provided, giving due consideration to the context of the sentence.

.... 1. Supposons qu'il y a deux gaz **auxquels** il faut ajouter un troisième.

.... 2. Voilà la méthode **dont** il a parlé.

.... 3. Prenons un événement **duquel** la probabilité est connue.

.... 4. Examinons le centre **auquel cette force** est dirigée.

.... 5. Voyons **en quoi** consiste l'enseignement médical.

.... 6. Pour bien connaître les choses, il faut **en** savoir le détail.

.... 7. L'animal se libère **en** abandonnant le bras qui est pris.

.... 8. **En** tout cas, ces faits nous suffiront.

.... 9. On a une urne; la probabilité d'**en tirer** une boule blanche peut être calculée.

.... 10. L'air est indispensable aux êtres vivants; **en outre** il est le véhicule du son.

II. Write the most common translation for each of the following essential words:

1. .... souvent   6. .... ensuite

2. .... plusieurs   7. .... jusqu'à

3. .... presque   8. .... ainsi

4. .... cependant   9. .... surtout

5. .... bientôt   10. .... au lieu de

III. Supplemental Auxiliaries (§60). Translate:

1. On **doit assurer** aux producteurs français un prix de l'énergie électrique comparable à celui à l'étranger. ....

....

2. Les examens psychotechniques ont pour objet de déterminer les aptitudes intellectuelles et techniques des recrues de l'armée; au moyen de ces tests on **peut éliminer** les personnes sans capacité. ....

....

....

....

3. Nous **allons** maintenant **déterminer** l'élasticité de ce coupon d'acier [*steel*].

....

4. On ne **peut** guère **réaliser** une production télévisée sans une moyenne de quinze répétitions — parfois davantage pour les grandes émissions dramatiques.

....

....

....

5. Les personnes qui ne disent pas la vérité **devraient avoir** une bonne mémoire.

....

....

6. Un chat **peut regarder** un roi.

....

7. Pourquoi **avez-vous laissé tomber** votre marteau, Alphonse?

....

8. Georges sait très bien **jouer** du piano, mais il ne veut pas.

....

NAME .... SECTION .... DATE ....
    Print Last   *First*   *MI*

I. Tense Discernment

Translate the following sentences, and identify the tense of the verbs in **boldface** type.

1. Le roi, qui **était** superstitieux sans vouloir l'avouer, **demanda** à l'astrologue de lui prédire le jour précis de sa mort.

....

....

(Tense of **était**: ....;   of **demanda**: ....)

2. Le professeur **parlait** au sujet de la littérature allemande quand cet élève

est entré. ....

....

(Tense of **parlait**: ....;   of **est entré**: ....)

3. L'astrologue **soupçonna** ce que le roi **voulait** faire.

....

(Tense of **soupçonna**: ....;   of **voulait**: ....)

4. Quand j'**étais** assez jeune, j'**allais** à Paris avec ma famille.

....

(Tense of **étais**: ....;   of **allais**: ....)

Why is **allais** used instead of **allai** or **suis allé**? ....

....

5. Bien des bâtiments **furent** détruits à Moscou par l'incendie de 1812.

....

(Tense of **furent**: ....;   Infinitive of this verb: ....)

6. Louis Pasteur mit au point une technique pour la purification du lait. ....

....

(Tense of mit: ....)

II. Expressions of Time (§§67, 69)

Underline the expressions of time, and translate the sentences.

1. Lawrence et Livingston perfectionnèrent le cyclotron il y a plusieurs années.

....

....

2. Il y a trois ans que mon frère étudie la médecine à l'université. ....

....

3. Nous étudions le français depuis douze semaines, à peu près.

....

4. Depuis quand êtes-vous dans la salle de classe? ....

....

5. Nous venons de lire quelques phrases en français.

....

6. Quand le chimiste est entré dans le laboratoire, un élève venait de détruire une
partie du bâtiment en faisant une expérience défendue.

....

....

....

7. Il est rare qu'un Américain se fixe pour toujours sur le sol qu'il occupe.

....

8. Dès que la pression est suffisante, on introduit une petite quantité d'un gaz déterminé.

....

....

222

NAME .... SECTION .... DATE ....
    Print Last   *First*   *MI*

I. Relative Clauses

Separate the **que** or **qui** clauses from the main clause by diagonals (/) as has already been done in the first example. Underline the main clause. Translate the sentences.

1. Candide,/que le baron chassa du paradis terrestre,/marcha longtemps sans savoir précisément où.

   ....

   ....

2. Voilà la machine à calculer qu'inventa Pascal au dix-septième siècle. ....

   ....

3. Napoléon, qui était de retour sur le continent depuis trois mois, fut vaincu par le général Wellington à Waterloo.

   ....

   ....

4. Voilà la tête du poisson que mangea Alphonse. ....

   ....

5. Voilà le lion qui mangea le professeur de français. ....

   ....

6. L'échantillon d'acier que nous avions examiné avait disparu. ....

   ....

7. Albert Einstein, le célèbre physicien et mathématicien qui travaillait à Princeton, était venu de l'Allemagne aux États-Unis.

   ....

   ....

II. *tout* (§72). Give English equivalents:

1. tous les jours .... 9. tout à fait ....

2. toujours .... 10. Il est tout fatigué ....

3. toutes les histoires .... 11. tous les végétaux ....

4. toute l'histoire .... 12. Je les aime tous. ....

5. tous les bâtiments .... 13. le livre tout entier ....

6. tout le bâtiment .... 14. Tout chien [*dog*] est un lion chez lui

7. tout de suite ....

8. tous les poissons ....

III. Sentence Drill. Translate:

1. Thomas Edison a découvert une méthode d'enregistrer le son, ce qui rend possible

   le phonographe moderne. ....

   ....

2. L'étude de la littérature anglaise offre un intérêt tout particulier. ....

   ....

3. C'est Jacques Cartier qui, en 1534, a découvert le Canada. ....

   ....

4. Notre globe est recouvert de masses de terre et d'eau. ....

   ....

5. La porte est ouverte; le professeur l'ouvrit hier. ....

   ....

6. Ouvrons nos livres pour examiner ce qui se trouve à la page cent cinquante-trois.

   ....

   ....

224

NAME .... SECTION .... DATE ....
      Print Last   *First*   *MI*

I. Adjective Drill. Translate:

1. Cette maison ancienne fut bâtie il y a cent vingt-sept ans.

....

2. Mon ancienne maison a été bâtie l'année passée.

....

3. Notre propre expérience ne vous regarde pas.

....

4. Notre laboratoire propre est tout sanitaire.

....

5. Votre expérience seule ne prouve pas le fait.

....

6. Nous avons obtenu les mêmes résultats que vous.

....

7. Nos mesures furent justes; c'est l'échantillon même qui n'était pas pur.

....

8. Un certain général français est célèbre pour les mots qu'il prononça pendant la première guerre mondiale: «Ils ne passeront pas.»

....

....

9. C'est une constatation certaine qu'Alphonse avait l'esprit pénétrant.

....

II. Sentence Drill. Conjunctions and *y*. Translate:

1. La Californie m'attire; néanmoins je n'y vais pas, faute d'argent. ....

....

2. Téléphone marqua un "X" sur le rebord du canot afin de pouvoir retrouver plus

tard le même endroit. ....

....

....

3. N'ayez pas peur: les soldats ne jetteront pas l'astrologue par la fenêtre avant que

le roi ne leur donne le signal. ....

....

....

4. C'est une question difficile que vous me posez; j'y penserai pendant deux ou trois

jours avant de vous donner ma réponse.

....

....

5. Jean joue-t-il au tennis? Oui, bien sûr, il y joue.

....

6. Allez-vous à Monte-Carlo pour devenir riche en appliquant les lois de la

probabilité qu'a créées Pascal? Oui, j'y vais. ....

....

....

7. Les trois fils de l'Arabe n'ont pas voulu désobéir au commandement de leur père.
Ils y ont obéi.

....

8. Les Étoiles de mer ne dînent pas comme les êtres civilisées.

....

NAME .... SECTION .... DATE ....
    Print Last   *First*   *MI*

I. Disjunctive Pronouns (§78)

Underline the disjunctive pronouns used in the following sentences; translate the entire sentence in each case. (If the disjunctive pronoun is used for *emphasis*, be sure that your translation conveys this fact.)

1. Moi, je parle français; Henri ne parle que l'anglais, lui. ....

....

2. Alain et moi, nous sommes allés au cinéma hier soir pour voir un film italien. ....

....

....

3. C'est lui qui a mis les livres sur la table; pas moi. ....

....

4. Connaissez-vous Pierre et Marie? Eh bien, ce microscope est à lui. ....

....

5. Le colonel, lui, n'accompagna pas les autres. ....

....

II. Imperatives (§79). Translate:

1. Supposons maintenant qu'il y ait trois électrodes. ....

....

2. Mettez l'appareil photographique sur cette longue table-là. ....

....

3. Soyez comme vous voudriez paraître. ....

....

4. **Les** candidats au doctorat? Qu'ils viennent me voir à trois heures vingt cet après-midi. ....

....

....

5. Finissons cette expérience! Il ne nous reste que dix minutes. ....

....

III. *aussi; aussi bien ... que* (§80). Translate:

1. La littérature française a beaucoup contribué à la culture du monde, **aussi** faut-il la lire. ....

....

....

2. C'est à Blaise Pascal que nous devons **aussi bien** la machine à calculer **que** le baromètre. ....

....

3. Georg Friedrich Händel était un célèbre compositeur allemand qui créa aussi bien des opéras que des oratorios comme *Israel in Egypt.*

....

....

....

4. Stéphane Mallarmé fut **aussi bien** professeur d'anglais **que** poète symboliste.

....

5. A l'Opéra on a installé des machines modernes grâce auxquelles on peut produire de magiques effets; **aussi** devrait-on les employer davantage.

....

....

NAME .... SECTION .... DATE ....
Print Last   *First*   *MI*

Translate into English:

1. Tout est possible: il se peut même que Napoléon soit venu en Amérique après la bataille de Waterloo, mais ce n'est pas vraisemblable.

....

....

....

2. Arthur Rimbaud, le poète symboliste par excellence, écrivit de la poésie exquise jusqu'à ce qu'il soit parti de la France à l'âge de dix-neuf ans pour mener la vie d'aventurier en Éthiopie.

....

....

....

3. Les poèmes de Walt Whitman sont parmi les plus longs que j'aie jamais lus; la

collection s'appelle *Feuilles d'herbe.* ....

....

....

4. Voilà le plus grand accélérateur linéaire qui existe aux États-Unis. ....

....

....

....

5. Nous regrettons vivement que cet acteur veuille aller à Hollywood; nous doutons qu'il revienne à New-York. ....

....

....

6. Les servo-moteurs sont les plus ingénieux que vous puissiez imaginer.

....

....

7. M. Levêque craint que nous ne finissions pas notre travail avant que l'heure sonne. ....

....

....

8. Le train pour Lyon part de la gare à Paris à 13 h. 20 et arrive à destination à 17 h. 10. ....

....

9. Ce train rapide s'appelle «Le Mistral»; il termine son voyage à Nice, où il arrive à 24 h. ....

....

10. Le messager de l'état-major était pressé; il est entré en courant.

....

....

11. D'habitude, pendant que je dors la nuit, mon camarade de chambre Pierre se trouve dans une boîte de nuit. [*nightclub*] ....

....

....

NAME .... SECTION .... DATE ....
    Print Last   *First*   *MI*

I. Compound Tenses

Underline both parts of any compound verbs in the following sentences. Translate the passages.

1. Le trait le plus charactéristique de l'œuvre de Lavoisier est d'avoir introduit dans la chimie l'esprit de la physique. La physique est essentiellement, comme l'astronomie, une science de mesures précises. Jusqu'au temps de Lavoisier, la chimie s'inquiétait très peu, en effet, de la mesure des phénomènes. Dominée par des préjugés, elle cherchait des corps nouveaux, des propriétés inconnues et magiques; elle croyait à des elixirs de longue vie et à la transmutation des métaux vils en métaux précieux.

....

....

....

....

....

2. Beaucoup d'Américains voudraient continuer à vivre enfermés dans leur société qu'ils trouvent bonne. Beaucoup de Russes voudraient peut-être continuer à poursuivre l'expérience étatiste à l'écart du monde capitaliste. Ils ne le peuvent et ne le pourront plus jamais. De même, aucun problème économique, si secondaire apparaisse-t-il, ne peut se régler aujourd'hui en dehors de la solidarité des nations. Le pain de l'Europe est à Buenos Aires, et les machines-outils de Sibérie sont fabriquées à Detroit. Aujourd'hui, la tragédie est collective. (Camus, *Actuelles* I)

....

....

....

....

....

....

3. Un voyageur qui avait passé toute la journée sous la pluie arriva un soir dans une petite ville.

....

....

4. Quant à vous, le nouveau, vous me copierez vingt fois le verbe *ridiculus sum*.

....

....

5. Rimbaud ne serait pas parti de Londres s'il n'avait pas été fâché contre Verlaine.

....

....

II. Interrogatives

Answer the questions in English on a separate sheet (Do not translate).

1. Pourquoi Napoléon n'est-il pas resté longtemps à Moscou?

2. Qu'est-ce qu'Alphonse a demandé à Téléphone de faire quand ils étaient dans le canot?

3. Quel voyageur français a décrit l'Amérique telle qu'il l'a trouvée au XIXe siècle?

4. Que faites-vous pendant le week-end?

5. Quand est-ce que la comète de Halley va reparaître?

6. Où peut-on aller en Amérique pour essayer de prouver la loi des probabilités?

7. Comment Lohengrin a-t-il prouvé l'innocence d'Elsa?

8. Pourquoi Candide fut-il chassé du château du baron?

9. Quel monument est-ce que Napoléon a visité en Egypte?

10. Combien de bras est-ce que l'Étoile de mer possède?

Vocabulary

The following abbreviations and symbols are used in this vocabulary:

Acad.	Academic	*Elec.*	Electrical	*nm.*	noun, masculine
adj.	adjective	*F.*	Future	*nf.*	noun, feminine
adv.	adverb	*fr.*	from	*PD.*	Past Definite tense
Arch.	Architecture	*Geog.*	Geography	*Phys.*	Physics
art.	article	*Geom.*	Geometry	*pl.*	plural
Astron.	Astronomy	*Imperf.*	Imperfect tense	*pn.*	pronoun
Biol.	Biology	*Mech.*	Mechanics	*pp.*	past participle (§21)
Bot.	Botany	*Met.*	Meteorology	*Pr.*	Present tense
C.	Conditional tense	*qqch.*	something (*quelque*	*prep.*	preposition
Chem.	Chemistry		*chose*)	*ps.p.*	present participle (§49)
conj.	conjunction	*Mil.*	Military	*sthg.*	something

Verb forms use the following symbols:

* * Irregular verb

* † False Friend

* ‡ Verb which is only slightly irregular in spelling. The only change may be the addition of an accent mark or the doubling of a consonant. No change in this type of verb is sufficient to make identification difficult.

* / The *slash* is used to separate the stem (on the left of the slash) from the infinitive ending, when the infinitive is listed.

* /— *vst.* The abbreviation *vst.* means *verb stem.* Only the stem is indicated before the slash; (this stem may be *any* irregular stem of an irregular verb.)

* / with English meanings. The slash calls for the appropriate adjustment of the English verb form to the subject being used. (The entry "want/" indicates that the basic meaning is "want"; if the subject is *he,* read *wants.*)

[vb. 2] This symbol is a reference to the Table of Irregular Verbs. The abbreviation vb. stands for "verb."

A

à *prep.* to; at, in (*a place, a city*); having (*a characteristic*), *e.g.,* un animal à quatre pattes a four-footed animal

à cause de because of, on account of

à côté de beside

à droite de on the right of

à gauche de on the left of

à peu près about, approximately

abaiss/er *v.* to lower; to drop; to be reduced

abol/ir *v.* to abolish

abondant, -e *adj.* abundant

abord: d'abord first of all; at first

abord/er *v.* to approach

about/ir (à) *v.* to end, to conclude (with, at)

abrég/er‡ *v.* to shorten, to abridge, to condense

abri *nm.* shelter

absolu, -e *adj.* absolute

absorb/er *v.* to absorb

abstrait, -e *adj.* abstract

abyssal, -e *adj.* abyssal

accélérateur *nm.* accelerator; — linéaire linear accelerator (*Phys.*)

accélératrice *adj. f.* accelerating

accélér/er *v.* to accelerate, to speed up

accident *nm.* irregularity (*Geog.*)

accidenté *adj.* irregular

accompagn/er *v.* to accompany; accompagné (de) *pp.* accompanied (by)

accompl/ir *v.* to accomplish

accord *nm.* agreement; — en phase phasing (*Phys.*)

accord/er *v.* to grant (*a request*)

accroissement *nm.* increase, augmentation

accroît/re* *v.* to increase; to add to

accru *pp.* (*fr.* accroît/re* increased; s'étant —(e) having increased

accumulateur *nm.* storage battery

achet/er‡ *v.* to buy

acier *nm.* steel; — inoxydable stainless steel

Açores Azores (*Geog.*)

acquier/— *vst.* (acquér/ir*) acquire(s)

acquis *pp.* acquired

actuel, -le† *adj.* present-day; current

actuellement† *adv.* currently; these days; now; at present

admett/re* *v.* to admit [vb. 14]

admet: on — que it is admitted that

afin de, afin que in order (to), (that)

agent (de police) *nm.* policeman

ag/ir *v.* to act; il s'agit de it concerns…; it is a matter of…

agit: il s' — de it concerns…(§32)

aid/er *v.* to aid, to help

aïeul (*pl.* aïeux) *nm.* ancestor

aill/— *vst.* (aller*) go(es) [vb. 1]

ailleurs *adv.* elsewhere; d'— moreover, anyway, besides; par — elsewhere

aimant *nm.* magnet

aimantation *nf.* magnetism

aim/er *v.* to like, to love

aîné *nm.* eldest

ainsi *adv.* thus, in this way; — que *conj.* as well as, in addition to; — de suite and so on, etc.; pour—dire so to speak

air *nm.* air; avoir* l'— to appear, to seem

aire *nf.* area (*Geom.*)

aisé *adj.* easy

ait *v.* (*fr.* avoir*) has; qu'il y — that there be

ajout/er *v.* to add

algue *nf.* alga, seaweed

Allemagne Germany

allemand, -e *adj.* German

all/er* *v.* to go [vb. 1]

allongé *pp.* elongated

allum/er *v.* to light, to ignite

alors *adv.* then, at that time; — que *conj.* whereas, even though

âme *nf.* soul, mind

aménagé *pp.* arranged

aménagement *nm.* utilization

amené (à) *pp.* constrained (to)

amen/er‡ *v.* to bring, to get, to produce, to lead, to attract

ami *nm.* friend

amiante *nm.* asbestos

amical, -e *adj.* friendly

amiral *nm.* admiral

amour *nm.* love (*pl. is f.*)

an *nm.* year; tous les ans every year

ancien, -ne *adj.* old, ancient; (*before the noun*) former

anglais, -e *adj.* English

anglais *nm.* English (*language*)

Angleterre England

anneau *nm.* ring

année *nf.* year

anse *nf.* small bay (*Geog.*); handle (*of a cup*)

antérieur, -e *adj.* anterior; prior (*time*)

août August

s'apercev/oir* (de) *v.* to notice, to perceive

aplati, -e *adj.* flattened

apparaît/re* *v.* to appear [vb. 18]

appareil *nm.* apparatus, equipment, instrument; — photographique camera

apparition *nf.* appearance

apparten/ir* *v.* to belong to [vb. 28]

appel/er‡ *v.* to call

s'appel/er‡ *v.* to be called, to be named; …s'appelle … is called

appliqu/er *v.* to apply

apport/er *v.* to bring

appréciation *nf.* increase

apprend/re* *v.* to learn, to teach [vb. 21]

apprentissage *nm.* apprenticeship

apprit (*fr.* apprendre*) learned

s'approch/er (de) *v.* to approach

appuyé *pp.* supported

après *prep. adv.* after; — quoi after which; d'après according to après-midi *nm.* or *nf.* afternoon

arbre *nm.* tree

arc *nm.* arch, arc

arête *nf.* edge (*of a knife,* etc); — vive sharp edge

argent *nm.* silver; money

arme *nf.* arm, weapon

armé *pp.* reinforced

armée *nf.* army; — du Salut Salvation Army

armure *nf.* armor

arrachement *nm.* stripping off

arrach/er *v.* to strip off

s'arrang/er *v.* to arrange

arrêt *nm.* stop; sans — ceaselessly, without stopping

arrêt/er *v.* to stop; s'— to halt, to stop

arrière: en — behind, towards the rear, astern

arriv/er *v.* to arrive, to happen (*uses auxiliary* être*)

as† *nm.* ace

assemblage *nm.* assembly

s'asse/oir* *v.* to sit down

assez *adv.* enough; (*before an adj.*) rather; — peu considérable rather small

assidu, -e *adj.* industrious, constant

assis, -e *adj.* seated

assise *nf.* layer, stratum; une — de briques a course of bricks

assur/er *v.* to assure

astre *nm.* star

atelier *nm.* workshop, studio

atmosphère *nf.* atmosphere

atome *nf.* atom

attach/er *v.* to attach, to tie

atteign/— *vst.* (atteindre*) attain, reach

atteind/re* *v.* to reach, to attain

atteint *pp.* reached, attained

attend/re *v.* to wait for

s'attend/re (à) *v.* to expect

attente *nf.* wait, waiting

attérage *nm.* shore, approach to land (*Geog.*)

attir/er *v.* to attract

s'attir/er *v.* to be attracted

attraction *nf.* attraction, gravitation (*Phys.*)

attribu/er *v.* to attribute, to award

au *prep.* to the, at the, in the; — bout de after (*time*); — milieu de in the middle of

aucun, -e *adj.* no, none

au-dessous de *prep.* below

au-dessus de *prep.* above

augmentation *nf.* increase

augment/er *v.* to increase

aujourd'hui *adv.* today

auprès de *adv.* close to, beside

aur/— *vst.* (avoir*) will have; would have

aussi *adv.* also; (*at beginning of a clause*) therefore (§80); — (ADJ.) que . . . as . . . as; — bien . . . que both . . . and

aussitôt *adv.* immediately

autant de . . . que as many . . . as; d'autant plus . . . que proportionately greater . . . as; autant que as long as

auteur *nm.* author

automne *nm.* autumn, fall

auto-moteur *adj.* self-propelled (*f.* auto-motrice)

autour (de) *adv.* around, about

autre *n., adj.* other; — part elsewhere

autrefois *adv.* formerly

autrement *adv.* otherwise, in another way; — dit in other words; il en est (tout) — it is (quite) otherwise

autrichien, -ne *adj.* Austrian

autrui *pn.* others, other people

aux to the (§19)

avait (*Imperf. of* avoir*) had

avance: en —, par — in advance, early

avant *prep.* before (*in time*); bien — well before; en — forward; — que *conj.* before (+ *subjunctive mood*)

avant-garde *nm.* advance guard, point

avec *prep.* with

avenir *nm.* future

avert/ir *v.* to warn

avertissement *nm.* warning, notice

aveugle *adj. and nm.* blind

avion *nm.* airplane; — à réaction jet plane; — en remorque glider

avis *nm.* opinion

avoir* *v. to have* [vb. *Appendix C*]; — besoin de to need, to have need of; — chaud to be warm, to be hot;

— envie de (faire) (qqch) to feel like (doing) (something); — l'air . . . to seem . . . ; — lieu to take place; — raison to be right; — retentissement to have repercussions; — tort to be wrong

avou/er *v.* to admit

ayant *ps.p.* (avoir*) having

ayons let's have

axe† *nm.* axis

azote *nm.* nitrogen

B

baie *nf.* bay

baign/er *v.* to bathe, to be immersed

baisse *nf.* reduction

baiss/er *v.* to lower, to reduce

balanc/er *v.* to weigh

banc *nm.* bench; bank (*finance*)

bas, -se *adj.* low; en — below, in the lower part

basilique *nf.* basilica, church

bataille *nf.* battle

bateau *nm.* boat

bâti, -e *pp.* built

bâtiment *nm.* building; (*rarely*) ship

bât/ir *v.* to build

bâton *nm.* stick

bâtonnet *nm.* rod (*of retina*)

batt/re *v.* to beat

beau, bel, belle *adj.* beautiful, fine, handsome; il fait beau it (*the weather*) is nice

beaucoup *adv.* much, many; (*after a verb*) greatly, very much; — de (*before a noun*) much, many

bel *adj. m.* fine, beautiful, handsome

belle *see* beau

besoin *nm.* need; avoir* — de to need, to have need of

béton *nm.* concrete (*material*); —armé reinforced concrete

bibliothèque *nf.* library; bookshelf

bien *adv.* well; (*before an adj. or adv.*) very; (*after some verbs*) indeed; — des many; — que although

biens *n.pl.* property, possessions

bientôt *adv.* soon

bilan *nm.* schedule, statistics

blanc, -he *adj.* white

bless/er *v.* to hurt, to wound

bleu, -e *adj.* blue

blindage *nm.* armor (*Mil.*); — protecteur protecting shield

bloc *nm.* block

boi/re* *v.* to drink

bois *nm.* wood, forest; en —, de — made of wood

boîte *nf.* box, can (of food); — étanche watertight, airtight box; — de nuit night club

bon, -ne *adj.* good (precedes noun); à quoi — (*m.*) what's the use?

bond† *nm.* bound, leap; d'un — suddenly

bonheur *nm.* happiness

bord *nm.* edge; à — on board (*ship*); au — de on the edge of

bore† *nm.* boron (*Chem.*)

Bosphore Bosporus

bouche *nf.* mouth

bouclier *nm.* buckler, shield

bougie *nf.* candle

boule *nf.* ball

boulevers/er *v.* to upset, to overthrow

bourgeois *nm.* and *adj.* a middle-class person; middle-class

bout† *nm.* end, piece; au — de (*time*) after (*time*)

bouteille *nf.* bottle

bouton *nm.* button

branche *nf.* branch, limb

bras *nm.* arm, sound (*Geog.*)

brièvement *adv.* briefly

brique *nf.* brick

brisé *pp.* broken

bris/er *v.* to break

bruit *nm.* noise, rumor

brûlé *pp.* burned (-out)

brûl/er *v.* to burn

brusquement *adv.* suddenly

but† *nm.* purpose, goal

C

ça (= cela) *pn.* that

cach/er *v.* to hide (à) from

c.-à-d. *abbreviation for* c'est-à-dire that is, i.e.

cadet *nm.* the youngest

Caire: le Caire Cairo

calcaire *nm.* limestone ($CaCO_3$); *adj.* calcareous

calcul *nm.* calculus; calculation

calcul/er *v.* to calculate

camion *nm.* truck

campagne *nf.* country (*as opposed to* city); à la — in the country

canal *nm.* channel, canal; (*Biol.*) duct

cap† *nm.* cape (*Geog.*)

car† *conj.* for, because

caractère *nm.* character, characteristic

carapace *nf.* shell, hood, carapace

carbone *nm.* carbon (*Chem.*)

carbonique: gaz — *nm.* carbon dioxide

carré *nm.* and *adj.* square

carrière *nf.* career

carte *nf.* card, map; **jou/er aux cartes** to play cards

cas *nm.* case

cass/er *v.* to break

cause *nf.* cause; à — de because of; **mettre* en** — to involve

caus/er *v.* to chat, to converse, to cause

ce, cet, cette *adj.* this, that; **ce . . . -ci** this; **ce . . . -là** that

ce *pn.* this, it; **c'est** it is

ce que *pn.* that which, what

ce qui *pn.* that which, what

ceci *pn.* this (*opposed to* **cela**, that)

cela *pn.* that

célèbre *adj.* famous

céleste *adj.* celestial

celle *pn. f. sing.* the one, that

celle-ci *pn. f.* the latter, this one

celles *pn. f. pl.* those

cellule *nf.* cell

celui *pn. m. sing.* the one, that; — **-ci** the latter; — **-là** the former

cendre *nm.* cinder

cent† hundred

centaines hundreds; **plusieurs** — **de** several hundreds of

cependant *adv., conj.* nevertheless, however

certain, -e *adj.* indisputable, certain (§74)

certitude *nf.* certainty

ces these, those (*fr.* **ce**)

cesse: sans — incessantly

cess/er *v.* to cease

c'est it is, he is, she is

c'est-à-dire that is, *id est*, i.e. (*abbreviated* **c.-à-d.**)

cet *adj.* (*alternate form of* **ce**) this, that

cette *adj.* (*f. form of* **ce**) this, that

ceux *pn. m. pl.* those (*pl. of* **celui**); — **-ci** the latter; — **-là** the former

Ceylan Ceylon

chacun(e) *pn.* each one, everybody

chair† *nf.* flesh

chaleur *nf.* heat

chambre *nf.* bedroom; — **de Wilson** Wilson chamber, cloud-chamber (*Phys.*)

chameau *nm.* camel

champ *nm.* field; **sur-le-** — immediately

chance *nf.* luck, chance; **avoir* de la** — to be lucky

chang/er *v.* to change

chantier *nm.* building-site (*Arch.*)

chapitre *nm.* chapter

chaque *adj.* each, every

charbon *nm.* coal

chargé (de) *pp.* charged (with), loaded (with)

charg/er *v.* to charge, to load

se charg/er (de) *v.* to take the responsibility for

charpente *nf.* carpentry, framing; à — timber, made of wood

chassant: en — by forcing out

chasse *nf.* hunt, chase; **faire* la** — to hunt

chass/er *v.* to drive out, to expel; to hunt

chat† *nm.* cat

chaud, -e *adj.* warm, hot; **avoir*** — to be hot (*person*); **il fait** — it is hot (*weather*)

chauffage *nm.* heating

chauff/er *v.* to heat, to warm up

chef *nm.* chief, leader

chemin *nm.* road; — **de fer** railroad

cheminée *nf.* fireplace

cher, chère *adj.* dear (*before noun*); expensive (*after noun*)

cherch/er *v.* to seek, to look for, to attempt, to get

chercheur *nm.* researcher

cheval *nm.* horse

chevelure *nf.* tail, coma (*of a comet*)

cheveu *nm.* hair

chez *prep.* at the home of; at the place of business of; in the case of; — **eux** in their case, at their house, among them

chien *nm.* dog

chiffre *nm.* figure, number

chimie *nf.* chemistry

chimique *adj.* chemical

chimiste *nm. or f.* chemist

chirurgie *nf.* surgery

chlorure *nf.* chloride

choc *nm.* shock

chois/ir *v.* to select, to choose

choix *nm.* choice

chose *nf.* thing; **quelque** — something; **peu de** — trivial

christianisme *nm.* Christianity

chute *nf.* fall, decline, drop, decrease

cible *nf.* target

ci-dessus *adv.* above (*in a book*)

ciel *nm.* sky, heavens

cieux (*pl. of* **ciel**) heavens, skies

ciment *nm.* cement, concrete

cinématographique *adj.* movie

cinq five

circonstance *nf.* circumstance

circonférence *nf.* circumference

circuit *nm.* circumference

cité *nf.* city; *pp. of* **cit/er** quoted

cit/er *v.* to quote, to cite

citoyen *nm.* citizen

class/er *v.* to classify

clef *nf.* key, wrench; — **anglaise** monkey wrench; — **de voûte** keystone

cliché *nm.* negative (*photography*)

climatisation (**de l'air**) *nf.* air-conditioning

cloche *nf.* bell

cloison *nf.* partition wall (*Arch.*)

cloître *nm.* cloister; **arc de** — square vault (*Arch.*)

clou *nm.* nail

cœur *nm.* heart

coin† *nm.* corner; **au** — **de** at the corner of

colère *nf.* anger; **se mettre* en** — to become angry

colline *nf.* hill

colon† *nm.* colonist

colonne *nf.* column (*Arch.*)

coloris *nm.* coloring (*Art*)

combien (**de**) how much, how many

combinaison *nf.* combination

combustible *nm.* fuel

comité *nm.* committee

commandé *pp.* controlled

comme like, as

commenc/er *v.* to begin

comment how; (*exclamation*) what!

commode *adj.* convenient

commodité *nf.* convenience

commun, -e *adj.* common

communément *adv.* ordinarily

communiqué *pp.* reported

communiqu/er *v.* to connect; — **à** to give to, to report to

compensateur *adj.* compensating

complet, complète *adj.* complete, full

complètement *adv.* completely

compliqu/er *v.* to complicate

comportement *nm.* behavior

comport/er *v.* to behave, to entail, to include, to consist of

composante *nf.* component part

composé *pp.* composed; *adj.* compound

compos/er *v.* to compose; **se** — **de** to be composed of

comprendre* *v.* to understand, to include [vb. 21]

comprend includes, understands

comprimé *pp.* compressed

comprim/er *v.* to compress

compris *pp.* (**comprendre***) included, understood; **y** — included (in it)

compromis *nm.* compromise

compte *nm.* account; **se rendre** — **de** to realize (*sthg*)

compt/er *v.* to count, to count on, to plan on

compte-rendu *nm.* report; minutes (*of a meeting*)

concentr/er *v.* to concentrate; **se** — to be concentrated

concevoir* *v.* to conceive [vb. 23]

conclu *pp.* concluded

conclu/re *v.* to conclude; **on en conclut** one concludes from this

concours *nm.* co-existence; competition

concurremment *adv.* simultaneously

concurrenc/er *v.* to compete with

conçut (*fr.* **concevoir***) conceived

conduire* *v.* to conduct, to lead [vb. 22]

conduis/— *vst.* (conduire*) conduct/

conduit *pp.* (conduire*) conducted, led

conduite *nf.* conduct, behavior

conférence† *nf.* lecture

confiance *nf.* confidence

confondu *pp.* confused

conforme *adj.* in conformity

connaissance *nf.* knowledge, acquaintance; les premières —s the fundamentals, the basic ideas

connaiss/— *vst.* (connaître*) know/; (*Imperf.*) knew

connaître* *v.* to know, to be acquainted with [vb. 2]

connu *pp.* known

conseil *nm.* advice

conseill/er *v.* to advise

conséquent *adj.* consistent; important; par — consequently

considérable *adj.* noteworthy, important, large

considér/er *v.* to consider; to contemplate

consign/er *v.* to set down

consommation *nf.* consumption, using up

consomm/er *v.* to consume

constamment *adv.* constantly

constatation *nf.* observation, verification

constat/er *v.* to establish, to ascertain, to verify

constituant *nm.* and *adj.* component

constitu/er *v.* to constitute, to consist of; se — to be developed

constitution *nf.* composition, make-up

construi/re* *v.* to construct [vb. 3]

construit *pp.* (construire*) constructed

conte *nm.* short story

contenir* *v.* to contain [vb. 28]

content, -e *adj.* contented, happy

contient *fr.* contenir* contains

continu, -e *adj.* continuous

continu/er *v.* to continue

contourn/er *v.* to follow along (closely)

contraint *pp.* (contraindre*) constrained

contraire *nm.* and *adj.* contrary; au — on the contrary

contrari/er *v.* to contradict

contre *prep.* against

contredire* *v.* to contradict [vb. 9]

contredit *pp.* contradicted

contrôle *nm.* testing

contrôl/er *v.* to test, to supervise

convainc/re* *v.* to convince

convainquant, -e *adj.* convincing

convenable *adj.* appropriate

convenance *nf.* propriety, appropriateness

convenir* *v.* to be appropriate; to agree [vb. 30]

convient: il — it is appropriate

convoi *nm.* convoy

copi/er *v.* to copy

coque *nf.* shell, hull

coquille *nf.* shell

corps *nm.* body, substance; — simple element (*Chem.*)

correspond/re *v.* to correspond

corrig/er *v.* to correct

cosmique *adj.* cosmic

côte *nf.* coast, shore

côté *nm.* side; à — de beside; — cible target side; — haute fréquence, — H.F. high-frequency side (*Elec.*); laiss/er de — to disregard

côtier *adj.* coastal (*Geog.*)

couche *nf.* layer, stratum

se couch/er *v.* to go to bed

coude *nm.* elbow

coul/er *v.* to flow, to pour

couleur *nf.* color; (*cards*) suit

couliss/er *v.* to slide

coup *nm.* blow, stroke; (*coins*) toss; — de foudre flash of lightning; — de grâce finishing stroke; — d'état revolution; — de pied kick; — de téléphone telephone call

coupable *adj.* guilty

coupe *nf.* cut, cross-section; — verticale cross-section (*Arch.*)

coup/er *v.* to cut

coupole *nf.* cupola, dome (*Arch.*)

cour *nf.* courtyard, yard; (*royal*) court; basse- — farmyard

couramment *adv.* currently, at present

courant *nm.* current (*water, electricity*); — alternatif alternating current; — continu direct current; — d'électrons electron stream

courbe *nf.* curve

courb/er *v.* to bend; se — sur to bend over

cour/ir* *v.* to run [vb. 4]

couronne *nf.* ring, annulus, corona

couronn/er *v.* to crown

cours *nm.* course; au — de in the course of; au long — of long duration; en — in progress; — d'eau watercourse

course *nf.* travel, race

court, -e *adj.* short

couru *pp.* (courir*) run

coût *nm.* cost

coût/er *v.* to cost; coûte que coûte regardless of cost

coûteux, coûteuse *adj.* costly

couvercle *nm.* cover

couvert, -e *adj., pp.* covered

couvrant *ps.p.* covering

couvr/ir* *v.* to cover [vb. 17]

crain/— *vst.* (craindre*) fear/

crainte *nf.* fear

crédit *nm.* support

cré/er *v.* to create; *pp.* créé created

creus/er *v.* to dig

creux, creuse *adj.* hollow

cri/er *v.* to shout, to call out

critique *adj.* critical

critiqu/er *v.* to criticize

croi/re* *v.* to believe [vb. 5]

crois/er *v.* to cross

croissant, -e *adj.* increasing

croît increases, grows

croyez believe

croyons we believe; let us believe

crut (*Past Def. of* croire*) believed

cuir *nm.* leather

cuisine *nf.* kitchen; cooking

cultivateur *nm.* farmer, grower

cultiv/er *v.* to cultivate

curieux, curieuse *adj.* curious, strange

cuve *nf.* vat, basin, chamber; — à réaction reaction chamber (*Phys.*)

cuvette *nf.* basin, pan

cygne *nm.* swan

D

d'abord *adv.* first of all, at first

d'ailleurs *adv.* besides, moreover, anyway

dame *nf.* lady

dangereux, dangereuse *adj.* dangerous

dans *prep.* in

d'après according to; adapted from

dalle *nf.* paving-stone; plate (*Arch.*)

daté *pp.* dated

davantage *adv.* more, still more

de *prep.* of, from, (*before an infinitive*) to, with; de . . . à from . . . to

débarrassé *pp.* relieved of, stripped of

débarrass/er (de) *v.* to rid (of)

debout *adv.* standing (up)

début *nm.* beginning, start, origin; au — at the beginning

décelable *adj.* discoverable

déchir/er *v.* to tear (apart)

décid/er *v.* to decide; se — à to make up one's mind, to decide

décontenanc/er *v.* to disconcert, to discountenance

décor/er *v.* to decorate

découl/er (de) *v.* to be derived (from); to pour (from)

découvert *pp.* discovered

découverte *nf.* discovery

découvr/ir* *v.* to discover [vb. 17]

décri/re* *v.* to describe [vb. 6]

décrit *pp.* described

décroissance *nf.* decrease

décroît/re* *v.* to decrease, to shrink

dedans *adv.* inside

dédui/re* *v.* to deduce

déduit *pp.* deduced; on — it is deduced

défavorable *adj.* unfavorable

défend/re *v.* to defend; to forbid

défini *pp.* defined, definite, specific; mal — poorly defined, unclear

défin/ir *v.* to define; se — to be defined

définitive: en — definitely

définitivement definitely

dégagé *pp.* released

dégagement *nm.* release, disengagement

degré *nm.* degree; step

dehors *adv.* outside; en — de in addition to, beyond

déjà *adv.* already

delà *prep.* beyond; au — de, en — de beyond

délai *nm.* delay

demain *adv.* tomorrow

demand/er *v.* to ask (for); se — to wonder

démesuré *adj.* unusually large

demeure *nf.* dwelling

demeur/er *v.* to remain; to reside

demi, -e *adj., adv.* half, one-half; demi-tour *nm.* half-turn; à demi-voix in a low tone (of voice)

démol/ir *v.* to demolish

démont/er *v.* to dismount, to disassemble

démontr/er *v.* to demonstrate

dent† *nf.* tooth

d'entre (eux) or (elles) among them

d'environ of about

départ *nm.* departure; starting-point; au — de at the exit of; dès le — from the outset

départagé *pp.* divided

dépass/er *v.* to exceed, to surpass

dépend/re *v.* to depend

dépens *nm.* expense

dépens/er *v.* to spend

dépit: en — de in spite of

se déplaçant moving

déployer *v.* to deploy, to exhibit

déposé *pp.* deposited

dépôt *nm.* deposit

depuis *prep., adv.* since; for (A TIME); from; — l'antiquité since ancient times; — lors since that time, since then; — que *conj.* since

dérang/er *v.* to disturb, to upset

dériv/er *v.* to drift downstream; to derive

dérobé *pp.* hidden

dernier, dernière *adj.* last; (*before noun* = final; *after noun* = most recent)

dernier *nm.* the latter; the last

dernièrement *adv.* recently

derrière *adv., prep.* behind, in back of

derviche *nm.* dervish (*member of a Moslem religious order*)

des some, of the; from the; with the; any

dès *prep.* starting with, since; — que *conj.* as soon as, when

descend/re *v.* to descend, to go down; to get off (*a vehicle*); to stop at (*a hotel*) (*uses auxiliary* être*)

désert, -e *adj.* deserted

désir/er *v.* to desire

désobé/ir (à) *v.* to disobey

désormais *adv.* henceforth

dessin *nm.* sketch, plan

dessinateur *nm.* sketcher, designer

dessin/er *v.* to sketch, to draw

dessous *adv.* below

dessus *adv.* above, over

destiné (à) *pp.* intended (for)

déterminé *pp.* specified, determined

détroit *nm.* narrows (*Geog.*)

détruit *pp.* destroyed

deuton *nm.* deuteron

deux two

deuxième second

devait (+ INFINITIVE) must have, was to have (DONE STHG)

devancier *nm.* predecessor

devant *prep.* before (*physical location*), in front of

développ/er *v.* to develop

deven/ir* *v.* to become [vb. 30]

dévié *pp.* deviated

devien/— *vst.* (devenir*) become/

deviendr/— *vst.* (devenir*) F. will become C. would become

devinrent (they) became

dévoil/er *v.* to reveal

devoir* *v.* to be obligated to; must, should; il a dû he had to [vb. 8] (§64)

devoir *nm.* duty; homework

diamètre *nm.* diameter

Dieu *nm.* God

différence; à la — de unlike

différenci/er *v.* to differentiate

difficile *adj.* difficult

difficulté *nf.* difficulty

digér/er *v.* to digest

digne *adj.* worthy

dilatation *nf.* expansion

diminu/er *v.* to diminish, to decrease

diminution *nf.* decrease, reduction

dîner *nm.* dinner

dîn/er *v.* to dine

di/re* *v.* to say, to tell; à vrai — in fact; c'est-à- — that is, i.e.; pour ainsi — so to speak

directrice *adj. f.* steering, directing

se dirigeant *ps.p.* moving

dirig/er *v.* to direct

disant *ps.p.* (dire*) saying; en — que by saying that

discut/er *v.* to discuss

disparaissent (*Pr. of* disparaître*) (they) disappear

disparaît/re* *v.* to disappear [vb. 18]

disparition *nf.* disappearance

disparu *pp.* disappeared

dispens/er (de) *v.* to obviate, to make unnecessary

disponible *adj.* available

dispos/er *v.* to arrange, to place; — de [N.] to have [N.] at one's disposal

dispositif *nm.* device, arrangement

disposition *nf.* arrangement

dissemblable *adj.* dissimilar, different

distingu/er *v.* to discern, to distinguish

dit *pp.* (dire*) said, told; l'on — it is said; autrement — in other words

dit, -e named, called

divers, -e *adj.* various

divis/er *v.* to divide

dix ten

dix-huit eighteen

dix-sept seventeen

dizaine about ten; "tens of" (*pl.*)

docteur *nm.* doctor

doit (*Pr. of* devoir*) must, should; owes

doigt *nm.* finger

doiv/— *vst.* (devoir*) should

domin/er *v.* to dominate

donc *conj.* therefore; (*after imperative verb = emphasis*) parlez donc DO speak!

donnée *nf.* datum; (*pl.*) data

donn/er *v.* to give

dont *pn.* whose, of which, of whom (§28)

dorm/ir* *v.* to sleep

d'où whence, from which

doute *nm.* doubt; sans — doubtless

doux, douce *adj.* sweet, gentle, soft

douze twelve

drame *nm.* drama

dress/er† *v.* to rise; se — sur to rise on

droit *nm.* right (*legal*); tax, fee

droit, -e *adj.* straight, just; une ligne droite a straight line

droite *nf.* right-hand (side); à — de on the right of

droite *nf.* a straight line

drôle *adj.* funny; strange

du *prep.* of the, from the; (*with singular noun, it may mean* some)

dû *pp.* (devoir*) due; il a — he had to [vb. 8]

duc *nm.* Duke

duquel (= de + lequel) of which

dur *adv. and adj.* hard

durée *nf.* duration

dur/er *v.* to last, to endure

dureté *nf.* hardness

E

eau *nf.* water; entre deux eaux slightly below the surface; — lourde heavy water

écart *nm.* deviation

échantillon *nm.* sample, specimen

échapp/er *v.* to escape (à) from

échauff/er *v.* to warm

échelle *nf.* scale; ladder

éclair/er *v.* to light, to illuminate

éclat *nm.* brilliance

éclat/er *v.* to explode; to break out (*war*)

écliptique *nm.* ecliptic; plane of the ellipse (*Astron.*)

école *nf.* school

écolier *nm.* schoolboy

écorce *nf.* crust; — terrestre earth's crust

s'écoul/er *v.* to flow; to pass by (*years, time*)

écout/er *v.* to listen

écran *nm.* screen

écras/er *v.* to crush

s'écri/er *v.* to exclaim, to shout

écrire* *v.* to write [vb. 6]

écrit *pp.* written; par — in writing

édifice *nm.* building, structure, edifice

éditeur† *nm.* publisher

effac/er *v.* to erase, to efface

effectu/er *v.* to execute (*plan*); to achieve, to carry out, to produce; s'— to occur, to take place

effet *nm.* effect, result; avoir* pour — to have as a result; en — in fact

efficace *adj.* effective

effondré *pp.* sunken, engulfed

effondrement *nm.* engulfment

s'efforc/er (de) *v.* to make an effort (to); to strive (to)

égal, -e *adj.* equal

également *adv.* equally; also

égal/er *v.* to equal

égalité *nf.* equality; à — de distance equidistant

égard *nm.* regard; eu — à considering, by comparison with

s'égar/er *v.* to stray, to wander

égaux *adj. pl.* (égal) equal

église *nf.* church

électroaimant *nm.* electromagnet

élève *nm.* or *nf.* student

élevé, -e *adj.* high; peu — low

élev/er *v.* to raise; s'— to be raised, to be built

élimin/er *v.* to eliminate

éloigné, -e *adj.* removed, distant

s'éloign/er *v.* to move away, to go away, to become more distant

émanation *nf.* emission

éman/er *v.* to emanate

embranchement *nm.* class, branch

embrass/er *v.* to include; to embrace, to kiss

émetteur *nm.* transmitter; — de haute fréquence high-frequency transmitter

émetteur *nm.* source; — de particules α source of Alpha particles

émett/re* *v.* to emit [vb. 14]

émis *pp.* emitted

empêch/er *v.* to prevent, to hinder

empirique *adj.* empirical

emploi *nm.* use, employment

employ/er‡ *v.* to use

employé *nm.* employee

emport/er *v.* to remove, to carry away, to take away; l'— (sur) to prevail (over)

emprunt/er (à) *v.* to borrow (from)

émule *nm.* imitator

en *prep.* in; — effet in fact; — ce qui insofar as; — dehors de outside of; — être to be advanced to a certain point; — face de opposite, across from; — passant in passing; *pn.* some

enceinte *nf.* enclosure

encore *adv.* again, still, yet; — une fois once again, once more

endommagé *pp.* damaged

endroit *nm.* place, location; par —s in places

énergie *nf.* energy; faible — low energy

enfant *nm.* or *nf.* child

enferm/er *v.* to include; to shut in

enfin *adv.* finally

enfoncement *nm.* penetration, encroachment, inroad, indentation

s'enfonc/er *v.* to sink

engin *nm.* machine

englobé *pp.* embodied, embraced

engrais *nm.* fertilizer

enlèvement *nm.* removal

enlev/er *v.* to remove

ennemi *nm.* enemy

énorme *adj.* enormous

enregistr/er *v.* to record

enrich/ir *v.* to enrich

enseignement *nm.* instruction, teaching

enseign/er *v.* to teach

ensemble *adv.* together; *nm.* set (*math.*); whole; tout l' — the whole of

s'ensuit results; il — it follows logically that

ensuite *adv.* then, next

entend/re *v.* to hear; to understand

entendu *pp.* heard; understood; bien — of course

enterr/er *v.* to bury

entier, entière *adj.* entire; dans son entier in its entirety; tout entier total, entire

entièrement *adv.* entirely

entouré (de) *pp.* surrounded (by)

entour/er *v.* to surround

entraîné *pp.* driven

entraîn/er *v.* to be accompanied by; to entail

entre *prep.* between; among; — eux among themselves

entrée *nf.* entrance

entrefer *nm.* gap (*of a magnet*)

entrepris *pp.* undertaken

entr/er *v.* to enter; il entre pour ... dans it makes up ... of

entreten/ir* *v.* to support [vb. 28] (§37)

entretien *nm.* maintenance

entretient (*Pr. of* entretenir*) supports

envah/ir *v.* to invade

envie *nf.* desire; avoir* — de to want to, to have a desire to

environ *adv.* about, approximately; d'— by about, of about

environnant, -e *adj.* surrounding, neighboring

envisagé *pp.* contemplated, considered

envoi/— *vst.* (**envoyer***) send/—; **on —** ... is sent [vb. 10]

envoy/er* *v.* to send; **— chercher** to send for [vb. 10]

épais, -se *adj.* thick

épaisseur *nf.* thickness

épaule *nf.* shoulder

épineux, épineuse *adj.* troublesome; spiny

époque *nf.* time, era, epoch; **à cette —** at that (this) time; **dès cette —** since that (this) time

épreuve *nm.* test

éprouv/er *v.* to experience, to feel; to test

épuis/er *v.* to exhaust

épure *nf.* final plan; design (*Arch.*)

erreur *nf.* error, mistake

escalier *nm.* stairs

espace *nm.* space

espèce *nf.* species, kind

espérer‡ *v.* to hope

espoir *nm.* hope, aspiration

esprit *nm.* mind; wit; spirit

essai *nm.* test, try, attempt; essay

essay/er‡ *v.* to try

essuy/er‡ *v.* to wipe off, to clean

est *nm.* east; *v.* (**être***) is

estimé *adj.* estimated; esteemed

estim/er *v.* to consider

estomac *nm.* stomach

et *conj.* and; **— ... —** both ... and

établ/ir *v.* to establish

établissement *nm.* establishment; construction

étage *nm.* floor (*level of a building*); stage; phase

étagé *pp.* in stages

étain *nm.* tin

était (*Imperf. of* **être***) was, used to be

s'étal/er *v.* to display, to spread out

étanche *adj.* watertight; **— à l'air** airtight

étant *ps.p.* (**être***) being; **— arrivé** having arrived, having happened

étape *nf.* step, stage

état *nm.* state; condition

état-major *nm.* staff (*Mil.*)

États-Unis *nm. pl.* United States (*abbrev.* É-U.)

été *pp.* (**être***) been; *nm.* summer

éteind/re* *v.* to extinguish; **s'—** to die out, to become extinct [vb. 11]

étend/re *v.* to extend; **s'— (sur)** to expand (upon), to extend

étendue *nf.* extent, expanse

étoile *nf.* star

étoilé *adj.* stellate, starry

étonn/er *v.* to astonish

étrange *adj.* strange

étranger, étrangère *adj.* foreign; **à l'étranger** abroad

être* *v.* to be; (*as auxiliary*) to have (§83c); **— de retour** to be back; **peut- —** perhaps; *nm.* a being, a creature

étroit, -e *adj.* narrow

étude *nf.* study, investigation

étudi/er *v.* to study

eu *pp.* (**avoir***) had

eurent (*fr.* **avoir***) had

eut (*fr.* **avoir***) had

eût had

eux *pn.* them

eV *abbrev.* electron-volts

évalu/er *v.* to evaluate

s'évanou/ir *v.* to faint; to fade away

événement *nm.* event

évidemment *adv.* obviously

évidence: mise en — *nf.* proof

évit/er *v.* to avoid

évolu/er *v.* to evolve, to develop

examen *nm.* examination; **passer un —** to *take* an examination

examin/er *v.* to examine

excès *nm.* excess

exécut/er *v.* to carry out (*a task*); to execute; **s'exécuter** to be carried out

exemple *nm.* example; **par —** for example

exerçant *ps.p.* exercising

exerc/er *v.* to exercise

exig/er *v.* to require

exogène *adj.* exogenous

expérience† *nf.* experiment; experience

expérimentateur *nm.* experimenter

s'expériment/er *v.* to become adjusted; to become experienced

explication *nf.* explanation

expliqué *pp.* explained

expliqu/er *v.* to explain

exposant *nm.* exponent (*Math.*)

expos/er *v.* to explain

exprim/er *v.* to express; **s'—** to express oneself; **s'— par** to be expressed by

expulsé *pp.* ejected

exquis, -e *adj.* exquisite

extrai/re* *v.* to extract; to draw out

extrait *pp.* (**extraire***) extracted; *nm.* extract

extrémité *nf.* end; extremity

F

face: en — (de) opposite

facile *adj.* easy

facilement *adv.* easily

facilité *nf.* ease

facilit/er *v.* to facilitate

façon *nf.* way, manner; **de cette —** in this way; **de — que** in such a way that; **de toute —** in every way

facultatif, facultative *adj.* optional

faculté *nf.* college

faible *adj.* weak, poor; **à — vitesse** at low velocity

faiblesse *nf.* weakness

faim *nf.* hunger; **avoir* —** to be hungry

faire* *v.* to make, to do (§53); **— partie de** to be part of; **— remarquer** to point out; **— semblant de** to pretend to; **— son possible** to do one's best; **— signe de** to give the signal to; **— voir** to show

faire (+ INFINITIVE) *v.* to cause (*sthg*) (TO BE DONE) (§55)

faisant *ps.p.* making, doing

faisceau *nm.* **— d'électrons** stream of electrons

fait *nm.* fact; **du — que** from the fact that; **en —** in fact

fait *pp.* (**faire***) made, done

falaise *nf.* slope

fallait (*Imperf. of* **il faut***) **il —** it was necessary

falloir* *v.* (*defective*) **il faut** it is necessary; **il ne faut pas** one must not; **il fallait** it was necessary; **il faudra** it will be necessary; **il faudrait** it would be necessary; **il a fallu** it was necessary

fallu *pp.* (**falloir***) *see under* **falloir,** *above*

famille *nf.* family

fantaisiste *adj.* imaginary

fass/— *vst.* (**faire***) do, make (*Subjunctive*)

fatigué *adj.* tired

faudra (*fr.* **falloir***) *F.* it will be necessary

fausse *adj.* false, wrong

faut: il — it is necessary; **il ne — pas** one must not

faute *nf.* mistake; **— de mieux** for lack of something better

faux, fausse *adj.* false

faveur: en — de in favor of

favorisant, -e *adj.* favorable

fécond, -e *adj.* fruitful; profitable

femme *nf.* woman; wife

fenêtre *nf.* window; **— coulissante** sash window (*Arch.*); **— à guillotine** sliding window

fer *nm.* iron; **chemin de —** railroad

ferme *nf.* farm

ferm/er *v.* to close

feu *nm.* fire; firing (*Mil.*); **au —** on fire

feuille *nf.* leaf; sheet (*paper*); foil

fibreux, fibreuse *adj.* fibrous

fier, fière *adj.* proud

se fi/er (à) *v.* to rely (on)

figure† *nf.* face

fil *nm.* thread; **— de fer** wire

filiation *nf.* affiliation, connection

fille *nf.* daughter; **jeune —** girl

fils *nm.* son

filtre *nm.* filter

fin† *nf.* end; **à cette —** for this purpose; **mettre* — à** to put an end to

fin, -e *adj.* fine, detailed; **réglage fin** fine adjustment

fin/ir *v.* to finish

fissible *adj.* fissionable

fixe *adj.* fixed, stationary

flacon *nm.* flask

fleur *nf.* flower

flottant *ps.p.* floating

flux *nm.* flow, flux

focalisation *nf.* focus

focalis/er *v.* to focus

foi *nf.* faith, trust

fois *nf.* time (*recurrence of an event*); **à la —** at the same time; **mille —** a thousand times; **une — pour toutes** once and for all; **une seule —** a single time; **encore une —** again, once more

folie *nf.* folly; madness

foncé *adv.* (*added to name of a color*) dark: **bleu foncé** dark blue

fonction *nf.* function; **en — de** as a function of

fonctionn/er *v.* to function

fond *nm.* bottom; back; background; **à —** thorough(ly); **examiner à —** to examine thoroughly; **un — froid** a cold front (*Met.*)

se fond/er (**sur**) *v.* to be based (on)

fond/re *v.* to melt

fondu *pp.* melted; cast (*foundry*)

font (*Pr. of* **faire***) (they) make, do; (+ INFINITIVE) cause

force: à — de by dint of

forêt *nf.* forest

forme *nf.* form; **sous — de** in the form of

form/er *v.* to form

formule *nf.* formula; equation

fort, -e *adj.* strong; **château — ** *nm.* castle

fort *adv.* (*before an adj. or adv.*) very

fortement *adv.* strongly, closely

fortifi/er *v.* to strengthen

fosse *nf.* depression, hole; moat (*Arch.*)

foud/re *nf.* lightning

Fougère *nf.* Fern (*Bot.*)

four† *nm.* furnace, oven

fourn/ir *v.* to furnish

fournissant *ps.p.* furnishing

fractionnaire *adj.* fractional

frais, fraîche *adj.* cool

français, -e *adj.* French

Français *nm.* Frenchman; **Française** *nf.* Frenchwoman

français *nm.* French (*language*)

franch/ir *v.* to cross; to pass (through or over)

frappant *ps.p.* striking

frapp/er *v.* to strike; to knock

fray/er *v.* to spawn

frein/er *v.* to brake; to slow down

frénateur, frénatrice *adj.* braking; damping; checking

fréquemment *adv.* frequently

fréquence *nf.* frequency; **— d'inversion** number of cycles (A.C.)

frère *nm.* brother; **beau-—** brother-in-law

froid *nm.* cold

froid, -e *adj.* cold; **avoir* —** to be cold (*person*); **il fait —** it is cold (*weather*)

front† *nm.* forehead; front

frontière *nf.* frontier

frottement *nm.* friction

fructueux, fructueuse *adj.* fruitful, profitable

fu/ir* *v.* to flee

fumée *nf.* smoke

fum/er *v.* to smoke

fur: au — et à mesure in proportion as

furent (*fr* **être***) (they) were

fusse (*fr.* **être***) were

fut (*fr.* **être***) was

G

gabarit *nm.* top profile (*Arch.*)

gagn/er *v.* to gain, to earn; to increase; to win

galerie *nf.* gallery; **— de peinture** art gallery

garçon *nm.* boy; waiter

gard/er *v.* to keep, to retain

garni (de) *pp.* equipped (with)

gauche: à — to the left

gaz *nm.* gas

géant, -e *adj.* giant

gênant, -e *adj.* troublesome

gên/er *v.* to annoy

génie *nm.* genius; spirit; **— civil** engineering

genou *nm.* knee

genre *nm.* kind, species, genre (*literary*)

gens *nm. pl.* people

gisement *nm.* deposit (*mineralogy*)

glace *nf.* ice

glissement *nm.* sliding

gliss/er *v.* to slip, to slide

golfe *nm.* gulf (*Geog.*)

goût *nm.* taste

goutte *nf.* drop (*of water, etc.*)

gouverné *nm.* governed (person); citizen

gouvernail *nm.* rudder

grâce *nf.* pardon; — **à** because of, thanks to

gradin *nm.* step; **à —s** in the form of steps

graine *nf.* seed

grand, -e *adj.* big, tall; **un grand homme** a great man; **un homme grand** a tall man

grand *nm.* a nobleman; a person of great influence

grandeur *nf.* size; greatness; quantity

grec, grecque *adj.* Greek

Grèce Greece

grenier *nm.* attic

grenu, -e *adj.* granular

grimp/er *v.* to climb, to clamber

gris, -e *adj.* gray

Groenland Greenland

gros, -se *adj.* thick, fat

grossi *adj.* enlarged

grossier, grossière *adj.* crude, rough; vulgar

guère: ne [VERB] — scarcely, hardly

guér/ir *v.* to heal, to cure

guerre *nf.* war

guett/er *v.* to watch attentively; to stalk (*prey*)

H

habitant *nm.* inhabitant

habit/er *v.* to inhabit, to live in

habitude *nf.* habit; **d'—** usually

haine *nf.* hate

hardiesse *nf.* boldness

hasard *nm.* chance; **les lois du —** the laws of chance

haut, -e *adj.* high, tall; advanced; **plus —** above (*in a book*)

haut *nm.* height; **de —** in height

haute en couleur rosy-cheeked

hauteur *nf.* height; **la — dont on se dispose** the height which is available

havre *nm.* harbor

herbe *nf.* grass; **mauvaise —** weed

hérissé (de) *pp.* bristling (with)

heure *nf.* hour; o'clock; **à l'—** on time; **de bonne —** early; **tout à l'—** just now, right away

heureusement *adv.* fortunately

heureux, heureuse *adj.* happy, fortunate

se heurt/er *v.* to collide with

hier *adv.* yesterday

hiver *nm.* winter

homme *nm.* man

homogène *adj.* homogeneous

horloge *nf.* clock

hors de out of; outside of; **hors d'usage** out of service; **hors programme** unplanned; unexpected

hôtel *nm.* mansion; hotel

huile *nf.* oil

huit eight; **— jours** a week

hypothèse *nf.* hypothesis

I

ici *adv.* here

idée *nf.* idea

identique *adj.* identical

il en est de même de . . . the same holds true for . . . ; **il n'en est rien . . .** it is not the case at all . . .

île *nf.* island

illimité *adj.* unlimited

illuminé *adj.* illuminated; *nm.* mystic (*sect*)

il y a there is, there are

il y avait there was, there were

imaginé *pp.* invented

imagin/er *v.* to invent; to imagine

imitateur *adj.* imitative

immerg/er *v.* to sink, to submerge

immeuble locatif *nm.* apartment house

immuable *adj.* immutable, unchangeable

impair *adj.* odd-numbered

imparfait, -e *adj.* imperfect

impasse *nf.* blind alley

important, -e *adj.* large, great, important

importe: il — de it is important to; **n'importe** it does not matter

imposant, -e *adj.* imposing, impressive

s'impos/er *v.* to become necessary

impressionant, -e *adj.* impressive

imprévisible *adj.* unforeseeable, unpredictable

imprimé *pp.* imparted; printed

imprim/er *v.* to impart, to exert; to print

imput/er *v.* to attribute

impureté *nf.* impurity

inattendu, -e *adj.* unexpected

incendie *nm.* burning, fire, conflagration

incessant, -e *adj.* ceaseless

incliné *pp.* inclined

incolore *adj.* colorless

inconnu *pp.* unknown

inconvénient† *nm.* disadvantage

inculte *adj.* uncultivated

incurvé *adj.* curved

indice *nm.* index

indiscutable *adj.* indisputable

indium *nm.* indium

individu *nm.* individual

inégal, -e *adj.* unequal

inférieur, -e (à) *adj.* less (than).

infime *adj.* tiny

infini, -e *adj.* infinite; à l'— endlessly

ingénieur *nm.* engineer

ingénieux, ingénieuse *adj.* ingenious

innombrable *adj.* countless

inodore *adj.* odorless

inoxydable *adj.* stainless

s'inquiét/er *v.* to worry

insaisissable *adj.* evasive

inscri/re* *v.* to register (*Acad.*)

inscrit *pp.* registered, enrolled

insensiblement *adv.* imperceptibly

s'insinu/er *v.* to creep in, to penetrate

insonorisation *nf.* sound-proofing

s'install/er *v.* to settle down

instruit, -e *adj.* instructed; learnèd

insuffisant, -e *adj.* insufficient

insupportable *adj.* unbearable

intelligence *nf.* understanding; knowledge

interdit *pp.* prohibited

intéressé *pp.* concerned; involved

intéress/er *v.* to interest; to concern; s'— (à) to be interested (in)

intérêt *nm.* interest; self-interest

intérieur *nm.* interior

intermédiaire *adj.* intermediate

s'interrog/er *v.* to wonder; to ask oneself

interrompu *pp.* interrupted

interven/ir* *v.* to intervene; to take effect [vb. 30]

intime *adj.* very close

intimement *adv.* closely, intimately, thoroughly

introduit *pp.* introduced

inusable† *adj.* inexhaustible

inversant: en — by reversing; by inverting

inverse *adj.* inverse; à l'— de contrary to; sens — opposite direction

s'invers/er *v.* to be reversed; to reverse; to invert

invraisemblable *adj.* incredible; improbable

iode *nm.* iodine

ionis/er *v.* to ionize

ir/— *vst.* (*fr.* aller*) F. will go; C. would go

irradiant *ps.p.* radiating

isocèle *adj.* isosceles

isolant, -e *adj.* insulating

isol/er *v.* to isolate

isotope *nm.* isotope

issu (de) *pp.* originating (from); derived (from)

J

jamais: ne (VERB) jamais never; à — forever

japonais *adj.* Japanese

jardin *nm.* garden

jet/er‡ *v.* to throw; que l'on jette which is thrown; — un soupir to heave (a sigh)

jeu *nm.* action; game; set; — de cartes deck of cards

jeune *adj.* young

joie *nf.* joy

joli, -e *adj.* pretty

jouant *ps.p.* playing

jou/er *v.* to play

jour *nm.* day; au — le — from day to day

journal *nm.* newspaper

journaux *nm. pl.* newspapers

journée† *nf.* day

jugement *nm.* judgment

jug/er *v.* to judge

juillet July

juin June

jusqu'à until, as far as; jusqu'ici until now, thus far; — nos jours up to the present

juste *adj.* just, exact

se justifi/er *v.* to be confirmed, to be substantiated

K

kilomètre *nm.* kilometer (about ⅝ of a mile); .62137 miles; 1000 meters

L

la *art.* the; *pn.* it, her

là *adv.* there; **là-bas** over there

laborieux, laborieuse *adj.* hard-working, industrious

là-dedans *adv.* in it

laissant *ps.p.* allowing, leaving; — **subsister** allowing to remain

laiss/er *v.* to allow; to leave; — **de côté** to disregard

laiton *nm.* brass

lame† *nf.* blade

lanc/er *v.* to throw, to launch

langue *nf.* tongue; language

laquelle (*f. of* **lequel**) *pn.* which

large† *adj.* wide

largement *adv.* greatly

largeur *nf.* width

lav/er *v.* to wash

le *art. m.* the; *pn.* (*before verb*) it, him

leçon *nf.* lesson

lecteur *nm.* reader

lecture† *nf.* reading

léger, légère *adj.* light; slight

légèrement *adv.* slightly

lendemain *nm.* the next day

lent, -e *adj.* slow; **lentement** *adv.* slowly

lenteur *nf.* slowness

lequel *pn.* which (§61)

les *art.* the; — **uns** — **autres** each other; both

leur(s) *adj.* their

leur *pn.* to them (*before a verb*)

lev/er *v.* to raise, to lift; **se** — to get up, to rise

liaison *nf.* bond, linking, connection; **énergie de** — bonding force

libre *adj.* free

lié *pp.* connected, related

li/er *v.* to link, to connect, to relate; to tie

lieu *nm.* place; **avoir*** — to take place; **donner** — **à** to cause; **au** — **de** instead of

lieue *nf.* league (*distance measure*)

ligne *nf.* line

linéaire *adj.* linear

lingot *nm.* ingot

li/re* *v.* to read

lit *nm.* bed

lit (*fr.* **lire***) reads

littoral *nm.* shore

livre *nm.* book

livre *nf.* pound (*wt.*)

livr/er *v.* to deliver

logé *pp.* lodged

logement *nm.* lodging, quarters (*Mil.*)

loi *nf.* law

loin *adv.* far; **voir plus** — see below; see farther on in the text

lointain, -e *adj.* distant, remote

loisir *nm.* leisure

Londres London

long, -ue *adj.* long; **le long de** along

longtemps *adv.* for a long time; **il y a** — a long time ago

longueur *nf.* length; — **d'onde** wave length

lors de concurrently with; at the time of

lorsque *conj.* when

lou/er *v.* to rent; to praise

Louisiane Louisiana

lourd, -e *adj.* heavy

lui *pn.* to him, to her, to it; (*after a preposition*) him

lui-même himself; itself

lumière *nf.* light

lune *nf.* moon

lutte *nf.* battle, struggle

luxe *nm.* luxury

lycée *nm.* lycée (*French secondary school*)

M

M. *abbr.* (**Monsieur**) Mr.; **MM.** Messrs.

Madère Madeira (*island north of Canary Islands*)

magie *nf.* magic

main *nf.* hand

maintenant *adv.* now

mainten/ir* *v.* to maintain

mais *conj.* but

maison *nf.* house

maître *nm.* master; — **d'œuvre** foreman

mal *adv.* badly

mal *nm.* evil

malade *adj. and n.* sick; sick person

malfaiteur *nm.* criminal, evildoer

malgré in spite of

malheur *nm.* misfortune

malheureusement *adv.* unfortunately

manche *nf.* channel; **La Manche** The English Channel

mang/er *v.* to eat

manière *nf.* manner, way; **à la —** in the way

manqu/er *v.* to miss; to fail; to be lacking in; **— le train** to miss the train

maquette *nf.* model (*Arch.*)

marais *nm.* swamp

marbre *nm.* marble

marchandise *nf.* merchandise

marche *nf.* progress; operation; motion; march; step (*of stairs*)

marché *nm.* market

march/er *v.* to march; to run (*machinery*); to walk

maréchal *nm.* Marshal (*Mil.*)

marqué *adj.* obvious; marked

marqu/er *v.* to mark; **— un but** to score a goal

mars March; Mars

masse *nf.* mass

massif *adj.* solid, massive

matériel (*pl.* **matériaux**) *nm.* material

matière *nf.* matter; subject (*Acad.*); **— première** raw material

matin *nm.* morning

matinée *nf.* morning

mauvais, -e *adj.* bad, poor (*quality*)

mécanique *nm.* mechanics; **— quantique** quantum mechanics

méchant, -e *adj.* wicked, bad, evil

médecin *nm.* doctor (M.D.)

médical, -e *adj.* medical (*m.pl.* **médicaux**)

médiocre *adj.* mediocre, small

méfi/er *v.* to beware

meilleur, -e *adj.* better (*comparative of* **bon**); **le (la, les) meilleur(e)(s)** the best

mélange *nm.* mixture

mélang/er *v.* to mix

même *adj.* (*before noun*) same; (*after noun*) very, itself; **de — que** the same as; *adv.* even

mémoire *nm.* article, paper (*Acad.*)

ménagé *pp.* arranged, provided

men/er‡ *v.* to lead

ment/ir *v.* to lie, prevaricate

mer *nf.* sea

mère *nf.* mother

méridienne *nf.* meridian (*Geog.*)

méridional, -e *adj.* southern (*m.pl.* **méridionaux**)

mésopotamien *adj.* Mesopotamian

mesure *nf.* measure; **à — que** gradually as, proportionately as

mesur/er *v.* to measure

métaux *n.pl.* metals

méthode *nf.* method

mètre *nm.* meter; 39.3701 inches; about 1 1/10 yards

mett/re* *v.* to put; to place; to spend (TIME); **— au point** to perfect; **— en doute** to cast doubt upon; **— en état de** put in a position to; **— en évidence** to demonstrate; **— en jeu** to produce; **se — à** to begin (§56)

meurt (*Pr. of* **mourir***) dies

meuvent (*Pr. of* **mouvoir***) (they) move

midi *nm.* noon, midday; **le Midi** the South (*usually southern France*)

mieux *adv.* better; **faute de —** for lack of something better

milieu *nm.* environment; medium, substance; **au — de** in the middle of, in the midst of

mille thousand

milliard *nm.* a billion (1000 million)

milliardième a billionth

milliers *n.pl.* thousands

mince *adj.* thin, delicate

minerai *nm.* ore

minéral *nm.* mineral

minime *adj.* slight, minimum

minuscule *adj.* slight, tiny

minuit *nm.* midnight

minutieusement *adv.* minutely, in detail, painstakingly

mirent (*PD of* **mettre***) (they) put

miroir *nm.* mirror

mis *pp.* (**mettre***) put, placed; **— à part** excepted, set aside; **— au point** perfected; **— en évidence** demonstrated, shown; **— en œuvre** put into operation

mise en évidence *nf.* demonstration

mise en œuvre *nf.* operation

Mlle *abbr.* (**mademoiselle**) Miss

modérateur *nm.* moderator

modér/er *v.* to moderate, to modify, to damp

moindre *adj.* less; le — the least; — que less than

moins *adv.* less; à — que *conj.* unless; au — at least; de — en — less and less; du — at least; — de (NUMBER) less than

mois *nm.* month

moitié *nf.* half, one-half

monde *nm.* world; tout le — everybody

montagneux, montagneuse *adj.* mountainous

montée *nf.* climb, rise

mont/er *v.* to climb; to rise; to go upstairs; to board (*a vehicle*) (*uses auxiliary* être* *when intransitive*)

montr/er *v.* to show, to demonstrate; se — to appear, to occur, to happen

morceau *nm.* piece, portion

mord/re *v.* to bite

mort *pp.* (mourir*) died; *adj.* dead; *nf.* death; *nm.* the deceased

mortier *nm.* mortar (*Arch.*) (*Mil.*); — de liaison mortar (*cementing*)

Moscou Moscow

moteur, motrice *adj.* motive (*force*)

motif *nm.* motive (*reason*); theme (*Music*)

motrice *adj. f.* (moteur) motive; installations —s engine installations

mou, molle *adj.* soft

mouche *nf.* housefly

moule *nm.* mould, matrix

moul/er *v.* to mould, to shape

mourir* *v.* to die (*uses auxiliary* être* *with pp.* mort)

mourr/— *vst.* (mourir*) F. will die; C. would die

mourut (*PD of* mourir*) died

mouvement *nm.* movement, motion

mouvoir* *v.* to move

moyen *nm.* means, manner, way; au — de by means of; les —s the means, the resources

moyen, -ne *adj.* average, medium, middle; vie moyenne half-life (*Phys.*)

muet, -te *adj.* mute, silent

muni *pp.* equipped (de) with

mur *nm.* wall; — mitoyen fireproof wall (*Arch.*)

muraille *nf.* wall

musée *nm.* museum

N

naissance *nf.* birth, beginning; après avoir pris — after originating; donner — à to produce

naître* *v.* to be born [vb. 16]; *pp.* né (*auxiliary* être*)

navigu/er *v.* to sail, to navigate

navire *nm.* ship

né *pp.* born

néanmoins *adv.* nevertheless

nef *nm.* nave (*of a church*)

néfaste *adj.* disastrous

négatif, négative *adj.* negative

ne . . . pas *negation of verb* (§33); ne . . . plus no longer; ne . . . que only

net, -te *adj.* clear, distinct

nettement *adv.* clearly

nettoy/er‡ *v.* to clean

neuf nine

neuf, neuve *adj.* brand-new

neutre *adj.* neutral

neuve *adj. f.* brand-new

nez *nm.* nose

ni . . . ni neither . . . nor

n'importe . . . qui anybody at all; — quoi anything at all; — quel(le) . . . any . . . at all

niveau *nm.* level (e.g., *of water*); — de la mer sea-level

nœud *nm.* knot

noir, -e *adj.* black

nom *nm.* name; sous le — de by the name of

nombre *nm.* number; — atomique atomic number

nombreux, nombreuse *adj.* numerous

nommer *v.* to name

non *adv.* no; — plus either

nord *nm.* north

Norvège Norway

notamment *adv.* especially

not/er *v.* to note, to notice

notre *adj.* our

nôtre *pn.* ours

nourr/ir *v.* to feed, to nourish

nourriture *nf.* food, nourishment

nouveau, nouvel, nouvelle *adj.* new; de nouveau again

nouvelle *adj. f.* new

noyau *nm.* nucleus

nu, -e *pp.* bare, stripped, naked

nuage *nm.* cloud

nuancé *adj.* discerning; specific

nucléaire *adj.* nuclear

nuit *nf.* night; la — at night, every night; la — se fait night is falling

nul, -le *adj.* no; nil; zero

nulle part *adv.* nowhere

numérot/er *v.* to number

O

obé/ir (à) *v.* to obey

s'objectiv/er *v.* to be demonstrated

objet *nm.* object

oblig/er *v.* to require, to oblige

observateur *nm.* observer

observ/er *v.* to observe

obten/ir* *v.* to obtain; s'obtient is obtained [vb. 28]

obtenu *pp.* obtained

obtien/— *vst.* (obtenir*) [vb. 28] obtain/

occasionn/er *v.* to cause

occidental, -e *adj.* western

occup/er *v.* to occupy; s'— de to devote oneself to, to be busy with

odorat *nm.* sense of smell, olfaction

œil *nm.* eye; (*pl.* yeux); à l'œil by the eye, with the eye

œuf *nm.* egg

œuvre *nm.* work

offert *pp.* offered, presented

offr/ir* *v.* to offer [vb. 17]

ogival, -e *adj.* gothic (*Arch.*)

oiseau *nm.* bird

ombre *nf.* shadow

ombré *pp.* shaded

on *pn.* one; we; "they" (§26)

onde *nf.* wave

ondulatoire *adj.* undulatory, wave; mécanique — wave mechanics

opère (*Pr.* opér/er) operates

opér/er‡ *v.* to operate; s'— to take place; to occur

opposé *pp.* opposite

s'oppos/er (à) *v.* to be contrasted (with)

or† now; but; now we know that . . . ; *nm.* gold

orbite *nf.* orbit

ordinaire *adj.* ordinary; d'— usually

ordonn/er *v.* to order, to command

ordre *nm.* order; de l'— de on the order of

oreille *nf.* ear

orgueil *nm.* pride

orifice *nm.* orifice, opening

origine *nf.* origin

ôté *pp.* eliminated, removed

où *adv.* where; when

ou *conj.* or

oubli/er *v.* to forget

ouest *nm.* west

oui yes

outre besides, in addition to; en — in addition to; — -tombe beyond the tomb

ouvert *pp.* (ouvrir*) opened; étant — being open

ouverture *nf.* opening, aperture

ouvrage *nm.* work (*literary or artistic*)

ouvr/ir* *v.* to open

ovation *nf.* acclaim; reception

oxygène *nm.* oxygen

P

pair *adj.* even-numbered

palais *nm.* palace

palpe *nf.* feeler, antenna (*insects*)

paquet *nm.* pack, packet, group

par *prep.* by; per; — exemple for example

paradis *nm.* paradise

paraiss/— *vst.* (paraître*) appear/—

paraître* *v.* to appear [vb. 18]

parce que *conj.* because

parcour/ir* *v.* to traverse; to travel through [vb. 4]

pareil, -le *adj.* such (a)

parcours *nm.* path, travel

parenté *nf.* relationship, kinship

parfait, -e *adj.* perfect

parfois *adv.* sometimes

parisien, -ne *adj.* Parisian

parl/er *v.* to speak, to talk

parmi *prep.* among

parole *nf.* word

part *nf.* part, share; **d'une** — ... **d'autre** — ... on the one hand ... on the other hand; **de toutes** —s from everywhere; **nulle** — nowhere; **quelque** — somewhere

partag/er *v.* to divide up, to share

partant (de) *ps.p.* starting (with *or* at)

particularité *nf.* characteristic

particule *nf.* particle

particulier, particulière *adj.* individual, unique, special; private (*as in* **maison particulière** private house); **en particulier** in particular

partie *nf.* part (*of a whole*); **faire*** — **de** to constitute a part of

partiellement *adv.* partially

part/ir* *v.* to depart, to leave (*uses auxiliary* **être***) [vb. 19]; **à** — **de** beginning with

partout *adv.* everywhere; **un peu** — almost everywhere

paru *pp.* (**paraître***) appeared

parut (*PD of* **paraître***) (it) appeared

parven/ir* *v.* to succeed (**à**) in [vb. 30]

parvien/— *vst.* (*Pr. of* **parvenir***) reach/, attain/

parviendr/— *vst.* (**parvenir***) *F.* will succeed; *C.* would succeed

pas *nm.* pace, step; pass, strait (*Geog.*); **Pas de Calais** Straits of Dover

pass/er *v.* to pass; to take (*an examination*); — **de** ... **à** ... to make the transition from ... to ...; **se** — to happen; to spend (*time*)

passion *nf.* enthusiasm, emotion

patte *nf.* foot (*of animals*)

pauvre *adj.* poor; (*after noun* = poverty-stricken; *before noun* = deserving of pity)

pauvreté *nf.* poverty

pay/er *v.* to pay (for)

pays *nm.* country (*political, territorial*)

paysan *nm.* country boy; peasant

pêche *nf.* fishing

pêch/er *v.* to fish

peind/re* *v.* to paint

peine *nf.* difficulty; **à** — hardly; **sans** — easily, without difficulty

peintre *nm.* painter

peinture *nf.* painting

pellicule *nf.* film, layer

se pench/er (sur) *v.* to be bent (over)

pendant *prep.* during; for (A TIME); — **que** *conj.* while

pendentif *nm.* pendentive (*Arch.*)

pend/re *v.* to hang, to suspend

pendule *nm.* pendulum; *nf.* clock

pénétrant, -e *adj.* penetrating; **peu** — non-penetrating

pensée *nf.* thought

pens/er (à) *v.* to think (of) (about) [*attention*]; (**de**) about [*opinion*]

pente *nf.* slope

percement *nm.* piercing

perd/re *v.* to lose

père *nm.* father

perfectionné, -e *adj.* perfected

périlleux, périlleuse *adj.* dangerous

période *nf.* period; half-life (*Phys.*)

pér/ir *v.* to perish

permett/re* *v.* to permit, to allow [vb. 14]

perse *adj.* Persian

personne *nf.* person; **ne** ... — nobody

perte *nf.* loss

pesanteur *nf.* weight; gravity — **universelle** gravity

pesée *nf.* evaluation; weighing

pes/er *v.* to weigh

petit, -e *adj.* small; **moins** — larger; **peu** — large; **plus** — smaller

pétrole *nm.* oil, gasoline; **moteur à** — oil engine (*e.g.,* Diesel)

peu *adv.* little; **à** — **près** approximately; — (+ ADJECTIVE) *translate by the antonym of the adj., e.g.,* **peu profond** shallow *or* not so (deep); — **à** — little by little; — **marqué** negligible; **un** — a little

peut (*Pr. of* **pouvoir***) can; **il se** — it is possible (**que**) that

peuvent (*Pr. of* **pouvoir***) can

phénomène *nm.* phenomenon

physicien† *nm.* physicist (*a physician is* **médecin**)

physique *nf.* physics; *adj.* physical

pièce *nf.* piece, part; room; play; document; — **polaire** pole (*of a magnet*) pied *nm.* foot (*as a measure,* 12.7892 *U.S. inches*); base (*Geom.*)

Pierre le Grand Peter the Great, Czar of Russia (1682–1725)

pignon *nm.* gable end (*Arch.*)

pile *nf.* reactor (*atomic*) (*Phys.*); — autorégénératrice "breeder" pile

pinceau *nm.* beam (*light*)

piqu/er *v.* to sting (*insect*); to inject (*hypodermic*); to prick (*with a sharp instrument*)

piscine *nf.* swimming pool

plac/er *v.* to place

plafonnement *nm.* maximum altitude; levelling-off place

se plaind/re* *v.* to complain

plai/re* (à) *v.* to please

plaît: on se — one enjoys; s'il vous — please (*abbr.* s.v.p.)

plan *nm.* plane (*Geom.*); map (*city*); floor-plan (*Arch.*); — horizontal (vertical) horizontal (vertical) plane; — médian mid-plane; au premier — in the foreground

plancher *nm.* floor

plaque *nf.* plate (*of a ship,* etc.) (*photographic*)

plat, -e *adj.* flat

plateau *nm.* plateau; platform (*of a scale*)

plein, -e *adj.* full

pleur/er *v.* to weep, to cry

pli/er *v.* to fold, to bend; se — (à) to adapt, to adjust (to)

plomb *nm.* lead (*metal*)

plongée *nf.* dive

plong/er *v.* to dive, to plunge

pluie *nf.* rain

plupart: la — des *adv.* most of the

plus *adv.* more; en — (de) in addition (to); de —en — more and more; ne . . . plus no longer; plus grand(e) que bigger than; — que jamais more than ever; — . . . — the more . . . the more

plusieurs *adv.* several

plutôt (que) *adv.* rather (than)

poésie *nf.* poetry

poids *nm.* weight

point: ne (VERB) point = ne (VERB) pas *simple negation*

poisson *nm.* fish

polissage *nm.* polishing

pompe *nf.* pump; — à vide vacuum pump

pondérable *adj.* weighable

pont *nm.* bridge; deck (*of a ship*)

poreux, poreuse *adj.* porous

porte *nf.* door

port/er *v.* to carry; to wear; que l'on porte which is brought

portique *nm.* porch (*Arch.*)

posé *pp.* asked, posed

pos/er *v.* to ask (*question*); to place

positif, positive *adj.* positive

posséd/er‡ *v.* to have, to possess

poste *nm.* station, post; — de haute fréquence high-frequency generator; — émetteur transmitting station, transmitter

poteau *nm.* pile (*Arch.*); post, pole

poudre *nf.* powder

pour *prep.* for; — cent per cent; — effet as a result; — (+ INFINITIVE) in order to . . . ; — 100 per cent; — que so that

pourchass/er *v.* to hunt, to pursue

pourquoi *adv.* why?

pourr/— *vst.* (pouvoir*) *F.* will be able; *C.* would be able

poursuivant *ps.p.* continuing

pourtant *adv.* however

pourvu (de) *pp.* provided (with)

poussé *pp.* developed; vide — high vacuum

poussée *nf.* thrust (*Arch.*); push

pouss/er *v.* to push; — un cri to cry out, to shout; — un soupir to heave a sigh

poussière *nf.* dust

poutre *nf.* beam (*Arch.*)

pouvant *ps.p.* being able to; capable of

pouvoir* *v.* to be able [vb. 20]

pouvoir *nm.* power

praticien *nm.* practitioner

pratique *nf.* practice; *adj.* practical

pratiqué *pp.* carried on, practiced

pratiquement *adv.* practically

pratiqu/er *v.* to carry out, to execute

préalable *adj.* prerequisite

précéd/er *v.* to precede

précis, -e *adj.* precise

précis/er *v.* to determine, to specify

précision *nf.* detail

préconisé *pp.* highly praised

premier, première *nm.* and *number* first

prenant *ps.p.* taking

prend/re* *v.* to take [vb. 21]; — **naissance** to originate; — **garde** to be careful

prenn/— *vst.* (**prendre***) take

prépar/er *v.* to prepare

près *adv.* near; **à peu** — approximately; **à** — nearly; **au (millième) près** almost to the (thousandth); **tout** — **(de)** very near (to)

près de *prep.* near (*location*); about to (*do an action*)

se présent/er *v.* to appear

presque *adv.* almost

se press/er *v.* to hurry, to be in a hurry

pression *nf.* pressure

présumé *pp.* presumed, assumed

prêt, -e *adj.* ready

prétend/re† *v.* to claim, to allege

prétendu *pp.* alleged, claimed

prétention *nf.* claim

prêt/er *v.* to lend; **se** — **à** to lend itself to . . .

preuve *nf.* proof; **faire** — **de** to give proof of

préven/ir* *v.* to forewarn, to warn, to alert [vb. 30]

prévoir* *v.* to foresee; to anticipate [vb. 31]

prévu *pp.* anticipated, foreseen, predicted

prière *nf.* prayer

primaire *nm.* primary

primitif, primitive *adj.* original

principe *nm.* basis, element, principle

printemps *nm.* spring (*season*)

pris *pp.* (**prendre***) taken, caught; — **pour** taken as; — **sur** taken from; (*mortar, cement*) hardened

prix *nm.* prize, price; **au** — **de** at the price of

procédé *nm.* process, procedure

procéd/er‡ *v.* to proceed

prochain, -e *adj.* next

proche (de) *adv.* near

produi/re* *v.* to produce [vb. 22]

se produisant *ps.p.* occurring

produit *nm.* product, material; *pp.* produced

profess/er *v.* to teach, to profess

profil *nm.* cross-section; — **surbaissé** segmental profile; — **surélevé** stilted profile (*Arch.*)

profond, -e *adj.* deep; **peu** — shallow

profondeur *nf.* depth

progrès *nm.* progress

proie *nf.* prey

projet *nm.* plan, project; **à l'état de** — in the planning stage

promett/re* *v.* to promise [vb. 14]

se propag/er *v.* to be propagated

propre *adj.* (*before noun*) own; *after noun*) clean; appropriate; — **à** peculiar to

proprement dit(e) *adj.* per se; proper; itself; **à proprement parler** actually, really

propriété *nf.* property; characteristic

prospection *nf.* prospecting

protection *nf.* shield

protég/er‡ *v.* to protect

protéide *nf.* protein

prouv/er *v.* to prove

provenance *nf.* source, origin

provenant *ps.p.* resulting

proven/ir* *v.* to originate [vb. 30]

provisoirement *adv.* tentatively

provoqué *pp.* produced

pu *pp.* (**pouvoir***) been able

public, publique *adj.* public

public *nm.* public; **le grand** — the general public

publié *pp.* published

puis *adv.* then, next

puis/er *v.* to derive, to get

puisque *conj.* since, inasmuch as

puiss/— *vst.* (**pouvoir***) can

puissamment *adv.* greatly, powerfully

puissance *nf.* power; **de faible** — low power(ed)

puissant, -e *adj.* powerful

puisse may, can

puits *nm.* well

pun/ir *v.* to punish

pur, -e *adj.* pure

Q

quadrilatère *nm.* quadrilateral

qualité: en — de in the status of

quand *conj.* when; — même *adv.* nevertheless, anyway

quant à as for . . . ; with regard to . . .

quantique *adj.* quantum

quantité *nf.* quantity; une toute petite — a very small quantity

quarante forty

quart *nm.* one quarter, ¼

quatre four

quasi *adv.* almost

que . . . ! *adv.* how . . . !

que *pn.* which, whom; that

que *conj.* that; (*in comparisons*) as, than

quel, -le *adj.* which, what

quelconque *adj.* ordinary; any; a given . . .

quelque *adj.* some; quelques a few, several; quelque chose something quelques-un(e)s *pn.* some

quelquefois *adv.* sometimes

quel(le) que soit [X] whatever [X] may be

quelqu'un(e) *pn.* somebody

qu'est-ce que? what . . . ?

qu'est-ce qui? what?

queue *nf.* tail; line

qui *pn.* who; which; that

quitt/er *v.* to leave, to depart from

quoi *pn.* what; après — after which

quoique *conj.* although

quotidien, -ne *adj.* daily; *nm.* daily (*paper*)

R

racine *nf.* root

racont/er *v.* to recount, to tell (*a story*)

rade *nf.* port, roads (*Naval*)

radio-élément *nm.* radioactive element

raide *adj.* steep, stiff

raie *nf.* ray; — spectrale spectral band (*Phys.*)

raison *nf.* reason; proportion; à — de at a rate of; avoir* — to be right; en — de as a result of; en — directe in direct proportion; en — inverse in inverse proportion; avec — rightly

raisonnement *nm.* reasoning

ralent/ir *v.* to slow down, to decelerate

ramass/er *v.* to pick up (again)

rameau *nm.* branch

ramen/er‡ *v.* to lead back

ramifi/er *v.* to branch out, to ramify

rang *nm.* rank

rang/er *v.* to arrange; to line up

se rappel/er‡ *v.* to recall, to remember

rappelons let us remember

rapport *nm.* relationship, connection; ratio; par — à as compared with, in relation to

se rapport/er (à) *v.* to be related (to); to be connected

rapproch/er *v.* to approach; se — de to approach

raréfi/er *v.* to rarefy, to thin out

rassembl/er *v.* to assemble, to collect

rattach/er *v.* to attach, to connect; se — à to be related to, to deal with

se ravis/er *v.* to change one's mind

ravitaillement *nm.* supply

rayon *nm.* ray; radius (*Geom.*); — d'action operating range; — lumineux light ray; —s X X-rays

rayonnement *nm.* radiation

réacteur *nm.* reactor

réactif *nm.* reagent (*Chem.*)

réaction *nf.* — en chaîne chain reaction

réagir *v.* to react

réalisation *nf.* accomplishment

réalis/er *v.* to accomplish; to create

réalité: en — in reality, really

récemment *adv.* recently; tout — quite recently

recevoir* *v.* to receive [vb. 23]

réchauff/er *v.* to warm up, to heat

recherch/er *v.* to do research; to analyze, to seek out

recherche *nf.* research; search; à la — seeking, looking for

récipient *nm.* container

reçoi/— *vst.* (recevoir*) receive/ [vb. 23]

recommand/er *v.* to entrust

recommenc/er *v.* to recommence, to begin (*sthg.*) again

reconnaît/re* *v.* to realize, to recognize; se — to recognize oneself [vb. 2]

recours *nm.* recourse

recouvert (de) *pp.* covered (with)

recouvr/ir* *v.* to cover (de) with

rectitude *nf.* accuracy

recueill/ir* *v.* to collect, to gather

récupéré *pp.* recovered

reçut received

redescend/re *v.* to go down . . . again

redevable *adj.* indebted

redresseur *nm.* commutator (*Elec.*)

réduire* *v.* to reduce [vb. 22]

réduit *pp.* (réduire*) reduced; — à néant reduced to nothing; destroyed

réel, -e *adj.* real, actual

réfectoire *nm.* refectory, dining-hall

se référ/er (à) *v.* to refer (to)

réfléch/ir *v.* to reflect

réflexion *nf.* reflection

réfractaire *adj.* fireproof; refractory

se réfract/er *v.* to be refracted

refroidi *pp.* cooled

refroid/ir *v.* to cool (off)

refroidissement *nm.* cooling

refroidisseur *nm.* cooling element

regard/er *v.* to look at; to regard; to concern; cela ne vous regarde pas that does not concern you

réglage *nm.* control, regulation; barre de — control rod

règle *nf.* rule

réglé (sur) *pp.* based (on)

règne *nm.* reign (*of a king,* etc.)

régn/er *v.* to exist

réitér/er *v.* to repeat, to reiterate

rejet/er‡ *v.* to throw back, to reject; to throw upwards

rejoign/— *vst.* (rejoindre*) rejoin/

relâch/er *v.* to release

relai *nm.* relay

relatif, relative *adj.* relative

relation *nf.* relationship

relativité *nf.* relativity

reliant *ps.p.* relating

relié *pp.* related, connected

reli/er *v.* to join, to tie

remarquable *adj.* remarkable

remarqu/er *v.* to notice, to observe

remarquons let us notice

remett/re* *v.* to remit, to give back; to postpone [vb. 14]

se remirent en route (they) started off again

remis *pp.* given back; — à neuf renovated

remont/er *v.* to go up again; to wind (*a clock*); to date back to (*a date*); — le courant to go upstream

remorqu/er *v.* to pull, to tow

remous *nm.* eddy; — atmosphériques atmospheric eddies

remplaçant: en — by replacing

remplacement *nm.* replacement

remplac/er *v.* to replace, to change (*a part of a machine*)

rempl/ir *v.* to fill (de) with

remport/er *v.* to win (*a victory*); to achieve

remu/er *v.* to move about, to be in motion

rencontr/er *v.* to meet, to encounter

rend/re *v.* to render, to make (= to cause to be); to bring; se — compte de to realize

rendu *pp.* rendered

renferm/er *v.* to contain, to include

renommé *pp.* famous

renouvellement *nm.* replenishment, renewal

renseignement *nm.* information (*pl. often used*)

rentr/er *v.* to go home; to re-enter

repand/re *v.* to spread

répandu *pp.* spread; widespread

reparaît (*Pr.* of reparaître*) reappears

réparation *nf.* repair

réparti *pp.* divided, shared

répart/ir *v.* to divide up; to distribute

repart/ir* *v.* to depart again

répartition *nf.* distribution

répét/er *v.* to repeat

repli *nm.* fold, crease

répliqu/er *v.* to reply

répond/re *v.* to answer, to respond, to correspond, to reply

repos *nm.* rest; au — at rest

repos/er (sur) *v.* to depend (upon)

repouss/er *v.* to repulse

reprend/re* *v.* to take up . . . again; to resume; to take back

représent/er *v.* to represent; se — to imagine, to picture

requis *pp.* required

resserr/er *v.* to constrict

résolu *pp.* resolved; solved

résolution *nf.* solution (*of a problem*)

résoud/re* *v.* to resolve; to solve

respir/er *v.* to breathe

ressembl/er *v.* to resemble

restant *nm.* remainder; *ps.p.* remaining

reste (*Pr.* rester) remains; il en — there
remain(s)

reste *nm.* remainder; du — moreover,
however

rest/er *v.* to remain (*uses* être* *as auxiliary*)

restreint *pp.* limited, restrained

résultant (de) *ps.p.* resulting (from)

résultat *nm.* result

retard *nm.* delay; en — late

retardé *pp.* delayed, retarded

reten/ir* *v.* to retain, to remember, to
keep [vb. 28]

retien/— *vst.* (retenir*) retain/

rétine *nf.* retina

retir/er *v.* to withdraw

retour *nm.* return; de — back

retourn/er *v.* to return; to turn around;
to turn over; se — to turn around

retrouv/er *v.* to rediscover, to find again

réun/ir *v.* to assemble, to join together, to
co-exist

réunion *nf.* meeting

réunissent (they) meet

réuss/ir (à) *v.* to succeed (in); — à un
examen to *pass* an examination

revanche: en — on the other hand

rêve *nm.* dream

réveill/er *v.* to awaken

révél/er *v.* to reveal

reven/ir* *v.* to come back, to return [vb.
30]

revêtement *nm.* casing, revetment

revêt/ir *v.* to cover

revien/— *vst.* (revenir*) reappear/

revoir* *v.* to revise, to review; to see . . .
again [vb. 31]

revue *nf.* magazine; review

richesse *nf.* wealth

rien *pn.* nothing; ne . . . rien nothing;
il n'en est — such is not at all the
case

rigoureusement *adv.* strictly

rigoureux, rigoureuse *adj.* strict; complete

rire* *v.* to laugh

risqu/er (de) *v.* to run the risk (of), to
threaten (to)

rivage *nm.* shore, bank (*of a body of
water*)

rive *nf.* shore, (*river*) bank

roche *nf.* rock

romain, -e *adj.* Roman

roman *nm.* novel (*literature*)

romp/re *v.* to break

roue *nf.* wheel; — directrice steering
wheel; — motrice drive wheel

rouge *adj.* red; (porter) au — vif (to
bring) to red-hot

roug/ir *v.* to blush

roul/er *v.* to roll

royal, -e *adj.* royal (*m.pl.* royaux)

rue *nf.* street

Russie *nf.* Russia

S

sa *adj.* his, her, its

sach/— *vst.* (savoir*) know/

sagesse *nf.* wisdom, sagacity

sais (*Pr.* savoir*) know

sais/ir *v.* to grasp, to seize

saison *nf.* season

sait: on — it is known

salé, -e *adj.* saline, salt

salle *nf.* room; — de théâtre auditorium

sans *prep.* without

Sargasse Sargasso (*seaweed*)

satisfai/re* *v.* to satisfy [vb. 12]

satisfaisant, -e *adj.* satisfactory

saur/— *vst.* (savoir*) *F.* will know, will
be able; *C.* would know, would be
able, could

saut/er *v.* to jump, to skip; to explode

sauv/er *v.* to save

saveur *nf.* taste, savor

savoir* *v.* to know, to know how to [vb.
24]

savoir: (*or*) à savoir: namely: . . .

schéma *nm.* schematic drawing

scindé *pp.* split

scrut/er *v.* to scrutinize

Scythe *nm.* Scythian

sec, sèche *adj.* dry

séch/er *v.* to dry

secours *nm.* help

sécurité *nf.* safety

sein *nm.* midst; heart (*of a machine*, etc.)

seize sixteen

séjour *nm.* visit, stay; habitat

sel *nm.* salt

selon *prep.* according to; depending upon

semaine *nf.* week

semblable *adj.* similar

sembl/er *v.* to seem

sens *nm.* sense, meaning; opinion; direction; en ce — que in the sense that; — inverse opposite direction

sensibilité† *nf.* sensitivity

sensible† *adj.* sensitive; noticeable

sensiblement† *adv.* obviously, noticeably

sent/ir* *v.* to feel; to smell

sépar/er *v.* to separate

sept seven

ser/— *vst.* (être*) F. will be; C. would be; (*as an auxiliary*) F. will have, C. would have

sériation *nf.* sequence, placing in series

série *nf.* series

sérieux, sérieuse *adj.* marked; serious; important

serment *nm.* vow, promise

serpentin *nm.* coil

serr/er *v.* to squeeze, to press tight

sert (*Pr.* servir*) serves

serv/ir* *v.* to serve (de) as [vb. 25]; se — de to make use of

serviteur *nm.*, servant

ses *possessive pl.* his, her, its

seuil *nm.* threshold

seul, -e *adj.* alone; (*before noun*) only, single

seulement *adv.* only

sévèrement *adv.* strictly

si *adv.* so; *conj.* if, whether; — ce n'est que except

siècle *nm.* century

sien, -ne *pn.* (*after a definite article*) his, hers

signal/er *v.* to point out

silice *nf.* silica

sillonn/er *v.* to furrow

sinon *adv.* if not; otherwise

sinueux, sinueuse *adj.* winding

sociaux *adj.* (*m.pl.*) social

société *nf.* company, organization, society

sœur *nf.* sister

soi *pn.* oneself

soi/— *vst.* (être*) be; soient let there be

soign/er *v.* to care for, to take care of

soin *nm.* care

soir *nm.* evening

soit that is, i.e.; be, will be; let (math); soit . . . soit either . . . or

soixante sixty

soixante-dix seventy

sol *m.* soil, ground

soldat *nm.* soldier

soleil *nm.* sun

sombre *adj.* dark

sommairement *adv.* briefly

somme *nf.* sum (*Math.*)

sommier *nm.* beam (*Arch.*)

son *nm.* sound

son *adj.* his, her, its

sonn/er *v.* to sound; to strike (*clock*); to ring (*bells*)

sonore *adj.* sonorous; sound-transmitting

sont (*Pr.* être*) are

sorte *nf.* kind, sort, species; de la — in this way; en — que so that; en quelque — in a way

sortie *nf.* exit; outlet, leaving

sort/ir* *v.* to leave, to go out of [vb. 26]

se souci/er (de) *v.* to be concerned (with) (about)

soudain, -e *adj.* sudden

soudé *pp.* fused, joined, attached

souffl/er *v.* to blow, to breathe, to whisper

souffr/ir *v.* to suffer

soulev/er‡ *v.* to raise

soulign/er *v.* to emphasize, to underline

soumett/re* *v.* to submit; to subject [vb. 14]

soumis *pp.* subjected (à) to

soupape *nf.* valve

soupçonn/er *v.* to suspect

souplesse *nf.* flexibility

sourire* *v.* to smile

sous *prep.* under; — -entendu implication

sous-marin *nm.* submarine

soustrayant *ps.p.* subtracting

soutien *nm.* support

souvent *adv.* often

souverain *nm.* sovereign, king

spectre *nm.* spectrum

spirituel, -le† *adj.* witty

stationn/er *v.* to park (*a vehicle*)

statuaire *nf.* statuary

sub/ir *v.* to undergo, to experience

subsist/er *v.* to remain, to exist, to subsist

subtil, -e *adj.* thin, rarefied

suc *nm.* juice

successif, successive *adj.* successive

sud *nm.* south

Suède Sweden

suffi/re* *v.* to suffice

suffisamment *adv.* enough, sufficiently

suffisant, -e *adj.* sufficient

suggér/er‡ *v.* to suggest

suisse *adj.* Swiss

suite: à la — de as a result of; following; continuing on from

suivant *prep.* according to, depending upon; *ps.p* following; — que *conj.* depending on whether, according as

suiv/re* *v.* to follow [vb. 27]

sujet *nm.* subject

superficie *nf.* area, surface

supérieur, -e (à) *adj.* greater (than); superior (to)

suppli/er (à) ... (par) *v.* to compensate (for) ... (by) ...

support/er *v.* to endure

suppos/er *v.* to suppose; supposons let us suppose, let us postulate

supprim/er *v.* to cancel

sur *prep.* on; (*dimensions*) by

sûr, -e *adj.* sure, certain; bien sûr sure!

surbaissée: voûte — segmental arch (*Arch.*)

surcroît: par — in addition, moreover

surélevée: voûte — stilted arch (*Arch.*)

surnommé *pp.* named

surtout *adv.* especially, primarily, above all

surveill/er *v.* to supervise

surven/ir* *v.* to arrive

survient along comes ...

susceptible (de) *adj.* capable (of) ...

suscit/er *v.* to arouse, to excite

système *nm.* system; — de référence system used as an example

T

tableau *nm.* picture, panel; — noir blackboard

taille *nf.* size, stature, dimensions

taill/er *v.* to trim

se taire* *v.* to fall silent

tandis que *conj.* whereas, while

tant *adv.* so much, so many; en — de insofar as

tard *adv.* late

tard/er *v.* to delay

tâtonnement *nm.* groping

tel, -le *adj.* such a ...; such and such a ...; — que such as

tellement *adv.* so much, so

témoign/er *v.* to substantiate, to attest; to witness

témoin *nm.* witness; evidence; comme — as a guide

temps *nm.* weather; time; de — à autre, de — en — from time to time

tend/re *v.* to stretch tight, make taut

ten/ir* *v.* to hold [vb. 28] (§37); se — to remain, to stay; — à to be anxious to; — compte de to keep an account of

tension *nf.* voltage, potential, gradient (*Elec.*); à haute — high tension; — redressée direct current; — superficielle surface tension

tente *nf.* tent

tent/er (de) *v.* to attempt (to)

tenu *pp.* (tenir*) held, bound

terme: au — de at the end of

termin/er *v.* to terminate, to end

terrain *nm.* building site (*Arch.*)

terre *nf.* earth, soil; Earth; par — on the ground

terre cuite *nf.* terra cotta

terrestre *adj.* terrestrial

tête *nf.* head

théâtre *nm.* theater; salle de — auditorium

théorie *nf.* theory

tien/— *vst.* (tenir*) hold/

tiers *nm.* one-third

tige *nf.* stem; trunk (*tree*); shaft, rod (*Mech.*)

tir *nm.* fire (*gun*)

tir/er *v.* to draw, to pull; d'en — to obtain (from it)

titre *nm.* title; composition; à juste — with good reason

toit *nm.* roof

toiture *nf.* roof, roofing

tomb/er *v.* to fall (*uses auxiliary* être*)

ton *nm.* tone; d'un — in a tone

tonne *nf.* ton

tort *nm.* wrong; à — wrongly; avoir* — to be wrong

tortue *nf.* turtle

toucher *nm.* sense of touch

touch/er *v.* to touch

toujours *adv.* always, still

tour† *nm.* turn (*to do sthg.*); à son — in its (his, her) turn; *nf.* tower

tourn/er *v.* to rotate, to turn; — sur (elle-) même to rotate on its own axis

tous *adj. m.pl.* (*tout*) all; *pn.* everybody, everything, all; — les deux both

tout, -e *adj.* all, every; du tout at all; pas du tout not at all (§72); tout à fait entirely, completely; tout ce qui, tout ce que everything; tout à l'heure recently, just now; tout au plus at the very most; tout autre quite otherwise; tout de suite immediately; tout le monde everybody

toutefois *adv.* nevertheless, in any case

tracé *nm.* layout, plan (*Arch.*)

tradui/re* *v.* to translate; se — is reflected

traité *nm.* article, treatise

traitement *nm.* treatment; usine de — processing plant

trait/er (de) *v.* to deal (with)

traître *nm.* traitor

trajet *nm.* travel

tranche *nf.* slice; slab (*Arch.*)

se transform/er (en) *v.* to be changed (into)

transport/er *v.* to transport

trapèze *nm.* trapezoid (*Geom.*)

travail *nm.* work, study (*pl.* travaux)

travaill/er *v.* to work

travailleur *nm.* worker

travers: à — *prep.* through; across

traversée *nf.* crossing; sweep

travers/er *v.* to cross, to traverse, to go through

très *adv.* very

triste *adj.* sad

trois three

se tromp/er *v.* to be mistaken

trop *adv.* too much

trou *nm.* hole

trouv/er *v.* to find, to discover, to invent; se — to be located, to be found, to be (*in a location*)

T.S.F. *abbr.* (téléphonie sans fil) radio; poste de — *nm.* radio receiver; poste émetteur de — radio broadcasting transmitter

tu/er *v.* to kill

tuile *nf.* tile

U

ultérieurement *adv.* later, subsequently

un(e) *art.* a, an; l'— ... l'autre one... the other; l'— par rapport à l'autre with relation to each other

uni, -e *adj.* smooth; joined, united

uniquement *adv.* only

un/ir *v.* to unify, to join, to smooth

unité *nf.* unit; — de masse unit of mass

univers *nm.* universe

universitaire *adj.* (*pertaining to university*) of higher learning; university

ultime *adj.* final, ultimate

usine *nf.* factory, plant; — de traitement processing plant

usuel, -le *adj.* usual

utile (à) *adj.* useful (for)

utilement *adv.* profitably, usefully

utilisant: en — by using

utilis/er *v.* to use, to utilize

V

vainc/re* *v.* to overcome; *pp.* vaincu

vainqueur *nm.* victor

vaisseau *nm.* ship, vessel; duct (*Bot.*)

valable *adj.* valid; reliable; valuable

valeur *nf.* value

valoir* *v.* to have value, to be worth; il vaut it is worth; — mieux to be preferable

vapeur *nf.* steam; vapor; — de l'eau water vapor

vari/er *v.* to vary

vase *nf.* mud, slime; *nm.* vase

végétal, -e *adj.* vegetable, plant

végétaux† *n.pl.* plants

véhiculé *pp.* transmitted

vend/re *v.* to sell

ven/ir* *v.* to come (*auxiliary* **être***) [vb. 30] (§68); — (+ INFINITIVE) to happen to (DO STHG.); — **de** (+ INFINITIVE) to have just (DONE STHG.) (§69); **en** — **à** (+ INFINITIVE) to go so far as to . . .

vent *nm.* wind

venu *pp.* (**venir***) come (*with auxiliary* **être***)

véritable *adj.* actual; correct

vérité *nf.* truth

verr/— *vst.* (**voir***) *F.* will see; *C.* would see

verre *nm.* glass (*container*)

vers *prep.* towards; about (*time*)

vertu *nf.* courage; virtue; **en** — **de** by virtue of

veuill/— *vst.* (**vouloir***) wish/; want/

veut dire *v.* (**vouloir* dire**) means, signifies

vide *nm.* vacuum; emptiness; — **parfait** perfect vacuum; — **poussé** high vacuum

vid/er *v.* to empty

vie *nf.* life; — **moyenne** half-life (*Phys.*)

vieil, -le *adj.* old, agèd (§15)

vien/— **de** (+ INFINITIVE) (**venir***) has just (DONE STHG.)

vien/— (*Pr.* **venir***) come/

viendr/— *vst.* (**venir***) *F.* will come; *C.* would come

vierge *nf. and adj.* virgin

vieux, vieil, vieille *adj.* old (§15)

vif, vive *adj.* lively, turbulent; **rouge vif** red-hot

vil, -e *adj.* vile, base

ville† *nf.* city; **petite** — town

virtuel, -le *adj.* theoretical

visiblement *adv.* obviously, visibly

visière *nf.* visor

vit (*fr.* **vivre***) lives

vite *adv.* quickly, fast; **moins** — slower

vitesse *nf.* speed; velocity

vitrage *nm.* windows

vivant, -e *adj.* living

viv/re* *v.* to live

voi/— *vst.* (**voir***) see/

voici *adv.* here is (are)

voie *nf.* way; path (*of action*); road; — **ferrée** railroad (right-of-way); — **respiratoire** respiratory tract; **en** — **de** in the process of

voilà *adv.* there is (are)

voir* *v.* to see; to understand [vb. 31]

voisin, -e *adj.* neighboring, nearby, near, in the neighborhood

voisinage *nm.* neighborhood, vicinity

voiture *nf.* car; vehicle

voix *nf.* voice; **à demi-** — in a low tone

volcan *nm.* volcano

vol/er *v.* to fly (*aircraft*); to steal

vorace *adj.* voracious

voul/oir* *v.* to want; to insist on [vb. 32]; — **dire** to mean, to signify

voulu *pp.* (**vouloir***) wanted

voûte *nf.* vault (*Arch.*); — **à plein cintre** semi-circular vault; — **d'arêtes** groined vault; — **de cloître** square vault

voûté, -e *adj.* vaulted, arched

voy/— *vst.* (**voir***) see

voyage *nm.* trip; voyage; — **de retour** return trip

voyag/er *v.* to travel

voyageur *nm.* traveller

voyant *ps.p.* seeing; **en** — upon seeing

vrai, -e *adj.* true; **à** — **dire** to tell the truth, in fact

vraisemblable *adj.* probable, likely

vu *pp.* (**voir***) seen

vue *nf.* view, purview; (sense of) sight

Y

y *adv.* there; **il** — **a** there is, there are; **il** — **avait** there were (was); **il** — **aura** there will be; **il** — **aurait** there would be; **y penser** to think of it (them); **y obéir** to obey it

yeux *nm. pl.* eyes (*fr.* **œil**)

Index